Elizabeth Bowen

The Cutting Edge:
Lesbian Life and Literature

The Cutting Edge:
Lesbian Life and Literature

Series Editor: Karla Jay

Lover
BY BERTHA HARRIS

Changing Our Minds: Lesbian Feminism and Psychology
BY CELIA KITZINGER AND RACHEL PERKINS

Elizabeth Bowen: A Reputation in Writing
BY RENÉE C. HOOGLAND

The Cutting Edge:
Lesbian Life and Literature

Series Editor: Karla Jay
Professor of English and Women's Studies
Pace University

renée c. hoogland

Elizabeth BOWEN

A Reputation in Writing

NEW YORK UNIVERSITY PRESS
New York and London

Grateful acknowledgment for permission to reprint material is made to the following:

From THE LAST SEPTEMBER by Elizabeth Bowen. Copyright © 1929, 1952 by Elizabeth Bowen. Reprinted by permission of Alfred A. Knopf, Inc., the Estate of Elizabeth Bowen, Jonathan Cape Limited, and Curtis Brown, London.

From THE HEAT OF THE DAY by Elizabeth Bowen. Copyright © 1948 by Elizabeth Bowen. Reprinted by permission of Alfred A. Knopf, Inc., the Estate of Elizabeth Bowen, Jonathan Cape Limited, and Curtis Brown, London.

From EVA TROUT OR CHANGING SCENES by Elizabeth Bowen. Copyright © 1968 by Elizabeth Bowen. Reprinted by permission of Alfred A. Knopf, Inc., the Estate of Elizabeth Bowen, Jonathan Cape Limited, and Curtis Brown, London.

From BOWEN'S COURT and SEVEN WINTERS by Elizabeth Bowen. Copyright © 1942. Reprinted by permission of Virago Press Limited.

From Elizabeth Bowen and Jocelyne Brooks [broadcast]; autobiographical note on manuscript; and GIRLHOOD [essay]. Reprinted by permission of The Harry Ransom Humanities Research Center, The University of Austin, Texas.

Extracts from "Out of a Book," "The Bend Back," "The Big House," and "Why Do I Write" by Elizabeth Bowen. Reprinted by permission of the Estate of Elizabeth Bowen and Curtis Brown, London.

Extracts from PICTURES AND CONVERSATIONS by Elizabeth Bowen. Copyright © 1975 by Elizabeth Bowen. Reprinted by permission of Curtis Brown, London.

NEW YORK UNIVERSITY PRESS
New York and London

Library of Congress Cataloging-in-Publication Data
Hoogland, Renée C.
Elizabeth Bowen : a reputation in writing / Renée C. Hoogland.
p.   cm.—(The Cutting edge: lesbian life and literature)
Includes bibliographical references and index.
ISBN 0-8147-3501-0 (cloth).—ISBN 0-8147-3511-8 (pbk.)
1. Bowen, Elizabeth, 1899–1973—Criticism and interpretation.
2. Lesbians' writings, English—Irish authors—History and criticism.   3. Feminism and literature—Ireland—History—20th century.   4. Women and literature—Ireland—History—20th century.
5. Lesbians—Ireland—Intellectual life.   6. Ireland—In literature.
I. Title.   II. Series: Cutting edge (New York, N.Y.)
PR6003.06757Z672   1994
823'.912—dc20   93-49675
CIP

New York University Press books are printed on acid-free paper,
and their binding materials are chosen for strength and durability.

Manufactured in the United States of America

10 9 8 7 6 5 4 3 2 1

for Loep

Contents

xii   Contents

Foreword

Despite the efforts of lesbian and feminist publishing houses and a few university presses, the bulk of the most important lesbian works has traditionally been available only from rare-book dealers, in a few university libraries, or in gay and lesbian archives. This series intends, in the first place, to make representative examples of this neglected and insufficiently known literature available to a broader audience by reissuing selected classics and by putting into print for the first time lesbian novels, diaries, letters, and memoirs that are of special interest and significance but that have moldered in libraries and private collections for decades or even for centuries, known only to the few scholars who had the courage and financial wherewithal to track them down.

Their names have been known for a long time—Sappho, the Amazons of North Africa, the Beguines, Aphra Behn, Queen Christina, Emily Dickinson, the Ladies of Llangollen, Radclyffe Hall, Natalie Clifford Barney, H.D., and so many others from every nation, race, and era. But government and religious officials burned their writings, historians and literary scholars denied they were lesbians, powerful men kept their books out of print, and influential archivists locked up their ideas far from sympathetic eyes. Yet some dedicated scholars and readers still knew who they were, made pilgrimages to the cities and villages where they had lived and to the graveyards where they rested. They passed around tattered volumes of letters, diaries, and biographies, in which they had underlined what seemed to be telltale hints of a secret or different kind of life. Where no hard facts existed, legends were invented. The few precious and often available pre-Stonewall lesbian classics, such as *The Well of Loneliness* by Radclyffe Hall, *The Price of Salt* by Claire Morgan (Patricia Highsmith), and *Desert of the Heart* by Jane Rule, were cherished. Lesbian pulp was devoured. One of the primary goals of this series is to give the more neglected works, which constitute the vast majority of lesbian writing, the attention they deserve.

A second but no less important aim of this series is to present the "cutting edge" of contemporary lesbian scholarship and theory across a wide range of disciplines. Practitioners of lesbian studies have not adopted a uniform approach to literary theory, history, sociology, or any other discipline, nor should they. This series intends to present an array of voices that truly reflect the diversity of the lesbian community. To help me in this task, I am lucky enough to be assisted by a distinguished editorial board that reflects various professional, class, racial, ethnic, and religious backgrounds as well as a spectrum of interests and sexual preferences.

At present the field of lesbian studies occupies a small, precarious, and somewhat contested pied-à-terre between gay studies and women's studies. The former is still in its infancy, especially if one compares it to other disciplines that have been part of the core curriculum of every child and adolescent for several decades or even centuries. However, although it is one of the newest disciplines, gay studies may also be the fastest-growing one—at least in North America. Lesbian, gay, and bisexual studies conferences are doubling and tripling their attendance. Although only a handful of degree-granting programs currently exist, that number is also apt to multiply quickly during the next decade.

In comparison, women's studies is a well-established and burgeoning discipline with hundreds of minors, majors, and graduate programs throughout the United States. Lesbian studies occupies a peripheral place in the discourse in such programs, characteristically restricted to one lesbian-centered course, usually literary or historical in nature. In the many women's studies series that are now offered by university presses, generally only one or two books on a lesbian subject or issue are included, and lesbian voices are restricted to writing on those topics considered of special interest to gay people. We are not called upon to offer opinions on motherhood, war, education, or on the lives of women not publicly identified as lesbians. As a result, lesbian experience is too often marginalized and restricted.

In contrast, this series will prioritize, centralize, and celebrate lesbian visions of literature, art, philosophy, love, religion, ethics, history, and a myriad of other topics. In "The Cutting Edge," readers can find authoritative versions of important lesbian texts that have been carefully prepared and introduced by scholars. Readers can also find the work of academics and independent scholars who write about other aspects of life from a distinctly lesbian viewpoint. These visions are not only various but intentionally contradictory, for lesbians speak from differing class, racial, ethnic, and religious perspectives. Each author also speaks from and about a certain moment of time, and few would argue that being a lesbian today is the same as it was for Sappho or Anne Lister. Thus no attempt has been made to homogenize that diversity, and no agenda exists to attempt to carve out a "politically correct" lesbian studies perspective at this juncture in history or to pinpoint the "real" lesbians in history. It seems more important for all the voices to be heard before those with the blessings of aftersight lay the mantle of authenticity on any one vision of the world, or on any particular set of women.

What each work in this series does share, however, is a common realization that gay women are the "Other" and that one's perception of culture and literature is filtered by sexual behaviors and preferences. Those perceptions are not the same as those of gay men or of nongay women, whether the writers speak of gay or feminist issues or whether the writers choose to look at nongay figures from a lesbian perspective. The role of this series is to create a space for and give a voice to those interested in lesbian studies. This series speaks to any person who is interested in gender studies, literary criticism, biography, or important literary works, whether she or he is a student, professor, or serious reader, for the series is neither for lesbians only nor even by lesbians only. Instead, "The Cutting Edge" attempts to share some of the best of lesbian literature and lesbian studies with anyone willing to look at the world through lesbians' eyes. The series is proactive in that it will help to formulate and foreground the very discipline on which it focuses. Finally, this series has answered the call to make lesbian theory, lesbian experience, lesbian lives, lesbian literature, and lesbian visions the heart and nucleus, the weighty planet around which for once other viewpoints will swirl as moons to our earth. We invite readers of all persuasions to join us by venturing into this and other books in the series.

Elizabeth Bowen was a writer whose life and work encompassed many marginalities. She was a married woman who had several lesbian affairs; she was an Anglo-Irish writer, who, like many other Englishwomen transplanted into Ireland, took on aspects of both cultures; she was a tangential modernist who went on to explore other forms of the novel. Furthermore, like many of the writers whose work has been covered or will be covered in this series (Djuna Barnes and Radclyffe Hall, for example), only some of her novels explored lesbian issues, and, were she still alive, she might be amazed to find herself situated under the rubric of "Lesbian Life and Literature," and she might even object to this label, despite her preoccupation with adolescent girls of questionable sexual persuasions. As Renée Hoogland's book so clearly points out, there are many lesbianisms, and Bowen is only one example of how other issues of class, race, ethnicity, and historicity shape perspective.

KARLA JAY
Professor of English and Women's Studies
Pace University

Acknowledgments

No text stands by itself: like any other, this one is the outcome of a process in which a large number of other texts as well as the inspiration, criticism, and support provided by many different people in many different contexts have played a critical part. I can mention only a few.

I am especially indebted to Marijke Rudnik-Smalbraak; without her commitment, criticism, and genuine friendship this book surely would not have been written. My thanks extend to Dominic Baker-Smith, who has generously allowed me to benefit from his literary sensibility and intellectual openness. I thank my friends Tineke Kalk, Dorelies Kraakman, Bev Jackson, Monique Hoogland, and Titia Coppes for the various forms of stimulation, inspiration, and encouragement they have offered me over the years. My colleagues and students at the departments of English and comparative literature, as well as the members of the Women's Studies Research Program of the University of Amsterdam have provided me with a pleasant working environment for which I am grateful. My sincerest thanks and love are due to Pamela Pattynama, who has rewarded everything but my virtue.

Introduction: Elizabeth Bowen—
A Story of Sorts

A novel which survives, which withstands and outlives time, does do something more than survive. It does not stand still. It accumulates round itself the understanding of all these persons who bring to it something of their own. It acquires associations, it becomes a form of experience in itself. . . . And like all experiences, it is added to by the power of different kinds of people, in different times, to feel and to comment and to explain.

—"Truth and Fiction"

One spends one's life objectifying one's inner life, and projecting one's thought and emotion into a form—a book. Which, once one's inside difficulties are overcome, is the exercise of an unchecked power. . . . It is hard for me (being a writer before I am a woman) to realize that anything— friendship or love especially—in which I participate imaginatively isn't a book too. Isn't, I mean, something *I* make what it is by my will that it shall be like that.

—Elizabeth Bowen to Humphrey House

The Anglo-Irish writer Elizabeth Bowen (1899–1973) considered herself to be in the most eligible position to write a book about Elizabeth Bowen. She did not live to complete the set of autobiographical sketches that were to become such a book. Entitled *Pictures and Conversations,* her retrospective self-inscriptions were posthumously published in 1975. However, undaunted by the author's claim to "unchecked power" over the story of her self, several persons have brought "something of their own" to Elizabeth Bowen. She has been the subject of a few (biographically informed) critical studies, one full-length and one short biographical work, and diverse memoirs. Commented on and explained, "added to by the power of different kinds of people," the story of Elizabeth Bowen appears to have so far "withstood and outlived time."

Bowen was not only well known, widely read, and greatly admired during her lifetime; her novels are still regularly being reissued in paperback today. If only in its prolificness and the span of time in which it was produced, her oeuvre is remarkable: in the course of nearly fifty years, she published ten novels, almost eighty short stories, a chronicle of her family, and a substantial body of (major and minor) critical and other nonfictional work. Still, her reputation as a writer has not kept up with the times, nor has her work received the serious critical attention it deserves. Often uneasily linked to other neglected women writers with whom she has little more in common than that they were contemporaries, Bowen's name generally survives as that of a minor writer, hovering in the margins of the Great Traditions that make up the landscape of twentieth-century English literature.

Although her autobiography ultimately remained unfinished, Bowen's life is well documented. She herself published the history of her family mentioned above, *Bowen's Court* (1942), which contains a wealth of information about the cultural context into and onto which she was born, as well as a memoir of her Dublin childhood in the form of a series of short sketches, *Seven Winters* (1942). Whereas she did not keep a formal writer's diary, the prefaces to several of her novels and collections of short stories, as well as numerous essays and articles, public correspondences, recorded lectures, and radio talks in which she explores her ideas concerning the art of fiction nonetheless jointly compose an illuminating account of the ways in which Bowen's views on writing and the writer's role in society developed, changed, and also persisted over the course of time. Victoria Glendinning's informative biography remains the most extensive narrative of the author's life to date.[1] Different emphases placed by literary critics on different aspects of Bowen's life furthermore provide useful complementary insights into what is, on all accounts, a complex story about an equally complex personality. The following outline is a necessarily partial composition indebted in varying measures to these intertexts.

A Life

Elizabeth Dorothea Cole Bowen was born to Anglo-Irish parents in Dublin in 1899, the only child of a middle-class Protestant Unionist family. Her ancestors, the apOwens, had come from Wales with Cromwell's army to settle in Ireland at the time of the Civil War. The first Bowen to acquire land in Ireland was a professional soldier making his home in the English province in 1653. It was his great-great-grandson who built Bowen's Court, the remote family mansion that the author, at thirty-one, was to inherit upon her father's death. The latter, Henry Bowen, disappointed his father by not fitting into the role ascribed to him as eldest son and heir; he chose to make his living practicing law in Dublin instead of pursuing the political and social power the Bowens had so successfully acquired. While Henry primarily emerges as a reflective, self-contained, and rather abstract intellectual, he nonetheless inherited the family tendency "towards strong will, obsessiveness, and fantasy." In 1890, at age twenty-nine, he married Florence Colley, five years his junior and also of Anglo-Irish descent. In contrast to the Bowens' isolated existence on their demesne in County Cork, the Colleys lived a far more sociable and cheerful life at Clontarf, near Dublin. Like her father, Bowen's mother was the odd one out within her family. Daughter to a "dominant, dynamic, anti-intellectual, confident" mother,[2] Florence was "capricious, elusive, gently intent on her own thoughts."[3] They made a happy match, it seems, he being the "more thoughtful" of the two, "living by philosophy," she the "more feeling" one, "living by temperament." These are the terms in which Bowen, looking back, describes her parents' marriage and her own position within it:

My father and mother must have made by their marriage, and lived in, a world of their own. This world was seldom impinged upon: times and happenings and the winter city of Dublin made round it a shadowy outer ring. Inside this world they each ruled their private kingdoms of thought, and inside it I, their first child, began to set up my own. My parents did not always communicate with each other, and I did not always communicate with them. They were both very independent of other people. I had been born, I see now, into a home at once unique and intensive, gently phenomenal.[4]

Her early days in the somewhat ethereal company of her parents resulted in a strong attachment to "places and things": these, Bowen concedes, rather than people, "detach themselves from the stuff of my dream."

Despite their peculiar personalities, Bowen's parents provided their daughter with a "classic Anglo-Irish" heritage. Blended of originally diverse national strands (Norman, Scottish, Welsh, and English), the Anglo-Irish made up the ruling Ascendancy class whose power came to an end when the Irish rebellion (also known as "the Troubles") resulted first in Partition and Home Rule (1920) and eventually in the Irish Settlement (1922). The Anglo-Irish were not in the strict sense a nationality, even after several generations of residence in Ireland. Yet as a distinct cultural group they produced their own national myths and characteristics. These went into the making of Bowen's character as much as they found their way into her fiction. The author herself made a great point of her ancestors' isolated position in a country where they remained geographically and politically outsiders, living their lives in their remote country houses, "in psychological closeness and under the strong rule of the family myth." Not unlike the lives of only children, those of the Protestant landed gentry were "singular, independent, and secretive." In their concentration around one place, Anglo-Irish families were connected by a "continuous, semi-physical dream," above which "successive lives show their tips, their little conscious formations of will and thought."[5] However, as Glendinning points out, there is, in addition to "melancholy tinged with self-irony," also something "more vital and attractive" about Anglo-Ireland: "Great style, and a verbal fluency that leaves the rest of us islands nowhere" (13). She somewhat cryptically adds that, within the "context of an enormous communicative-ness," the Anglo-Irish have a "tact and sensitivity" that is some-times taken to a "baroque point where it almost becomes some-thing else." Bowen, while reticent about personal matters, in line with the norms of her race and her class, fully shared the (more Irish than Anglo-Irish) characteristic of a "natural warmth and gregariousness." Offset against the "nervous Bowen heritage," her gift for friendship, her hospitality, and her ability to live in the present were what she inherited from her mother's family, the Colleys (14).

Launched into what would become a lifelong itinerant exis-tence, the author divided her first seven years between Dublin and Bowen's Court: summers were spent at the family estate while her father's law practice kept the family in Dublin during winters. In view of his exacting professional obligations, Henry Bowen cannot have been a prominent presence in these early days. The relation-ship between mother and daughter was "very intense," however. Though generally absent-minded, Florence was not actually vague as a mother. When Elizabeth was five, her father suffered a mental breakdown. He went to England for treatment, but when he re-turned the following year, his condition had not improved. His doctors recommended that Florence and Elizabeth leave, for Henry's good. He committed himself to a mental hospital near Dublin and Elizabeth and her mother departed for the English south coast, where they were to dwell the following five years, shuttling between Edwardian seaside villas and assorted Anglo-Irish relatives. Thus thrown together, mother and daughter developed an exceedingly close relationship. The violent disruption of her primary habitat must have seriously affected the author, but the effect was apparent only in the development of a stammer that was to mark her otherwise dazzling conversation throughout her adult life. The transplantation "into a different mythology" further resulted in what Bowen describes as a "cleft between my heredity and my environment." The Anglo-Irish, she declares, have an "undertow of the showy," which explains why "primarily we have produced dramatists, the novel being too life-like, humdrum to do us justice":

There is this about us: to most of the rest of the world we are semi-strangers, for whom existence has something of the trance-like quality of a spectacle. As beings, we are at once brilliant and limited; our unbeatables . . . accordingly, have been those who best profited by that: Goldsmith, Sheridan, Wilde, Shaw, Beckett. Art is for us inseparable from artifice: of that, the theatre is the home.
Possibly, it was England made me a novelist.[6]

While her Anglo-Irish heredity remained the "more powerful," it was the environment provided by the English landscape and social scenery that implanted in Bowen a sense of history that would become one of the hallmarks of her fiction. Arriving at an "early though conscious age" in an all but alien culture, it was as if she had taken up her part in a "non-stop historical novel." Even if becoming a writer "knocked a good deal of nonsense out of [her] system," there persisted a "residuum" of this "daydream":

As a novelist, I cannot occupy myself with "characters," or at any rate central ones, who lack panache in one or another sense, who would be incapable of a major action or a major passion, or who have not at least a touch of the ambiguity, the ultimate unaccountability, the enlarging mistiness of personages "in history." History, as more austerely I now know it, is not romantic. But I am.[7]

While accounting for Bowen's fascination with the "dark horse" as far as her characters are concerned, the chanciness, the dislocations, and the fundamental temporary quality of her early life are also reflected in the often haphazard and violently disruptive plots of her fictions.

The romantic daydream was rudely shattered. In 1912, Henry Bowen appeared sufficiently recovered to allow his family to return to Ireland. So they did, but only to spend what proved to be their last summer together at Bowen's Court: in September Florence died of cancer. Elizabeth was thirteen. Never completely getting over the loss, her stammer became more severe, and she was never again able to speak about her mother. Henceforth, the responsibility for her upbringing and education—which had always been intermittent—was taken over by a deputation of aunts, female Colleys living scattered about England. The bereaved girl first attended Harpenden Hall in Hertfordshire, enjoying her father's company during the summer holidays in Ireland. While academically not a great success, Elizabeth became, during these years, a voracious reader. In 1914, she was sent to Downe House, a boarding school for girls in Kent. Reigned over by a powerful headmistress with an all-pervasive personality, Downe was to have a lasting impact. Pupils were not allowed to indulge in any form of "girlish" behavior; indeed, upon their arrival they were told that "it did not matter if [they] were happy as long as [they] were good." Bowen later reflected that she "learnt to define happiness as a kind of inner irrational exaltation having little to do with morals one way or the other." Dressed in a "uniform dictated down to the last detail" and constrained by a "self-imposed rigid emotional snobbishness" that precluded the "more direct means of self-expression," the girls articulated themselves through "foibles" and "mannerisms": these were "exaggerated most diligently." The "ever difficult business of getting oneself across" was, the author avers, at this age "most pressing" of all: "Personality came out in patches, like damp through a wall."[8]

The war was keenly felt inside the walls of the boarding school. Bowen remembers the "moral stress" as "appalling": "We grew up under the intolerable obligation of being fought for, and could not fall short in character without recollecting that men were dying for us." During these so-called formative years, the author, like her fellow students, expected to marry early, "partly because this appeared an achievement or way of making one's mark, also from a feeling it would be difficult to settle to anything else until this was done." While they were "not in love with each other at all constantly," few girls "anticipated maternity with either interest or pleasure." Indeed, Bowen admits, though some did become mothers, this "still seems inappropriate." She goes on to suggest: "Possibly, however, we were not natural girls."[9] Not encouraged to be ambitious, the girls yet all expected to "distinguish" themselves in some way. The author herself took to the "curious, quick, characteristic psychological pace" of Downe, beginning to develop traits that would structure her adult character: she became observant and analytical, sympathetic and understanding, with a keen awareness of what was funny and what was tragic.[10] She left Downe in the summer of 1917, instilled with an "overstrained" sense of honor and with the manners and style of a lady.

In 1918, Henry Bowen, who had continued to retain his mental health, remarried. Elizabeth was still mainly living in England but spent much time with her father and his new wife—whom she greatly liked—at Bowen's Court. Although she had by this time started writing, she wanted to become an artist and went to the London County Council School of Art in London. After two terms, she was forced to admit that she would never be a really good painter. Bowen took a course in journalism, began sending out stories to the editors of various periodicals, and "haunted the fringes of literary London."[11] Through her old headmistress she met Rose Macaulay, who, already well established as a critic and novelist at the time, recommended her work to Naomi Royde-Smith, the editor of the *Saturday Westminster*. The stories that were first printed in this periodical were later collected and published by Sidgwick and Jackson: *Encounters* appeared in 1923, the same year Bowen married Alan Cameron.

Cameron, an assistant secretary for education, was a talented administrator, not an intellectual. While generally considered generous and kind, he also often appeared quite out of place in the literary circles in which the young author started to move. But even if remembered by some of her friends as a rather hearty Colonel Blimp, Cameron provided Bowen with the secure emotional and home base that had practically always been lacking in her life. Their relationship constituted a true and warm friendship but was not of a sexual or passionate nature. In the first years of their marriage, Bowen wrote two more books: another collection of stories, *Ann Lee's* (1926), and her first novel, *The Hotel* (1927). Though extremely funny, both the novel—which deals with its adolescent protagonist's search for a sexual identity in the context of her relationship with an older woman—and most of the stories are characterized by an atmosphere of tenseness and restlessness, situated in the (interconnecting) areas of violence and sexuality: "I was beating myself against human unknowableness; in fact, I made that my subject—how many times? The stories are questions asked: many end with a shrug, a query, or, to the reader, a sort of over-to-you."[12]

By 1925, Cameron's work had taken the couple to Old Headington, near Oxford. Here Bowen met and befriended John and Susan Buchan, who in their turn established her contact with Virginia Woolf and Rosamund Lehmann. Other professionals with whom she became acquainted were the Oxford don/literary critic Lord David Cecil and the philosopher Isaiah Berlin, while Maurice Bowra became an intimate friend. With her straightforward attitude, forthright opinions, her gift for intelligent conversation, wit, and satiric sensibility, Bowen was an instant success in the intellectual and artistic community of 1920s Oxford. Losing her insecurity about her appearance and sexual attractiveness, she became handsome in an unusual fashion: large-boned and tall, Bowen used her exceptional sense of style in manner, speech, and dress, her strong features acquiring rare charm and distinction. Professionally, socially, and emotionally, the author came into her own during the ten years in Oxford. In 1929, she published two books, a third collection of short stories, and her second novel, *The Last September*. While the stories in *Joining Charles* are rather uneven in quality, the novel shows how she further perfected what became an inimitable descriptive style. Again presenting female pre-adulthood in connection with the figure of a powerful older woman, the novel fully established the exploration of female sexual identity as one of the author's central themes. Even so, as Glendinning correctly points out, in Bowen's early fiction, "passion and terror lie beneath, partly controlled, partly controlling" (67). Its essential quality is what the author herself was to call with respect to Jane Austen's work, "life with the lid on." Rather than representing a limitation, however, she argues that her famous predecessor successfully "dispels . . . the fallacy that life with the lid off . . . is necessarily more interesting than life with the lid on." [13]

The following year, Henry Bowen became ill again. He died in May 1930, leaving the responsibility for Bowen's Court and the management of the estate in the hands of his daughter and only heir. Until financial difficulties would force her to sell her inheritance, Bowen continued to divide her life between the two countries in which she had originated. Alternately staying in Oxford (increasingly also in London) and in County Cork, she led the life of an exile. Whereas England provided her with the high-spirited intellectual and social milieu she needed, Bowen returned to Ireland in order to rest, to enjoy the sense of home, and to exert her generous hospitality toward the friends she constantly entertained. In the rather spartan circumstances offered by a house lacking any modern amenities, the author numbered among her most frequent guests well-known literary figures such as William Plomer, Sean O'Foalain, Cyril Connolly and his wife, as well as her beloved cousin Audrey Fiennes. Virginia Woolf once stayed at Bowen's Court, and later regulars were, among others, Rosamund Lehmann, Stephen Spender, Iris Murdoch, and Eddy Sackville-West. Although she loved the very old-fashionedness of the austere mansion, Bowen's Court proved a great burden. Furthermore, since the Irish Settlement, the position of the Anglo-Irish had come in for a great deal of discussion, and the financial anxiety it caused strengthened the author's ambivalence about the power and prestige her male ancestors had derived from her property's imposing presence in the Irish countryside.

Bowen was as swiftly taken up by the grand chain of literary Londoners in the 1930s as she had been in Oxford in the 1920s. Political turmoil increasingly began to consume her attention. Though never involved in party politics, she started to contribute regularly to magazines such as the *New Statesman* and the *Tatler,* writing sharply focused critical articles on the contemporary cultural and political scene. Her international reputation was established with the publication of *Friends and Relations* in 1931, and *To the North* the following year. With visits to Rome, Italy, and New York, an ever-expanding social life, her work, and her life with Alan, she had little time to spend in Ireland. Bowen's next novel, *The House in Paris,* was published in 1935. Centering on two children, the narrative revolves around what had become the author's recurring themes: passion, desire, and power, the effects of which are played out in the context of an entrapping motherhood. It was in the 1930s that the author's preoccupation with sexuality also took a sharp turn in her personal life. Bowen fell passionately in love and embarked on an affair with Humphrey House, a lecturer in English at Oxford. Though the affair soon ended—House was engaged to be married—the overpowering sexual intensity of the experience left the author with a radically changed sense of self. Allowing her to discover the strength of her hitherto restrained passions, it furthermore taught her that writing was fundamental to her life. From then on, Bowen continued to engage in a series of short-lived affairs, mostly with men but occasionally also with women, while simultaneously succeeding in keeping her relationship with Alan not only intact but well balanced.

Alan's new job with the British Broadcasting Company brought the couple more or less permanently to London: they bought a house on Clarence Terrace, Regent's Park, which is conspicuously featured in what is probably Bowen's best-known work, *The Death of the Heart* (1938). Bowen's literary and social influence grew steadily in the years preceding World War II. Just as she herself had earlier been taken up by such figureheads as Lady Ottoline Morell and Virginia Woolf, so young American woman writers like Carson McCullers and May Sarton came to stay at Bowen's Court to enjoy the company and friendship of the now-celebrated author. With the outbreak of war, one of the most exciting periods of Bowen's life began. With all the pent-up intensity of her personality she responded wholeheartedly to the disruption of the social order, assuming her part in the war effort as an Air Raid Precaution warden while continuing to publish short fiction and critical essays. She also worked for the Ministry of Information, traveling to Ireland and writing intelligence reports on its sociopolitical situation. In the early days of the war, she met Charles Ritchie, a Canadian diplomat who became her lover and lifelong friend. The sense of betrayal pervading the social climate, the breakdown of cultural traditions, the destructive material effects of moral abstractions, and the operations of sexual difference within these sociopolitical developments were to become the controlling themes in *The Heat of the Day* (1949), Bowen's wartime novel, which she was only barely able to finish five years after the war had officially ended.

In the postwar years disenchantment about England set in: a

culture on the decline and Alan's deteriorating health led Bowen to spend more and longer periods at Bowen's Court. She also started lecturing for the British Council, mainly in the United States, and began giving radio broadcasts. She received an honorary doctorate of literature from Trinity College in Dublin in 1949, and wrote a chronicle of its Shelbourne Hotel. In 1952, Alan died. Bowen suffered the loss of a nurturing and devoted companion, the reassuring presence of a sympathetic and generous friend: once again, she found herself homeless. The novel on which she had been working before Alan fell ill, *A World of Love,* became a somewhat wistful exploration of fantasies and memories revolving around sexuality and death. Resuming her lecture tours and accepting fellowships at colleges in the United States, the author spent the following years traveling, visiting friends—among whom her favorite was Eudora Welty—and meeting Charles Ritchie occasionally, but rarely staying anywhere for very long. In 1960, she was no longer able to bear the strain produced by her financial anxiety over Bowen's Court. She could not afford its upkeep, even though she was writing frantically for (better-paying) American magazines such as *Holiday, American Home, Mademoiselle, House and Garden,* as well as for the *New York Times Book Review* and the *Saturday Review of Literature.* She sold the house rather abruptly, expecting the buyer to turn it into a residence for himself and his family. This was not to be: soon after its contents had been auctioned, Bowen's Court was demolished. Bowen at once returned to America.

In these final dislocated years, Bowen wrote two further novels, *The Little Girls* (1964) and *Eva Trout* (1969). Both represent radical departures from her earlier stylistic methods and narrative techniques. While far less well received than any of her previous work, these texts, in which powerful subversive forces can be felt to be cracking through the surface, reveal the abiding strength of her creative and critical imagination. In 1965, the author had bought a modest cottage in Hythe, on the coast of England. A compulsive smoker throughout her life, she contracted lung cancer in 1971. Bowen was working on a new novel when she died on February 22, 1973.

A Reputation

It is perhaps precisely the fact that novels and life stories alike accumulate around themselves what others have brought to them that has landed Bowen in the shadowy regions of the literary map. As a result of their usually unmanageable scope, literary histories necessarily tend to reproduce themselves, to rewrite the same overedited stories about a (limited) number of authors over and over again. Despite shifting concerns and preoccupations, literary historians make it exceedingly difficult to disentangle the threads that have gone to the making of officially acknowledged vignettes, to retrace the lines and contours that, rather than allowing for a recreation, reassessment, or re-cognition of a given writer's accomplishment, tend further to congeal established images and stock evaluations. Elizabeth Bowen is a case in point. In 1952, Jocelyn Brooke published a short pamphlet in which he categorized Bowen as a "writer of sensibility."[14] Highlighting the pictorial quality of her work, he defines her style as "highly wrought" and "convoluted" and singles out as Bowen's major preoccupation the disruption of "civilized behaviour" caused by a conflict between a rebellious nature and "Philistine middle-class" society. Stylistic mannerisms, merging with an "occasional use of the supernatural," Brooke suggests, serve as "means for effect" in texts he eventually designates "satirical comed[ies]" (5–9). He voices his concluding praise by volunteering that Bowen distinguishes herself favorably from "many women novelists" who have "too boldly . . . ignored the limitations which . . . are implied by the mere fact of being female." Indeed, Bowen forms a laudable exception in that she "confined herself . . . to the themes which she feels to be safely within her range as a woman novelist" (30).

When we look up Bowen's name in recent literary histories we find strikingly similar and equally reductive classifications that, in one way or another, reinforce standard practices of sexual stereotyping still prevailing in literary canonization. Back in 1962, however, Mary McCarthy already appeared to echo Brooke when she observed:

The fictional experiments of the twentieth century went in two directions: sensibility and sensation. To speak very broadly, the experiments in the recording of sensibility were made in England (Virginia Woolf, Katherine Mansfield, Dorothy Richardson, Elizabeth Bowen, Forster), and America was the laboratory of sensation (Hemingway, and his imitators, Dos Passos, Farrell). The novel of sensibility was feminine, and the novel of sensation was masculine.[15]

Rosalind Miles, to whom I owe this fragment, quotes McCarthy's reflections disapprovingly. She goes on to suggest that, given the constraints imposed by the sexual paradigm (in which, incidentally, the alignment of a male homosexual on the side of the "feminine" goes all but unnoticed), it is "hardly surprising that women writers in the past have not been able either confidently to create new traditions, or even to hang on to what had been achieved."[16] Qualifying Elizabeth Bowen as a "classic case" among women writers who have dropped from public view while their reputations were "in their own day not merely respectable but towering," she repeats precisely the kind of constraining gestures that her book purports to denounce, albeit in terms of class rather than sex. Reducing Bowen's "gift" to the "evocation of class romance," Miles rejects what she misreads as "unexamined social assumptions," which—and here sex obliquely reenters the discussion—also underlie the work of Rosamund Lehmann, "though her subject-matter and technique are not otherwise comparable with those of Elizabeth Bowen"(30). Since Miles does not elaborate on such differences as she may have perceived between these two authors, we are left with an impression that has continued to accumulate around Bowen: that she was a class-conscious if not snobbish writer of sensibility whose work, due to the mutually reinforcing constraints of both her class and her sex, is narrow in scope, romantic, and technically conventional.

Such vignettes tend to cling to a writer's name with great tenacity once they have been inscribed. While clearly written from an entirely different perspective than Miles's attempted reconstruction of a female literary tradition, Douglas Hewitt's *English Fiction of the Early Modern Period* (1988) yet echoes the unexamined assumptions underlying and voiced by, among others, Mary McCarthy and, in a different guise, Miles herself. Hewitt numbers Bowen among those "novelists who established themselves in the late 1920s and 1930s" and whose "works are still read." He points out that, however diverse, writers like Ivy Compton-Burnett, Richard Hughes, Henry Green, Evelyn Waugh, and Elizabeth Bowen "mostly seem to have chosen deliberately smaller subjects and to have turned their backs on technical innovation." These "minor" writers produced narratives "limited" in "social and emotional range," even if some of them seemed "gifted . . . with everything required for a serious and major novelist." A figure such as Bowen, who, it is implied, cannot be considered either serious or major, is filed away as a traditional novelist who published "a number of delicate small-scale post-Jamesian studies, mostly of children and adolescent girls."[17] This repetitive pattern of reductionism is all the more surprising when we note that Hewitt mentions Hermione Lee's critical study of Bowen's work in his suggestions for further reading.[18] The premise on which the latter's thoroughly researched—if ultimately unsatisfying—argument rests is (quite contrary to what Hewitt proposes) that her subject occupies an "exceptional" as much as a "central" position in the tradition of English literature:

Elizabeth Bowen is an exceptional English novelist because she fuses two traditions—that of Anglo-Irish literature and history, and that of a European modernism indebted to Flaubert and to James. Her idiosyncratic, highly mannered style is a product of this fusion, as much as of a temperamental opposition between romanticism and severity. But she is a central, as well as an unusual, figure, in that the personal, emotional concerns of her novels and stories are consistently deployed for a critique of the English middle-classes. Elizabeth Bowen's analysis of what she takes to be a "disinherited" society is the austere basis of her romantic, witty, evocative treatment of manners and feelings. (11–12)

In her final paragraph, Lee hopefully suggests that Bowen is one of those writers who, "now that the dust is beginning to clear around Virginia Woolf and Katherine Mansfield," will "have their due" (239). In view of the self-perpetuating practices inherent in the process of canonization, this is perhaps an overly optimistic conclusion. Even so, both Lee's and a number of other studies do appear to have begun to acknowledge Elizabeth Bowen's great gifts as a writer, her stylistic talents, her intellectual acuity, and her sharply satirical wit. In contrast—or perhaps in response—to such (dis)qualifying consensus as is presented by literary histories, these critics have characterized the author in highly disparate if not contradictory terms.

Published before Bowen produced her remarkable later work, William Heath's introduction to her novels remained for many years the only full-length study of her fiction.[19] He places his subject firmly in the tradition of social realism, the dominant literary mode of what we now refer to as liberal humanist culture. In common with all twentieth-century artists, Heath suggests, Bowen struggles with the difficulty of reconciling the "romantic will," "innocence" and the "imagination" with external reality. Her fiction is an approach to reality: form is a means for survival, a way of applying patterns of coherence to a fragmented and chaotic reality. Rendering Bowen's writing practice very much a moral art, this, he submits, also allows her to define herself as a writer within an established tradition. Shifting the emphases of his argument, Heath proceeds by positing that such a position is a "function of her moral concern and aesthetic practice as well as of her literary knowledge" (15, 16). However, while art may enable the imaginative individual to live, the artist "cannot crudely substitute art for life and live with sanity," for what is at stake is a "sense of reality." Revealing the stakes of his own argument, Heath in the end defines Bowen's novels as "novels of proposition," in which the "insistence on fatality, circumstance, predestination is overtly paralleled by her apparent conviction that character is inevitably determined by action and that the social individual is subordinate to his circumstance" (157, 159).

In a study appearing fourteen years later, Harriet Blodgett forthrightly repudiated Heath's assumptions about the strictly social-realist nature of Bowen's work.[20] She tentatively qualifies the author as a "psychological realist who must use symbolic methods" (8). Discerning a Jungian tendency in the novelist's aesthetic, she conceives of Bowen's world as one in which the individual must find meaning through her/his imagination and by perfecting her/his moral identity. Jung's "process of individuation" is introduced as a parallel to Bowen's controlling theme of growth, which implies "growth into consciousness" as well as "expanding awareness." Such evolutionary processes, Blodgett contends, include the emergence of cultural and emotional values out of originally biological drives, leading to eventual self-realization—to what she defines as the "actualization of the numinous *Self*" (12, 16, 17). Inferring from this "sense of the numinous" a "religious sensibility," Blodgett ends up categorizing Bowen as an essentially Christian writer, a "modern myth-maker" whose central myth is that of the Fall. As the author's "unescapable subject," the human struggle for perfection through ascending to higher levels of consciousness is considered to represent a redemption for the world's Fall from God's Grace (18–20). Bowen's novels are thus "offerings to the imagination, heightenings of actuality, and transmutations of the literal" (24).

Hermione Lee's comprehensive and intelligent discussion of all of Bowen's fiction succeeds in setting aright many of the erroneous notions Bowen's work had gathered around itself. The focus of

Lee's study is, as the passage quoted earlier conveys, the author's central if unusual inscription in both the Anglo-Irish and the European modernist literary traditions. Lee traces the "quality of wistfulness" and the "satirical coolness" characterizing Bowen's work straightforwardly to the former (17). The specific kind of humor, "always verging on the grotesque," as well as the extreme and unexpected violence punctuating her narratives are also presented as part of the author's Anglo-Irish heritage (21). At the same time, it is Bowen's outstanding ability to scrutinize, record, and criticize "pre-war, wartime, and post-war England and Ireland" that places her "firmly in the tradition of Jane Austen, George Eliot, Henry James, and E. M. Forster" (12). In line with Heath, Lee argues that Bowen further deserves recognition as a modern writer "for her analysis of dislocation, unease, and betrayal" in a thoroughly disenchanted culture. Lee suggests that by applying "elaborately formal methods to chaotic, inexpressible experience," Bowen played her "part in the modernist paradox" through the "precise charting of a loss." Foregrounding the crucial relations between "place and plot" (132) in Bowen's fiction, Lee highlights the historical background of the author's critiques of class convention and her concomitant preoccupation with a declining civilization. She admires Bowen's earlier fiction and her original methods of "controlled . . . analysis of motive and emotion," but finds fault with the later novels' preoccupation with the "abnormal" and the unconscious, surfacing in their obsession with "involuntary recall, nonverbal communication, retardation, infantilism, and fantasy life" (192). Because they fall outside the limited scope that forms the underlying (and unquestioned) traditional critical framework of Lee's discussion, Lee denounces the disruptive narrative strategies and technical experiments increasingly featured in these later texts in favor of the more reassuringly "modernist" texts of the 1930s and 1940s.

Indicative of the elusive quality, or rather, the fundamental ambiguity of her work, such dissenting views point to what I consider one of Bowen's most outstanding features, that is, her refusal to be classified in terms of established generic and/or stylistic categories. When I first came upon Bowen's novels several years ago, I was immediately taken by both their subject matter and their idiosyncratic style, as well as by the thoroughly puzzling effects these jointly produced. Indeed, every one of her narratives left me with a sense of unease, a decidedly disconcerting ambivalence. None of the existing critical appreciations offered satisfactory answers to the probing questions raised by and in these texts. Introductory rather than analytic in character, and in the main traditional in their manner of approach, these investigations are inadequate, if not ultimately reductive, assessments of Bowen's accomplishment. Although I am, one way or another, indebted to every one of the critics just mentioned, I do not think that these studies duly recognize Bowen for what she also is: a truly radical, innovative, and critically practicing feminist. Their virtual gender blindness and their unwillingness to engage in any but rather sketchy terms with Bowen's destabilizing sexual subtexts has led earlier critics to disregard what seems to me one of the central issues problematized in/by the author's texts. By obscuring the operations of gender on the thematic as well as the discursive levels of her novels, they actually have deprived Bowen of her radical edge.

More recently, a feminist appreciation of a selection of Bowen's novels has appeared. Phyllis Lassner's short but pertinent reevaluation of the author's texts from a feminist perspective was clearly long overdue.[21] This critic begins by pointing out that "viewing a woman writer as a connecting link in a primarily patriarchal tradition" diminishes and conceals "what is exceptional about her work," then proceeds to locate Bowen's resistance to classification firmly in the issue of gender (142). The focus of Lassner's argument is the myth of femininity as represented by dominant cultural discourses as well as by the conventions of "English domestic fiction for women." The constraining effects of these discursive regimes are connected to the "struggles with autonomy, dependence, and self-expression" of Bowen's female protagonists (153). By exploring the author's fiction "in the context of her marginality," Lassner maintains that her critical response to narrative traditions "reflects her position as an outsider both culturally and as a woman of her time" (145). While Lassner's emphasis on language and power in relation to female subjectivity is both apt and relevant, her insistence on female marginalization and her concentration on gender as a merely oppressive social function seem too one-sided to account for the complex and intertwined ways in which both sexuality and gender surface in Bowen's fictions. What is more, like her critical predecessors, Lassner prefers to overlook the configurations of lesbian sexuality emerging on various levels of these idiosyncratic texts. Assuming that Bowen's subversive potential resides in precisely this area, I decided to (re)read a selection of her novels from a lesbian feminist perspective. Poststructuralist and deconstructive theory provided me with the analytic and interpretive framework I was looking for. It has, I believe, proved sufficiently flexible to accommodate a type of fiction that escapes conventional generic boundaries and at the same time comprehensive enough to allow for an exploration of the wide range of moral, epistemological, psychological, and political questions addressed in Bowen's narratives.

By approaching Bowen from a lesbian feminist angle, I do not wish to suggest that she herself would have defined her work in such terms. Indeed, the author considered what "must inevitably be called ... feminism" in her admired fellow writer Virginia Woolf to be a "bleak quality, an aggressive streak, which can but irritate, disconcert."[22] A few lines preceding this denunciation, however, Bowen had raised the question, "Whence ... this obsession of hers that women were being martyrized humanly, inhibited creatively, by the stupidities of a man-made world?" Intensely verbal and articulate, ambitious, self-aware as well as knowledgeable about precisely the "stupidities of a man-made world" (in which she identified herself as "a writer before [being] a woman"), Bowen obviously could not subscribe to a notion of her sex as helplessly victimized by an oppressively patriarchal culture. While her confidence in the range of the authorial will, her belief that anything in which she engaged imaginatively was "something *I* make what it is by my will that it shall be like that," suffered severely in the course of her experience, her position toward (the exertion of) discursive power in relation to gender is more complicated than either her own or Lassner's comments convey.

Since my understanding of the operations of literary texts is largely shaped by feminist theory, I inevitably bring to Bowen's novels those analytic and critical tools that—to recall the opening epigraph—function as "forms of experience" in themselves and thus provide me with the most effective means "to feel and to comment and to explain" the complex problems they present. "Participating imaginatively" in the semiotic process in which writer, text, and reader are inevitably joined so as to prevent the power of each from going entirely "unchecked," I have sought to recreate yet another Elizabeth Bowen by "projecting" my "thought and emotion" into "form": this book constitutes the reflection of my undertaking. Central to the textual analyses is the question of female sexual identity, which is considered in relation to discourse and to symbolic agency. Different theoretical emphases have led to divergent angles of vision on these overriding themes. Chapters 2 and 3 focus on one of Bowen's early novels, *The Last September* (1929). As a bildungsroman, or novel of development, the text gives rise to an examination of the psychological and ideological underpinnings of the concept of (female) adolescence in general, and of the function of writing adolescence by a female author in particular. Chapters 4 and 5, organized around Bowen's war novel *The Heat of the Day* (1949), seek to demonstrate how the author's increasing awareness of the discursive, and thus contingent, nature of both history and morality affected her views on the precarious position of the female speaking subject within the power structures determining both. In chapters 6 and 7, Bowen's last and perhaps least accessible novel, *Eva Trout* (1969), is placed within a psychoanalytic perspective. The discussion is aimed at tracing the textual inscription of sexual excess and of the primordial mother/daughter bond in its constitutive function in the process of female subjectivity/sexuality. The concluding chapter centers on the stylistic aspects of Bowen's discourse, arguing that the subversive desire operative on the various levels of her texts legitimates the author's transfer from a marginal to an ex-centric place in the literary field.

2

Technologies of Female Adolescence

Nothing can take place nowhere.
—"Notes on Writing a Novel"

The Ideological Timespace of The Last September (1929)

Fictionalization/Factualization. In her preface (1952) to the American edition of *The Last September* (1929; hereafter *LS*), Elizabeth Bowen remarked upon a number of respects in which this, her second novel, deviates from any of the others she had written so far. Set in County Cork at the time of the Irish Troubles (1920), it is one of the two novels whose action takes place entirely in Ireland. It is also the only one "set back deliberately, in a former time." Clearly reminiscent of her own girlhood summers, *LS* is, as Bowen avers, a "work of instinct rather than knowledge" and, "to a degree, a 'recall' book." Although she considered it to be "nearest to [her] heart," having sprung from a "deep, unclouded, spontaneous source," the author warns against reading the novel as autobiography, for it is "at many, many removes" from that (96).

This warning is not to suggest that Bowen maintained a strict and straightforward separation between fiction and what she, in fact, called "'real' life."[1] Indeed, she discounted the traditional distinction, both on account of its untenability and on literary grounds. Still, as a writer extremely conscious of her artistic and professional responsibilities, Bowen found it impossible to dismiss the opposition life/literature as simply irrelevant. The many direct or indirect observations on the issue in her nonfictional writings testify to her awareness of its problematical implications. Bowen tackled the problem of (un)tenability by coining the phrase "transposed autobiography." She first used this phrase in the preface (1949) to the American edition of *Encounters* (1923; hereafter, *E*) in an attempt to account for the "blend of precocity and naïvety" she retrospectively perceived in some of her early stories.[2] This presumed flaw was partly attributed to her youthful age. In her early twenties, the author concedes, she ransacked literary texts for their "power to express, reflect, magnify and give body to states of feeling" she was only then becoming gradually conscious of in herself. At the time, "reality meant the books [she] had read." It was not that Bowen's own sensations were new to her; rather, it was that she newly gained awareness of them, an awareness that could be cultivated through (other people's) language. By means of what she defines as "synthetic language," the young writer felt able to "express what *was* real and true to [her] nonetheless."[3] This suggests that Bowen discerned that one's sense of reality, and thus one's sense of oneself, does not derive from so-called raw experience so much as from its textualization, in "real life" as in literature. This assumption is borne out by her assertion that the characters in these early stories had a "'realness' for which [she] could not account." The implicit suggestion is that the relations between life and literature are fully reciprocal, or more precisely, intrinsically dialogical. For, imparting a realness to her fictional characters that was as yet "beyond her ken," Bowen was capable of creating a sense of meaningful reality in fiction that she was only beginning to feel in "real life."[4] Borrowing meaning from literary texts that, filtered through her own developing consciousness, in turn served to create a realness unknown to her in actual experience, Bowen thus constructed first and foremost an *extra*-fictional sense of reality. By establishing a connection between between Self and (the) Other/s, she forged her own reality, a reality whose meaningfulness could only obtain in/ through language.[5]

Her initially "brigandish" attitude toward literature allowed Bowen to accumulate a "synthetic" language that could gradually develop into a voice of her own. The stories in *Encounters,* she observes, already display a keen "susceptibility to places, particular moments, objects, and seasons of the year."[6] It nonetheless took several years of living and writing before Bowen attained the profound awareness of the interpenetration of language, self, and world that enabled her to give meaning to what she ten years later identified as her own "unique susceptibility to experience."[7] By modifying this notion with the assertion that the writer's susceptibility is identical to her/his experience, Bowen underscores a concern central to postmodern thought, that is, that there is no such thing as a *direct* experience of reality. This holds true for identity as well, for, as she explains, the "susceptibility is, equally, the writer." In other words, any experience of self or world is mediated, and the primary means of mediation is language, or rather, discourse. This leads Bowen to the conclusion that a "writer can never be absent from what he writes."[8] The ineluctability of this insight results in what at first sight appears to be a contradictory position. For while she acknowledges that "impersonality in . . . writing is, for me certainly, impossible," she finds herself objecting most strongly to "stories which reek to me of myself by exhibiting sentiments—or betraying them." She rejects stories that seem "yoked to [her] personality" by declaring that she is "dead against art's being self-expression."[9] Although the paradox remains ultimately unresolved, Bowen is far too self-conscious a writer to leave matters at that. She therefore returns to the question of "the personal" by picking up the phrase used earlier in a very restricted sense, expanding the notion of "transposed autobiography" to encompass fiction in general:

> To return to the matter of the personal, I repeat that one cannot wholly eliminate oneself for a second, and also sufficient, reason: any fiction . . . is bound to be transposed autobiography. (True, it may be this at so many removes as to defeat ordinary recognition.) I can, and indeed if I would not I still must, relate any and every story I have written to something that happened to me in my own life. But here I am speaking of happenings in a broad sense—to *behold* and *react*, is where I am concerned a happening; speculations, unaccountable stirs of interest, longings, attractions, apprehensions without knowable cause—these are happenings also.[10]

The passage suggests that "happenings in the broad sense" determine the texture of the writer's susceptibility. Her/his unique susceptibility, is, as my emphasis shows, fundamentally a way of looking at and responding to the world. Such angles of vision have, in their turn, been shaped and spurted into awareness by/through other texts or, in discourse, in dialogue with (the) Other/s.

Bowen's phrase "transposed autobiography" provides more than a useful way of approaching her stories or novels, for it can justifiably be extended to cover all of her work. Allowing me to read Bowen's "fiction" in relation to her many "nonfictional" writings, "transposed autobiography" therefore neatly describes the guiding principle underlying my readings of the novels in this and the following chapters. Such a form of intertextual reading naturally does not stop here. Since it is by *beholding* and *reacting* that a writer's susceptibility—which is identical to her/his experience—is constituted, it is essential to take the text of history, that is, the cultural conditions in which the texts were produced, equally into account. This is not to suggest that I intend to create a convincing picture of Elizabeth Bowen as a human being, of what she was "really like." Rather, I will explore the interconnections between these various texts and try to delineate the "author-effect" they jointly produce.[11] I also intend to show that Bowen's novels are more than explorations of certain themes in a particular style

or idiosyncratic manner. A lesbian feminist poststructuralist perspective enables me to read the novels as incisive critiques of
patriarchal and heterosexist ideologies, as complex cultural texts
whose radicalness has been obscured by traditional appreciations
of the author's work. I will furthermore read the texts as the sites
of discursive struggle. As struggles not only for artistic expression
but also for a position from which to speak at all as a writer and
as a woman, they are elaborations on (discursive) power as such.
Located at the intersection of the author's self and the world, the
novels reflect a quest for identity *in* and *through* language. As I
hope to make clear, it is precisely a growing awareness of the
precarious and contingent basis of subjectivity in discourse that
emerges as the overriding Bowen theme.

Dialogism and Authorship. Bowen's acknowledgment of the critical function of literary discourse in the formation of subjectivity is
in itself not so remarkable. What is remarkable is her appreciation
of the fact that the most profoundly felt (private) experiences can
obtain reality value only within a discursive set of interrelations,
within an essentially *public* context. In other words, what Bowen
recognizes is that (a sense of) identity is not so much modified or
even determined as virtually *constituted* in discourse, that is, that a
sense of self as well as of the world comes into being not only
within the system of language but *through* language itself. The
assumption of the intertextual nature of identity poses a problem
when placed in relation to the notion of (female) authorship. How
does Bowen's insight into the discursive basis of subjectivity relate
to the authoritative—and explicitly moral—stance taken up by
the majority of her narrators? This question calls for a closer look
at the notions of "dialogism" and "answerability" as proposed by
Mikhail Bakhtin (1895–1924).[12]

Bakhtin considers ethical activity to exist in/of deeds of the
individual in the world. Since the subject derives her/his unique
position in life from the ever-changing conditions of time and place

in which s/he finds her/himself,[13] existence is not a passive state of being so much as an activity or event.[14] The ethical aspect resides in the process of creating or, more accurately, of authoring this event—be it in physical action, thought, utterance, or written text. Ethical values, then, are articulated in deeds, deeds performed in answer to others and to the world. The individual's life amounts to nothing but a series of shifting positions in response to specific yet altering circumstances. This implies that s/he is not only answerable *to* the world but also answerable *for* her/his responses. From the notion of the Self as performance in response to (the) Other/s it follows that authorial activity, that is, the creation of (literary) texts, is not merely representative but paradigmatic of the activity of being: "The architectonic activity of authorship, which is the building of a text, parallels the activity of human existence, which is the building of a self."[15]

A concept of human existence as an endless string of communicative acts between Self and (the) Other/s leads to a central place for the utterance, which, in addition to words and texts, occurs in thoughts and deeds. To accommodate the comprehensiveness of this process, Bakhtin developed his theory of dialogism. Positing that the human being is never complete or whole, he sees the Self as fundamentally a gift of (the) Other/s, for the individual's response to her/his environment *is* life itself. No individual can be in complete possession of her/his identity, or fully understand or know her/himself, since the physical restraints imposed on the means of perception prevent any individual from perceiving her/himself as a whole. It is our temporal and spatial placement that provides us with our unique vantage points on both the world and ourselves.

Bakhtin conceives of language as both subjectivity and communication.[16] The paradox of the human condition, then, is that the means for expression of the self, its so-called markers, are essentially noncoincidental with it. This radical noncoincidence accounts for the inability of all aspects of language to merge with the human subject. Within Bakhtin's "architectonics," the subject derives her/his definition from her/his adjustment to and positions within the "heteroglossia" of social discourses available in a given society at a certain moment in history. The only (self-)consciousness of the subject is her/his consciousness of the fact that s/he can never fully *be*. In other words, achieving a sense of oneself or acquiring an "identity" is an activity never to be completed. Just as the self is a ceaseless project, so is the world. "Reality" has no meaning in itself for it is only through values articulated in deeds that human beings give it its meaning(s). The Bakhtinian term "answerability" serves to bridge the gap between consciousness and the world. And this, as we have seen, is closely connected with the notion of authorship.

Authorship is the organizing principle of the texts of the self and the world. It operates through the creation of characters and dialogue. Since the author of literary texts is not a human being but a textual effect to be (re)constructed by the reader, the sense of self that the individual "authors" is no more than a subject-effect, never whole or identical to her/him and only to be perceived as a whole in/by others. Since the subject is constituted in discourse, and since discourse is impossible without the sign, the materiality of the word—as an intersection of diverse textual surfaces—is crucial to her/his meaning(s). To put it differently, since being involves a perpetual process of temporary fixing(s) in that which is Other so as to construct fictions of correspondence or identity, the alterity between self and the material world—both sign and social reality—is intrinsic to subjectivity. For Bakhtin, visualizing a Self through (the) Other/s is coterminous with consciousness: the end of the dialogue means the end of existence. Since one always exists within a multiplicity of discourses, one's self is fundamentally multiple, deriving its distinctive features from the heteroglossia by which it is (provisionally) defined.

Bakhtin's theory of dialogism is a philosophy of plenitude and abundance. His concept of authorship justifies, in the present post-

Derridean era, a reading of the (literary) text that, in addition to bringing to the surface its unsaid, focuses on what the text *does* say, on tracing the effects of its smallest intelligible units or "ideologemes."[17] Moreover, the idea of authorship makes it possible to conceive of the subject as not just an ontological but also an ethical category by defining her/his constitutive responses to (the) Other/s in terms of moral responsibility. As such, the concept at once guarantees a certain independence of action for the individual to meet her/his answerability *and* the possibility of transformation. This, among other things, explains the importance of Bakhtin's thought for feminism. It also signifies his relevance to an indisputably moral writer such as Bowen.

The theoretical significance of the combined notions of authorship and answerability notwithstanding, it is in the entirely positive, indeed celebratory employment of these terms that the limitations of Bakhtinian dialogism emerge. Furthermore, his extrapolation of the authoring of literary texts to the authoring of a self and vice versa implies a degree of autonomy and freedom of choice that seems, if not altogether unwarrantable, at least somewhat naïve. Within a lesbian feminist critical perspective, surely the oppressive aspects of discursive power and authority must also be taken into account. Louis Althusser's theory of ideology hence provides a useful complement to Bakhtin's dialogism.

Subjectivity and Ideology. In "Ideology and Ideological State Apparatuses," Althusser defines ideology as the representation of the "imaginary relationship of individuals to their real conditions of existence."[18] This illusory structure always exists in actions or practices performed by the individual within the social. Such practices serve to secure specific interests of particular social groups. Embedded in social institutions (the media, the educational system, the family) Ideological State Apparatuses (ISAs) (re)produce *illusory* social relations and obtain in material practices in which both dominant and dominated groups participate. The essential question remains why "men [*sic*] 'need' this imaginary transposition of their real conditions of existence in order to 'represent to themselves' their real conditions of existence" (37). This question gives (the notion of) the subject a central place in Althusser's theory.

There can be no ideology without subjects. Ideologies, however, are not merely effected and constituted *by* subjects, for, as Althusser points out, the "category of the subject is only constitutive of all ideology insofar as all ideology has the function (which defines it) of 'constituting' concrete individuals as subjects" (45). Ideology, therefore, while needing the subject as its final destination, at the same time "*interpellates concrete individuals as concrete subjects,* by the functioning of the category of the subject*" (47). Like the ostensible transparency of language, the "obviousness" of the individual subject's "uniqueness" issues directly from the operation of ideology. Subjective identity is no more than an ideological effect, for it is a "peculiarity of ideology that it imposes (without appearing to do so, since these are obviousnesses) obviousness as obviousness" (46). Since every subject is *always already* inscribed in ideology, any knowledge of this operation can only be obtained "while speaking in ideology, and from within" (47).

Although any discursive activity is by definition ideological, to appreciate the fact that there is no "outside" to ideology does not mean that no consciousness of its operations is possible. Various minority groups have more or less successfully contested dominant ideologies in the relatively short history of Western capitalist society. This shows that even in its most invisible operations, ideology does not form an impenetrable screen of intransigent forces of power. Indeed, it is the growing awareness of the operations of dominant discourses that has enabled the (lesbian) feminist critique of (heterocentric) patriarchy. Hence, while exposing ideology as a force of structural oppression, Althusser also insists that ideology is the site of discursive struggle, and therewith of potential social change. Instead of analyzing ideological apparatuses as violent distorters of reality, as (abstract) powers imposing themselves on individual subjects, he emphasizes the ambiguity of their doubly constitutive function. After all, ideologies need material practices— and thus individual subjects—for their inscription. It is this very ambiguity that is borne out by, or more accurately defines, the concept of the subject.

The subject is both a theoretical category, a precise though abstract notion never to be fully realized by any one individual, and the specific configuration of ideological effects constituting the individual woman or man. The individual is a subject even before s/he is born, for her/his existence as a human being is prefigured by the discursive system in which s/he is quite literally delivered. In this sense, the term "subject" designates our state of subjection to a system that preexists us and exceeds our control; at the same time, however, the term signifies a "free subjectivity, a centre of initiatives, author of and responsible for its actions." [19] The ambiguity of the term, and the contradictory nature of its produced effect, is most clearly exemplified in the system of language/discourse, the ideological apparatus par excellence.

In line with Bakhtin and Althusser, contemporary poststructuralist theorists insist on the discursive construction of subjectivity. This necessarily implies a central place for the act of enunciation. In order to be able to speak, to become an agent in the symbolic order, the enunciating subject must adopt a position within the discursive network constituting the social. Not all positions within a given society, however, are equally available to all subjects. Michel Foucault has pointed up the inextricable links between the forces of power and the structures of discourse.[20] Focusing on the intertextual nature of discursive formations, he argues that all systems of meaning and knowledge are essentially contingent, historical, and thus discontinuous. The ideological grounding of all forms of meaning/knowledge allows dominant groups to use the strategies of exclusion and assimilation in order to suppress that which threatens social stability, those radical discourses whose heterogeneity cannot be fitted into the homogeneous interpretation of reality, the official ideology upon which established power structures rest.[21] Even so, the very existence of minority discourses in the margins of the central discourse betray the inherent fallibility of the structures of dominant power. Laying bare the interconnections between power, discourse, and suppression, Foucault's project both allows for detailed feminist analyses of the operations of phallogocentrism and creates a space for radical change—on the level of consciousness as well as in society.

Engendered Subjectivity and Patriarchal Ideology. The feminist analysis of the discourses of patriarchal power (e.g., law, science, religion) extends to exposing the "masculist" bias of theoretical discourses.[22] Thus, Teresa de Lauretis criticizes Althusser and Foucault for their virtual gender blindness. Ignoring gender, these "radical" theorists implicitly reinscribe the founding myth of patriarchy, failing to take into account that subject-positions are distributed differentially against a set of power structures not only along the lines of class and race but also along those of gender. The notion of the subject as an ideological effect displaced across a range of heterogeneous discourses is therefore not sufficient to account for *gendered* subjectivity.

In "The Technology of Gender,"[23] de Lauretis begins by suggesting that the conceptualization of gender as "sexual difference" appears to have become a "limitation, something of a liability to feminist thought."[24] Whether gender is seen as deriving from biological differences or differences in socialization or as the effect of signification, thinking of gender in these binary terms implies an extension of the conceptual framework of dominant ideology. In this way, sexual difference remains the demarcation line that divides women from men, or, when regarded as the result of discursive effects, it "ends up being in the last instance a difference (of woman) from man" (1). Establishing that "gender is not sex," de Lauretis then follows Althusser to introduce an elaborated version of the "sex/gender system," a notion that serves to designate the ideological apparatus by which gender is produced and maintained in a given society at a given moment in history.[25] Like all ideologies, the sex/gender system is a meaning-producing system, and as such, it is closely connected with sociopolitical power structures. Insofar as gender refers primarily to a set of social relations, it is thus both a sociocultural construct and a semiotic apparatus. The meaning-producing function of gender derives from the fact that individuals can (re)present themselves only within the existing sex/ gender system and therewith assume a position within the social order. By taking up these positions we acquire a sociocultural meaning/identity. The sex/gender system, however, also "engenders" the individual in the ideological process of "interpellation."[26] This implies, in the words of de Lauretis, that a "social representation is accepted and absorbed by an individual as her (or his) own representation, and so becomes, for that individual, real, even though it is in fact imaginary" (12). Just as subjectivity generally is a produced/producing effect of ideology, so is the "construction of gender . . . both the product and the process of its representation" (5). Gender is thus the "variable configuration of sexual discursive positionalities" whose social representation and subjective construction are mutually effective/affected (7). The latter aspect ensures a certain degree of subjective agency and the possibility of social change.

What de Lauretis calls the "ambiguity of gender" thus resembles the ambiguity of subjectivity, for there is no outside to the sex/ gender system—not even for feminism. Indeed, as she continues to point out, the characteristic feature of feminism since the early 1980s has been its consciousness of its complicity with gender ideology (11). The "subject of feminism" is therefore a theoretical construct that operates both inside and outside gender ideology. From such a position of double inscription, feminist discourse today should, according to de Lauretis, seek to account for the processes whereby the (female) subject—as "distinct from Woman

. . . the *representation* of an essence inherent in all women" as well as from "women, the real historical beings and social subjects"— is constructed in both discursive and material practices (9–10).

Where it is de Lauretis's explicit objective to move beyond Foucault in her (re)conceptualization of the sex/gender system, so that her main focus is on the constitution and function of gender in Western culture, I would equally like to foreground the Foucauldian analysis of sexuality as a "set of effects produced in bodies, behaviours, and social relations by a certain deployment deriving from a complex political technology."[27] While underscoring de Lauretis's objections to a view of gender as sexual difference, I think that the notion of the sex/gender system has in its turn become a "limitation, something of a liability to feminist thought." For even in its putatively "problematized" version,[28] the feminist analysis of the patriarchal sex/gender system has led on the one hand, as Judith Butler argues, to a reinscription of the "immutable character of sex" and, on the other, to a further or renewed obscuring of the structures of psychosexual differentiation operative within and across this system.[29]

In *Gender Trouble,* Judith Butler adopts Foucault's method of "genealogical critique" to identify compulsory heterosexuality and phallogocentrism as the two "regimes of power/discourse" constitutive of both masculist and feminist gender discourses.[30] The poststructuralist destabilization of identities and their meanings entails that the notions male/female can no longer be taken to be "natural facts," as distinct from culturally or "artificially" produced genders. Indeed, she asks, is it not "naturalness" itself that is "constituted through discursively constrained performance acts that produce the body through and within the categories of sex?" (x). The assumption of a sexed body, or an anterior sexual difference, onto which the (insidious) effects of cultural gender discourses are differentially displaced and inscribed, Butler points out, rests on "the state of nature hypothesis." It is this very hypothesis that, in its contemporary guise as the "ontological integrity of the subject before the law," provides the legitimating ground of liberal humanist philosophy and Western metaphysics (3). Since the sex/gender distinction underlying much feminist critical discourse "suggests a radical discontinuity between sexed bodies and culturally constructed genders," sex itself continues to function as a fixed or given category of which gender forms the "multiple interpretation" (6). But, as the Bakhtinian concept of being-as-activity implies, the "duality of sex" is not a biological or ontological given so much as a discursively established construct. This leads Butler to the assumption that the binary options of "natural" sex per se might in effect be no more than a "variable construction." Such a denaturalization of sex results in a further problematization of the notion of gender:

> Gender ought not to be conceived merely as the cultural inscription of meaning on a pregiven sex . . . ; gender must also designate the very apparatus of production whereby the sexes themselves are established. As a result, gender is not to culture as sex is to nature; gender is also the discursive/cultural means by which "sexed nature" or a "natural sex" is produced and established as "prediscursive," prior to culture, a politically neutral surface *on which* culture acts. (7)

The notion of sex as a stable or natural given serves to maintain existing gender relations, for the "hegemonic discursive/epistemic model of gender intelligibility" assumes that there must be a "stable sex expressed through a stable gender" (151). The ostensibly natural facts of sex, oppositionally and hierarchally defined, Butler infers, can therefore be considered to be discursively produced "in the interests of other political and social interests" (7). These interests are first and foremost *sexual* interests. For, as Monique Wittig has contended, the basis of the contract upon which the maintenance of the social order depends is the institution of heterosexuality: "To live in society is to live in heterosexuality. In fact, social contract and heterosexuality are two superimposable notions."[31] The existence of the separate categories of men and women, prior and/or exterior to the social order, is preconditional for the prevalence of "natural" heterosexuality. It is therefore only within the context of what Butler terms the "heterosexual matrix" that the "category of women [can] achieve stability and coherence" (5). Heterosexuality, Wittig reminds us, is not a "natural" disposition but a sociocultural institution, a "nonexistent object, a fetish, an ideological form which cannot be grasped in reality, except through its effects, whose existence lies in the mind of people, but in a way that affects their whole life, the way they act, the way they move, the way they think."[32] And, as I have argued earlier, it is in its very "presumptive heterosexuality" that the feminist critique of the sex/gender system becomes exceedingly problematical for a lesbian feminist practice of cultural analysis.

Underscoring "mainstream" feminism's implication in the structures of (heterosexual) gender ideology, Jane Gallop submits that the "internalized heterosexuality" of much feminist theory may indeed be read "symptomatically" as part of the "heterosexual teleology" implicit in both Western culture and the practice of literary theory.[33] Rhetorically asking whether "we prefer sexual difference because this particular difference conventionally promises narrative solution," Gallop analyzes the desire underlying much feminist theoretical practice as a fundamental desire for "a happy ending" within a cultural plot of otherwise irreducible differences. The feminist focus on gender can thus be seen to reinstate the promise of what Cora Kaplan has called the " 'inevitable resolution' " to the plot of heterosexuality, the dominant cultural scenario in relation to which other social/theoretical divisions and deviations operate as mere " 'narrative backdrop or minor stumbling-block[s].' "[34] Since, as we shall see, the story of heterosexual romance functions as a central, if disrupted, intertext in Bowen's novels, my foregrounding of sexuality will seek both to illuminate the sexual underpinnings of her heroines' negotiations for a gendered subject-position within their narrative "timespaces" and to denaturalize the categories of sex in the theoretical perspectives on gender that form the intertexts of my discussions.

One final remark before I go on to explore these issues in the context of *LS*. Insofar as all products of consciousness are inscribed in ideology, both institutional discourses such as theory and technologies of gender such as cinematic or literary texts produce and "implant" representations of sexualities and gender relations that are experienced as "real" by individual subjects.[35] To define the "complex of meaning effects, habits, dispositions, associations, and perceptions resulting from the semiotic interaction of self and outer world," Teresa de Lauretis, following C. S. Peirce, uses the term "experience." Her description of gender experience as the shifting "constellation or configuration of meaning effects" produced by the "sociocultural practices, discourses, and institutions devoted to the production of men and women"[36] shows a remarkable similarity to Elizabeth Bowen's notion of "so-called real life" as a series of "happenings in a broad sense." We recall that Bowen defines a writer's experience/susceptibility as the "speculations, unaccountable stirs of interest, longings, attractions, apprehensions without knowable cause" that in one form or another find their way into fiction as "transposed autobiography." The correspondence between these respective conceptualizations of experience/reality suggests the potential significance of radical theories of gender such as de Lauretis's for a critical (re)reading of Bowen's work.

The Interpellation of the Adolescent

Adolescence as a Technology of Gender. In traditional generic terms, *The Last September* can be classified as a social comedy that satirizes the manners and morals of the Anglo-Irish landed gentry and the English upper-middle classes.[37] Depicting the quest for identity of its adolescent protagonist, Lois Farquar, it could also be defined as a novel of development, or bildungsroman. The main narrative events are sufficiently undramatic for some critics to pay special attention to the novel's political background. These generally foreground Bowen's ambivalence toward the Anglo-Irish Ascendancy, as articulated in her family history, *Bowen's Court* (1942), and in a number of critical essays.[38] The violence of the Troubles is so muffled, however, that we may safely assume different issues to be central in *LS*. Written in a style at once taut, precise, and impressionistic, the novel's narrative voice is characteristically authoritative. The typical Bowen narrator emerges as rational, intelligent, witty, and aloof yet benevolent. The often-comic dialogues are sometimes oblique, occasionally obscure to the extent that necessary referential information is elided. This device forces the reader actively to engage in the process of meaning construction, and to bring to bear on the narrative events the implications of the evocative descriptive passages. The characters' occupations during this lazy month in late summer are of a decidedly prosaic nature: their activities range from the reception and entertainment of house guests to tennis parties, dances, and casual conversation. The novel yet emanates throughout a sense of urgency and impending crisis for which neither its stylistic concentration nor the violence in the background can satisfactorily account.

Hermione Lee observes that Bowen's "talent for expressing unease, a constant sense of peril," exploited to great effect in many of her short stories, successfully "inculcates a sense of nervousness into the reader" of *LS*. Lee associates the sense of doom pervading the novel to the "pull of fatality" introduced by the presence of death, which she identifies as the "true reality" behind the "transient" history of the narrative.[39] To support her assumption, she quotes a passage in which the narrative voice merges with the main character's consciousness to proclaim that "life, seen whole for a moment, was one act of apprehension, the apprehension of death" (*LS*, 202). Read with a different emphasis, the passage leads to a possibly even more disconcerting conclusion: that it is not the threat of death but life itself that is an unremitting enactment of crisis. Such an interpretation links up with the presentation of the adolescent quest of the novel's protagonist. Instead of providing a "very good example of Elizabeth Bowen's talent for presenting pre-adulthood,"[40] the character of Lois Farquar then represents, as William Heath has also suggested, the "prototype . . . to set the pattern for all Miss Bowen's heroines," characters in crisis irrespective of their age.[41] The crisis structure of adolescence thus assumes a far wider significance than Lee appears willing to concede. I will come back to this.

The first of *LS*'s three long chapters opens, as the title announces, with "The Arrival of Mr and Mrs Montmorency" upon the scene of Danielstown, one of Ireland's Big Houses, owned by Sir Richard and Lady Naylor.[42] Staying at Danielstown are Myra Naylor's nephew Laurence, down from Oxford for the summer, and Sir Richard's nineteen-year-old orphaned niece Lois, daughter of his late sister Laura. Added to this company are Hugo Montmorency, one-time lover of Laura's and old friend of Sir Richard's, and his sickly wife, Francie. The arrival of the "long-promised visitors" create in Lois a sense of "happiness, of perfection" that makes her wish to "freeze the moment and keep it always." Setting the tone of the protagonist's quest, her reaction conveys a conflict, for despite a yearning for "things to happen," she is also moved by a need for stability and permanence. Having just left school, Lois finds herself in that twilight zone of transience between childhood and adulthood generally known as adolescence. She is tossed about by bouts of extreme self-consciousness and a sense of doom springing from the suspicion that "nobody notice[s]" or "would take the trouble to understand her" (7–8). This is the kind of tension customarily associated with the experience of adolescence.

The concept of adolescence as a stage of development with explicitly sexual connotations is of relatively recent date.[43] With the dissemination of (Freudian) psychoanalytic theory or, in Foucauldian terms, with the "invention of sexuality" at the end of the nineteenth century, adolescence became generally regarded as by far the most crucial stage in identity formation precisely on account of its sexual overdetermination. But since identity is not an objective to be achieved so much as a shifting configuration, a process of endless (re)contextualization, the discourse on adolescence has come to function as a "technology" of gender in its own right. By positing a direct and causal relationship among the biological body, gender, and (hetero)sexual desire, the institution of adolescence acts as an ideological apparatus ushering children into their positions as (hetero)sexual subjects. As such, it operates as a measure of containment. At the same time, the concept is a semiotic apparatus by means of which children of either sex are prepared for their future social roles as gendered sexual beings. A variety of cultural discourses serve to ensure social stability by defining the period of adolescence as one of licensed rebellion, as a necessary phase of emotional and mental confusion and of (sexual) experimentation and irresponsibility. Such instability is, at least within Western societies, never allowed to reemerge in adult subjects—with the possible exception of artists and lunatics. Thus, while the locus of twentieth-century definitions of identity in the first instance appears to reside in a person's sexuality, the institutionalization of nineteenth-century medico-scientific discourses has paradoxically resulted in a shift away from sex (as a "natural" given) to gender (a cultural position). With the acquisition of a (hetero)sexual gender identity—that is, with the internalization of *symbolic* representations of normative "masculinity" or "femininity," individuals become the coherent subjects that (patriarchal) ideology needs to sustain itself. As we have seen, any subject is in her/his turn equally dependent on her/his gender identity in order to attain that sense of self-mastery that s/he needs to assume a position in the social order. While betraying the essentially constructed nature of the "obviousness" called adolescence, this double inscription also explains the ambivalent feelings aroused by the phenomenon in retrospect. Once gendered adulthood has been successfully realized, adolescence represents a period of intense anxiety, sexual confusion, and an often daunting sense of nonexistence, while at the same time marking the individual's definitive subjection to the constraints and demands of a given symbolic order.

Since adolescence is fundamentally about the acquisition of heterosexual gender identities, the operation of the technologies of gender is particularly felt during any number of years between the ages of fourteen and twenty to twenty-four. Teresa de Lauretis observes that identity is "interpreted or reconstructed by each of us within the horizon of meanings and knowledge available in the culture at given historical moments."[44] This entails that adolescence directly confronts the individual with both normative heterosexuality and the differential accessibility of available subject-positions unequally distributed along, among others, gender lines. This point needs stressing for, while generally acknowledged as forming a process of differentiation in the interplay between the psychic and the social, adolescence is conventionally analyzed in primarily psychological terms. Given the overall neglect of the sociohistorical level within psychoanalytic theory, it is not surprising to find that traditional psychological discourse tends to collapse male and female adolescence. This assimilation of the girl's experience to that of the boy's renders female adolescence, and therewith the gender inequality both in society and within theoretical discourse itself, virtually invisible.

Only recently has clinical psychoanalysis turned its focus to female sexual development as in many ways a crucially different process from its male counterpart.[45] The feminist theoretical engagement with psychoanalysis has also led to shifts in traditional notions of (female) adolescence. In the present context, it is furthermore interesting to note that the only two—unresolved—cases of Freud's involving female adolescents both center and founder on the operation of lesbian sexuality in his patients' histories, a fact that Freud first fails to notice and then relegates to his (retrospectively added) footnotes.[46] Indeed, as Jane Gallop aptly stipulates, for Freud, homosexuality as such was "an adolescent stage, a stage of development prior to adult reproductive heterosexuality."[47] Both the sexual overdetermination of the adolescent crisis and the wider cultural associations of sexual ambivalence surrounding the female adolescent place the prototypical value of the preadult Bowen heroine in a significant light.

These considerations further provide some indication about the causes underlying the "sense of peril" or "unease"—noted but unsatisfactorily accounted for by Hermione Lee—inspired in the reader of *LS*. For the produced/producing effects of signification, hence the double inscription of the subject in language and by extension in literary texts, entails that the sexual indeterminacy marking the protagonist's quest is carried over onto the reading subject herself. This supposition is indirectly confirmed by clinical psychologist Katherine Dalsimer, whose exploration of female adolescence turns to literary texts because of the "power of [their] insights into particular situations, which language delivers and which the reader, with a shock of personal recognition, acknowledges to be just."[48]

Interpellating Forces in Absentia. Erik Erikson notes that adolescents are "sometimes morbidly, often curiously, preoccupied with what they appear to be in the eyes of others as compared with what they feel they are, and with the question of how to connect the roles and skills cultivated earlier with the ideal prototypes of the day."[49] Although he takes care to insert the adolescent's feelings in this assessment of his/her conflictual sense of self, the presumed contrast between an "apparent" identity (in relation to others) and a "real" or anterior one (harbored by the adolescent her/himself) signals Erikson's moorings in traditional liberal humanist thought. Indeed, the underlying premise of his overall argument is a notion of individual consciousness as an essence gradually unfolding itself in accordance with its increasing engagement with the outside world. As we have seen, Bakhtinian dialogism and the critique of ideology refute such a concept of subjectivity. It is not so much the individual's investment in the exterior world of an as-yet "hidden" essence—patiently lying in wait for proper opportunities to reveal itself—that constitutes identity, but the interiorization of specific external meaning structures and symbolizations. Such internalization of cultural representations results in a sense of self by which the individual subsequently comes to "know" her/himself.[50]

The earliest "significant others," according to Erikson, are the young person's parents, at least in Western societies based on the nuclear family. Rather than mere role models or objects of identification, such others have been exposed by Althusserian and poststructuralist theories of ideology as exerting a fundamentally interpellating influence, an influence so profound that it inculcates a sense of self that seems wholly "natural" on both the psychic and the social levels of experience. It is important therefore to consider Lois Farquar's orphaned state. About the fate of her father the text does not give any explicit information. All we learn about "poor Walter" is that something "terribly sad" has happened to him, but this, as Lady Naylor informs us, "was what we always expected" (17). The cause of his wife's death remains equally unclear, but Laura figures quite prominently in the minds of the novel's characters. Though Lois's mother is absent from the narrative scene, her character therewith acquires particular significance. What is more, as Erikson notes, it is primarily the "encounter of maternal person and small infant" that initiates the child into the "cultural patterns" of the symbolic order into which it is born.[51]

As elusive as Laura Farquar-Naylor may be in her textual presence, equally as inscrutable does she appear to have been before she died—characteristically "without giving anyone notice of her intention" (19). Remembered as wild and rebellious, Laura lives on in her daughter Lois's restlessness. According to Hugo Montmorency, Laura "was always lovely. But she was never happy at all, even here [at Danielstown]. She never knew what she wanted— she was very vital" (19). Lois's state of high-strung tension reminds Hugo of her, for "next to Laura, [Lois] was the most fidgety person from whom he had suffered." There is, however, a difference in quality:

Laura's unrepose had been an irradiation, a quiver of personality. She was indefinite definitely, like a tree shining, shaking away outlines; a bay, a poplar in wind and sunshine. Her impulses—those incalculable springings-out of mind through the body—had had, like movements of branches, a wild kind of certainty. He had been half aware of some kind of design in her being of which she was unaware wholly. (63)

The passage suggests that Laura's wildness resided in her indefinite sexual identity: it was precisely her confusion in this respect that made her "never real in the way" Hugo wanted. He and her brother Sir Richard express their frustration about this in remarkably similar ways: " 'Talk and talk and you'd never know where you had her.' " The emphasis on the discursive nature of sexual positioning in these male characters' sense of reality suggests that Laura, who is throughout described in predominantly physical terms, refused to subject herself to their symbolic power, hence to adopt the role of Other to the male Self. Not willing to fit within established cultural patterns, Laura would, as Hugo observes, "start a crying-fit" if "she thought you had her" (19). In order to escape such constraints, Laura was "very remote" and eventually ran away. She nonetheless remains a haunting presence in the very atmosphere of the house upon which she has left her mark.[52] This unequivocally emerges from Laurence's nocturnal fantasies.

The young man is, despite his intellectual manner, highly susceptible to the residing mood of sexual rebellion Laura has left behind. Her impassioned nonconformism tickles his imagination:

[Laura's] confusion had clotted up in the air of the room and seemed, in that closest darkness under the ceiling, to be still impending. Here, choked in the sweep of the bed-curtains, she had writhed in those epic rages; against Hugo, against Richard, against any prospect in life at all; biting the fat resistant pillows, until once she had risen, fluttered at her reflection, dabbed her eyes, buttoned a tight sleek dress of that day's elegance over her heaving bosom, packed her dresses in arched trunks (that had come back since to rot in the attics) and driven off, averting from the stare of the house an angry profile. (107)

Laurence astutely perceives why the constant reminder of Laura's fickleness is threatening to the inhabitants of Danielstown. Instead of going north and marrying Farquar—the "rudest man in Ulster . . . with a disagreeably fresh complexion and an eye like a horse" (107)—Laura could have "done otherwise." But, and here Laurence's thoughts merge with the narrative voice, "there is a narrow and fixed compulsion . . . inside the widest ranges of our instability" (107). It is this compulsion to instability (with its resounding sexual connotations) that the adult characters in *LS* have taken great pains to ward off.

For Lois, Laura embodies the very ambivalent feelings to which she is currently prey. She is eager to learn more about her mother, whose actions "seemed so natural" and who figures prominently in the "kindly monolith of her childhood" (11, 27). While suggestive of the close bond between mother and daughter, this childhood, depicted as undifferentiated oneness, is at the same time shown to be invested with a "rather rare gloom" (13). The intense associations evoked by Laura's memory are connected with Lois's sensual experience of the sound, smell, and feel of nature. This makes for an extremely menacing effect, for Lois is vaguely aware that Laura's sexuality, her "naturalness," is precisely what turned her into an outcast. While susceptible to the attraction of the unrestrained impulse, she simultaneously feels profoundly lonely when she suspects "for herself a particular doom of exclusion." This issues in a strong desire to belong, to be "in a pattern . . . to be related" (23, 98). The connection between nature and Laura and the conflicting desires it evokes in Lois are brilliantly brought to the fore when the latter one evening defiantly turns her back on the family and walks into the garden alone:

A shrubbery path was solid with darkness, she pressed down it. Laurels [!] breathed coldly and close: on her bare arms the tips of leaves were timid and dank, like tongues of dead animals. Her fear of the shrubberies tugged at its chain, fear behind reason, fear before her birth; fear like the earliest germ of her life that had stirred in Laura. She went forward eagerly, daring a snap of the chain, singing; a hand to the thump of her heart, dramatic with terror. She thought of herself as forcing a pass. In her life— deprived as she saw it—there was no occasion for courage, which like an unused muscle slackened and slept. (33)

While highlighting the strength of Lois's sensual yearnings, the sequence goes on to stress her equally strong need to belong: when Lois next looks up to the house and sees the family "sealed in lamplight, secure and bright like flowers in a paperweight," they seem "desirable, worth much of this to regain." Her predicament is fully articulated when, the "laurels deserting her groping arm," the heroine recognizes that she has reached a point where "two paths crossed" (33): her physical desires "cross" the borders of the cultural "patterns" in which she must secure a place for herself.

William Heath rightly identifies the typical Bowen character "at the cross-roads" as a recurring theme in all of the author's novels. Regarding the conflict as one in which the individual's romantic will finds itself rebelling against the material constraints imposed by a corrupt society, he describes the situation in terms of "Innocence and Experience."[53] The conflict is not as straightforwardly oppositional as Heath suggests. In Bowen, "innocence," or Nature—which, as her consistent capitalization of the word suggests, is no more of a prediscursive given than its implied counterpart—

is never an explicitly positive term as opposed to a negative concept of "experience," or Culture. Assuming the tension between the senses and rationality, she rather insists on the continuing *struggle* between these two "modalities of being," a "living of the contradiction" that she sees as a primarily moral imperative. In her essay "Out of a Book," the author reflects on the issue in the context of reading.[54] The child, Bowen maintains, reads "unthinkingly, sensuously" until education enforces a change in attitude. The "young person is then thrown out of Eden," and "for evermore his brain is to stand posted between his self and the story." The reference to the garden of Eden underscores, on the one hand, that it is "carnal knowledge" that installs the subject in the sociosymbolic order, and, on the other, that the individual's insertion into the "story" of culture is premised on the radical noncoincidence of the self and its markers. The loss of this prelapsarian or presymbolic bliss is not to be deplored. Indeed, "it becomes an enormity, within the full-sized body, to read without the brain." The stakes involved are moral ones, for as Bowen contends, "It is not only our fate but our business to lose innocence, and once we have lost that it is futile to attempt to picnic in Eden" (265). This does not mean that the early sensations can or should be forgotten. Only in (discursively produced) "synthetic experience"—which "involv[es] valid emotion," "imagination" as well as the "brain"—does the possibility of "vision" exist, both ethically and aesthetically (269). By "doubl[ing] the meaning" of concrete events in material reality, fiction exposes the "insufficiency of so-called real life to the requirements of those who demand to be really alive" (264). Bowen concludes by claiming that the "process of reading is reciprocal" (267).

When we extend the author's ideas on reading the fictional text to the "text of reality," we are led to infer that it is in the active experience of precisely the tension between the senses and the brain that the individual's moral responsibility, or, in Bakhtinian terms, her/his "answerability," lies. In other words, since subjectivity is constituted at the intersection between self and world, and the fundamental discontinuity between them is hence a necessity, the contradiction can never be resolved. The conflict must be lived—at least by those who "demand to be really alive"—for it inheres in the doubly inscribed nature of subjectivity itself.

Dominant ideology obscures the crisis lying at the heart of subjectivity by relegating it to its margins in order to ensure acceptable social behavior. Instability belongs to adolescence, to art, crime, madness, and similar discursive niches. While institutionalized discourses provide the individual with a sense of meaningful identity, they thus inevitably also operate as measures of containment by excluding the potentially disruptive excesses to rational consciousness.[55] As mentioned earlier, it is usually only at the end of puberty that the subject, with her/his increasing engagement in wider social structures, becomes consciously aware of the restraints imposed on her/him by (gender) ideology. Since the adolescent is not yet fully "affixed" to a specific subject-position, s/he simultaneously recognizes the precariousness of such positions, in particular the instability of the categories of sex. It is not surprising, therefore, that despite their different positions in relation to the Law, Laurence, being of similar age, to some extent shares Lois's sense of standing "at the cross-roads." Their mutual plight sets them apart from the older generation, who seem firmly established in their adult identities.

The sense of dislocation Laurence and Lois have in common is placed at the center of the narrative by being reflected in the novel's sociohistorical setting, metaphorically foregrounded by the violence of the Troubles. Indicative of the gulf dividing the Anglo-Irish from the native Irish, this war will eventually lead to the destruction of the colonizing power of the Anglo-Irish landed gentry, of the Ascendency itself, and of the way of life it still barely upholds. Founded on unequal power relations embedded in an outdated class system, the Anglo-Irish community is shown to have rendered itself virtually obsolete. This in turn is intimated by Lois's and Laurence's relative indifference to the threat of the political upheavals. As the drawn-out ending of a story in which they feel they have no part, the war yet keeps them in thrall and thwarts them in their search for the meanings of their own "historical present":[56]

To Laurence and Lois this all had already a ring of the past. They both had a sense of detention, of a prologue being played out too lengthily, with unnecessary stress, a wasteful attention to detail. Apart, but not quite unaware of each other, queerly linked by antagonism, they both sat eating tea with dissatisfaction, resentful at giving so much of themselves to what was to be forgotten. The day was featureless, a stock pattern day of late summer, blandly insensitive to their imprints. The yellow sun ... seemed old, used, filtering from the surplus of some happy fulfillment; while, unapproachably elsewhere, something went by without them. (118)

Since each confronts the other with her/his unfixed position in this historical moment and its corollary, a lack of symbolic power that precludes their giving a twist to a no-longer-relevant cultural scenario, the bond between the cousins is one of antagonism. Laurence, on his part, hides his vulnerability by "being intellectual," holding up a shield of "clever conversation" in order to pretend to have "no emotional life" (9). Lois, in contrast, has no Oxford to fall back on. As a girl, she has no sociocultural framework empowering her to conceal her sense of dislocation and instability or to forego the challenge of her bewildering inner conflicts. Laurence's protective shield, however, also exacts its price. While preventing him from being ensnared—he "escape[s] by sitting always with a social alert expression between two groups; when one tried to claim him he could affect to be engaged by the other"—it simultaneously leaves him in a state of limbo (41). Determined to remain impervious to the demands of an eroded social system, he renders himself ineffectual within it. As a result, he ends up "beating the bushes vaguely" (42).

Laurence's "unsympathy" is precisely what gives Lois a sense of comfort in his presence. She is reassured by his complete "indifference to every shade of her personality." Initially, Lois had been intent on impressing her cousin as an "intellectual girl." His blunt advice to "read less and more thoroughly and, on the whole ... talk less," however, had induced her to change her attitude. She subsequently "reattained confidence, expanding under his disapproval." Such ease is unattainable with any of the other inhabitants of Danielstown. As Lois clearly perceives, it is "those tender, those receptive listeners to whom one felt afterwards committed and sold" (11). This somewhat puzzling insight springs directly from the ambivalent nature of subjective interpellation: once one has been "received" in the preexisting discursive slots in/through which the process of subjectivity obtains, one is also bound to their constraining effects. The instability of the adolescent's sense of psychosexual self enhances her/his awareness of the interdependence inherent in the relations between Self and (the) Other/s. As Erikson observes, during the adolescent stage of identity formation the subject is most willing to "put his [*sic*] trust in those peers and leading, or misleading, elders who will give imaginative, if not illusory, scope to his aspirations." At the same time, however, the adolescent "fears a foolish, all too trusting commitment" (129). Considering the severe restraints imposed by her sociocultural context, what exactly are the options for Lois? What "imaginative" possibilities are offered to her by her "peers and leading elders"?

Negative Presences. In the absence of Lois's real parents, the Naylors appear as eligible substitutes. Sir Richard seems sufficiently generous and kind, but he does not show any active concern for his niece. His lack of interest obviously does not spring from his responsibilities as the Anglo-Irish landowner, since his tasks do not seem to be particularly exacting. His wife does not stop pointing out, however, that "Sir Richard is easily worried" (182). She takes great pains to prevent her husband from encountering anything potentially upsetting. Sir Richard's equilibrium is a precarious affair and the slightest disruption of his accustomed ways is cause for inordinate distress. This is at once established when he comes down for dinner the night of the Montmorencys' arrival. He is annoyed to find Francie already in the dining room, for "Sir Richard was very much worried by visitors who came down early for dinner; evidently he had not expected this of Francie" (22–23). His irritation increases when the ensuing conversation leads to a "suspicion of something somewhere" regarding his late sister's relations with Hugo. Sir Richard chooses to suppress the unwelcome sensation induced by the mere suggestion of "something" sexual by flatly chatting away to Francie. Eventually, it falls to Lois to "check the couple in their career of inanity" (22). Sir Richard's temperament is clearly not one to rise to any occasion. He prefers not to notice Lois's restlessness, just as he refuses to let the impending devastation of Anglo-Ireland unsettle his equanimity. His feebleness and lack of moral energy are confirmed by his reaction to the only explicitly emotional event in the novel. When the death of an English soldier is announced, a young man whom he knows to have been involved with his niece, Sir Richard turns out to have "slipped away quietly; he was an old man, really, outside all this, and did not know what to do" (203).

The portrait of his wife, Myra, forms a striking contrast to the picture of (sexual) impotence represented by Sir Richard. Her character forms at once a splendid piece of social comedy and a sharp indictment of Anglo-Irish and upper-class narrow-mindedness. In addition to her presence as a formidable figurehead, Lady Naylor provides an outspoken instance of thwarted ambition cast in explicitly gendered terms.

Francie reflects that Myra, before her marriage, used to be "interesting," someone cultivated who "sketched beautifully, knew about books and music" and had been "to Germany, Italy, everywhere that one visits acquisitively" (14). The narrator discloses Lady Naylor's view on her own young self:

Lady Naylor thought all young people ought to be rebels; she herself had certainly been a rebel. But since the War, they had never ceased mouching.

She herself had had a deep sense of poetry; she remembered going to sleep with Shelley under her pillow. She used to walk alone in the mountains and hated coming in to meals. (120)

With Myra's accession to adult womanhood, her adolescent "rebelliousness" was conclusively brought to an end. As Lady Naylor she feels a certain responsibility toward her husband's charge, but she repeatedly emphasizes that Lois is "not her own niece at all" (182). Her reasons for keeping her distance from this potential source of commotion are directly related to her own aborted desires. While she impresses on Lois that she herself at "nineteen, was reading Schiller," being "intensely interested in art" (167), it is clear that married life has neither met Myra Naylor's sexual desires nor fulfilled her romantic yearnings and artistic aspirations. The link between her lately acquired "terrible habit of shutting doors" and her sex is astutely discerned by Laurence. Musing about an alternative life for his aunt, he envisages her "enjoy[ing] a vigorous celibacy" (106). Forced by the exigencies of her gender role and Sir Richard's impotence to suppress her ambitions and stifle her passions, Myra Naylor has more or less ossified in her position as the Lady of the House. The success of her attempts at suppressing her desires reveals the abiding strength of her "romantic will." Such ruthless ardor has left its unmistakable traces:

Her bright grey eyes, with very black, urgent pupils, continued in a deep crease at each outside corner. High on the curve of her cheeks, like petals, bright mauve-pink colour became, within kissing distance, a net of fine delicate veins. Her eyebrows, drawn in a pointed arch, suggested tragic surprise till one saw the arch never flattened, the face beneath never changed from its placid eagerness, its happy dissatisfaction. (16)

Thoroughly internalized, the cultural constraints belonging to her sex have inscribed themselves onto Lady Naylor's body. Francie notices "something set now in Myra; she was happier, harder" (17). In addition to marking the strength of the woman's determination, these physical signs indicate the extent and the force of ideological operations. Deprived of social agency, what is left to

Lady Naylor are her limited domestic powers. These she exerts vigorously, in a high-handed, imperious manner and with a steady, almost unscrupulous perseverence.

An additional outlet for Aunt Myra's frustration and suppressed anger is provided by the elaborate British class system. Her (class) arrogance and bigoted nationalist views allow Bowen to display her exquisite talent for social satire. The main target of the Irish lady's scorn are the English upper-middle classes:

I always find the great thing in England is to have plenty to say, and mercifully they are determined to find one amusing. But if one stops talking, they tell one the most extraordinary things, about their husbands, their money affairs, their insides. They don't seem discouraged by not being asked. And they seem so intimate with each other; I suppose it comes from living so close together. Of course they are very definite and practical, but it is a pity they talk so much about what they are doing. I can't think why they think it should matter. (134)

Lady Naylor's embrace of these hierarchical discourses empowers her to exploit her superior position within them. She is able to overrule the laws of gender when dealing with men socially beneath her, expertly drawing on the sophisticated codes by which dominant and nondominant groups mutually uphold their relations. She thus interferes effectively with the young English subaltern's (aptly called Lesworth) wishes to marry Lois. Myra Naylor's muffled rage is less explicitly vented when it comes to the men of her own class. In her relations with Sir Richard, she successfully follows a strategy of neutralization by containment. While allowing her to organize life at Danielstown according to her own indomitable will, this also reveals her contempt for her husband's impotence and the inefficacy of upper-class men generally. The complex ways in which the intersecting discourses of gender and class operate are perhaps most strikingly expressed in the fact that the only person proving a match to Lady Naylor's powerful temper is a female subordinate. The cook Kathleen, "who resembled her mistress in personality so closely that their relation was an affair of balance, who had more penetration than Lady Naylor and was equally dominant," apparently offers Aunt Myra her only substantial challenge (169). In the safety of class hierarchies, the staunch lady thus finds a rare significant other in a member of the same sex.

Lady Naylor's admonition to Lois not to marry ("There's a future for girls outside marriage") is undoubtedly sincerely felt. So are her motives for advocating a different course, which she articulates with the "inspiring" exclamation: "'Careers—how *I* should have loved one'" (174). These exhortations, however, spring more from her own sense of frustration than from an actual recognition of Lois's needs. The possible alternatives to marriage that she suggests, for example, a "school of art," or "taking up" French or German, are offered indiscriminately and in such an off-hand manner as to sound quite fatuous. Lady Naylor's strategy of (self-)containment has inevitably led to nearly absolute indifference. Her fervent endeavors to keep any potentially disturbing element at bay is poignantly reflected in her attitude toward the political situation. As she tells her visitors: "'From all the talk [about the war], you might think almost anything was going to happen, but we never listen. I have made it a rule not to talk, either'" (26). Her long-standing practice of (self-)repression has made Aunt Myra incapable of any deep affection or empathy. The nearest she gets to showing emotion is when she insists that Lois "knows better" than to marry. It is on this occasion that she can give Lois "one of her rarest, most charming, direct and personal glances" (174). But her response to the announcement of Gerald Lesworth's death reveals that Aunt Myra is as emotionally crippled as her husband. Since the challenge of compassion is beyond her, her only option is dodging it altogether:

Lady Naylor thought firmly: "Now I must go and find Lois. But she did not go; things seemed to delay her. She looked into the drawing-room to see whether something—she wasn't certain what—was there. Francie, red-eyed, looked guiltily over the back of the sofa. They did not say anything. The room became so sharply painful that Lady Naylor almost exclaimed: "Lois has not done the flowers!" (203)

The moral cowardice resulting from emotional desiccation and sexual inertia as embodied by the Naylors represents a constant preoccupation in Bowen's work. In an interview with Jocelyne Brooke broadcast by the BBC in 1950, the author commented on what she considered to be misleading notions that had gathered around her best-known novel, *The Death of the Heart* (1938; hereafter, *DH*).[57] Her statements on this novel's theme and its central characters are equally relevant to *LS*:

I've heard [*DH*], for instance, called a tragedy of adolescence. I never thought of it that way when I wrote it and I must say I still don't see it in that way now. The one adolescent character in it, the young girl Portia seems to me to be less tragic than the others. She at least, has a hope, and she hasn't atrophied. The book is really a study, it might be presumptuous of me to call it a tragedy of atrophy, not of *death so much as of death sleep*. And the function of Portia in the story is to be the awake one, in a sense therefore she was a required character. She imparts meaning rather than carries meaning. (Italics mine.)

While underscoring the significance of the female adolescent as a destabilizing figure in the (lethal) story of (heterosexual) convention, these remarks should not obscure the fact that the Naylors do not present as bleak a picture of a lost civilization as the disaffected Quaynes, the central characters in *DH*. The Naylors cling to cultural patterns that are being eroded by their own and their era's failure to provide the moral vigor necessary for revitalizing them. The Quaynes are emotionally and morally dispossessed by lacking a sociocultural framework entirely. The Naylors' "atrophy" is nonetheless undeniable. Lois, whose sense of incoherence forces her to perceive how "she and those home surroundings . . . penetrated each other mutually in the discovery of a lack," recognizes the fundamental decenteredness of both subjectivity and dominant culture (166). She fulfills her role as the "awake one" by experiencing and exposing the fundamental lack at the heart of the established power/meaning structures—symbolized by Danielstown—in which she is compelled to negotiate a position.

Such a concept of adolescence as I have outlined above allows us to discern that Lois, on account of her sexual indefiniteness and her unfixed gender identity, "imparts" meaning by embodying the subject-in-process within ideology. Her crisis, reflected in the violence of the novel's sociopolitical setting, represents the struggle of the individual in her/his dialogic relationship with the world. The Naylors shirk their *moral* responsibility by recoiling from the challenge of their "answerability." Their "happy dissatisfaction" stems from their unwillingness—or rather, their inability—to "be really alive," to engage in the heterogeneity of experience that forms the ground of semiosis, of giving meaning both to one's self and to reality. Their recoil signifies a foregoing of what Bowen calls the "struggle for life." It is this unremitting struggle, she adds, that "may be said, in fact, to *be* life itself, and [that] should not therefore have anything terrible about it."[58] The Naylors' "death sleep" is more than a personal tragedy. The ambivalence of their isolated position in Ireland and their willful ignorance thereof will ultimately result in the destruction of both Danielstown and the Ascendency. This indicates that their personal moral failure is also fundamentally a sociopolitical one.

The Inscription in Experience. Preceding the narrative of *LS,* we find a line from Marcel Proust's *Le Temps Retrouvé:* "'Ils ont les chagrins qu'ont les vierges et les paresseux.'" Serving as the novel's motto, the line condemns the Naylors to the category of *les paresseux* for their reluctance to embrace experience in its destabilizing multiplicity. Underlining the ambivalence of the concept of "innocence," the factual lack of (first and foremost sexual) experience in *les vierges* is equally reproved. The distinction between these forms of *chagrin* yet supports a reading of the adolescent protagonist as the "awake one" of the story. Although Bowen describes her as a "creature still half-awake, the soul not yet open, nor yet the eyes," she also asserts that Lois, "like it or not . . . acquiesced to strife, abnormalities and danger," since "violence was contained in her sense of life, along with dance-music, the sweet-pea in the garden, the inexorable raininess of days."[59] As yet wavering in her sexual orientation and unfixed in her gender identity, the adolescent cannot but actively engage in whatever dialogical relations she is launched into.

Lacking a place within the traditional family triangle, Lois is particularly dependent on the wider context of sociocultural relations in which she is to position herself. Her sense of dislocation is reinforced rather than alleviated within the Anglo-Irish community. However unstable the political situation may be, all of her relatives emphatically define themselves in national(ist) terms. This strengthens Lois's sense of exclusion. She realizes that there is "something else that she could not share: she could not conceive of her country emotionally" (34). The multiple character of subjectivity is foregrounded by the simultaneous and intersecting operations of these various power structures in the context of the adolescent quest. The connections between the discourses of nationality, class, and gender acquire full articulation in Lois's relationship with Gerald Lesworth. Since psychosexuality forms a (if not the) major substructure of subjective identity, I will primarily focus on the heroine's "struggle for life" in this respect.

As we have seen, a sense of Self is essentially a "gift" of (the) Other/s. The concept of significant others as it is used by Erikson is therefore, as I have already suggested, somewhat misleading. His emphasis on (the) Other/s' function as mere role models presupposes a degree of autonomy and choice that the fundamental ambiguity of ideological interpellation clearly refutes. Precisely the tension created by the need to be authenticated by (the) Other/s and simultaneously to resist the constraints of such "hailing" forms the crux of Lois's predicament. The conflict emerges most conspicuously in "those incalculable springings-out of mind through the body" that find expression in her "intense brimming wandering look" set against a chin showing "emphasis," seeming "ready for determination" (28). The gendered nature of Lois's ambivalence appears when the adults insist that she must be having a "wonderful time" now that she has "grown up":

"Oh, well . . . " said Lois. She went across to the fireplace and rose on her tiptoes, leaning her shoulders against the marble. She tried not to look conscious. She still felt a distinct pride at having grown up at all; it seemed an achievement, like marriage or fame. Having a wonderful time, she knew, meant being attractive to a number of young men. If she said, "Yes, I do," it implied "Yes, I am, very—" and she was not certain. She was not certain, either, how much she enjoyed herself. "Well, yes, I do," she said finally. (21)

Such recognition is thus both pleasing, reassuring Lois of her adult position, and cause for doubt because of the questionable meanings of the position itself. Even so, Lois's misgivings do not prevent her from discerning the semiotic importance of discursive positioning: "Not to be known seemed like a doom: extinction" (34). Nor is she unaware of the constructed character of what she has learned to regard as her "personality":

She could not hope to explain that her youth seemed to her also rather theatrical and that she was only young in that way because people expected it. She had never refused a role. She could not forgo that intensification, that kindling of her personality at being considered very happy and reckless, even if she were not. (32)

These sequences capture the very paradox of identity and its determining categories, which, as Judith Butler points out in a recent essay, "tend to be instruments of regulatory regimes, whether as the normalizing categories of oppressive structures or as the rallying points for a liberatory contestation of that very oppression."[60]

While underscoring the gendered meanings of adolescence, Lois's recognition of the theatrical aspects of her youth and her role as an object of male desire attests to the performative nature of gendered sexuality. But the second-cited sequence also shows that such a recognition does not mean that she can simply forego the process of subjective interpellation effected by "regulatory" discursive practices. Given the sociohistorical context, the immediate route to adult identity is channeled through the discourses of love and marriage. Love, with its "gift of importance," presents itself as at least something concrete to Lois, as a means to fulfill her profound need to belong (23). Gerald Lesworth's attraction hence resides precisely in his "eagerness and constancy." At the same time, however, the young men who play their assigned gender roles seem unimportant. They "block her mental view by their extreme closeness" and "move shadowless in a kind of social glare numbing to the imagination" (13). Lois's feelings reveal that it is the heterosexual teleology implicit in the dominant cultural scenario that forms the major "stumbling-block" in her quest for her self.

An overheard conversation between Lady Naylor and Francie Montmorency simultaneously suggests to Lois the political and social interests involved in the maintenance of the heterosexual contract and confirms that it is their internalized heterosexuality that defines female subjects' complicity in the system of phallogocentrism:

The voices spoke of love; they were full of protest. Love, [Lois] had learnt to assume, was the mainspring of woman's grievances. Illnesses all arose from it, the having of children, the illnesses children had; servants also, since the regular practice of love involved a home; by money it was confined, propped and moulded. Lois flung off the pillows and walked round the room quickly. She was angry; she strained to hear now, she quite frankly listened. But when Mrs Montmorency came to: "Lois is very—" she was afraid suddenly. She had a panic. She didn't want to know what she was, she couldn't bear to: knowledge of this would stop, seal, finish one. Was she now to be clapped down under an adjective, to crawl round lifelong inside some quality like a fly in a tumbler? (60)

Since even the most "provisional totalization" of the self in language entails a radical exclusion of that which exceeds such a determination, Lois shirks from being defined in any terms.[61] Having prevented Francie from finishing her sentence, she realizes that now she "would never know" what she "*was*." This will not stop her wondering, however, for she realizes that she cannot remain forever in a state of "indefiniteness" (60).

While it is psychologically impossible to live without some sense of coherent identity, the very ambivalence of language also implies that no marker of the self can in effect be "final." Indeed, as Butler contends, the noncoincidence of subjectivity entails that in any performative act serving to identify oneself, that which is excluded "remains constitutive of that determination itself." In other words, any identificatory statement exceeds its determination and "even produces that very excess in and by the act which seeks to exhaust that semantic field" of the self.[62] To put it in Bakhtinian terms, the irreducible indeterminacy of subjectivity springs from the inability of all aspects of language to merge with the human subject. The dialogical basis of identity implies that the self is a ceaseless project constituted in otherness. Since achieving a sense of oneself is an activity never to be completed, Lois's struggle cannot be judged in terms of failure or success.[63] The contradiction between her need for definition and her desire to escape from the restrictions imposed by the regulatory regimes of established power/knowledge structures is not a specifically adolescent phenomenon. Being inherent in the process of subjectivity itself, the conflict is ultimately unresolvable. Still, the assumption that the contradiction is therefore always suspended or maintained should not be allowed to obscure the gendered operations of ideological discourses. These place specific limitations on the female adolescent.

Hailing Peers and the Discourse of Love The second group of "significant others" identified by Erikson are the adolescent's peers. Hence the importance of Lois's friends Viola and Livvy Thompson. These two characters might be said to function at the opposite ends of the axis upon which Lois's thoughts about love

and marriage revolve. Not actually appearing on the narrative
stage, the heroine's former schoolmate Viola performs the role of
alter ego, available only in discourse, in the intimacy of their
correspondence. Precisely her physical absence signals the character's representative function as the cultural ideal of "femininity."
Figuring in Lois's story as the personification of heterosexual womanhood, she operates as the standard of psychosexual "normality"
that, as Teresa de Lauretis reminds us, "is only conceivable by
approximation, more in the order of a projection than an actual
state of being."[64] Livvy, in contrast, lives within riding distance of
Danielstown and her rather too close presence invites a certain
reserve in Lois. Livvy being Irish and slightly common, the differences in their respective classes and social positions nonetheless
place the character at the necessary distance so as to provide a
counterbalance to the English schoolmate, whose sophistication
Lois finds quite intimidating. The moment of their parting, "anxious between the enormous past and future," marks Lois's keen
sense of the difference between herself and Viola. The memory
locates her anxiety squarely in the issue of gender:

They had left school the day before. Yet the new life had been impatient
for Viola, drawing her away from Lois in the taxi, appropriating her with
certainty. She had stepped from their taxi toppling with school trunks
with a kind of solemnity, as on to a carpet stretched for her festal approach from the kerb to the doors of her home. Next day, when they said
goodbye, her hair was in place already, woven into her personality. Her
pigtail had been the one loose end there was of her, an extension of her
that had independence, a puppyish walloping thing with nerves of its own.
Now the hair was woven in bright sleek circles over her ears, each strand
round like an eel's body. The effect completed her; Lois knew she had
been missing or else discounting something all these years. Viola must
have played at being the schoolgirl just as Lois would have to play at
being a woman. (50)

Lois's unnerving recognition at the end of this sequence corroborates the poststructuralist concept of the self as a produced/produc-
ing effect, articulated and realized in material practices. Using the

very same terms of "playing-at-being," Butler, in the essay cited earlier, argues that (lesbian) sexuality is a "certain performance and production of a 'self' which is the *constituted effect* of a discourse that nevertheless claims to 'represent' that self as a prior truth."[65] To say that "to be a lesbian" is to "play at being one," however, does not deny the "reality" of sexual identities, for, she maintains, this is "deep-seated, psychically entrenched play":

This is not a performance from which I can take radical distance . . . *and this "I" does not play its lesbianism as a role.* Rather, it is through the repeated play of this sexuality that the "I" is insistently reconstituted as a lesbian "I"; paradoxically, it is precisely the *repetition* of that play that establishes as well the *instability* of the very category that it constitutes. For if the "I" is a site of repetition, that is, if the "I" only achieves the semblance of identity through a certain repetition of itself, then the I is always displaced by the very repetition that sustains it. (18)

Since the self is constituted in the repetition of contextually significant and socioculturally determined meaningful performances, it follows that there is no anterior self that "precedes the gender that it is said to perform" (18). While Butler's focus is on lesbian sexuality, this equally holds true for that which was in fact "created as a counterpart of homosexuality," that is, naturalized heterosexuality.[66] Only by a compulsory repetition of itself, by being always "in the process of imitating and approximating its own phantasmatic idealization," can heterosexuality produce the effect of itself as the natural, the original.[67]

We recall that it is only by presupposing the "natural" categories of "man" and "woman" that gendered heterosexuality can produce itself as "normal" and, vice versa, that it is only in the context of the heterosexual matrix that such stable sexual categories obtain. Heterosexual gender identities are thus the "theatrically produced effects" of the entirely interdependent regulatory regimes of phallogocentrism and compulsory heterosexuality.[68] This is at once reflected in Lois's appreciation of the theatrical character of her role as a grownup and in her ambivalent reactions to her two friends' endeavors to play at "being" women. The sense of inferiority incurred by Viola's "adult" personality is not unqualified, for Lois clearly perceives that her friend's instant womanhood implies the loss of what little independence she had as a schoolgirl. Her own reluctance to be "clapped down" under one of the identity categories sustaining the binary system of heterosexualized genders, however, leaves her with no recognizable, meaningful sense of self at all. She therefore feels incapable of countering the "married-womanish tone of encouragement" of Viola's letters with something equally self-assured of her own. Displacing her ambivalent feelings about womanhood onto Livvy, she regards the Irish girl's eagerness to practice her "feminine sensibility" with silent scorn (38).

Both Livvy and Viola prove worthy subjects to the gender ideology prevalent within their respective sociocultural surroundings. Livvy gets secretly engaged to an English subaltern, which at once makes her feel "all the soldiers' woman" (39). Viola, having "two expensive young men's photographs . . . on her mantelpiece" (whose positions seem "regularized magically by the putting up of [her] hair"), embarks upon her career as gendered subject by attending balls and successfully making "various people . . . seem intrigued" (50–51). By adopting their prescribed roles in the social contract, Lois's friends not only conform to but in effect reinforce the regimes of compulsory heterosexuality and phallogocentrism subtending it. Despite her need to be recognized, to "be in a pattern," our heroine is incapable of such a wholehearted embrace of her assigned place within the established power/knowledge system. Sensing the aridity of the marriages around her, Lois astutely discerns the limitations imposed on the individual spouses by the institution of heterosexuality itself. Wanting no part of that, she can alleviate her fear of being "locked out" by the elder generation by deriving a "feeling of mysteriousness and destination" from the thought that she will "penetrate thirty years deeper ahead into Time than they could" (29). She cannot so easily afford to distance herself from her peers, however. Succeeding the now "lost" leading elders, Viola and Livvy are the others on which Lois depends for confirmation of her precarious sense of self. Her conscious reservations notwithstanding, she feels compelled to follow them in trying to be a "pleasant young person," which, she has learned, entails being "attractive to a number of young men." She therefore hesitatingly accepts Gerald Lesworth's persistent attentions.

From the outset, Lois understands that she and Gerald are preserving an "illusion both were called upon to maintain" (33). Her insight into the fictional character of the heterosexual plot initially strengthens her need for his dependability. Gerald's "nice-minded" self-assurance—he "smiled everywhere . . . went every-where"—contrasts sharply with her own sense of unreality, of being "nowhere" (35). Lois's very susceptibility to the fact that she is no more than acting her prescribed role in an endlessly repeated cultural play equally allows her to understand that she will never be acknowledged by Gerald as a person in her own right. When she observes him "watching her as though she were an entirely different person," she is led to reflect: "Some idea he had formed of herself remained inaccessible to her; she could not affect it" (48). In this scenario she can merely function as the Other to his Self.

Indeed, Gerald's ostensible reliability is a direct result of his unquestioning incorporation of meanings and values produced by established power/knowledge structures. The narrator's look into his "inner landscape" discloses the ideological basis of the most "private" aspects of subjectivity. While additionally drawing attention to the success with which ideologies obscure their own operations, the narrative irony underlines the constraining effects of prevailing notions such as "romantic love." Living in a world in which affections are "rare and square . . . unrelated and positive,"

[Gerald] did not conceive of love as a nervous interchange but as some-thing absolute, out of the scope of thought, beyond himself, matter for a confident outward rather than anxious inward looking. He had sought

and was satisfied with a few—he thought final —repositories for his emotions: his mother, country, dog, school, a friend or two, now—crown-
ingly—Lois. Of these he asked only that they should be quiet and positive,
not impinged upon, *not breaking boundaries* from their generous allotment. His life was a succession of practical adjustments, into which the
factor of personality did not enter at all. His reserve—to which one was
apt to accord a too sensitive reverence—was an affair of convenience
rather than protection. Pressed for a statement, he could have said, "I love
her," to ... anyone there, without uneasiness, without a sense of the
words' vibrations of alarm at a loud impact on something hollow. (41;
italics mine)

In his unself-conscious embrace of various modes of totalizing
thought, Gerald undoubtedly belongs to *les paresseux*. But whereas
the Naylors' complacency is condemned in relatively moderate
terms, the damaging implications of the young English subaltern's
lack of self-awareness are far more bluntly brought to the fore.

Gerald's phallocratic and bigoted views on personal relations
not surprisingly extend to his fixed notion of "civilization" and the
colonialist discourse to which he adheres in order to justify the
English army's presence in Ireland. His naïve but by no means
harmless nationalism—"no one could have a sounder respect than
himself and his country for the whole principal of nationality"—
barely allows him "some awareness of misdirection, even of paradox, that he was out here to hunt and shoot the Irish" (93).
Such thoughts contrast sharply with Laurence's reflections on the
political situation, a disparity that is underlined by the narrator's
shifting attitude toward these respective characters. Gerald's "baffled" state of mind is, as shown above, analyzed with searching
irony. Without a shade of ironic distancing, the narrative voice
then merges with Laurence's thoughts to define "civilization" as a
"rather perplexing system of niceties ... an unemotional kindness
withering to assertion selfish or racial." In this "silence cold with a
comprehension in which the explaining clamour died away," we
are told, the "end of art, of desire, as it would be the end of battle"
is to be foreseen (93). While signaling the devastating effects of the

prevailing regimes of power/knowledge, the text thus underscores the fully interdependent relations between the private and the public, between subjective experience and objective "reality." In the character of the English subaltern the destructive consequences of an unquestioning internalization of dominant values are suggested to be the result of moral inadequacy, to derive from a lack of self-consciousness—in personal as well as political terms.[69]

Gerald's failure critically to "behold and react," to assume his "answerability," renders him all but oblivious to Lois's erotic desires. In the absence of any (self-)reflexive tendencies in her lover, Lois, on her part, is initially primarily impressed with Gerald's physical presence. Looking "as though his thoughts were under his eyelids," he seems to represent "emotion . . . unclothed in the demi-decency of thought; nakedness, not a suggestive deshabille" (52). Gerald not only seems to offer a solution to her fear of exclusion but also promises the fulfillment of her dawning sexual needs. Attracted by his "beautiful body" and his "round, smooth head," she excitedly recollects dancing with him on the lawn, "his hand slid[ing] up between her shoulders; then, as she steadied back to the rhythm, down again" (33). Her susceptibility to the potentially constraining power of words induces Lois to desire Gerald in his very "earthy vitality." Her lover's unequivocal (physical) presence, however, does not automatically signify that he is capable of erotic interaction. Since the engagement in what Bowen designates "synthetic experience" involves valid emotion, imagination as well as the brain, Gerald's moral blindness and lack of (self)reflection preclude any mode of dialogic exchange. Lois correctly traces the source of his inability to "take in a word [she] say[s]" when she exclaims: "I do wish you wouldn't, Gerald—I mean, be so *actual*" (88). The apparent contradiction reveals that she recognizes the annihilating effects imposed on herself by Gerald's need to suppress anything that might "break boundaries." The ambivalence of Lois's idea of Gerald as "at once close and

remote, known and un-personal," issues from her double inscription in gender ideology (153). Dancing, she can enjoy his closeness
"under the lovely compulsion of movement," for such physicality
seems to keep her temporarily out of the "net" of verbal discourse,
the "little twists of conversation knotted together" that make her
feel that "one can't move, one doesn't know where one is." Locked
together in a cultural context that forbids her, as it did her mother
before her, to express herself sexually, Lois considers it a "nightmare that even [Gerald] should begin to talk" (191). Since he fails
to see that the "only way across" for them is physical communication, he either "ignore[s] or reject[s]" Lois's wordless appeal. The
paradoxical result is a feeling of impotence and desolation on the
latter's part (190).

It is Lois herself who establishes the connection between the
phallogocentric gender and nationalist discourses personified by
Gerald. Her sense of frustration enables her to disclose their fully
intertwined operations as oppressive and exclusionary practices:

It's all this dreadful idea about self-control. When *we* [the Anglo-Irish] do
nothing it is out of politeness, but England is so moral, so dreadfully keen
on not losing her temper, or being for half a moment not a great deal
more noble than anyone else. Can you wonder this country gets irritated?
It's as bad for it as being a woman. I can never see why women shouldn't
be hit, or should be saved from wrecks when everybody complains they're
superfluous. (49)[70]

Her words, however, resoundingly bounce off against the impenetrable hollow of her lover's personality. Gerald's "belief in [Lois's]
perfection as a woman," his conviction that "she was his integrity," reduce her to what is no more than a function in prevailing
cultural scenarios. The fact that she is a "woman" explains "exactly why it wasn't to be expected or desired she *should* understand." Since he regards the relations between the sexes as an
"affair of function," he feels that a "possible failure in harmony, a
sometimes discordant irreverence" in the girl must chivalrously be

"excused" (49–50). Such putative magnanimity beautifully exemplifies the strategy of containment by which hierarchical gender relations are traditionally sustained.

Lois is forced to acknowledge that Gerald's thorough internalization of an ideology of self-control has made it in fact impossible for him to meet the demands of her desire. After their first kiss, she reflects: "So that was being kissed; just an impact, with inside blankness." The ensuing sense of disenchantment—"she was lonely and saw there was no future"—first induces Lois to close her eyes and try "to be enclosed in non-entity, in some ideal no-place, perfect and clear as a bubble." The next moment she is filled by a yearning to be "at a party, unreal and vivid, or running on hard sands" (88–89). The conflictual impulses explain Lois's frequent associations of Gerald, and the sexual desires he evokes in her, with both death and her mother Laura. Echoing her earlier sensations of mixed excitement and fear, "fear behind reason, fear before her birth," these associations are directly linked to the attractions and dangers of the engulfing safety of the maternal womb: "She thought of death and glanced at his body, quick, lovely, present and yet destructible. Something passed sensation and touched her consciousness with a kind of weight and warmth; she glimpsed a quiet beyond experience, as though for many nights he had been sleeping beside her" (89). Lois's "quick response to [Gerald's] beauty" and his picture in her "mental eye . . . as though he were dead, as though she had lost him" (52) confirm the connection between death and desire. Recalling the end of the infant's dyadic unity with the mother, the compulsory split upon which, according to Lacan, the subject's entry into the symbolic order depends, Lois's associations signify a reevocation of the loss of her first love object, the mother. Paradoxically, it is a feeling of loss at "*not* being compelled" by Gerald's touch that inflicts Lois eventually with a sense of oppression that is to propel her away from him (190; italics mine). It is not Lois's presumed inability to love that puts an end to their relationship but Gerald's overall failure to respond, his lack of, in Bakhtinian terms, "dialogic imagination."

Lois is filled with a feeling of wistfulness and deprivation when she reflects that she "would have loved to love" Gerald. The causes for the failure of their relationship are firmly located within the ideological context, in the system of compulsory heterosexuality and its curtailing effects:

If there could only be some change, some movement—in her, outside of her, somewhere between them—some incalculable shifting of perspectives that would bring him wholly into focus, mind and spirit, as she had been bodily in focus now—she could love him. Something must be transmuted. . . . Or else, possibly, if he would not love her so, could give her air to grow in, not stifle imagination. (52)

The discursive inscription of subjectivity accounts for the fact that the stillness between Lois and Gerald is, in the final instance, of decisive importance. Since subjectivity can only obtain in dialogue with (the) Other/s, that is, within the symbolic order, this additionally explains why the ostensible safety of Gerald's womblike dependability is, in effect, lethal. The critical function of discourse in the production of a self is furthermore underlined when Lois sees Gerald as a "foreigner with whom by some failure in her vocabulary all communication was interrupted" (190). It is not Lois's failure to communicate, however, but the recognition that her lover has "nothing to do with expression" (153) that finally forces her to turn away from him. In the next chapter we shall see to what Others Lois turns in her quest for her Self, and in what ways their potential for offering alternative modes of being is also, though differently, subject to ideological constraint.

3

Authoring Sexual Identities

> Experience is the reaction to what happens,
> not the happening itself.
> —"Sources of Influence"

Sexual Position(ing)s

Lesbian Desire and Cultural Intelligibility. It should be clear by now that the constitutive function of ideology does not allow Lois to simply "withdraw" from the heterosexual contract in which both Gerald and her friends so forcefully urge her to implicate herself. The restrictive social codes of the Anglo-Irish community make any deviation from established patterns of behavior, let alone a transgression of heterosexual gender boundaries, a risky affair. With the intrusion of the outside world upon the secluded world of Danielstown in the form of Miss Marda Norton, potential alternatives nonetheless appear to offer themselves. Comprising the second and middle chapter of *LS*, "The Visit of Miss Norton" functions as a pivot in the novel's structure as a whole, and hence underlines the critical role of this figure in the heroine's quest. Marda is, Lois has gathered, someone who "annoys Aunt Myra by being unfortunate in ways that are far more trying for other people than for herself." Years ago, she had been the cause of a great deal of "fuss and bloodiness" at a children's party at Danielstown, where she has since then continued her career of disruption (75). On this occasion, the unknown woman begins her visit by seriously distressing Sir Richard when she leaves one of her suitcases on the train. Marda's tendency to create disorder in the orderly pattern of life at Danielstown immediately turns her into an object of attraction for Lois.

My focus on the novel's characters in the preceding chapter has led me to neglect the role of the Big House itself. "Manifestly a writer for whom places loom large,"[1] Bowen succeeds in attributing to Danielstown's "vast façade ... star[ing] coldly over its mounting lawns" the living aspect of a character (7).[2] At one point beheld by Lois as at once a "reservoir of obscurity" and a "magnet to [her] dependence," Danielstown embodies the very stakes involved in her quest (67). While representing the stability and security she craves, the Big House is also the personification of the immutable sociocultural patterns from which she yearns to break away. Marda Norton's function as a disruptive agent highlights Danielstown's symbolic value as the seat of phallocratic power. Her prominent presence at the core of the narrative thus underscores the central place taken up by the questions of gender and sexuality in the adolescent process and in the novel's thematic framework as a whole.

Before Lois encounters Marda in the flesh, she is confronted by the material attributes of the mysterious woman's personality. She is duly impressed with the sophistication and the lifestyle these paraphernalia appear to convey. Lois's response to Marda's possessions lying scattered about the hall adequately testifies to the imitative character of gendered subjectivity. Regulatory discourses transmitted by mass media such as fashion magazines interpellate the subject in her/his *gender* identity by inviting her/him to (re)constitute a self in an endlessly repeated series of performative acts:

Lois sat on the hall table to look at the *Tatler*. Early autumn fashions reminded her—this was an opportunity to try on the fur coat. She hoped for the proper agony, finding a coat she could not live without. . . . Her arms slipped silkily through; her hands appeared, almost tiny, out of the huge cuffs. "Oh, the escape!" she thought, pressing her chin down, fading, dying into the rich heaviness. "Oh, the *escape* in other people's clothes!" And she paced round the hall with new movements: a dark, rare, rather wistful woman, elusive with jasmine. "No?" she said on an upward note; the voice startled her, experience was behind it. She touched the fur lightly, touched the edge of a cabinet—her fingertips drummed with foreign sensitiveness. And the blurred panes, the steaming changing trees, the lonely cave of the hall no longer had her consciousness in a clamp. *How* she could live, she felt. She would not need anyone, she would be like an orchestra playing all to itself. "Is it mink?" she wondered. (76–77)

While the sequence exposes the Self to be an effect produced by/in what is essentially Other, the scene's spatial setting underlines the connection between Lois's sense of oppression and the patriarchal power represented by the Big House. With its "square black eye" and its hold on her consciousness, it is Danielstown from whose "whole cold shell" Lois longs to escape (86–87). One of the reasons why Marda is such an eligible object of her fascination is precisely the latter's rebelliousness, which directs itself against the house and what it stands for. This point is made quite explicit when Marda tries to account for the disturbing effects on Danielstown of her usually efficient presence by ascribing to the house itself a "kind of fatality." Lois is struck by a sense of recognition: such an appreciation of the coercive power exerted by Danielstown makes an "approach seem possible, imminent" (77).

Marda's appearance and her independent attitude promise the possibility of escape. Her "sophistication open[s] further horizons" to Lois. But the heroine is not the only one to be affected by Marda's dazzling presence: all Danielstown's residents are jolted into various forms of self-awareness. Since, as the narrator explains, Marda's "stronghold of . . . indifference" turns her every speech into a "lightning attack on one's integrity," the effect is a "heighten[ing of] one's own consciousness." Marda's markedly androgynous appearance indicates that her destabilizing power is of a decidedly sexual nature. With her back "like a young man's in its vigorous slightness," her body "escape[s] the feminine pear-shape." By blurring the distinction between male and female bodies and, a fortiori, by challenging the "natural categories" of "man" and "woman," the figure not only defies the traditional system of gender relations but calls into question the very "fact" of sexual difference underlying this cultural scenario. In her masculine tallness, Marda forces the other characters—sitting "fixed in their row"—to look up to her, inflicting them with a "vague sensation of being abandoned." By undermining the "integrity" of their sexual identities, the figure destabilizes their overall consciousness of themselves *as* selves (79–80).

Marda's assessing eye immediately detects Hugo's "lameness of thought," Lady Naylor's "despairing optimism," and the "disappointments" they all are to Lois, whom she perceives to be "sick with eagerness" for something "fatal" to happen (81, 83). She does not hesitate to shatter the married couples' complacent composure. Having swiftly established that "to be loved is not [Lois's] affair at all," Marda declares that "love" itself is "quite irrelevant . . . at any age": its staying power can only be explained on the grounds that "one has those ideas" (83). The unsparing lucidity with which she exposes the fiction of heterosexual romance does not mean, however, that Marda can as easily debunk the concrete, material consequences of the ultimate social contract. The circumstance that she, at twenty-nine, has "not brought anything off" (as Livvie Thompson crassly puts it) is cause for true anxiety glinting occasionally through her "defence of manner" (118). Still, Marda's visit to Danielstown turns out to have been prompted by her engagement to the English stockbroker Leslie Lawe (!). Her reluctance to announce this news to the Naylors—whom she suspects of thinking her engagements "fantastic" for having "all come to

nothing" (85)—reveals that Marda's keen eye for the degrading
effects of the Law does not preclude her from being subordinated
to its sway. Although she correctly senses the dangers of nonexistence springing from her unwillingness to "play at being a woman,"
she, unlike the other adults surrounding Lois, is painfully conscious of the limitations imposed by prevailing ideological regimes.
This (self-)consciousness explains why Marda, as yet another dis-
gruntled character in the novel, presents a particularly trenchant
portrait of disenchantment.

Marda's detachment impresses Lois as indicative of her "brilliant life." She assumes that the visitor's air of awareness is a token
of the "polish and depth of experience" (96). Marda, in contrast
to the other adult residents of Danielstown, feels no need to ward
off the unnerving signs of and destabilizing effects produced by
Lois's condition of transience: she frankly acknowledges her own
state of disaffection and consequent sense of dislocation. Not rebuffed by the customary self-protecting gestures, Lois feels free to
express her secret misgivings about her appointed cultural role to
the older woman: " 'Being grown up seems trivial, somehow. I
mean, dressing and writing notes instead of letters, and trying to
make impressions. When you have to think so much of what other
people feel about you there seems no time to think what you feel
about them. Everybody is genial at one in a monotonous kind of
way' " (97). These frank remarks reveal why Lois's lack of (sexual)
experience, and the resultingly indeterminate position she occupies
in the field of power/knowledge, holds an intolerable threat of
exposure. Her palpable naïvety permits her to question exactly
those "realities" that *les paresseux* cannot afford to let go, enabling
her to expose the precarious nature of, in effect, all truths and
meanings. This allows her to say things whose implications may be
positively startling. She remarks, for instance, that "surely love
wouldn't get so much talked about if there were not something in
it." Suggesting the discursive and thus illusory nature of one of
the mainstays of the social order, Lois continues by declaring

reassuringly: " 'I mean even soap, you know, however much they advertise . . . ' " (97). Marda responds by perfunctorily admitting that Lois is probably right, that "there must be" (something in it). Although this may suggest that she, too, betrays Lois by not taking her seriously, Marda's reply does not convey the penchant for self-delusion of *les paresseux*. Her reaction is motivated by her failure to defeat the oppressive ideological forces whose operations exceed her control, by her bleak recognition that the "fruit of her own relation to experience, unwisdom, lacking the sublimer banality," is "meaningless and without value" to Lois (100).

Marda's profound cynicism springs from the fact that socioeconomic pressures have forced her finally to subject herself to the laws of patriarchy. Her need for Leslie Lawe signifies a humiliating resignation to the politically and socially interested regulatory regimes of phallogocentrism and compulsory heterosexuality. Her engagement means a loss of self of which she is fully aware. She tells Lois: " 'If you never need anyone as much you will be fortunate. I don't know for myself what is worthwhile. I'm sick of all this trial and error' " (101). Her sense of frustration has issued in a thorough scepticism toward intersubjective relations; her sense of ineffectuality has convinced her that the "infinite variance" of the relation between self and experience "breaks the span of comprehension between being and being." To Marda, any "attempt at sympathy" seems to be destined to accomplish no more than the "merest fumbling for outlet along the boundaries of the self" (100).

Lois as yet lacks the experience that has hardened Marda's disenchantment. Although she admits that "personal relations make a perfect havoc" of her, she realizes that she depends on relating to others for her sense of self. Her present "difficulties," she informs Marda, spring from being expected to be "beginning" with this only to discover that she does not "seem to find young men inspiring, somehow" (97). At once signaling the centrality of gendered (hetero)sexuality in the process of subjectivity, as well as the indeterminacy of that necessary fiction called self, she nonetheless continues to insist on her need to "be in a pattern . . . to be related," appreciating that "just to *be* is so intransitive, so lonely" (98). Lois herewith confirms de Lauretis's notion of subjectivity as "not . . . the fixed point of departure or arrival from which one interacts with the world," but rather the "effect of that interaction." De Lauretis emphasizes, however, that the experience of self is not simply produced by "external ideas, values or material causes." She foregrounds instead that only one's "personal, subjective engagement in the practices, discourses, and institutions that lend significance to the events of the world" can give the individual a sense of her/his meaningfulness.[3] It is precisely the gender-determined restrictions imposed on such meaning-producing "subjective engagement" that have resulted in Marda's embittered resignation to the Law. Her insight into the constraining force of dominant regulatory regimes is reflected in her urging Lois not to "expect to be touched or changed—or to be in anything that you do. One just watches. Pain is one's misunderstanding" (102).

Lois suffers a "shock of flatness" when she learns about Marda's engagement. She sharply perceives "how anxious to marry Marda must really be . . . how all her distantness and her quick, rejecting air must be a false effect, accidental and transitory" (100). Seeing her formerly vague misgivings about womanhood thus confirmed in her new friend, Lois emphatically professes to "hate women." The binary frame of sex does not leave her much option, however, and she admits that she "can't think to begin to be anything else" (99). In her need to disengage both herself and Marda from the male/female paradigm, Lois feels suddenly "certain that Leslie would die or break off the engagement." She also resolves that she herself must be a "woman's woman" (103). Having thus reassured herself, she feels "more alone with Marda, and nearer." Her subsequent sensation of "movement . . . as though she were on the prow of a ship" is nonetheless abruptly brought to an end when Laurence appears on the scene. He ruth-

lessly puts Lois back into place by pointing out that her involvement with Marda will never exceed attending her wedding in the
role of a bridesmaid. Both Lois's resolutions and her subversive
fantasies show that the duality of sex can only be ensured by
compulsory heterosexuality. That sexual difference is a highly unstable precondition for the patriarchal social contract is abun-
dantly clear from the ideological overkill and the very insistence
with which a wide range of institutional discourses seek to "naturalize" this culturally produced, and thus contingent, effect. The
remarkable fact that Laurence, who has consistently demonstrated
his otherwise complete indifference to Lois's personality, steps in
to lay down the Law at the very moment when she has decided to
be a "woman's woman" and appears to enter into nonnormative
relations with Marda thus signals the precariousness of the founding structure of society.

Marda's defeat in the face of the overpowering strength of
dominant gender ideologies is undeniably a disappointment to
Lois. Their friendship yet strengthens her self-confidence, for it
involves a degree of intimacy and truly dialogic exchange formerly
unknown to her. Newly confronted with Livvie Thompson's success with the English soldiers, Lois now envisages herself as "very
singular, distant, and destined" (110). Although such detachment
enables her rather disdainfully to denounce her friend's conform-
ism, her position "at the crossroads" does not allow for a complete
alleviation of her anxious feelings. Her stance towards the Irish
girl's engagement remains ambivalent: Livvie seems to be "at once
in a pit and upon a pinnacle" (118). The perils of exclusion are still
lurking everywhere, and the thought of "anybody doing anything
without her" continues to fill Lois with "vivid and deep disappointment" (113–14). These recurring fears invariably issue in a
renewed determination that she "must marry Gerald." Lois's as
yet frail sense of self is clearly most alarmingly shaken by the mere
thought of a position outside patriarchy's founding myth.

Even if Marda cannot fulfill the promise of release Lois had hoped for, she does play a crucial role in the heroine's quest by bringing about its moment of revelation. One morning the two decide to take a walk in the company of Hugo, who has meanwhile rather feebly fallen in love with Marda. Instead of being a sign of restored vigor, this merely confirms Hugo's emotional deficiency: to accommodate his secret passion, he has had to create "some kind of non-existence," a fantasy world in which he "could command [Marda's] whole range imaginatively" (176). In suggesting that the heterosexual plot is essentially a male fantasy, the text prepares the ground for the subsequent inscription of a different sexual scenario. Exploring the fields, the three strollers come upon an abandoned mill that sits "staring, light-eyed, ghoulishly, round a bend of the valley" (122). The intimation of death is at once linked up with sexuality. To Hugo the "idea of escape appear[s] irresistible," while in Lois the mill evokes a "fear she didn't want to get over, a kind of deliciousness." Marda tantalizingly calls her a "shocking little coward," therewith luring Lois into entering this "nightmare." When they investigate the mill together, the scene acquires both the attributes and the significance of an initiation rite.[4]

The connection between sexuality and death, previously established in the context of Lois's memories of her mother and in her (frustrated) desire for Gerald's "womblike" body, conveys the ambivalence of the sexual impulse itself, in both its engulfing and its differentiating aspects, and underlines the subject's primary desirous investment in the female body. Marda's pressure in conducting Lois into the mill—in sharp contrast to Gerald's failure to "compel" her—facilitates the release of the protagonist's hitherto repressed desires:

Marda put an arm round her waist, and in an ecstasy at this compulsion Lois entered the mill. Fear heightened her gratification; she welcomed its inrush, letting her look climb the scabby and livid walls to the frightful stare of the sky. Cracks ran down; she expected, now with detachment, to see them widen, to see the walls peel back from a cleft—like the house of Usher's. (123–24)

The suggestive verbal detail and the evocative imagery of the passage clearly locate the dynamics of the scene in an active female same-sex, or lesbian, eroticism. While Marda's solicitude and Lois's confidence in subjecting herself to her guidance underline the initiatory aspect of the event, any moment of relaxation in their interchange is succeeded by another onrush of fear and desire. The discursive movement of the text thus reflects the ebb and flow of a sexual practice that, in its lack of closure, distinguishes itself from heterosexual coitus. The following sequence illustrates Bowen's superb talent for presenting such intricately intertwining themes with great subtlety:

The sun cast in through the window sockets some wild gold squares twisted by the beams; grasses along the windows trembled in light. Marda turned and went picking her way through the nettles; there was a further door, into darkness—somewhere, a roof still held. . . . Shuddering exaggeratedly, leaping in a scared way over the nettles, Lois also made for the dark doorway, eager for comment, contempt, consolation. She was a little idiot—appealing, she felt quite certain, to a particular tenderness. (124)

While the "particular tenderness" appealed to by Lois signifies the nonnormative quality of her sexual desires, the nettles acquire explicit significance as a symbol of female heterosexuality when the two discover a man sleeping in the mill. Lois notices that the man's "fist . . . strayed to a clump of nettles" and figures that his "knuckles must have been stung quite white." But since he is lying face down as though he "could not feel the nettles," she is amazed to find that he is obviously insensitive to them (124). Indicative of man's inability to perceive female sexuality except in relation to his own, this supports the feminist concept of the male gaze as fixing Woman in her position as Other to his Self.[5] This suggestion is soon confirmed.

The shell of female same-sex intimacy is rudely shattered by the intrusion of the male element. A Sinn Feiner apparently on the run from the Black and Tans, the man verifies the violence of phallogocentric power by pointing a gun at Lois and Marda. "Embarrassed by this curious confrontation," they sense that the bond between them, having been forged on the exclusion of Hugo (still sulking and smoking outside) to begin with, is now broken from within. The connection between female subordination and the male gaze is made explicit: "Framed" by the Sinn Feiner's look, "as though confronting a camera," Lois and Marda are forced to regain their temporarily suspended consciousness of themselves as "women." Since Marda is thoroughly practiced in her gender role, she is quick to resume her accustomed position. Lois, however, at once feels "quite ruled out." The conviction that "there was nothing at all for her here" lands her with full force back into her dilemma: "She had better be going—but where?" Her recognition that she does not fit within the heterosexual matrix leaves her quite literally with no discursive site in which to articulate herself, and with nowhere to go. By falling outside the "grid of cultural intelligibility that regulates the real and the nameable,"[6] lesbian sexuality is indeed quite effectively "ruled out," rendered invisible, unnameable and hence unthinkable within the dominant cultural domain. Since there is no outside to the field of discursive power/knowledge, the only recourse Lois can think of is, once again, that she "must marry Gerald" (125).

Under the threat of his phallic power, Lois and Marda are forced to swear their silence to the Sinn Feiner about the events at the mill. Subordinated to the political interests structuring the historical plot, their own "dialogue" is thus erased from the larger cultural scenario. When the man's gun goes off by accident, the bullet scrapes the back of Marda's hand. The fact that it is Marda and not Lois who is injured indicates that the conclusion of the adolescent protagonist's sexual initiation simultaneously marks the older woman's definitive subjection to the Law. Her willingness to silence her transgressive sexuality and to take up her proper gender position is suggested to be no less than an act of self-mutilation, a wound inflicted by the sway of the powerful phallus. Freud, in fact, describes the process of becoming "feminine" quite explicitly in terms of "injury": adult "femininity" is the point at which a woman, acknowledging the "fact" of her castration, has become "aware of the wound to her narcissism," as a result of which she "develops, like a scar, a sense of inferiority."[7] Marda's irrevocable conversion to "true womanhood" is underlined by Hugo's ineffective but vehement reaction to the incident. By thus betraying his secret longing for her, Hugo establishes his masculine Self in its dependence on feminine Otherness.

Instead of implicating the protagonist in a "conspiracy of adultery," as Heath would have it, the "emotional shock" Lois suffers at this point issues from her recognition that male self-presence requires the "injury" of femininity as its guarantee. She infers that it is this that makes Hugo, set on "transgressing the decencies," into an encroachment upon her own sexuality/subjectivity. Observing "how the very suggestion of death" causes him to bring about "this awful unprivacy," Lois tries to recapture the bond between Marda and herself. In mutual recognition of the predatory nature of male sexuality, the two "acknowledge silently" that their sex constitutes a "stronghold" against the inroads of (male) violence. But, while their unLawful sexual relations may serve as a valuable protective shield, their gender identity within the Law confines them to a position in which their subjective agency is reduced to passive resistance only. The reassuring thought that "traditionally, one could always retreat on collapse" hence simultaneously marks a recognition of their inevitable subordination to phallocratic dominance (127).

As we have seen, for Marda, the adventure at the mill turns out to have been a final act of defiance in terms of sexual deviancy. Falling in with the prevailing myths by which lesbian sexuality is relegated to the margins of Western culture, and in particular to the adolescent period, she maintains that from now on, "one won't be girlish again." She reveals, however, that she is fully aware of what her subjection to the Law(e) in entering into adult femininity entails:

She expected, some forty-eight hours ahead, to be walking with [Leslie Lawe] in a clipped and traditional garden, in Kentish light. Under these influences, she would be giving account of herself. Leslie's attention, his *straight* grey gaze, were to modify these wandering weeks of her own incalculably, not a value could fail to be affected by him. *So much of herself that was fluid must, too, be moulded by his idea of her.* Essentials were *fixed* and *localized* by their being together—to become as the bricks and wallpaper of a home. (129; italics mine) [8]

Since lesbian sexuality falls quite literally outside the phallogocentric economy, the violent conclusion of the scene at the mill is here confirmed to entail the relinquishment of much more than Marda's social independence. Even so, her chilling resignation to womanhood should not obscure the positive significance of the experience for Lois.

Conscious of a sense of loss as a result of her revelation, Lois concedes that she "was too damned innocent" before (129, 128). Having been initiated into "carnal knowledge," Lois is no longer the *vierge* whose "business" it is to be "thrown out of the garden of Eden," to lose her innocence. In psychoanalytic terms, both the subject's entrance into the symbolic order and the adolescent crisis are wholly centered on loss. As the reemergence of the oedipal crisis in which the infant is forced to give up its first love object, adolescence reevokes this primary loss upon which the subject's entry into the symbolic order depends. With the loss of the Real, the child is compelled henceforth to repress its desire for the mother. Heterosexual gender stratification seeks to ensure that, when this repressed desire reawakens at the onset of puberty, the adolescent's search for a secondary object is "normally" directed at members of the opposite sex. Since the primary loss involves the loss of the maternal figure for male and female infants alike, their respective attempts at recovery necessarily take radically different forms. While both must give up the mother as a love object, the heterosexual paradigm allows the boy merely to postpone his desire until adulthood. The continued focus of his desire on a female object is both ensured and fully sanctioned by dominant ideology. In contrast, the female adolescent is obliged both to give up her original object and to redirect her desire into an entirely opposite direction. The girl's normative course of heterosexual development is thus far more complicated in that it prescribes a complete withdrawal of desire from the female figure. It is hence far more likely that the adolescent girl would invest her reemerging desire in a member of the same sex.

Indeed, the insistence with which both literary and psychoanalytic texts suggest that the female adolescent's "crush" on an older woman is in fact quite "normal" signals the precarious foundations on which the heterosexual gender system rests. By almost unexceptionally situating the phenomenon of the same-sex crush strictly within the adolescent phase, these discourses function so as to naturalize what is clearly a rather unstably "fixed" standard: that which may be considered to be healthy or "normal" during an earlier stage of subjective development becomes "abnormal," regressive, and/or pathological once this period has officially ended.[9] We may therefore fairly assume that it is primarily the enforcement of heterosexual gender ideology that compels the female adolescent to turn to a male secondary object instead.[10] What is more, the girl's "forbidden" object from then on represents the negative (female) to the positive (male). The discourses of phallogocentrism and compulsory heterosexuality thus interact in such a way as to reinforce each other. The inescapability and compelling force of ideological interpellation is perhaps most strikingly foregrounded by the otherwise unaccountable circumstance that the majority of female subjects "willingly" assume their positions within the heterosexual matrix. This is even more amazing when we consider that, in addition to being denied access to women as objects of her own desire, the adolescent girl learns that she herself belongs to this "negative" category—a fact that not seldomly leads to a sense of inferiority if not to virtual self-hatred.

These considerations attest to the critical significance of the mill scene as the heroine's initiation into a nonnormative, subversive sexuality. They also highlight the female adolescent's cultural function as a figure of sexual indeterminacy, and, by extension, qualify its value as a prototypical character in Bowen's fiction. Lois has gained insight into the close links between sexuality and death as well as access to her own reemerging sexual desires, and the experience with Marda has allowed her to set up a female subject in the position of "self-giving" other, a position ideologically reserved for a member of the opposite sex only. Since Lois's loss of the maternal object has in fact been "doubled" by the premature death of Laura—a sexual rebel in her own right, whom Lois primarily recollects in sensual terms—it is not surprising that she finds a worthy secondary object in a female subject. This is not to say that Lois can henceforth simply sidestep heterosexual gender ideology. Gerald's importance lies in the security he represents in sociocultural terms, and these cannot be so easily discounted. However, we have seen this potential secondary object turn into something of a stumbling block in Lois's "struggle for life." Instead of providing her with an outlet for her sexual desires, the young man has consistently curtailed Lois's attempts at self-definition in this as much as in any other respect. Having triumphed over the revived oedipal depression (on which the continuation of the subjective process depends) through her sexual encounter with Marda, Gerald has in fact become quite irrelevant to the heroine's psychosexual development. Taking into account, however, that the setting of the novel is the Anglo-Ireland of the 1920s, the hazards of transgressing cultural boundaries by rejecting the narrative of heterosexual romance would yet seem fatal to the adolescent's quest for a social identity. Even if Lois's sexual initiation therefore does not allow her to abandon her role in this dominant cultural scenario, a change of vision has definitely been achieved.

The erotic encounter with Marda has taught Lois to apprehend her sexuality as distinct from femininity. Her gender no longer merely represents a liability from whose social consequences she needs to break away: it has been revealed to be a potential source of strength and vitality as well. This recognition is underlined when Marda ostensibly inconsequentially remarks that she would "hate to be barren," therewith articulating the contrast between her sexual potential and Hugo's (male) sterility (128). Lois's initiation into "carnal knowledge" entails an altered view of herself, which makes it harder for her to "imagine what [she]'ll be doing or where [she] shall be" tomorrow. Her uncertainty is enhanced by the fact that Marda, in relation to whom she has defined her new self, will by that time have departed into her own rigidly defined "straight" future. But because she can carry away the "perfect secret" of her sexual awakening, Lois is also relieved that "at present, the mill [is] behind her." She reassumes her quest with an intensified sense of agency: "As though breaking a spell," she "shift[s] away down the parapet" and "put[s] her feet to the ground" (129). The fact that she has broken the spell of the "illusion" that she had felt called upon to maintain in her relationship with Gerald does not imply, however, that the resulting shift in perspective extends beyond Lois's own sense of herself. Instead of bringing about the overall transmutation she had hoped for, the world around her generally, and Gerald in particular, do not appear to be in any way affected by the expanse of her personality. While Lois can now bring Gerald "wholly into focus," she does so in a way that is contrary to what was once the intended effect of such focus (52). The "loss of her innocence" has rendered him even less eligible as the object of her desire than before. The incontrovertible proof of Gerald's superfluousness in the narrative of Lois's quest is reflected in the title of the novel's third chapter, "The Departure of Gerald." This casual phrase refers to the young subaltern's almost equally casual death in an ambush.

The Lure of Disintegration. Following the highly charged central chapter, the events in the novel's concluding section are somewhat of an anticlimax. Instead of continuing to focus primarily on Lois's development, the narrator takes the action out of the enclosed setting of Danielstown, a widening of scope that is in itself significant with regard to the protagonist's itinerary. The main scene of the chapter is set in one of the English officers' huts near the village of Clonmore. Depicting a party organized by several of the officers' wives, the scene forms a sharply satirical attack on the vulgarity of the English middle classes. The highly unsympathetic narrative tone of voice stands in marked contrast to the mildly critical terms in which, throughout the novel, the eccentricities and snobbery of the Anglo-Irish are presented. Both the ruthless quality of the sociocultural critique and the widening of the narrative scene turn the party into a suitably tense background to the next stage of the protagonist's quest. Displaying her talent for creating a compelling atmosphere, Bowen succeeds in setting the perfect stage for Lois's unnerving encounter with a senior subaltern called Daventry.[11]

Daventry is a shell-shocked World War I veteran who is ready to go "over the edge" but for a great deal of whiskey and his vigorous hatred of the Irish (145). In the hut, buffeted by a fierce storm sending "shudders" down its walls "like a lunatic," he is evidently in his element. "Elegant, tall and a shade satanic," Mr. Daventry is the odd one out in this room "sticky with strawberry light." While the dancers appear to be "moving slowly in jam," he emanates an air of desperation to which Lois feels curiously drawn. Whereas Gerald might, for all she knows, have been "sealed up permanently in tin, like a lobster," Lois detects in this diabolical ghost of a man a quality for which she "could have loved" him (146). Still caught between her transgressive desires and her need to belong, she feels nonetheless urged to go along with the dance and is rather anxious whether she will in fact be "claimed" by Gerald. But since the spell of the "illusion" of love has been broken, it is impossible for her to abandon herself to the evening, which is running along with a "high impetuousness out of everybody's control." Daventry, with his "discomforting . . . intensity," gives her access to an aspect of herself that she realizes Gerald will never even begin to recognize (149, 156–57).

Daventry's principle attraction is his instability and the threat of disintegration he embodies. Although she senses the difference from the fearful "deliciousness" provoked in her by Marda, Lois is "startled to meet the dark look" in the man's eyes "*on a level*" with her own (156; italics mine). She perceives that what Daventry has to offer her is not the gift of her self in dialogic exchange. Since there is "not a man here, hardly a person," it is clear that the subaltern has nothing to give. Yet, in his total detachment from the play being enacted around them, he allows Lois a space in which to *be,* a space that Gerald's "actuality" simply cannot accommodate. Because she feels "framed" by the "generous allotment" the latter has granted her, Lois's sense of "not being understood" by him is reinforced when she discovers that she, in her turn, cannot "see" Gerald, for "there was nothing, in fact, to which to attach her look" (158). By not appealing to her in conventionally romantic terms, Daventry opens Lois's eyes to the lack of passion in her response to Gerald's first kiss: "She could not remember, though she had read so many books, *who* spoke first after the first kiss had been, not exchanged but—administered. The two reactions, outrage, capitulation, had not been her own" (152). Trying to play by the rules of the heterosexual contract, Lois had faked a "natural" feminine response. When she realizes her mistake, Lois has already promised to marry Gerald. Her desperate question— " 'What have I done?' "—is therefore swiftly succeeded by the hopeful thought that "perhaps it will seem natural tomorrow" (158). Her recently acquired knowledge, however, prevents Lois from naturalizing what obviously is not "natural" to her at all. While no longer a *vierge,* the adolescent is, in her role as the "awake one," unlike *les paresseux,* and hence unable to suppress her desires or to curb the widening of her consciousness for the sake of expediency. On the contrary, her newly attained insights give rise to searching questions that extend from her own sexual identity to the ideological practices by/in which such categories are produced. Increasingly "shy of [Gerald's] uncomprehension of a particular notion of living she seemed only now to have formed," Lois's (self-) scrutiny irrevocably leads her to question the regimes of power/knowledge making up the social field: "Where was the flaw? Or was Gerald, sublimely, the instrument of some large imposture?" The paramount "imposture" of dominant ideology is suggested to be the "naturàlness" of heterosexuality. This is underlined when Lois, after another confrontation with Gerald's agonizing "singleness," gives vent to her utter frustration by expressing the wish that "he were a woman" (172).

Lady Naylor's determination to interfere with Gerald's designs is undoubtedly informed by her own sense of (sexual) frustration. By an act of subtle scheming, she succeeds in inducing Lois to break the cultural contract. In a splendid piece of social satire, the young man shows his willingness to subject himself unequivocally to the hierarchical class system that legitimizes Lady Naylor's presumed superior power. It is this surrender—though entirely in character—that convinces Lois that she must try and "transmute" perspectives without Gerald. Although the young soldier's ensuing death may seem shocking in its abruptness, it is not a tragedy; it forms, rather, the inevitable conclusion to a fully substantiated course of (narrative) events.

When the news of Gerald's death is (quite appropriately) conveyed to her by Daventry, Lois is led to the reflection quoted at an earlier point, where the narrator merges with the heroine's consciousness to assert that life is "one act of apprehension, the apprehension of death." This, I have argued, is not the ultimate expression of despair (as Lee suggests), but a deliberate and conscious acceptance of the challenge of life. Lois belongs to the people Bowen classifies as "those who wish to be really alive": she cannot but opt for facing the challenge. Concisely summing up Gerald's character—' "He loved me, he believed in the British Empire' "—she subsequently rejects Laurence's supposition that "one probably gets past things." Pointing out that this is precisely what she "do[es]n't want to" (203), Lois voices the author's conviction that the "struggle for life," being a "struggle" by necessity, "should . . . not have anything terrible about it."[12] By thus consciously assuming her role as a subject answerable to the world, and answerable for her own responses, the heroine concludes her appearance on the narrative scene.

The Adolescent Paradigm. The conclusion of Lois's quest underlines that, within Bowen's ethical framework, the individual can only live up to her/his potential by actively engaging in the experience of life generally, and of sexuality in particular, in all of its destabilizing multiplicity. The crucial influence of the "here and now" on the protagonist's search for a sense of meaning/self foregrounds the subject's inscription in materiality, and, a fortiori, the inscription of her/his identity in deeds and actions. Attesting to the contingent nature of subjectivity/sexuality, the novel unequivocally advances a notion of life as a never-ending activity, of the self as an endless process of (re)constitution performed in the field of discursive power/knowledge. Since nothing is fixed once and for all, life is essentially a matter of negotiation and compromise. Or, as the narrator in another of the early novels avers: "One has to live how one can."[13] In Bowen, the "business" of living is, as we have seen, losing one's innocence by/in experience. This entails that to try to remain a *vierge* is not only a cause for personal *chagrin;* it is a fundamentally moral flaw and thus unacceptable. Nor can one shirk one's responsibility by taking up a position among *les paresseux.* Although "very few remain ennobled" in the process of "experience,"[14] it is in only in the dialogue between Self and (the) Others/s that the subject's answerability—which is life itself—is located.

My discussion so far has attempted to show that it would be reductive to regard Lois's adolescent struggle in traditional terms, that is to say, to regard its characteristic sexual indeterminacy as a crisis in identity restricted to a given period of one's life. Nor would the frequency with which the young girl appears in Bowen's novels validate a categorization of the character as merely a typically Bowenesque picture of preadulthood. Beginning with her war novel *The Heat of the Day* (1949), Bowen's heroines gradually "grow older," more or less in line with the novelist's own advancing age.[15] All her protagonists face crises similar to Lois's, however. This allows us to approach the adolescent character as a figure of sexual ambivalence and indeterminacy with a far wider significance than dominant regimes of knowledge are willing to concede. As my readings in the following chapters will confirm, the female adolescent functions as a prototype in Bowen's work, as a representative figure through which she could explore the conflicts and contradictions lying at the heart of female sexuality/subjectivity as such. Lois's predicament is undeniably linked to her lack of experience; this is what makes her, in contrast to the adult characters in *LS*, critically susceptible to the influence of external (sociocultural) conditions. But the general state of sexual instability and psychic dislocation in which she is presented is not exceptional so much as inherent in the perpetual struggle called life. Bowen underlines this central insight as follows in one of her autobiographical sketches: "I have thriven . . . on the changes and chances, the dislocations and . . . the contrasts which have made up so much of my life."[16] The adolescent generally, but the female adolescent in patriarchal culture in particular, is unquestionably in an eminent position to experience such dislocations and contrasts intensely. This is why Lois's quest so adequately reflects the process of (female) sexuality, for this concerns precisely the negotiation of a position within a myriad of constraining and often conflicting ideological discourses. Since the typical Bowen character is consistently shown to be "in transit *consciously,*" the heroine of *LS* is a representative instance of what Bowen calls "sensationalists," those individuals who are "able to reexperience what they do, or equally, what is done to them, every day," and who "tend to behold afresh and react accordingly." [17]

Defined as such, the adolescent emerges not only as the prototype of the Bowen character but also as the fictional representation of (the concept of) the subject-in-process whose (sexual) identity is never determined once and for all but rather endlessly displaced in a series of performative acts. As an instance of what Gayatri Chakravorty Spivak calls "'non-expository' theory in practice," [18] the novel delineates a quest that is the condition of gendered subjectivity per se. The heroine is presented as a site of contradiction, shown to be "perpetually in the process of construction, thrown into crisis by alterations in language and in the social formation," and therefore also "capable of change." [19] As a textual configuration of sexual indeterminacy, the adolescent acquires further significance on the extrafictional or extradiegetic level of the text, and therewith sheds significant light on the narrative's concluding scene. [20]

Interpretation, Transference, and Authorial Control

(Auto)biographical Inscriptions. The narrative of *LS* does not end with Lois's off-stage departure into an appropriately indeterminate future—she has finally not entered a school of art but has gone on "tours," "for her French," as Lady Naylor two weeks later reports to her friend Mrs. Trent (204). The novel's closing scene centers on Danielstown. The Big House, its inhabitants' desiccated way of life, and its symbolic value as the seat of patriarchal power hence receive full dramatic emphasis. All its summer guests having left, Danielstown's "now settled

emptiness" seems to have "gained composure." But both Mrs. Trent's "uneasy, exposed look" and Lady Naylor's "restlessly, lightly folded hands" express the abiding atmosphere of subdued tension and impending crisis. And justifiably so, the narrator confirms, since the "two did not . . . again see Danielstown at such a moment, such a particular happy point of decline in the short curve of the day, the long curve of the season," for "by next year light had possessed itself of the vacancy, still with surprise" (205–6). Set to fire by Irish nationalists, Danielstown shares a fate suffered by many other such big houses. Although to their owners it seems as if an "extra day, *unreckoned,* had come to abortive birth that these things might happen" (206; italics mine), the acts of destruction are presented as part of an irreversibly evolving design.

The end of the Ascendency, of the Anglo-Irish community and its cultural tradition, is not to be taken as an act of God—however suggestive the all-consuming flames may be. It is definitely not His final day of "reckoning" that is referred to here. The "death—or execution rather" of the big houses is accomplished by human hands, and it is the executioners whom the Anglo-Irish had not reckoned with. By closing their eyes to themselves, these *paresseux* have been living within a state of unawareness personally harmful, but their complacency has also prevented them from recognizing their constituting/constituted roles within the larger sociopolitical field. As a consequence, they have failed to notice the gradually multiplying cracks in the structure of their seemingly timeless cultural order. The short description of the night that sees Danielstown burning succinctly captures these implications and conveys them in all their ambivalence:

The roads in unnatural dusk ran dark with movement, secretive or terrified; not a tree, brushed pale by wind from the flames, not a cabin pressed in despair to the bosom of night, not a gate too starkly visible but had its place in the *design of order and panic.* At Danielstown, half-way up the avenue under the beeches, the thin iron gate twanged (missed its latch, remained swinging aghast) as the last unlit car slid out with the execution-ers bland from accomplished duty. The sound of the last car widened, gave itself to the open and empty country and was demolished. Then the first wave of silence that was to be ultimate flowed back, confident, to the steps. Above the steps, the door stood open hospitably upon a furnace. (206; italics mine)

The closing sentence of the novel reaffirms the inextricable link between the private and the public, the personal and the political, the subjective and the objective, the Self and (the) Other/s. Moving from the house standing prey to the devouring flames, the narra-tor's all-purveying look into the future shifts to zoom in on the Naylors, therewith establishing a straightforward connection be-tween the exposure of Danielstown's feeble foundations and its owners' moral lassitude. Equally ruthlessly exposed, "Sir Richard and Lady Naylor, not saying anything, did not look at each other, for in the light from the sky they saw too distinctly" (206).

Articulating an unequivocal moral stance and passing a pointed political judgment, this closing scene provides a suitable ending to the sustained ideological critique couched within a narrative pervaded by an unremitting atmosphere of suspended crisis. How-ever, the burning of Danielstown additionally demands attention on what I have called the extradiegetic level of the text. What ulterior motive may Bowen have had to conclude this "work of instinct rather than knowledge," this "recall" book, with such an act of willful violence? Indeed, why does the novel end with the destruction of the house that beyond any doubt *is* her family home? Historically speaking, the event is plausible enough, for a number of big houses in Bowen's Court's immediate neighborhood were in fact burned by the Irish at the time of the Troubles. Still, although Bowen later wrote, "So often in my mind's eye did I see it burning" that the "terrible last event in *The Last September* is more real than anything I have lived through," in reality Bowen's Court "stayed untouched" at the time.[21] It would be both facile and beside my point to dispatch the matter by putting it down as the author's personal act of "reckoning" with her parents and/or her Anglo-Irish girlhood. After all, when Bowen wrote *LS*, she was thirty years old, had been living in England for over ten years, and was fully established as a writer. What I would like to dwell on, then, are the possible meanings of the novel's conclusion in the context of the paradigmatic significance of the adolescent crisis and its relation to the notion of authorial control. This takes me back to the author's preface to *LS*, and in particular to a point mentioned at the beginning of the previous chapter.

We recall that *LS* is the only of Bowen's novels that is "set back, deliberately, in a former time." In all others, she "wanted readers to contemplate what could be the immediate moment—so much so, that to give the sense of the 'now' has been, for me, one imperative of writing" (96).[22] These emphases suggest that an intertextual reading, linking up the theme of adolescence, Bowen's autobiographical reflections, and her observations on the art of writing, offers a constructive approach to the question. I will therefore make a short detour through these various intertexts.

Considering her obvious preoccupation with the phenomenon, it is surprising to find that Bowen seldom explicitly refers to the crisis structure of adolescence. In one of the very few instances in which she uses the term in relation to herself, she flatly denies having experienced any "overpowering onslaught of adolescence," maintaining that it "apparently by-passed me—or if I ever did have it, I got off light." The context in which these assertions are made is revealing. What Bowen is trying to account for here is her sudden transformation from a bright child into a "dunce" girl at the age of thirteen. She almost casually posits that her "stupidity may have been due to denied sorrow," since it manifested itself a few weeks after she had suffered the terrible loss of her mother.[23] The preceding five years, we recall, Bowen and her mother had been traveling together in England. The enforced intimacy must have made the impact of Florence Bowen's death on the young Elizabeth particularly devastating. Leaving her in a prolonged state of shock, it apparently urged her to continue her earlier-embarked-upon "career of withstood emotion" with renewed vigor.[24] Afterward, Bowen discloses, she "could not remember her [mother], think of her, speak of her or suffer to hear her spoken of."[25] Such silencing was to result in an exacerbation of the stammer that became a striking feature of her adult personality.[26] In order to screen herself from the "sense of disfigurement, disgrace, mortification" that followed her "total bereavement," Bowen became a "high-ranking initiator of school-crazes." In this "lifeless time in [her] own life, something outstanding and startling was what [she] needed."[27] While still allowing for her "farouche" nature to express itself, we can safely assume that her "carnival of bravado" served to protect Bowen against unbearable emotions. The display of "sensation" that, as distinct from emotion, is something the author claims to "have never fought shy of or done anything to restrain" was clearly set up as a shield against inexpressible feelings of grief. It appears equally viable that it deflected the experience of any "tormenting nameless disturbances, conflicts, cravings" Bowen associated with adolescence.[28]

Looking back on her girlhood, Bowen primarily remembers her preadult years as a period during which "I asked myself *what* I should be, and when?"[29] This agonizing question, we recall, is almost literally echoed by her protagonist Lois. At the time when she was writing the preface to her second novel in 1952, however, the author was in a position to reflect also on the period separating this former self from the one who assembled her into a fictional character. It is these years, between twenty and twenty-five, which Bowen identifies as "often important, packed with changes, decisive." If we read this statement as merely reflective of a forced postponement of adolescence—whose destabilizing effects had earlier been too much to bear—we fail to take into account its far-reaching implications. The shift signifies more than a displacement of a critical phase in the process of identity formation. For, having been transposed to a different spatio-temporal setting, the *mean-*

ings of this transformative phase had decisively altered as well. When Bowen sat writing *LS* in Oxford, "1920 seemed a long time ago":

> I myself was no longer a tennis girl but a writer; aimlessness was gone, like a morning mist. Not an hour had not a *meaning,* and a *centre.* Also changes had altered my sense of space—Ireland seemed immensely distant from Oxford, more like another world than another land. Here I was, living a life dreamed of when, like Lois, I drove the pony trap along endless lanes. Civilization (a word constantly on my 1928 lips) was now around me. I was in company with the articulate and the learned. (97; italics mine)

Remarkable about this passage is first of all the implicit recognition that meaning and coherence are acquired only in experience, with the subsidiary acknowledgment of the constitutive role of time and space in the process of self-construction. Secondly, and more importantly in the present context, the retrospectively perceived transformation is defined not in terms of sexuality or gender, but is explicitly cast as a coming-into-being as a *writer.* Bowen's sense of dislocation in the wake of her mother's death was reinforced by her having been "in and out of the home of my relatives" and "shuttling between two countries" ever since. This issued in the "sub-merged fear that I might fail to establish grown-up status." We have seen such anxiety to be directly reflected in Lois's *gender-*oriented predicament. It was precisely this fear, Bowen assumes, that "egged [her] on to writing: an author, a grown-up, must they not be synonymous?" Unlike Lois, therefore, who cannot "think how to begin to be anything else" but a "woman," Bowen does not locate the center of her sense of adult identity in the first instance in her gender, but in her sociocultural position as author. Furthermore, by assuming a place among the "learned and the articulate," she firmly situated herself within what even today is, but certainly in the 1920s was, a male-dominated section of "civilization." All this would seem to suggest that, as a consequence of her emotional "nonexistence" during preadulthood,

Bowen took on the struggle for identity *consciously* only when she was already fully embedded within the sociocultural order. It was in the world of discourse par excellence that she found a position from which to speak and articulate herself with authority.

This of course is not to suggest that Bowen simply "skipped" adolescence, or did not pass through the process of gender acquisition. It is nonetheless clear that she first and foremost identified her self as a writer, to the extent that she tended to separate these two aspects of herself. In a letter written to V. S. Pritchett in 1948, Bowen declares: "I do not know exactly what is involved in the being of a full-time intelligent person. I am fully intelligent only when I write. I have a certain amount of small-change intelligence, which I carry round . . . for the needs of the day, the non-writing day. But it seems to me that I seldom purely *think*."[30] She elaborates on the contrast between "thinking" and "living" by differentiating her public from her private selves. While beginning by casting this split in terms of sexual difference, Bowen at once demolishes the separation, calling into question the distinction as such: "For me personally, as a woman, any sort of kindness or being wished well or thought well of is the breath of life. Nor is that need wholly personal, womanish: it exists in the writing part of me too."[31] Whereas the personal is connoted as "womanish," the implied contrast is not extended to a definition of writing as "mannish" or masculine. If not exactly an opposition, surely there is a conflict between these two aspects. Bowen's ambivalent sense of self would appear to reflect the internalized contradiction of phallogocentric discourses in which power and authority are as a rule predicated on the possession of a penis. This may explain why she invariably refers to the writer in male terms—even when she is expressly discussing herself.

The conflict in Bowen's self-perception as a "woman writer" attests to the tenacity of the dominant myth underlying all binary oppositions, the "natural fact" of the duality of sex. In spite of the resulting tensions, the author's self-awareness precluded any subscription to notions whose untenability she was too astute not to discern, such as the relegation of the emotional/intellectual aspects of her identity to her gender/authorial roles, respectively. From the conviction that "thought exceeds consciousness," she infers that thought and emotion are in the final instance inseparable. This leads her to assume that "perhaps one emotional reason why one may write is the need to work off, out of the system, the sense of being solitary and farouche," for "solitary and farouche people don't have relationships: they are quite unrelatable." Since it is only through our inscription in a given sociocultural context that we acquire meaning, the act of positioning ourselves within a network of dialogic relationships is an ontological imperative. For Bowen, writing served as a "substitute for . . . a so-called normal relation to society," forging the necessary link between her Self and (the) Other/s: "My books *are* my relation to society."[32]

In her letter to Pritchett, Bowen's main concern is the role of the writer in society.[33] She argues that the writer, by creating fictional patterns, is capable of giving meaningful shape to an otherwise meaningless reality. This constitutes the writer's gift to the reader:

Shapelessness, lack of meaning, and being without direction is most people's nightmare, once they begin to think. . . . To the individual, the possibility that his life should be unmeaning, a series of in the main rather hurting fortuities, and that his death should be insignificant, is unbearable. Temporarily, for the reader . . . art puts up a buttress against that—or, still more important, makes a counter-assertion.[34]

While conceiving of the writer in a position of authority over both text and reader, Bowen does not conceal that the writing subject is equally in need of meaningful form. Positing that a writer is "simply trying to trace out some pattern around himself," or to "uncover a master-pattern in which he has his place," she acknowledges that her fictional discourse is also a mode of self-construction. Pressing the matter further, she wonders: "Couldn't it be that the wish, the demand for shape is more than individual, that it's a mass thing? Or rather, the mass's wish or demand not to have to go on being a mass merely?"[35] Bowen here clearly approaches the poststructuralist notion of the subject as interpellated by the same discursive structures upon which s/he depends for her/his self-differentiation and self-determination. The point is made even more explicitly in her autobiographical sketch "Pictures and Conversations" (1975):

A main trait of human nature is its amorphousness, the amorphousness of the drifting and flopping jellyfish in a cloudy tide, and secret fears (such as fear of nonentity), discouragement and demoralising misgivings prey upon individuals made aware of this. There results an obsessive wish to acquire outline, to be unmistakably demarcated, to take *shape*. (58–59)

Bowen's consistent choice for an omniscient narrator, "unmistakably" in control of her fiction, is thus not merely a matter of narrative strategy or technique: it is essentially a defense against the fear of "nonentity." And, as Heath correctly points out, the author's "concept of a saving pattern" is a central theme in all of her novels.[36]

Bowen's reflections on the interconnections between art and reality validate my speculations on the relations between her "postponed" adolescent crisis and her authorship. For is not the essential "amorphousness" of human nature most strikingly contrasted to the writer's authority in the literal extinction of Danielstown at the end of *LS*? The imaginary experience apparently not only served to subdue the author's fear that her family home might thus be destroyed but also to deflect the destabilizing effects the envisaged event would have on her. Furthermore, Bowen's belief in fiction as "realler" than life entails that the act of fictionalizing allowed her a kind of control that so-called real life certainly could not supply. As an author "playing God" over her fictional world she created her own, reassuringly meaningful reality. Bowen's exertion of her authorial power in the closing section may seem an overly dramatic move on the narrative level of *LS*. On the extradiegetic level, however, it enabled her to prove her "overlordship" over her characters and thus to come to terms with the irreducible lack of meaning at the heart of subjectivity. That this intrinsic shapelessness finds its locus in sexuality, is, as I have argued, most undisguisedly brought to the fore in the adolescent quest. By enacting sexual dispersal at its narrative level, by writing the story of the subject-in-process, the text itself therefore simultaneously undermines the author's control. Seen in this perspective, the tension pervading *LS* would seem to mirror the contradiction that defined the author's sense of her self.

Textual Transference. The narrator's authority surfaces most palpably in the irony and satire qualifying the novel's closing pages. Stressing its function as a measure of containment, Heath finds fault with Bowen's imposition of a "saving pattern" here, as "too explicit a defense against the loss of control."[37] The sense of unease expressed by this comment suggests the value the adolescent, as a paradigmatic figure of sexual instability and "unmeaning," obtains in relation to both writer and reader. By shifting Heath's emphasis in the opposite direction, we can read the contradiction between the diegetic and extradiegetic levels of the text in its irreducibility. This, in turn, would enable us to account for the disconcerting ambivalence that the equally irresistible pulls of disintegration and control create in the reader of *LS*.

In "The Adolescent Novel" (1990), Julia Kristeva approaches the relation between the author of the novel of development and her/his subject matter from a psychoanalytic perspective. She argues that these contradictory pulls are inherent in the writing of adolescence generally.[38] Employing a notion of the adolescent as a product of the imaginary, Kristeva defines this mythic figure as "less an age category than an open psychic structure." This allows her to consider writing adolescence as an act of "interrogating oneself on the role of the imaginary" (8). She begins by noting that adolescence can be called a *crisis structure* "only through the eyes of an ideal, stable law"—that is, from within dominant (clinical) discourse—and goes on to posit that adolescence involves a resurgence of the (repressed) imaginary "in the aftermath of the oedipal stabilization of subjective identity." The reemergence of the repressed leads to a renewed questioning of the individual's identifications "along with his [sic] capacities for speech and symbolization." As an open-structure personality, the adolescent in this sense "maintain[s] a renewable identity through interaction with another." Consequently, the imaginary activity of writing fiction can "permit a genuine inscription of unconscious contents within language" (9) while simultaneously protecting the subject "from phobic affects," since fictionalizing enables her/him to "reelaborate his [sic] psychic space" (10). What Kristeva defines as the two psychic "registers" of writing coincides exactly with the aspects of destabilization and control structuring the discourse of *LS*.

In Western societies, Kristeva asserts, the adolescent has a "right to the imaginary," while to the adult this right is granted "only as a reader or spectator . . . or as artist." She narrows her discussion to the genre of the novel, because, as an open structure par excellence, novelistic discourse is "largely tributary . . . to the 'adolescent' economy." Narrative fiction generally can thus be viewed as the "work of a perpetual subject-adolescent" (11). Hence, several early (fifteenth-century) adolescent novels single out the "*topos* of incompleteness that is also that of all possibilities" as the defining feature of the genre. Tracing the French novel of development through the centuries, Kristeva locates the emergence of the "question of sexual difference as an unresolved problematic" in the eighteenth-century variety of the genre. We recall that, in psychic terms, the adolescent, as yet unfixed in her/his object choice, directs her/his quest at the recovery of a (second) love object. The fictional inscription of adolescent perversion or insanity, functioning as the novelist's "powerful screen against madness" (20), can therefore be seen to be increasingly expressed in terms of "sexual ambiguity, disguise, polynymia" (18). The gradual establishment of the inner psychic space that was to become characteristic of the nineteenth-century psychological novel is, Kristeva maintains, initially set up as "delirium, chaos, or emptiness." Since such a space needs a powerful ordering principle, the author subsequently took up a position of unrestrained power over characters, action, and plot. The full development of the novelistic genre can hence be argued to reflect the birth of adolescence *as* crisis.

The novel form serves to accommodate the reemergence of repressed unconscious contents as well as their recollection in a process of psychic reorganization—usually called identity formation. Kristeva concludes that the figure of the adolescent is central to narrative fiction both as the "emblem of a subjectivity in crisis" and as a "means to display the psychic breakdown up to the point of psychosis and at the same time to recollect it, to unify it within the unity of the novel" (15, 18). It is the essential polyvalence or, to use a Bakhtinian term, polyphony of the novelistic genre that allows for these conflicting impulses to coexist and operate simultaneously. In carrying over onto the reader the intrinsic precariousness of the authorial "triumph" over the reemerging oedipal depression, the adolescent novel forces the reader also fully to experience the threat of disintegration underlying her/his own sense of self. Furthermore, because of the sexual overdetermination of the adolescent crisis, reading such a text affects her/him first and foremost in her/his sense of sexual identity. This, incidentally, would seem to provide a convincing explanation of Heath's uneasy objections to the closing part of *LS*.

Kristeva's unwavering bias for male-authored texts prevents her from considering any female adolescent novels. Nor does she explore the gendered aspects of either adolescence or authorial control. Even so, her general argument would seem to substantiate my reading of the tension sustained in the discourse of *LS*. There is a further element in the psychoanalytic account of adolescence that appears relevant to Bowen's novels. As an open structure enacted by/in its discourse, the adolescent novel presents an illuminating perspective on the writer's psychic investment in her/his protago-

nist's search for a second love object. Kristeva maintains that the
fictional representation of adolescence provides the writer with a
means to express her/his "own latent exhibitionism or homosexuality." There is, moreover, also a "certain identification of the
narrator with his seductress or seducer."[39] Adolescents, she explains, "escape all categories—even those of coded perversions—
and impose themselves on novelists as metaphors for what is not
yet formed: metaphor of what awaits the writer, of what calls to
him, the mirage of prelanguage or unnamed body" (21).[40] Because
it constitutes a primarily suggestive and implicit eroticism, the
representation of adolescence is an "erotic game" in which "nothing but . . . allusions to junctions of detours," "nothing but *signs*"
are articulated. This, of course, is what the novelist her/himself is
basically concerned with: the "effort to name, to make uncertain
meaning appear at the frontier of word and drive" (21–22). We
have seen the erotic tension in *LS* accumulate in the middle section
upon which the novel hinges, during "The Visit of Miss Norton."
Kristeva's observations enable us to discern that this tension is
structurally inscribed as unequivocally a lesbian eroticism, operating on the narrative level between Lois and Marda, and on its
extradiegetic level between the author and her created seduc-
tress(es). Bearing in mind that Bowen wrote within a heterosexist
as much as a phallocentric cultural context, we can thus read
the sexual indeterminacy, enacted by/in the figure of the female
adolescent and equally reflected in the novel's discourse, as the
expression of the author's own (conflictual) same-sex desire.

Kristeva assumes the interaction between writer/text/reader to
be a dynamics involving both "transference and interpretation." It
follows that the desirous investment on the writer's part is displaced onto her/his text and, similarly, carried over onto the
reader. The object of the reader's desire is located in the figure of
the adolescent and by extension in the novelistic *form*, for the text
itself constitutes the "writing-mimesis of a structure essentially
open, incomplete." As the "semiotic elaboration" of reawakened

imaginary material, the adolescent novel, Kristeva contends, can for the reader be "anything but a drug" (22). The implications of the transference effect suggest that her own exclusive focus on male adolescent novels is perhaps more than simply a matter of convenience or established practice.[41] Lee's curious silence on the sexual quality of Lois's encounter with Marda, and her failure generally to explore the lesbian aspects of Bowen's work, are herewith also cast in somewhat of a different light.[42] It hardly needs pointing out that the transference effect to some extent explains and, I may hope, sufficiently validates the emphases I have been placing in (re)constructing the meanings of *LS*. I have tried to show that rather than a nostalgic return to the past, Bowen's "recall" book is a novel of adolescence and subversive sexual desire, as well as a thoroughly moral/political work. The author's growing preoccupation with the technologies of gender in relation to discursive power will be the focus of my next chapter, where these issues will be linked up with history and the movement of narrative.

4

Histories of Narrative Desire

There cannot be a moment in which nothing happens.
—*The Heat of the Day*

The Fictitious Reality of The Heat of the Day (1949)

Fragmented Figments. In *LS*, Bowen presents an as yet unformed character trying to negotiate her position within fixed and oppressive ideological structures. Embodied in the figure of the female adolescent, gendered subjectivity itself represents the unstable, disruptive, or indeterminate element. In her war-time novel, *The Heat of the Day* (hereafter, *HD*), the same themes of dislocation and dispersal emerge, but the roles of agency have been reversed: it is not internal but external forces that are in flux and that set in motion a process of destabilization in the middle-aged protagonist. Although not an adolescent in the clinical sense, Stella Rodney faces a dilemma similar to Lois's when she finds herself surrounded by a world in which no structure, material or ideological, appears to hold.

HD's heroine is newly exposed to the crisis inherent in the process of subjectivity when the sociocultural frameworks that define her quite literally break down. The question of subjectivity is approached from a different angle: it is not the individual's struggle to demarcate herself in relation to external structures but the de(con)struction of a constituted sense of female self that is central to the novel. Whereas identity is exposed as a "necessary fiction" within a contingent set of discursive power/knowledge relations, the text focuses on what happens when this network is violently obliterated, while the heterosexual contract underpinning it still holds. The sense of suspended crisis pervading *LS* reaches a point of explosion and acquires a gruesome actuality in the almost ephemeral quality of *HD*'s setting: bombed-out London after the Blitz. By situating the forces of destabilization in the material "timespace" in which the story unfolds, the text brings the historical basis of gendered subjectivity to the fore in an extremely disturbing manner. Recognition of the operations of time and narrative history on the individual subject's sense of reality forces Stella Rodney to reconsider her experience of self as well as the moral order in relation to which she has thus far defined this self. Whereas lesbian sexuality plays a minor role on the representational level of the text, being largely confined to one of the novel's subplots, such narrative displacement and the novel's radical critique of the intertwining systems of phallogocentrism and compulsory heterosexuality nonetheless invite a lesbian feminist reading of *HD*. Before moving on to the narrative proper, I will briefly discuss some of Bowen's (nonfictional) observations on the war and war-time writing so as to contextualize *HD* in the author's continuing effort at "transposed autobiography."

Appearing in 1949, *HD* was Bowen's first full-length novel to be published in eleven years. Although she had finished the first five chapters by 1944, the upheavals of the times made it impossible for her to maintain the sustained concentration necessary for the completion of a work of such length and complexity. Throughout the war, she worked as a journalist and as a reporter for the Ministry of Intelligence and, in addition, published an autobiographical account of her childhood in Ireland, the previously mentioned history of her family, and a work of literary criticism,[1] while at the same time carrying out her duties as an ARP warden. Prevented from completing *HD*, Bowen restricted her writing of fiction to the short story. Collected in *The Demon Lover* (1945; hereafter, *DL*), her wartime stories feature a "snapshot" quality, which she later accounted for by declaring that "you cannot render, you can only embrace . . . something vast that is happening right on top of you."[2] In an essay written in 1942, Bowen explained what the "closeness" of the war-time events implied:

There is at present evident, in the reflective writer, not so much inhibition or dulling of his own feeling as an inability to obtain the focus necessary for art. One cannot reflect, or reflect on, what is not wholly in view. These years rebuff the imagination as much by being fragmentary as by being violent. It is by dislocations, by recurrent checks to his *desire for meaning,* that the writer is most thrown out. The imagination cannot simply endure events; for it the passive role is impossible. Where it cannot *dominate,* it is put out of action.[3]

As we have seen, Bowen had always regarded writing as a means to create patterns in an otherwise incoherent and meaningless reality, as a dialogic/discursive process involving both writer and reader. The passage cited here does not, therefore, suggest that the war suddenly introduces fragmentation and violation in a heretofore homogeneous and amenable world. What it does indicate is that fragmentation on the level of empirical reality effects a measure of disintegration that transgresses the limits of subjective comprehension. The war produced a degree of meaninglessness that fell outside anyone's imaginative scope.

The stories Bowen produced between the spring of 1941 and the late autumn of 1944 were all written on commission, as if she felt entitled to indulge in the private act of writing on public demand only. Yet it was in the practice of her art that the author's views on the social basis of subjective experience or, in Bakhtinian terms, the dialogic nature of the self, were reaffirmed. As she observed about her war-time stories in retrospect: "they were flying particles of something enormous and inchoate that had been going on. They were sparks from experience—an experience not necessarily my own."[4] Having elsewhere defined experience as the "reaction to what happens, not the happening itself," and, we recall, as a writer's "unique susceptibility" that in its turn constitutes her/his subjectivity, Bowen apparently continued to use writing as a protective shield against the fear of "shapelessness" that had induced her to become a writer in the first place.[5] Bowen's discursive powers enabled her to survive the chaos that threatened annihilation—physically as much as mentally. By giving symbolic form to the "things—ideas, images, emotions—[that] came through with force and rapidity, sometimes violence" as soon as she sat down to write, Bowen "authored" her bewildering experience. Unable to "dominate" entirely an intellectually unaccountable "objective" reality, she continued to feel ambivalent about her attempts to impose order and form upon it. Later she was to assert that her war-time stories had "their own momentum, which [she] had to control," the "acts" in them having an "authority which [she] could not question."[6] By linking authorship to the desire for meaning and the will to power, both here and in the passage quoted above, Bowen reveals that the magnifying effects of the war, while adding to the urgency of her fictions, gave new impetus to her ideas about the relations between power, language, and subjectivity.

Bowen conceded that she "would not have missed being in London throughout the war for anything: it was the 'most interesting period of [her] life.' "[7] One of the reasons why the war was so fascinating was that its amplifying force affected everyone on the subjective level. Or, as a character in one of the war-time stories asserts: " 'Whatever you are these days, you are rather more so. That's one thing I've discovered about this war.' "[8] A "sensationalist" like so many of her protagonists, whose "imagination . . . [was] most caught, most fired, most worked upon by the unfamiliar," Bowen lived through the war "with every pore open."[9] The major preoccupations controlling her prewar fiction accordingly became more pronounced: her "own values" were "accentuated rather than changed."[10] Still, a noticeable shift did occur in the author's views on her relation to society. As we have seen, Bowen had always maintained that she was "quite unrelatable."[11] In the postscript to the first U.S. edition of her collection of war-time stories, she dwells on the change the war effected in this respect. Her "sense of the abnormal," having always been "acute" in "so-called 'normal' times," was temporarily alleviated by the collapse of everything "normal." As "more a territory than . . . a page of history," Bowen describes the war climate as one in which "we all lived in a state of lucid abnormality." Her "feeling of slight differentiation" was suspended: she felt "one with, and just like, everyone else." The violent breakdown of social barriers and boundaries made Bowen feel that she "lived many lives, and still more, lived under the repercussions of so many thousands of other lives."[12] This resulted in an expansion of what she had termed "synthetic experience," formerly used only with reference to the "layers of fictitious memory," the "overlapping and haunting of life by fiction" she considered necessary "to make oneself."[13] From the inference that "almost no experience" finding its way into her war-time work was to be "vouched for as being wholly [her] own," the notion of "synthetic experience" came, under the pressure of war, to comprehend so-called real life. Such a blurring of the boundaries between fact and fiction or, more precisely, between Self and (the) Other/s, signifies that Bowen fully appreciated the profoundly psychic level on which the phenomenon of what Bakhtin designates dialogism occurs: "During the war the overcharged subconsciousnesses of everybody overflowed and merged."[14]

The war confirmed that ideology and subjectivity are contingent processes that operate in/through material practices and actions. The importance of material frameworks had been borne in on Bowen from her early childhood onward. Her personal history, full of emotional and physical upheavals, had produced in her an ingrained sense of exile.[15] Her sense of place and its function as a defense (in the psychoanalytic sense) against disintegration had always been acute. The crucial function of material reality is rendered explicit by the narrator in *The Death of the Heart:*

> After inside upheavals, it is important to fix on imperturbable *things.* Their imperturbableness, their air that nothing has happened renews our guarantee. Pictures would not be hung plumb over the centres of fireplaces or wallpapers pasted on with such precision that their seams make no break in the pattern if life were really not possible to adjudicate for. These things are what we mean when we speak of civilization: they remind us how exceedingly seldom the unseemly or unforeseeable raises its head. In this sense, the destruction of buildings and furniture is more palpably dreadful to the spirit than the destruction of human life. . . . Only outside disaster is irreparable. (207–8)

The passage was written in 1938. Rather than appearing "painful" in the "light . . . of what happened so soon after,"[16] we may safely assume that Bowen's conscious acknowledgment of the material inscription of subjectivity enabled her to deal with the "most palpably dreadful" when the "unseemly" came about in the form of World War II. Such an awareness allowed her to consider the social and moral implications of the war and, at the same time, to give artistic expression to its effects on the inter- and intrasubjective levels.

Bowen's perception of the almost grotesque forms that human behavior may take under extreme circumstances deepened her understanding of the interdependence of fiction and so-called real life. She saw that the constrictions of living in a city under siege meant that "self-expression in small ways stopped . . . small ways [that] had been so very small that we had not realized how much they amounted to." Signifying practices were shown to constitute rather then merely demarcate (self-)identity: "You used to *know what you were* like from the things you liked, and chose. Now there was not what you liked, and you did not choose."[17] If Bowen had, in 1938, insisted that the imperturbableness of material reality serves as a guarantee against the possibility of the individual subject's essential meaninglessness, by 1945 she had come to the conclusion that it is only within concrete sociohistorical contexts that some form of coherent subjectivity can come into existence at all. As means of (self-)representation, the (provisional) meanings of material objects amount to the meaning of the individual her/himself: "People whose homes had been blown up went to infinite lengths to assemble bits of themselves—broken ornaments, odd shoes, torn scraps of the curtains that had hung in a room—from the wreckage." The war, by disrupting the symbolic process, threatened the total extinction of the self. This recognition gave further significance to Bowen's views on the psychological function of literature and language. Noting that people "assembled and checked themselves from stories and poems, from their memories, from one another's talk," she retrospectively maintained that "all wartime writing is . . . resistance writing."[18] By creating fictional worlds, assembled both from the past and from the "anaesthetized and bewildered present," the writer puts up a defense against the threat of total disintegration:

Every writer during this time was aware of the personal cry of the individual. And he was aware of the passionate attachment of men and women to every object or image or place or love or fragment of memory with which his or her destiny seemed to be identified, and by which the destiny seemed to be assured.[19]

Instead of undermining Bowen's notion of the "insufficiency of so-called real life," the constant "desiccation" of daily life that the war entailed foregrounded the critical function of fiction. Particularly in a period of full-scale disaster, when all "direction" is lost, the writer seems still capable of offering the "possibility of shape."[20]

When she was preparing the collection of her stories after the war, Bowen saw reflected in them a "rising tide of hallucination." She emphasized that these "hallucinations . . . are not a peril; nor are the stories studies of mental peril. The hallucinations are an unconscious, instinctive, saving resort on the part of the characters." The creation of these "small-worlds-within-worlds of hallucination" functioned as a "saving resort" for characters, readers, and author alike: they were Bowen's way of answering to a reality in which "what was happening was out of all proportion to our faculties for knowing, thinking and checking up." Recognizing the stakes of all forms of signifying practice to be subjectivity itself, she asserts that in all these "little dear saving illusory worlds," it is "the 'I' that is sought—and retrieved at the cost of no little pain." By constructing patterns—"the conventional pattern one does not easily break, and is loath to break because it is 'I' saving"—the writer, we may infer, is trying to give meaning to inchoate reality as much as to her/himself.[21]

Constructed Realities. The war gave focus to Bowen's thoughts on history and historiography. She recognized that her fictional reconsiderations of the past were essentially acts of self-(re)construction. Returning to *HD* in 1945, she found it "far the most difficult" novel she had attempted so far. The "enormously comprehensive" scope she intended it to have led her far beyond a historical period that in itself was already difficult to grasp.[22] Writing to her lover Charles Ritchie, she complained: "[*HD*] presents every possible problem in the world . . . almost anything that happens round me contributes to it."[23] She professed that she "would not in the least mind" if this were her "last shot," if she "never wrote anything else again." Anticipating that a number of Bowen's major themes would converge in *HD*, these comments attest to the pivotal position of the novel in her oeuvre as a whole.

As indicated earlier, Bowen had, in literature as much as in real life, always been explicitly concerned with the operation of the past in the here and now. In "The Bend Back," an essay written in 1951, she discusses the significance of the prevailing mood of nostalgia in postwar literature.[24] Casting back over the century, the author traces the "decline of love for the present" and the concomitant "loss of faith in it" back to 1914. The psychological climate following World War I, she argues, gave rise to a "literature of contemporary sensation" that proved so ephemeral as to have disappeared even before World War II obliterated whatever "confidence in living" may still have remained. The postwar writer, she claims, in turning to the past, in "loving life by loving it at one remove," is trying to recover the "prepossession with living" rather than extend the "vacuum" left by predecessors. The active engagement with the past is not a "compromise" so much as an ontological necessity, for it is only thus that the "life-illusion" can be sustained. Bowen clarifies the point by emphasizing that "one invests one's identity *in* one's memory. To re-live any moment, acutely, is to be made certain that one not only was but is."[25] Shifting her focus to the historic as distinct from the personal past, Bowen contends that this, too, can only be known by being "re-created in terms of art." Such a claim almost literally articulates one of the basic tenets of postmodern thought: that both history and reality are accessible only through their textual inscriptions.

As new historicist Hayden White points out, historical "facts" are constituted rather than given.[26] What historians choose to say (describe and interpret) about the world is not only determined by their socioeconomic contexts but also by discursive codes. To historicize is to naturalize or familiarize perceptions into patterns of coherence. Since the impulse to mythologize is inherent in language, in discourse, it is "by figuration that the historian *constitutes* the subject of the discourse."[27] Writing history is thus not simply reduction (through selection) but is in fact a distortion of the phenomena it is presumed to describe. Writers of fiction and historians alike produce ideologically determined representations of some sort of "reality." White's theory of history implies that both present and past are discursive constructs—whether cast in terms of society or of individual subjectivity. It is precisely such a view that emerges from Bowen's essay "The Bend Back." In order to construct reality, she maintains, the writer must bring into play "factitious memory," that is, s/he must make us "seem to remember that which we have not actually known" (56). Since it is "not the past but the idea of the past" that is being recreated in discourse, the historian deals in "illusions" just as the writer of fiction does. Moreover, as a consequence of the "very necessity to compose a picture," both the historian and the fiction writer "cannot but eliminate, edit—and so, falsify." This is why both historiography and the writing of fiction are directly linked to the regulatory regimes of power/knowledge: that which can be said as much as the ways in which it can be said depends on the distribution of positions of discursive authority in a given society at a given time. As Bowen puts it: against "the favoured few" to whom positions from which to speak are available, there are the "millions ... leaving behind no trace," whose "brutalising humiliations" are therefore simply "forgotten."[28]

These views anticipate Foucault's argument in *The Archeology of Knowledge and Discourse on Language* (1969), where he maintains that "in every society the production of discourse is at once controlled, selected, organised, and redistributed according to a certain number of procedures," among which are, first and foremost, the "rules of *exclusion*":[29]

We know perfectly well that we are not free to say just anything, that we cannot simply speak of anything, when we like or where we like; not just anyone, finally, may speak of just anything. We have three types of prohibition, covering objects, ritual with its surrounding circumstances, the privileged or exclusive right to speak of a particular subject; these prohibitions interrelate, reinforce and complement each other, forming a complex web, continually subject to modification.... In appearance, speech may well be of little account, but the prohibitions surrounding it soon reveal its links with desire and power. This should not be very surprising, for psychoanalysis has already shown us that speech is not merely the medium which manifests—or dissembles—desire; it is also the object of desire. (216)

The inextricable links among desire, power/knowledge, and discursive practices form, as will be clear, one of the central preoccupations within Bowen's preoccupation with the past. Her concern with these issues did not suddenly arise during or after World War II.[30] She had, in effect, started working on her major historical work *(Bowen's Court)* in the early summer of 1939 and developed most of her ideas in the area of historiography while tracing the history of her own family. The horrifying events of the war highlighted the pertinence of her considerations and gave them a dreadful actuality. As she was to explain in the afterword (1963) to *Bowen's Court:*

I have stressed as dominant in the Bowens factors I saw as dominant in the world I wrote in—for instance, subjection to fantasy and infatuation with the idea of power. . . . Fantasy is toxic: the private cruelty and the world war both have their start in the heated brain. Showing fantasy, in one form or another, do its unhappy work in the lives of my ancestors, I was conscious at almost every moment of nightmarish big analogies everywhere. Also, the idea of the idea of power governed my analysis of the Bowens and of the means *they* took—these being, in some cases, emotional—to enforce themselves on their world. (454–55)

The implications of the presumed interconnections among ideas, fantasy, and the will to power will emerge in the course of this and the next chapter. What I want to emphasize at this point is that Bowen's study of the past, her look into the "microcosmic" society of her Anglo-Irish family, intensified her awareness of the contextual inscription of the subject in history, impressing her anew with the fundamental reciprocity of these processes:

I begin to notice . . . the pattern [the Bowens] unconsciously went to make. And I can see that that pattern has its relation to the outside more definite pattern of history. . . . My family, though notably "unhistoric," had their part in a drama outside themselves. Their assertions, their compliances, their refusals as men and women went, year by year, generation by generation, to give history direction, as well as colour and stuff. Each of the family, in their different manners, were more than their time's products; they were its agents. (452)

The extremity of the times deepened Bowen's appreciation of the operation of the past and strengthened rather than weakened her engagement in the present:

The war-time urgency of the present . . . seemed to communicate itself to one's view of the past, until, to the most private act or decision, there attached one's sense of its part in some campaign. . . . The past—private just as much as historic—seemed to me . . . to matter more than ever: it acquired meaning . . . details leaped out with significance. Nothing that ever happened, nothing that was ever even willed, planned or envisaged, could seem irrelevant. War is not an accident: it is an outcome. One cannot look back too far to ask, of what? (454)

Central to *HD* is this question concerning the interdependent operations of both private and public history, which at their constantly shifting points of intersection constitute the individual subject who, in her/his turn, leaves her/his own meaning-engendering traces on the map of "reality." Thus *HD* brings together several by now familiar Bowen themes. While providing a distinct link between her work and current critical theory, the war novel's focus on the interrelations between power and discourse gains particular relevance since Bowen—unlike Foucault—pays specific attention to the structuring role of sexual difference in these various processes of narrativization.

Inscribing the Self. HD brought Bowen her greatest popular success: it at once sold forty-five thousand copies and has become one of the classic novels in English literature about World War II.[31] Even so, the book has provoked mixed responses, both immediately after its publication and among later critics.[32] One of the problems *HD* presents is its unwillingness to be fitted into any traditional novelistic genre. As an evocation of a pivotal period in English culture, the novel combines elements of a spy story with a narrative of psychological development couched in what Bowen herself called the "point-blank melodrama" of a love story.[33] *HD* is by no means a spy story in the ordinary sense; its suspense derives from psychology rather than plot.[34]

Stylistically, the novel is also problematic. The disruptive techniques featuring in Bowen's previous work—double negatives, inversions, broken syntactic order, and unconventional passive constructions—acquire such frequency and prominence that they may seem signs of affectation. As a result, *HD* has been variously criticized as "strained" and "contorted," its textual surface as "distracting" and "evasive."[35] When Jocelyne Brooke expressed such criticisms in an interview with the author in 1950, Bowen responded that "a certain overstrain which you felt, which a great number of other people have been aware of probably came from a too high tension from my trying to put language to what for me was a totally new use, and what perhaps was, showed itself to be, a quite impossible use."[36] Although a novelist can never be the final authority on her work, I consider this comment valuable in that it supports my claim that the idiosyncratic stylistic contortions in *HD* are closely entwined with the novel's thematics.[37] Rather than showing a loss of control, the textual eccentricities form an intrinsic part of the continuing discursive "struggle" that the novel represents in the author's writing practice.

There is also the problem of scope. As my introductory comments suggest, *HD* deals with a wide range of complex issues. One of the questions it addresses is the functioning of plot and plotting. The intricate ways in which plot operates are problematized on the intra- as well as on the extradiegetic levels of the text. The main plot, concerning Stella's quest, is offset by two subplots. Although interrelated, these various story lines are not fully integrated. The fragmented structure and the comprehensiveness of the novel's scope give the text as a whole a fundamentally disjunctive aspect. My attempt at delineating some of the major problems it poses has occasionally become an experience of profound disorientation; this in turn will no doubt have found its way into the following (re)construction of the text's operations.

Narrativization and Historical Time. Its disruptive style and disjointed structure notwithstanding, *HD* was Bowen's "most 'narrative' novel to date."[38] Temporally set against a clearly defined historical period, the story unfolds in a series of scenes whose spatial settings operate like the changing scenery in a theater, each acquiring a role of agency similar to that of the dramatis personae. The novel opens in September 1942 and ends exactly two years later with the beginning of the Allied victory in Europe. Situated for the larger part in the darkest middle period of the war, it depicts a few months of the drawn-out lull after the Blitz, the time around Montgomery's victory in Egypt and long before the establishment of the Second Front. Any major incident or shift in the development of the narrative coincides with an incisive event upon the larger stage of history. With the exception of a number of flashbacks into the recent and the more distant past, the story follows a chronological progression. The closing section is marked off from the rest of the text by a time gap occurring just after the Allied landings in North Africa. The intervening historical events are summarized by the narrator. Foregrounded by a chain of references to clocks and watches, frequent indications of the times of day and night, and an evocative rendering of the movement of the seasons, the emphatic presence of time produces an overall atmosphere of sustained tension. The strict time scheme furthermore creates an effect of ostensible realism that sits particularly oddly with the surreal spatial settings. Time and the inscription of the individual within the text of history are thus highlighted from the start.

We have seen that Bowen, when pushed to the defense of *HD*, stressed that its center is a love story from which the "rest of the plot germinates." She added that "love, especially when it is coupled with fear, any kind of fear, makes its own scene, makes the landscape again; a Caligari-like subjective, exaggerated, highly defined, perhaps slightly out of the true world."[39] The novel's narrator, in contrast, ascertains that the love affair of Stella Rodney and Robert Kelway is not "out of the true world." Having met each other during the early days of the war, the lovers could not "have loved each other better at a better time," for "at no other would they have been themselves" (195). Being "creatures of history,"

They were not alone, nor had they been from the start, from the start of love. Their time sat in the third place at their table. . . . [Their] coming together was of a nature possible in no other day—the day was inherent in the nature. Which must have been always true of lovers, if it had taken till now to be seen. The relation of people to one another is subject to the relation of each to time, to what is happening. . . . The more imperative the love, the deeper its draft on beings, till it has taken up all that ever went to their making, and according to what it draws on its nature is. . . . War at present worked as a thinning of the membrane between the this and the that, it was a becoming apparent—but then what else is love? (194–95)

By disrupting the linear development of the historical plot, the war not only destroys the material social order but calls into question the very ideologies of linearity and coherence underlying both. Since history is written from within the same desire for meaningful integration as any other form of narrative, the war exposes the contradictions inherent in the interdependent operations of mythical and historical time.

In "Desire in Narrative" (1984), Teresa de Lauretis explores the crucial function of sexual difference in the operation of narrative time.[40] Recapitulating Jurij Lotman's theory of plot, defined as a "text-generating mechanism . . . coextensive with the origin of culture itself," she maintains that mythical texts engendered by this mechanism are "subject to an exclusively cyclical-temporal movement," within which human life is seen as a "recurrent, self-repeating cycle" (116–17). Serving to "construct a picture of the world in which the most remote phenomena could be seen as intimately related to one another," such mythical texts could "play the role of science," creating "invariant images" or fixed distinctions to which diversities and varieties could be reduced. Anything in life "contravening ... the mythically established order of things" therefore requires a text-generating mechanism that functions as a "counterpart" to the central one. This countermechanism results in "plot-texts," fictional narratives in which phenomena are "organized according to a linear, temporal succession of events." Lotman's analyses show that the "mythical-textual mechanics" structure the world along the lines of a "simple chain of two functions, open at both ends and thus endlessly repeatable: 'entry into a closed space, and emergence from it' " (118). Since the "closed space" or obstacle is invariably connoted female, the mythical hero is, de Lauretis infers, by definition male. As a consequence,

Opposite pairs such as inside/outside ... or life/death appear to be merely derivatives of the fundamental opposition between boundary and passage; and if passage may be in either direction ... nonetheless all these terms are predicated on the *single* figure of the hero who crosses the boundary and penetrates the other space. In so doing the hero, the mythical subject, is constructed as human being and as male; he is the active principle of culture, the establisher of distinction, the creator of differences. Female is what is not susceptible to transformation, to life or death; she (it) is an element of plot-space, a topos, a resistance, matrix and matter. (119)

The primary distinction upon which mythical thought rests is, de Lauretis concludes, sexual difference, which, we have noted, is in effect *heterosexual* difference.

Lotman posits the modern narrative text as the product of the "reciprocal influence of the two typologically older kinds of texts." These conflicting aspects function in a relation of mutual interdependence. Plot ultimately "mediates, integrates and ... reconciles the mythical and the historical, norm and excess," and the modern narrative text—on which the "mythical or eschatological schema" continues to be imposed—takes over the task of the mythical subject in constructing differences. De Lauretis hence asserts that the "work of narrative" has become the "mapping of differences, and specifically, first and foremost, of sexual difference into each text" (120, 121). The tension resulting from the joint operation of cyclical/mythical and linear/historical time in the text of *HD* immediately establishes a link between the interlocking plots and the inscription of (hetero)sexual difference in the movement of the narrative. The disintegration of the phallogocentric system of power/knowledge (the organizing principle of the symbolic order) effected by the war therefore implies a recasting of both traditional historical and mythical notions. The text's focus on the "myth of heterosexual romance" confirms the central place of sexual difference within the novel's plot as much as in the text of history. Presenting a protagonist "younger by a year or two than the century," *HD* problematizes the question of gender in relation to narrativization at several intersecting textual levels.

As an "instrument of her century," Stella Rodney is forced to recognize her answerability as a female subject in/to a "true world" whose (masculine) plot has at the same time produced her (25). On the face of it, *HD*'s narrative form conforms to the pattern of the mythical plot, or rather, to that of the novelistic genre in which such a plot structure has been traditionally reinscribed, the so-called novel of awakening.[41] Stella's quest begins when a man called Harrison comes to her furnished flat in Weymouth Street. Identifying himself as engaged in counterespionage, he accuses Stella's lover, Robert Kelway, of spying for the Germans from his position at the War Office. Harrison offers to keep his incriminating information secret on condition that Stella take himself instead of Robert as a lover and companion. This proposition immediately alerts us to the complications to which the operation of heterosexual difference in narrativization gives rise once the subject of a narrative is gendered female instead of male.

We are dealing with a female protagonist whose itinerary of self-discovery motivates the story's development. Genre conventions would lead us to expect a resolution in the form of Stella's "awakening." After all, as Jonathan Culler reminds us, the "hermeneutic code" within classic realist fiction works primarily through suspense or mystery. Paraphrasing Roland Barthes, Culler clarifies that "one could bring under this heading [of mystery] anything which, as one goes through the text from beginning to end, seems insufficiently explained, poses problems, arouses a desire to know the truth."[42] The central function of the "moment of revelation" within such a narrative line is underscored by the frame of the spy plot in which Stella's search for identity is cast. But if the desire to know is indeed the structuring force within the story of her psychological development, the hermeneutic code is at the same time confused by the fact that Stella is implicated in a spy plot in which not she but two *male* characters perform the roles of subjective agency. Rather than moving the story "inevitably towards *closure* which is also disclosure, the dissolution of the enigma through the reestablishment of order,"[43] the contradictory organization of gender roles in *HD* actually precludes a resolution of either the heroine's quest or the spy plot. Such a frustration of the hermeneutic code is not accidental. The text emphatically employs the two additional features that, Catherine Belsey points out, characterize classic realism, that is, *"illusionism"* and a *"hierarchy of discourses"*—which works "by means of a privileged discourse which places as subordinate all the discourses that are literally or figuratively between inverted commas."[44] Therefore the unresolved ending of either story in effect constitutes a deliberate act of subversion. By rendering the resolution of the male plot ultimately irrelevant, the text foregrounds the dual role of the female protagonist in the myth of masculinity—in which plot structure she is necessarily inscribed as both subject and object—and denaturalizes the mythical plot of heterosexual difference.

The Historical Inscription of the Self

Emplotment. Harrison's scheme evolves from the movement of masculine desire. De Lauretis contends that the passage of the mythical subject into manhood constructs Woman as the topos of obstacle or object. The quest for (self-)knowledge, inscribed both in narrative and in the text of history, thus implies that the symbolic order itself, organized around the Same/Other opposition, is an economy of the same. The social or heterosexual contract is—to use Luce Irigaray's term—in fact a system of "hom(m)osexuality," translating the function of Woman as Other into women's status as the objects of male (symbolic) exchange.[45] In sociopolitical terms, it is women's limited access to knowledge and power that sustains the phallogocentric order. *HD* both reinscribes and undermines dominant gender discourses. Unwillingly drawn into Harrison's plot, Stella is, while continuing to function as the subject of the narrative quest, also transformed into the object of male exchange. By positioning her in these conflicting functions, the text at once sustains and subverts the movement of masculine desire. Although this movement is, as I have suggested, eventually defeated by the text's lack of closure, the discursive nature of subjectivity entails that Stella's itinerary necessarily partakes of the "hom(m)osexual" economy from which the male characters obtain their power. The duality of the heroine's position is additionally foregrounded in that she is herself employed in "secret, exacting, not unimportant work": she is "not a woman who does not know where to go" in order to check up on Harrison's credentials. But even if Harrison's story strikes Stella as highly implausible, there is something about this man, who seems "not to be accounted for in any other way," that prevents her from doing so (26, 40, 39). Increasingly compelled to subject herself to the structuring of his plot, Stella stalls its denouement by neither rejecting nor accepting the "truth" of Harrison's accusations.

When Harrison confronts Stella on the "first Sunday of September 1942," we have already met him in the evocative opening pages of the novel. The scene is Regent's Park, where a crowd has gathered to attend an outdoor concert. Harrison, whose "excessive stillness gave the effect not of abandon but of cryptic behaviour," is accosted by lonely and naïve Louie Lewis, whose struggles with sex and language I will discuss in more detail at a later point (8). The young woman is rudely rebuffed, for Harrison sees "no behaviour as being apart from motive, and any motive as worth examining twice" (10). The man is established as at once "interesting" and threatening:

One of his eyes either was or behaved as being just perceptibly higher than the other. This lag or inequality in his vision gave [Louie] the feeling of being looked at twice—being viewed then checked over again in the same moment.... This was a face with a gate behind it.... A face, if not without meaning, totally and forbiddingly without mood." (12)

The words "meaning" and "mood" alert us to the character's existence as the product of his (verbal) actions and, by extension, to the discursivity of subjectivity per se. Harrison, we are soon to learn, is a calculator who has "never yet not come on a policy which both satisfied him and in the end worked" (14). He deals with human beings as though "thinking out a succession of moves in chess"; the war, in fact, forms part of his "calculations" (26, 34). He points out to Stella: " 'What you see now is what I've seen all along.' " (33) The latter instantly discerns what makes her persecutor dangerous. From the fact that Harrison seems "impervious to everything she felt" she infers that something has been "left out of [his] composition" (30); the semantic value of this subject-effect is unqualified by "mood." Indeed, Harrison himself is the first to admit that love, to him, is a "bit of the spanner in the works," since he has "no feeling" (22, 31). This, Stella infers, is what makes him difficult to "tape." Underlining the inextricable links between life and literature, she reflects that Harrison is, as a "character 'impossible,'" which, in turn, prevents her from "giv[ing] him any possible place in the human scene" (140). Confronted with her tormentor's "psychic, his moral blindness," the heroine gradually comes to an understanding of the sociopolitical effects of such "emotional idiocy" on the part of individuals (42, 142). Furthermore, the fact that war is Harrison's element (" 'This is where I come in' ") enhances Stella's awareness of her own contextualized position in history (34).

Harrison's affinity with the times shows that the traditional separation of the private from the public is an ideological illusion. Up until now, Stella has only engaged herself with the "world, the time whose creature she was," by not blaming it for any of the "deception[s]" she has suffered (133). Passively watching a "clear-sightedly helpless progress towards disaster" in the story both of the world and of her self, she has come to believe that the "fateful course of her century seemed more and more her own." Her stance toward either, however, has remained equally inactive and submissive. Harrison's threats simultaneously reinforce and give a twist to Stella's identification with the times. Her feeling of dislocation in a thoroughly dislocated world is enhanced by the possibility of a further loss of self in the face of his attempted blackmail. She feels as if "together she and [the world] had come to the testing extremities of their noonday" (133–34). Since the figure of the counterspy underscores the artificial nature of the boundaries between Self and (the) Other/s, he compels Stella to reconsider her implication in the historical present. When Harrison aptly observes: " 'War, if you come to think of it, hasn't started anything that wasn't already there' " (33), such a recognition of complicity becomes positively devastating:

To [Stella], tonight, "outside" meant the harmless world: the mischief was in her own and in other rooms. The grind and scream of battles, mechanized advances excoriating flesh and country, tearing through nerves and tearing up trees, were indoor-plotted; this was a war of dry cerebration inside windowless walls. No act was not part of some calculation; spontaneity was in tatters; from the point of view of nothing more than the heart any action was enemy action now. (142)

The passage makes clear that the discourse of violence revolves around the issue of emotion, or rather, the lack of it. This is not to suggest, however, that the text sets up a straightforward opposition between "dry cerebration" and "the heart," the traditional dichotomy extrapolated from the binary frame of sex. Nor is Harrison, as the almost grotesque personification of mechanized thought, placed in the position of being simply Stella's opposite, as male versus female. In the end, it is this "nobody" who will convince Stella that "below one level, everybody's horribly alike" (138). The heroine's dilemma is thus not that she faces a choice between "the heart" and destructive "calculation": no such either/or choice is available to her; nor, indeed, is such a dichotomy tenable at all, for "in a fallen world," we recall, it is "no use to attempt a picnic in Eden."

The contradictory position of the female subject in phallogocentric culture, at once inside and outside the dominant field of power/knowledge, acquires particular poignancy in the war context. This is revealed when Stella sums up her options to Harrison: "'I'm to form a disagreeable association in order that a man be left free to go on selling his country'" (36). Because Stella is the other within a "hom(m)osexual" system of symbolic exchange, her investments in notions such as "love" or "country" are fundamentally divided. This immediately pertains to the level of objective reality, for in her professional capacity Stella actively participates in this "war of dry cerebration"; and, as Harrison submits, the "funny" thing about the war is the "way everybody's on one side or the other." As it happens, Stella is in this respect on Harrison's side, and is hence an "enemy" of her traitor-lover Robert (31). But the conflict also affects her on the subjective level, for if the text would seem to suggest that the heroine's character represents emotion as opposed to Harrison's calculation, it soon turns out that Stella's capacity for acting upon her feelings is of fairly recent date. It is, in effect, a direct consequence of the war: only with the breakdown of established cultural patterns and social structures has Stella allowed this long-repressed faculty to (re)emerge.

Contradictory Pulls. When Harrison first confronts Stella, she is still convinced that "life had supplied to her so far nothing so positive as the abandoned past." Having "come loose from her moorings" at an early age, she has assumed the position of the "hybrid" and accordingly has formed no attachments except with her son Roderick (115). Such a repudiation of commitment is reflected in the interior of her London flat. Accentuating Stella's imbrication in the texture of history, the furnished flat epitomizes the chilling outcome of scientific thought, of discursive practices that "mean" without "mood." As such, it reflects the "dry cerebration" that characterizes the times. Permanently blinded, the room lacks the "apprehension of time. Inside it the senses were cut off from from hour and season. . . . Sealed up in its artificial light, [it] remained exaggerated and cerebral" (56).

It hardly needs pointing out that Harrison is much impressed by the flat's efficient arrangements. But the symbolic value of this space is not as straightforward as it may seem. The text's problematization of either/or choices generally, and its highlighting of the "complificating" factor of binary gender-relations within them,[46] is rendered concrete in that this artificial space, where Stella can enjoy the "irritation of being surrounded by somebody else's irreproachable taste," at the same time symbolizes her defiance of the patriarchal Law that would confine her as a woman and mother to the home (24). Hence her son Roderick's astute observation: this room, in which any piece of furniture is "without environment," definitely does "not look like home" (47–48). Lacking the "music of the familiar," his mother's flat constitutes, he is forced to realize, a "scene in which he could play no part" (47, 52).

Though preceding her "emotional rebirth," Stella's rejection of the traditional female role is nonetheless of similarly recent date. Only when her son was called into the army did she feel at liberty to seize the "opportunity to make or break, to free herself of her house, to come to London to work" (25). While calling attention to the liberating effects that the disruption of the social order has entailed for (at least some) women, this is not to suggest that Stella has benefited from the war in the same way as brazen opportunists such as Harrison have. With always "two or three places where [he] can turn in," Harrison's life is essentially organized around his lack of ties: in this respect, he is hardly affected by the current grand-scale dislocation. Stella, in contrast, is caught between the conflicting pulls of her responsibilities as a mother and her desire to break away from the constraints of patriarchal convention. The psychological cost of such a conflict is trenchantly brought to the fore when Roderick comes to spend a short leave at her flat.

Her son's presence makes Stella suddenly aware of the "unreality of the room." Apprehending that the "absence of any inanimate thing [he and she] had in common set up an undue strain" between them, she perceives that even the most personal relationships acquire meaning only by their inscription in material, that is, public contexts. Both she and Roderick are filled with a sense of "instinctive loss" that they both know to be more than the "romantic dismay of two natures romantically akin." This loss is, as the narrator points out, "a sign, in them, of the impoverishment of the world" (55–56):

Wariness had driven away poetry: from hesitating to feel came the moment when you no longer could. Was this war's doing? By every day, every night, existence was being further drained—you, yourself, made conscious of what was happening only by some moment, some meeting such as tonight's. (55)

The text goes on to question whether it is not the failure of civilization per se that has resulted in the "ban, the check, the caution as to all spending and most of all the expenditure of feeling." Evidently, the discourse of violence has rendered the subjects it produces as seriously lacking as it has shown itself to be, insofar as the violations it generates find their ultimate destination in the individual. The crisis of the times both reflects and is reflected in the "impoverishment" of intersubjective relations.[47] Stella's sense of loss and guilt is related to the fact that both she and Roderick are produced by and dependent on phallocratic technologies. If Stella's inside/outside position allows her, to a limited extent, to defy their constraints, her son—literally the armed defender of the Law—is clearly not in a position to do so. The social disintegration that has brought her a degree of relative autonomy as a woman demands its price precisely in the field in which Stella's position is most contradictory, in her role as a mother—which, in phallogocentric terms is almost synonymous with femininity.

Her sharp insight into the interpellating operations of ideology surfaces explicitly when Stella reflects that Roderick has apparently come to seek "some identity left by him in her keeping." She dreads a "dissolution inside his life ... never to be repaired," fearing that her "son might possibly disappear ... in the course of a process, a being processed" in the army (48–49). Stella furthermore knows that her own and her son's investments in the symbolic order are in the final instance irreconcilable. This realization forms the background to her self-searching questions:

[Stella's] anxiety mingled with self-reproach—how if he came to set too much store by a world of which she ... had deprived him? He would have esteemed, for instance, organic family life; she had not only lost his father for him but estranged herself (and him with her) from all his father's relations. (61)

Whereas Stella has, if not quite deliberately at least self-consciously distanced herself from the established order, Roderick has been taken up by a war that has "denied meaning" to a world in which he had as yet "never engaged himself" (49). Like Lois and

Laurence in *LS,* he is, at seventeen, exceedingly amenable to the interpellating powers of ideological agents. His limited subjective investments are divided between Stella and his army friend Fred. Her son's "unconscious purpose to underline everything he and [Stella] had in common" is therefore countered by an equally strong need to relate to his peers. As true defenders of the patriarchal order, his fellow soldiers are "all for the authoritarianism of home life"—the "last thing they wished was Liberty Hall" (52). Recognizing the dangers of such formative influences, Stella is increasingly "alarmed" by her son's "idealization of pattern":

She could perceive, too, that Roderick was ready to entertain a high, if abstract, idea of society—when he had been a baby she had amused him by opening and shutting a painted fan, and of that *beau monde* of figures, grouped and placed and linked by gestures or garlands, he never had, she suspected, interior sight. The fan on its fragile ivory spokes now remained closed: she felt him most happy when they could recreate its illusion in their talk. (61)

Foregrounding the fragile quality of the illusion called "society," this sequence signals a connection between Roderick's "idealization of pattern" and the war discourse of "dry cerebration." The point of intersection is located in the (in)capacity for truly "dialogic exchange" that the boy and Harrison have in common: while the latter treats people as if they were pieces on the chess board, the only thing the former likes about people is the "order in which they could be arranged" (61). Roderick remains "passive in his relations with people"—as distinct from "myths or objects" (60). Faced with Harrison's "emotional idiocy," Stella's anxiety about what she has thus far regarded as her son's "only-childishness" increases. Harrison teaches her that the differences between his "moral blindness," Roderick's emotional "oddness," and her own inclination toward disengagement are differences of degree rather than kind. Her doubts about her role as a Self-giving Other in relation to her son turn out to be not entirely unjustified. Such expanding self-consciousness leads Stella back to her "abandoned" past, a past, moreover, into which Roderick is unexpectedly fitted by his inheriting Mount Morris, the Irish estate of his late father's cousin Francis.

The Myth of Heterosexual Romance. Like so many Big Houses in Bowen's work, Mount Morris plays an important part in furthering the novel's plot. Its function in the narrative present is inaugurated by two significant points in the recent and in the more distant past. Some months before the moment at which the novel opens, Stella had been notified about Cousin Francis's death. The news had initially done "little more than stir up unwelcome memories" in her. The invitation to attend his funeral, however, had obliged her to "present . . . some sort of face to her once relations-in-law" (66). Vaguely conscious of doing him a wrong, Stella had kept Roderick ignorant of Francis's death, telling herself that her decision to do so had sprung from a need to protect him against the possibility of being treated like a "bad mother's fatherless son" (71). It is nonetheless clear that she primarily seeks to protect herself. Her success at surviving the "early failure of her early marriage" had, we are given to understand, required her to break off all relations with the past and to develop a "sort of hardiness as a poor resource" (25). Since the "world in which one could still be seen as *déclassée* was on the whole ignored by her, but not yet quite," the unexpected obligation to face the past means a threat to Stella's shield of protection (71). But Roderick's inheritance also forges the connection between her and Harrison: at Francis's funeral Stella first encounters him "stepping cranelike over the graves" (66). Although she does not know him, she allows herself to be placed in association with the intruder for, "delinquent in being known who she was, she could not fail to recognize [him] as a fellow-delinquent in being not known to be anyone" (72). Regarding herself as a social outcast, she thinks it is "like her to have attached this person," who "from every point of view [is] the last straw" (78).

The suggestion of a link between Harrison and Stella is reinforced when, at a later point, it is to him rather than to her lover
Robert that the heroine divulges the exact circumstances of her
divorce from Victor (!) Rodney. The story testifies to the critical
operations of the discourses of love and marriage in ensuring that
the female adolescent assumes her adult position within the heterosexual matrix. Looking back, Stella perceives that it was precisely
her need to fit into a pattern that made her think—like Lois in
LS—that marriage would provide her with such an anchor point:

"Half-baked, bottomlessly unconfident in myself as a woman, frenziedly
acting up. Not having found myself, at a time when—how boring it was,
how little it matters now!—it was really exceedingly difficult to find
anything. Having been married by Victor, having had Roderick like anyone else, made me think I *might* know where I was. Then, this [the
divorce] happened—so, no: apparently not." (223–24)

The heroine's use of the passive voice at the end of this sequence is
in itself revealing about "woman's proper place" within the social
contract. While Stella's retrospective appreciation of the performative nature of heterosexual gender may induce her to think that it
"matters little" to her now that she failed in properly "acting" her
part, at the time when Victor left her for another woman, the
prospect of being regarded as a failure in her primary function as a
gendered subject meant, quite literally, the threat of erasure. Such
dreaded "loss of face" prevented her from contradicting the "opposite story . . . of how [she] walked out on Victor," once it started
to go round:

"Whoever the story *had* been, I let it be mine. I let it ride, and more—it
came to be my story, and I stuck to it. Or rather, first I stuck to it, then it
went on sticking to me: it took my shape and equally I took its. So much
so that I virtually haven't known, for years now, where it ends and I
begin—or cared." (224)

This account provides a splendid illustration of the ways in which
the reciprocal process of discursive interpellation works. Rather

than "look a fool," Stella had preferred "sound[ing] a monster."
Cast in the gender role of the femme fatale, she had fully internalized this stereotypical (self-)image. By adopting the identity of the
whore—the only alternative to the woman who fails in her role as
madonna—Stella had achieved a measure of autonomy and social
independence that would have been impossible had she appeared
both to the world and to herself as the "boring pathetic casualty,"
the "'injured' one," which she might otherwise have become (224).

While explaining Stella's reasons for breaking away from the
past, these revelations do not resolve the question of her emotional
withdrawal. Why she should have felt the need to efface herself in
a much more profound manner than she apparently could foresee
when she took recourse to a "sort of hardiness as a poor resource"
emerges when Harrison asks her whether she had loved her
husband:

> "He said not. And he said he was the one to know. If I imagined I loved
> him, he said, that was simply proof that I had not, as he'd for some time
> suspected, the remotest conception what love was—could be. I said, oh
> hadn't I? and he said no, I hadn't. I said had he, and if so, how? He said,
> yes he had; he had been loved and he could not forget it. So then he told
> me about the nurse. I said, if there always had been the nurse, nothing
> perhaps was really so much my fault then, was it? He said, he was sorry
> but that was just his point: if I had been, ever, anything he had hoped he
> could have quite forgotten her—he had meant to, tried to. . . . I had
> seemed the person to be his wife; and he had given me—he implied if he
> did not say—a very fair trial. Somehow I had not made it. Almost any
> other woman he could have married, other than I, he said, could have
> made him forget the nurse: unhappily, I and my shortcomings had had the
> reverse effect. The idea of what it *had* been like to be loved haunted
> him." (223)

By not at any point addressing his own ability to love, the line
of Victor's argument identifies the function of both Woman and
"romantic love" as primary means in authenticating Man's existence. Rejected for failing in her appointed gender role at a time
when this seemed the only way to acquire a subject-position, Stella,

not surprisingly, was seriously "taken aback." Seventeen years later she is still afflicted by the psychological assault in which her sustained practice of emotional self-mutilation originates. Left with the sense that the "wind [had been] knocked right out of [her] sails," she also ended up with a deep suspicion of the notion of love itself (223). When the war appeared to have a liberating effect on heterosexual relationships—in other words, when the dissolution of the Law entailed a shift in symbolic authority as to the *meanings* of love—Stella hesitantly accepted the possibility of herself cast in the role of "lover"—as distinct from "wife."

Underlining his critical function in the novel's love story, Harrison accelerates a crisis that had already been set in motion by Stella's affair with Robert Kelway. Back in 1940, she remembers having had the sensation of "lightness . . . of loving no particular person now left in London" (93). Living like an "onlooker with nothing more to lose—out of feeling as one can be out of breath," Stella was affected in spite of herself when an "instinctive movement to break down indifference while there was still time" began to pervade the city (92, 94). Falling in love with Robert had put an abrupt end to her carefully preserved state of placid composure. Waking one morning to "find the lightness gone," she experienced a "shock which could be the breaking down of immunity" and realized that "*something* final had happened" (93).

The triangular nature of the main characters' interrelations is given further edge when Stella and Robert, like Harrison, are said to have found their "element" in the chronotope of war. Gravitating toward each other in the "heady autumn of the first London air raids," the prospective lovers had instantly recognized in each other a "flash of promise, a background of mystery" (90). The atmosphere of detachment had allowed each of them to enter into the "habitat" their affair was soon to become; Robert, too, had been living in a state of emotional limbo after his discharge from the army. Their shared fear of commitment had been alleviated by the "chanciness" of life in that "climate of danger." In the "canvas-like impermanence" of air-raided London, when "feeling stood at full tide," they gave themselves over to the "rising exhilaration of kindred spirits" (96), enjoying the "complicity of brother and sister twins," being "counterpart flowerings of a temperament identical at least with regard to love" (96).

As these descriptions with their incestuous ring suggest, the affair is consistently presented in highly ambivalent terms. Its grim setting in itself produces an ominous effect, since the liberating atmosphere enabling Stella and Robert to love is quite deceptive: as the narrator points out, what to the lovers is "more than a dream" stands in stark contrast to a "reality" in which "there were no holidays" (91). Even so, the opportunity to "draw from some inner source" when "no virtue [is] to be found in the outward order" is simultaneously suggested to form a protection against the "deadening acclimatization" that set in soon after the Blitz (93, 92). This apparent contradiction signifies that it is not love per se but rather the regulatory regimes molding it in particularly constraining patterns that is the object of the narrator's critique. Stella's retrospective feelings are equally equivocal. Recalling 1940 in terms of "sensations" rather than "thoughts," she remembers "something inside her head, never quite a thought" making itself felt as a "sort of imprisoned humming" the moment she had realized that the "departure she was about to take" had a "finalness not to appear till later" (94, 95). The allusions to the inception of love as the "closing of a gate," as the "demolition of an entire moment" (96), and as an event "arrest[ing] the movement of everything" (97) signal a shift away from Stella's personal equivocations to an emphasis on the closed and enclosing nature of the heterosexual contract generally (100). Such an implicit critique of the fiction of romance is further articulated by the narrator's contention that "war time, with its makeshifts, shelvings, deferrings could not have been kinder to romantic love" (100). The lurking awareness of a connection between the dominant discourses of violence and love informs Stella's abiding doubts.

Thriving in a context that also breeds "all that [is] most malarial," love is clearly not to be taken as an unqualified and/or positive notion (92). As indicated by the narrator's comments on the lovers' inevitable inscription in history (in the passage quoted earlier in this chapter), the insidious aspects of the myth of heterosexual romance lie in the fact that it can only be (re)produced in a conceptual universe in which the private and the public are ideologically separated. Paradoxically, the breakdown of cultural boundaries accentuates the persistence of the tenets of binary thought underlying this and similar dichotomies. The flaw in what seems to be the perfect love affair is precisely that it rests on its seclusion from "London's organic power" (91). Resembling the "ideal book about nothing," Stella's and Robert's "narrative of love" is entirely inwardly directed: it "stay[s] itself on itself by its inner force" (90). The lovers live in a dream of timelessness, a fantasy that is both unwarranted and harmful. Having met each other at a time when "vacuum as to the future was offset by vacuum as to the past," they retreat into the "hermetic world" of their love (90). Since it is dominant ideology that sets up romantic love as a phenomenon with an idealized autonomy, splitting it off from material reality so that it appears to "belie time," the safety into which they withdraw is both illusory and thoroughly sociopolitically interested (97). That the stultification resulting from such interiorization is punctuated by the amplifying effect of war is clear when it seems to Stella as if the "extraordinary battle in the sky transfixed" Robert and herself (96); her first glimpse of her lover strikes her as "one shot" left "frozen, absurdly, on to the screen" due to the "breakdown of projection" (98). Vaguely aware of the dangers inhering in its deceptive self-sufficiency and its potentially constraining effects on her self, she nonetheless devotes herself wholeheartedly to the "plan of love . . . go[ing] on unfolding itself" (100).

We note that the fictitious aspect of romantic love is underscored by a chain of references to words, stories, and narrative. These are also the terms in which Stella's misgivings obliquely surface. She believes, for instance, on the first date with her lover, that she is "going to a rendezvous inside the pages of a book." By questioning Robert's "fictitious" identity she reveals herself to be aware of the untenability of the separation of (private) romance from (public) reality (97). Such acknowledgment of the mutual inscription of fiction and reality a fortiori attests to the structural influence of the past upon the present as well as to the textual nature of both. Stella's lingering sensitivity to the values of the established order renders her particularly susceptible to the seductive illusion that it is yet possible to ignore the past and its stories. The atmosphere of concealment prevailing in war-time London makes it seem as if "life-stories were shed as so much superfluous weight"—a circumstance that, "for different reasons, suit[s] both her and [Robert]" (95). However, the artificial separation of the present from the past and the concomitant disengagement from the historical present that form the condition of their love also constitute the "time-bomb" underlying it from the beginning. It is precisely because she had deliberately remained unacquainted with what "went to Robert's making" that Stella will eventually be unable to assess the validity of Harrison's accusations. As if to foreshadow the implications of such willful ignorance, the lovers forget the first words they exchange: this gives them the "significance of a lost clue" (96).

During the early stages of their affair, Stella is happy to maintain her position of relative independence. She and Robert grow "into living together in every way but that of sharing a roof" (99). Her realization that it is the collapse of established institutions that allows them to do so nonetheless alerts her to the fact that the disintegration of society succeeds in strengthening the fiction of heterosexual romance. Her long-standing suspicion toward the regulatory discourses of love and marriage therefore continues to trouble her. In the course of time,

[Robert's] experience and [Stella's] became harder and harder to tell apart; everything gathered behind them into a common memory—though singly each of them might, must think, exit, decide, act; all things done alone came to be no more than *simulacra* of behaviour: they waited to live again till they were together, then took living up from where they had left it off. Then their doubled awareness, their interlocking feeling acted on, intensified what was round them—nothing they saw, knew, or told one another remained trifling; *everything came to be woven into the continuous narrative of love*; which, just as much, kept gaining substance, shadow, consistency from the imperfectly known and the not said. For naturally they did not tell one another everything. Every love has a poetic relevance of its own; each love brings to light only what is to it relevant. Outside lies the junk-yard of what does not matter. (99; italics mine)

On the face of it, the narrator's foregrounding of the unique "poetic relevance" of love seems a vindication of the romantic enclosure as a "safe haven" and of the ideological separation of the private from the public. But by underlining the dialogic nature of meaningful experience and by defining the lovers' lives in the outside world as "simulacra of behaviour,"[48] the text emphatically blurs the boundaries between private "habitat" and public context. Moreover, the notion of romantic love as impervious to the operations of sociohistorical conditions is further critically challenged when—as my emphasis seeks to suggest—both "everything" and "love" are located in the text of narrative, or rather, in the texture of ideology. Although representative of different levels of experience, these concepts form part of the network of heterogeneous discourses in which the process of subjectivity occurs. It is with the material intrusion of the outside world in the guise of Harrison that Stella is forced to step out of her and Robert's secluded existence. No longer able to disregard the outside world, she turns to her lover's past in order to (as Harrison puts it) go "look at the first place where rot could start" (131). Cracking the cherished cocoon of their habitat, the heroine accompanies Robert on a visit home. By placing him in a wider context, Stella also repositions herself in relation to her lover as well as with regard to her own past.

Paranoid Discursive Circles. The visit to Robert's home is an exquisite example of Bowen's talent for rendering place to great narrative effect. Inserting itself in a long tradition of the literary gothic, the scene depicts annihilating domesticity in such a way as to set up a straightforward connection between, on the one hand, the traditional image of Woman as obstacle or closed space (which, as de Lauretis posits, is "morphologically female and indeed, simply, the womb") and on the other, the "hom(m)osexual" relations between Robert and his persecutor Harrison.[49] As a topos of femininity-cum-domesticity, the house represents the apparent opposite of *das Heimliche:* what Freud termed "the uncanny" or *das Unheimliche.*[50] The contradictory associations converging in the sensation of "the uncanny" paradoxically evoke the ultimate "home" of human beings, the womb. Robert's *unheimliche Heim,* as will appear shortly, plays a central part in the spy plot as well as in the story of his subjectivity. But since the subject of this narrative quest is gendered female instead of male, it is the heroine who is forced to explore this "uncanny house" (which Patricia White identifies as a central topos in classic horror movies) in its symbolic value as the "dark continent" of female sexuality.[51] Stella's passage through Holme Dene serves not to set her up in the role of "mythical subject" in her own right, however, but rather to uncover the hidden plot lying beneath such dominant cultural myths. Couched in a critique of the desiccated life of the upper-middle classes, the episode centers on the issues of secrecy and concealment in/through discourse, laying bare the connections between dominant regimes of power/knowledge and culturally repressed or "taboo" sexualities. The sequence thus highlights the effects of phallogocentric ideology on both the subjective and the objective levels of reality. It also further confuses the distinctions between mythical and historical time. The implications of these issues acquire acute significance in the wider context of the novel's plot.

The first "intimation" of Holme Dene's hidden existence is a "notice saying CAUTION: CONCEALED DRIVE" (105).[52] The house presents a "façade . . . partially draped with virginia creeper, now blood red," surrounded by a "tennis pavilion, a pergola, a sundial, a rock garden, a dovecote, some gnomes, a seesaw, a grouping of rusticated seats, and a bird bath" (106). Unlike Danielstown with its "vast façade star[ing] coldly over its mounting lawns," this house is clearly not the blunt and outspoken seat of patriarchal power, but rather (the male fantasy of) enigmatic female sexuality.

Already confused by such a distracting jumble of attributes, Stella is positively disconcerted when Robert's rambunctious elder sister arrives on the scene. Ernestine's high-strung energy and her obsessive involvement in the Women's Voluntary Service convey the general atmosphere of nervous tension pervading this haunted house. Giving off the air of "having been torn, or having . . . torn herself away from some vital wartime activity," Ernie sends Stella a look in which the "absence of human awareness [is] quite startling" (107). The heroine's rising sense of perplexity increases upon entering the house:

The lounge of Holme Dene could be seen into from the entrance porch, through an arch. It had three sizable windows; but was so blackly furnished with antique oak, papered art brown and curtained with copper chenille as to consume, with little to show, their light. Some mahogany pieces, such as a dining-table, a dumb-waiter and an upright piano, could be marked as evacuees out of other rooms; the grandfather clock, on the other hand, must have stood here always—time had clogged its ticking. The concentrated indoorness of the lounge was made somehow greater rather than less by the number of exits, archways, and outdoor views; the staircase, lit from the top and built with as many complications as space allowed, descended into the middle of everything with a plump. In the evident hope of preventing draughts, screens of varying heights had been placed about. (107–8)

At once extending the initial intimation of its "screened" existence and the disorienting effects it produces on its visitors, the cluttered decoration of Holme Dene confirms the home's function as the paradoxical opposite of *das Heimliche*. While reflecting the tangled minds of its inhabitants, the baffling contortions in the house's architectural design are shown to be inherent in the cultural myths by which bourgeois society sustains itself. Faced with the tasteless propriety of middle-class convention and the "self-evident position of their own" that the Kelways accordingly assume, Stella—"born to some idea of position" so that she "seldom asked herself what her own was now" (115)—is newly confounded by the moral economy of the English class system:

The English, she could only tell herself, were extraordinary—for if this were not England she did not know what it was. You could not account for this family . . . by simply saying that it was middle class, because that left you asking, middle of what? She saw the Kelways suspended in the middle of nothing. She could envisage them so suspended when there *was* nothing more. Always without a quiver as to their state. Their economy could not be plumbed: their effect was moral. (114)

Securely interpellated in the positions assigned to them by dominant ideology, the Kelways have lost all consciousness of themselves outside the set of meanings and values concurring with their allotted identities and become trapped in the maze of their own obsessions. Stella's recognition of her own as much the Kelways' unconscious internalization of prevailing myths heralds the first stage of her (self-)exploratory itinerary.

The domain over which Mrs. Kelway—since her husband's death the official head of the family—rules with iron hand exposes the stifling effects of a life entirely turned in upon itself. Such inner-directness disturbingly transpires the dangers implied in the lovers' own habitat. What is more, the figure of Mrs. Kelway alerts Stella to the paranoid aspects of the lethal self-sufficiency of both this enclosure and the one in which she and Robert have sought refuge. Underscoring her symbolic value as the annihilating maternal womb, it is by a "silence, more than a sound" that Mrs. Kelway— "muttikins," as she is called by her adult children—invites Stella to meet her "sceptical" look. Seated in an armchair "posted midway across the floor," from which "strategic position" she "command[s] all three windows," Mrs. Kelway is the embodiment of (castrating) omnipotence (108). The intimidating matriarch momentarily threatens Stella in her own sense of identity:

[Stella] was now confronting, with a submerged tremor, with a momentary break in her sense of her own existence, the miniature daunting beauty of that face. Mrs Kelway's dark hair, no more than touched with grey, was of a softness throwing into relief the diamond-cut of her features. The brows, the nose, the lips could not have been more relentlessly delicate, more shadowlessly distinct. If Ernie's regard had held unawareness, her mother's showed the mute presence of an obsession. For, why *should* she speak?—she had all she needed: the self-contained mystery of herself. Her lack of wish for communication showed in her contemptuous use of words. The lounge became what it was from being the repository of her nature; it was the indoors she selected, she consecrated— indeed, she had no reason to go out. . . . If her power came to an end at the white gate, so did the world. (109–10)

Explicitly identified as the "self-contained mystery" called femininity, the figure of Robert's mother thus reinscribes one of the staple images of Woman: the frightful incarnation of castrating power. It is nonetheless clear that the matriarch is no more than the product of a phallogocentric collective unconscious, for, as White points out, while psychoanalytic notions associating "the uncanny" with the womb find their way into cultural texts ranging from "the western to the melodrama," it is always the "woman [who] provokes the uncanny; her experience of it remains a shadowy area."[53] The text of *HD* upsets the conventional scheme in that it is a female "hero" who is set to explore the "closed space," the "matrix/matter" of female sexuality. This allows for an exposure of the hidden subtext of prevailing myths.

Robert, it emerges, has never actually departed from the closed space of his youth: the habitat he shares with Stella is an extension of the maternal enclosure he has never been able definitively to leave behind. He compulsively returns to Holme Dene, no matter how much he professes to hate its annihilating force. Psychoanalysis shows that, as projections of the male fear of the "shadowy" female body, the fantasies of "the uncanny" that inscribe paranoia signal the "hom(m)osexual" investments in them. Freud in fact submits that the paranoid obsession itself serves as an "attempted defence against an unduly strong homosexual impulse."[54] Linking "regard for the father," "attachment to the mother," and "narcissism" to the fear of castration, he maintains that the (male) paranoid patient betrays his repressed homosexual wish in a "hysterical phantasy, an obsessional idea, or a delusion."[55] The displacement of the male fear of castration onto the female body hence forms the cultural inscription of the taboo on (male) homosexuality. The complexities of such a reaction-formation are reflected in the literary image of the *unheimliche Heim*.[56] Since it is Stella who is exploring the "obstacle" in her lover's story, the novel, rather than merely reinscribing this phallogocentric myth, superimposes an incisive sociopolitical critique on the psychosexual subtext underpinning it, therewith exposing the myth *as* myth.

The confusion of gender roles in the narrative thus enables us to see not only that Mrs. Kelway functions as the silent "matrix" of her son's psychosexual makeup but also that her unwillingness to communicate issues directly from women's "muted" position within the Law.[57] Having been denied social agency, she exerts her limited power within the confines of the realm of the middle-class housewife: the nuclear family or, to use a more old-fashioned but less obscuring term, the "paternal home." Venting her frustration on the system by which her subjective authority is categorically curbed, Mrs. Kelway nurtures a contempt for language and reigns through silence, repression, and concealment. The consequences of such a thwarted will to power show in the behavior of both Mrs. Kelway and her children, who "communicate with one another with difficulty," the "recurrence of a remark show[ing] that yet another circle around the subject had been completed" (252).

Bowen here shows in terms of gender what she has elsewhere discussed in the context of class relations, that is, the perils of "dispossession":

For these people—my family and their associates—the idea of power was mostly vested in property (property having been acquired by use or misuse of power in the first place). One may say that while property lasted the dangerous power-idea stayed, like a sword in its scabbard, fairly safely at rest. . . . Without putting up any plea for property—unnecessary, for it is unlikely to be abolished—I submit that the power-loving temperament is more dangerous when it either prefers or is forced to operate in what is materially a void. We have everything to dread from the dispossessed. In the area of ideas we see more menacing dominations than the landlord exercised over the land.[58]

Not the most horrifying of numerous sinister and diabolic elderly women appearing in Bowen's fiction,[59] the character of Mrs. Kelway is precisely so significant because her rebellious response to, or rather, her guerilla warfare against, phallocratic domination locates the latter's operative force irrevocably in discourse. In her symbolically constrained hands, all language has become "dead currency" (252).

Since the text highlights the sociocultural groundings of the uncanny home's symbolic value, it is evidently not only at Holme Dene that the "ticking" of the "grandfather clock" has been "clogged" by time. Illustrating the condition of—presently collapsing—established social structures, Robert's home reflects the consequences of an eroded system of Law. The "rot" within this family is the "rot" incurred by oppressive regimes of power/knowledge. The self-defeating results of phallogocentrism and compulsory heterosexuality are embodied in the figure of the treacherous Robert. Conflating his mother's putative omnipotence and the domestic scene that forms the "repository" of her "nature," he conceives of his childhood home as a "man-eating house." He tells Stella that his father's death had come as a "cracking relief" to him: it had allowed him to repress his conflictual desire for a man gradually reduced to "impoten[ce] . . . in all but one sense" and to displace it in a paranoid fantasy onto his emasculating "muttikins" (118–19). Repression is not elimination, however, and the termination of Mr. Kelway's "derisory" existence has not prevented "the indignities suffered by the father" from remaining "burned deeply into the son's mind" (257–58). Although Robert attributed the "broken spring" in his father's eyes exclusively to his mother's castrating power, the text indicates that husband and wife were equally enthralled by/in the binary frame of sex, acting as accomplices in the maintenance of its technologies: after his death, Mr. Kelway's "fiction of dominance was, as he would have wished, preserved by his widow and his daughters" (258).

The war of nerves within the Kelway family has quite appropriately been fought out in the field of discourse, for the battle between the sexes is fundamentally a struggle over meaning: it is only within the linguistic system of differential relations that (gender) identities come into existence. We recall that the dialogic constitution of the subject implies that the identity of the Same is defined by and depends on its difference from (the) Other/s: in terms of patriarchy, it is through the absence or marginalization of the female subject that the male subject can—and indeed must—be affirmed in his presence and centrality. If Mrs. Kelway represents the fantasmatic image of the voraciously man-eating woman, she simultaneously belies the connotations of conventional womanhood by mocking its attributes of passivity and helplessness. She has thus doubly succeeded in subverting the connotations of agency and power attached to its opposite term. For Robert, not surprisingly, "masculinity" has lost its traditionally reassuring meanings. What is more, since he ascribes his father's disgrace to his mother's abuse of symbolic power, Stella's lover has become deeply suspicious not only of those he considers to have corrupted its constructive potential but also of the discursive system itself.

Under the sway of his delusions, Robert considers paternal dominance to have been turned into a farce by his mother and sisters.

Even though he could not rely on their ability to cast him into his masculine position, his distrust of their emasculating power did not relieve him of his dependence on them as interpellating others. The spectacle of his "boyhood's den," in which "manly comforts" are "interspersed with fictions of boyishness," shows that they, in their turn, have not neglected their appointed roles in this respect. When Stella is met by the "striking" sight of "sixty or seventy photographs, upward from snapshots to crowded groups . . . [hanging] in close formations on two walls" (116), all featuring Robert, she correctly surmises that his mother and sisters are responsible for this "exhibition" of her lover's personality. Still, by never having "taken them down," Robert shows that he has not been able to come to terms with his distrust of such endeavors to supply him with a masculine identity. In other words, he has not, as de Lauretis puts it, "cross[ed] the boundary [of the closed space] and penetrate[d] the other space" and hence has not succeeded in constructing himself as a "male" subject. When Stella observes that the overstuffed attic room "feels empty," Robert responds: "'It could not feel emptier than it is. Each time I come back again into it I'm hit in the face by the feeling that I don't exist—that I not only am not but never have been'" (117).

Insisting that the photographs prove that there have at least been moments at which he existed, Stella is faced with her lover's utter lack of trust in the "realness" of his masculinity. What she calls "moments" are for him "'Imitation ones. If to have gone through motions ever since one was born is, as I think now, criminal, here's my criminal record. Can you think of a better way of sending a person mad than nailing that pack of his own lies all round the room where he has to sleep?'" (118). The courtroom vocabulary suggests the unLawful underpinnings of Robert's obsessional ideas. What he even now considers to be "wrong with him" is the fact that he has been deprived of a "genuine" male identity (117). Since an image of one's self as a fiction or fake is ultimately psychologically untenable, Robert has displaced his fears onto Holme Dene and, in a further act of displacement, set off in his mind this closed space as a deceptive imitation of the outside world that it has so successfully barred from its premises.

Holme Dene itself, I have suggested, reflects Robert's twisted state of mind. Despite its substantial space, it appears to have been "planned with a sort of playful circumlocution—corridors, archways, recesses, half-landings, ledges, niches, and balustrades combined to fuddle any sense of direction." Ideally suited for Mrs. Kelway's silent "intelligence service," it strikes Robert as "flockpacked with matter—repressions, doubts, fears, subterfuges, and fibs" (256). The uncanny home's value as a fiction deeply embedded in the cultural unconscious is underscored by its having "practically always" been "for sale" (120). When Stella wonders how "anyone [can] live ... in a place that has for years been asking to be brought to an end," Robert almost casually replies: "'Oh, but there will always be somewhere else, ... everything can be shifted, lock, stock, and barrel. After all, everything was brought here from somewhere else, with the intention of being moved again—like touring scenery from theatre to theatre. Reassemble it anywhere: you get the same illusion.'" Confirming the enthralling power of (the fantasy of) castrating woman as one of the most pervasive culturally inherited myths, Robert shows how keenly he grasps the concrete effects of symbolic operations when, with a "movement of bitter carelessness," he adds: "'What else but an illusion could have such power?'" (121).

To see the connections between Robert's boyhood experiences and his treachery we have to jump ahead to a later point in the narrative. We learn that his adult life has strengthened his suspicions regarding the castrating powers of "the feminine." Having sought himself in the most unmistakable of "manly" pursuits, that is, serving the mother country, Robert has suffered the army's defeat and humiliating withdrawal from Dunkirk. The experience has reinforced his neurotic fears, for, as Freud points out, "neurosis will always produce its greatest effects when constitution and experience work together in the same direction."[60] "Real life" having been turned into no less of an emasculating conspiracy than his *unheimliche Heim,* any notion upon which the maintenance of the established order depends has become meaningless to Robert. When Stella asks him why he is against this country, he maintains that he does not know what she is talking about: " 'I don't see what you mean—what *do* you mean? Country?—there are no more countries left; nothing but names' " (267). Showing his "madness" in a grandiose fantasy of future "overlordship," Robert maintains that what he is after is "on altogether another scale," something for which "there's so far no measure that's any use, no word that isn't out of the true" (268), that is, an absolute Truth beyond the boundaries of the symbolic order per se:

"If I said 'vision,' inevitably you would think me grandeur-mad: I'm not, but anyway vision is not what I mean. I mean sight in action: it's only now I act that I see—What is repulsing to you is the idea of 'betrayal,' I suppose, isn't it? In you the hangover from that word? Don't you understand that all that language is dead currency? How they keep on playing shop with it all the same: even you do. Words, words like that, yes—what a terrific dust they can still raise in a mind, yours even: I see that. Myself, even, I have needed to immunize myself against them; I tell you I have only at last done that by saying them to myself over and over again till it became absolutely certain they mean nothing. What they meant once is gone. (268)

The phrase "dead currency" links Robert's "disaffectedness" (271) directly to Mrs. Kelway's contempt for language, and a fortiori to the mother's function as a source of castration anxiety. The effects of women's dispossession of symbolic agency, which enable the male fantasy of their enigmatic power, are therewith shown to extend into society as a whole: having taken root in him as a boy, Robert's displaced fears have taken their corrupting course in his position as man manqué.

Within the context of a war in which, as Stella's son at one point asserts, "conversations are the leading thing" (63), Robert's rejection of words would to some extent appear to be justified. It is, after all, his perception of the discrepancy between dominant discourses and the actual circumstances in which people live their lives that has erased what lingering faith in symbolic values he might still have preserved. Despite his nominal role as the "bad guy" of the novel, Robert's function within its overall moral framework, and especially his stance toward language, is therefore ambivalent. Moreover, the character set up as his loathsome counterpart, the one who is politically speaking on the "right" side, is Harrison: a counterspy, a glib talker who cunningly exploits the ambiguity of words to his own advantage. Robert's arguments against the social order cannot be simply dismissed as the inconsequential gibberish of a lunatic—however contorted his ideas in the final instance turn out to be. What he rejects is the "racket" of liberal humanism, that is, the originating grounds of both subjective and objective reality:

"Freedom. Freedom to be what?—the muddled, mediocre, damned. . . . Look at it happening: look at your mass of 'free' suckers, your democracy—kidded along from the cradle to the grave. 'From the cradle to the grave, save, oh, save!' Do you suppose there's a single man of mind who doesn't realize *he* only begins where his freedom stops?" (268)

These words show that, while selling itself on the premises of "freedom" and "democracy," such an ideological system is as much founded on inequality and (dis)possession as any other form of societal organization. This is what having joined an "army of freedom" only to end "queueing [*sic*] up to be taken off by pleasure boats" has induced Robert to apprehend (272). Taken up by the chief antidemocratic discourse of the day, his disillusionment prompts him to think in terms of absolute notions such as law and order. To Robert the Germans have merely "started something . . . the beginning of a day . . . a day on our scale" (274). At this point, the text no longer invites us to sympathize with what has indeed become a dangerously megalomaniacal discourse of destruction.

Still, the careful exploration of his motives and the ambiguity of his backstage disappearance from the narrative—he either "fall[s] or leap[s] from the roof" of Stella's apartment—do not allow us simply to classify Robert as a morally reprehensible character from whom we can complacently distance ourselves (291). While this sort of (self-)righteousness would be particularly easy with the hindsight of history, it would also obscure that Robert's paranoia is not merely the unfortunate issue of his "personal" history but is first and foremost the product of a phallogocentric culture.

The links between Robert's disaffection, the "hom(m)osexual" economy, and the dominant regimes of power/knowledge become even more pronounced when he explains what his treacherous activities have come to mean to him:

"It utterly undid fear. It bred my father out of me, gave me a new heredity. I went slow at first—it was stupefying to be beginning to know what confidence could be. To know what I knew, to keep my knowing unknown, unknown all the time to be acting on it—I tell you, everything fell into place around me. Something of my own?—No, no, much better than that: any neurotic can make himself his corner. The way out?—no, better than that: the way on! *You* think, in me this was simply wanting to get my hand on the controls? . . . Well, it's not: it's not a question of that . . . to feel control is enough. It's a very much bigger thing to be under orders." (273)

The perils inhering in the reciprocity of discursive operations are illuminated when Stella expresses her abhorrence of Robert's twisted ideas. He retorts: " 'I didn't choose them: they marked me down. They are not mine, anyhow; I am theirs.' " The text clearly locates the forces of corruption in the contextual determinants of Robert's psyche. To underscore that subjectivity is not merely effected by but also affects the very structures by which it is produced through/by its own agency, Robert continues: " 'Would you want me simply to be their prey? Would you want me simply to be a case? Would you have wanted me not to fight this war?' " (272). By exposing the destructive consequences of the cultural taboo lying behind Robert's paranoia, the text underlines the origins of the male fantasy of the "castrating" woman. Still, the emphasis on the ambivalence of subjectivity also foregrounds the individual's moral responsibility, or more precisely, her/his answerability in/to the world. This is confirmed when Stella points out that there is nothing new in being "under orders." To this Robert replies: " 'But I don't mean orders, I mean order' " (273). The fatal distinction indicates that here a level of abstraction has been reached where Robert's contentions become morally intolerable: his absorption of and identification with a set of highly dangerous idealist notions are here unambiguously denounced.

Stella's role as the exploring subject of the narrative quest entails that the "enigma" of "femininity," concealed in/by the closed space of Holme Dene is shown to be *the fantasmatic product* of a paranoid male imagination. In her final conversation with her lover, Stella gradually begins to acknowledge the implications of what the visit to Robert's home has allowed her to perceive. Her heightened awareness of the groundings of his "madness" in turn forces her to realize her own function as matter/matrix in the male spy plot, and, a fortiori, in phallogocentric history. The implications of these realizations will surface in the course of the next chapter.

5

The Discourse of Suspension

> Permanence is an attribute of recalled places.
> —*Pictures and Conversations*

Heterosexual Materials

Linking Plots. Stella's last dialogue with Robert appropriately takes place in the enclosure of her blacked-out flat. "Bathed in a red appearance of heat from the electric fire," the room forms a suitably "infernal" setting to the crushing exposure of her lover's political and moral leanings (267). Listening to his voice, "familiar only in more and more intermittent notes," she is beginning to grasp "some undercurrent in it, hitherto barely to be detected, all the time forbidden and inadvertent" (269). It is this subtext in the narrative of love that the heroine is presently forced to recognize and peruse.

Pervaded by a profound sense of estrangement, Stella, at this "bare, irrefutable moment," is forced to ask herself whether "it had been terror of the alien, then, ... all the time" that had induced Robert to forge the spurious shelter of their habitat (274). But she also realizes her own complicity in the cultural myths that went to her lover's making. Acknowledging the fallaciousness of the separation of themselves from the world, it seems to her that "all love stood still in one single piercing illusion of its peace . . . unlived time was no more innocent than the time lived by them" (272). Understanding that the very possibility of the gift of the Self through (the) Other/s, instead of being dependent on its exclusion, consists in each individual's relations to the outside world, she wonders: "Rolled round with rocks and stones and trees—what else is one?—was this not felt most strongly in the quietus of the embrace?" (274). These rhetorical questions explain why Stella cannot take in Robert's nihilistic claims nor accept his off-hand repudiation of language as "dead currency." She appreciates that he has sought to contain his "terror of the alien" within the sanctuary of romantic love in order to rationalize his disaffection and to underpin his paranoid fantasies of an order on "an another scale." Robert's assertions, however, that they have "seen law in each other" and that "[she] has been [his] country" (271, 273) negate Stella's own experience of having "trodden every inch of a country with him," a country of which she "did not know how much was place, how much was time" (274). Her current reflections take up the narrator's earlier comments on the interpenetration of love and historical time:

She could not believe they had not, in those two years, drawn on the virtue of what was around them, *the* virtue peculiar to where they were— nor had this been less to be felt when she was without him, was where he was not, had not been ever, might never be: a perpetual possible illumination for her, because of him, of everything to be seen or be heard by joy. Inside the ring of war. . . . there had come to be the nature of Nature, thousands of fluctuations in their own stone country. Impossible that the population, the other people, should at least be less to be honoured than trees walking. (275)

Stella is compelled to recognize the common origins of Robert's love for her and his treachery. Her insight into his disordered mind leads to what is perhaps the most trying moment of her quest, when she finds herself torn between her "revulsion against . . . his act" and the realization that Robert's face "for ever dissolved for her into the features of love." Her conflict cuts far more deeply than a struggle of divided loyalties: rejecting him not only as a spy but also as her Other would imply not only the loss of a lover but first and foremost a loss of her Self.

Stella locates Robert's duplicity in his "twisted aspiration, a sort of recalcitrance in the energy, romanticism fired once too often." Realizing her own contextualization in history, she perceives that the standards of morality by which she is inclined to judge him are not transhistorical but are, in effect, as contingent as both their subjective identities. Robert is "right" in at least one sense: recognizing his face as that of a "latecomer," Stella grasps that in terms of meaning and value, "time makes the only fatal differences of birth" (277). If she cannot but condemn Robert in one fatal respect, she simultaneously comprehends that it need not mean that she has to renounce her love for him. She is thus able to discern the connections between what to her must remain two incompatible aspects of Robert's character. These are unambiguously traced to their joint point of origin in the experiences of his boyhood, and by extension, to the entwined discourses of phallogocentrism and compulsory heterosexuality.

Like his absolute notion of romantic love, the abstraction of danger has made Robert feel "secure" and "encased." Both have served to reconcile him to a deeply felt sense of "being set apart from people." His equation of female sexuality with secret (emasculating) power has urged him to seek in "danger" his own tool of control, "an attribute of one's own, a secret peculiarity one can keep in play." Plainly referring to the phallic power that he fears has always been the object of his mother's and sisters' voracious desires, Robert reveals that his castration anxiety has compelled him to deal with "unknown knowing" as a means of masculine self-authentication. Convinced that it "never suited them that [he] should be a man" (278), he has had to "be a man in secret." He assures Stella that this is what has given him a "sort of celebrity in reverse" (279). Inadvertently disclosing the repressed homosexual wish underpinning his obsessive fears, Robert admonishes her that she "must re-read [him] backwards, figure [him] out" (270). Stella begins to comprehend the ways in which Robert has implicated her in his terrible "masculine," or rather, "hom(m)osexual" plot: when she sees "his smile as the smile of one who has the laugh," it seems to her that "it was Robert who had been the Harrison" (275).

The ostensibly unaccountable confusion of the two male characters becomes less of a paradox when we consider that Harrison deals in secret knowledge just as much as Robert does. Strictly speaking each other's enemies—in political terms as well as in their relations to Stella—the men are united in their quest for power in both of these nominal fields of manly antagonism. When Harrison at the end of the novel reveals that his Christian name, too, is Robert, it is evident that he and Kelway are in effect two sides of the same coin—stamped phallocratic power.[1] This dawns upon Stella when she, locked inside her "infernal" flat with Robert, "pictures [Harrison] by some multiplication of his personality all around the house" (277). But the relations between the two male characters are not merely shown to be "hom(m)osexual" in socio-symbolic terms. Harrison proclaims from the start that it is not Robert's undoing he is after. He repeatedly points out to Stella: " 'I should feel bad if I let you ruin the chap. . . . I'd be in a way sorry to have things happen to him' " (38, 35). At one point he frankly admits: " 'I haven't a thing against him' " (39). This remarkable indulgence amounts to more than the odd sense of solidarity between victimizer and victim. The reciprocity of such sentiments indeed suggests otherwise: Robert also reveals himself to be capable of stirring up sympathy for the man whom he quite rightly could assume to be his lethal enemy. Indeed, when Stella, vexed by the thought of Harrison standing outside to catch a glimpse of the lovers together, in an impulse of anger threatens to defy and hurt him, her lover displays a striking sensitivity to his persecutor's feelings: " 'If he is down there, that's why he *is* down there. Imagine it's being gay for him, with his thoughts?' " (286). These manifestations of empathy betray the homosexual undercurrents of Robert's paranoia. Freud argues that it is the very appearance of a same-sex persecutor that signals the homosexual subtext of the paranoid patient's illness by "pointing back to a narcissistic object-choice." He continues: "Patients suffering from paranoia are struggling against an intensification of their homosexual trends . . . the persecutor is at bottom someone whom the patient loves or has loved in the past."[2] Considering Robert's identification with his father—" 'There'd been always X—who had always had to be *someone*' " (271)—and the narcissistic wound he has suffered on this account, this would appear to explain the otherwise rather puzzling affective investments of the male characters in each other.

In addition to providing further evidence of the psychosexual underpinnings of Robert's "disaffection," the suggestion of a degree of narcissistic identification between the two men sheds further light on the stakes of the "hom(m)osexual" power/knowledge game, and therewith on Stella's involvement in it. Foucault defines power/knowledge as follows:

Power and knowledge directly imply one another . . . there is no power relation without the correlative constitution of a field of knowledge, nor any knowledge that does not presuppose and constitute at the same time power relations. These "power-knowledge relations" are to be analysed, therefore, not on the basis of a subject of knowledge who is or is not free in relation to the power system, but, on the contrary, the subject who knows, the objects to be known and the modalities of knowledge must be regarded as so many effects of these fundamental implications of power-knowledge and their historical transformations.[3]

Foucault elsewhere points to the hierarchical organization of society, which ensures that different individuals are differently situated within the power/knowledge system. The spy plot of *HD*, thematically as well as narratologically controlled by a struggle over knowledge, thus links up with the novel's overarching theme of the dis/possession of power. Since the system in relation to which

Harrison and Robert operate is primarily, though not solely, organized around heterosexual difference, their attitude of forbearance
indicates that their game specifically revolves around *phallic*
power. Harrison correctly identifies the Law upon which his phallocratic scheming rests when he declares that he has "*got* to like
the chap" (35; italics mine). Since the underlying premise upon
which the surface hostilities between him and Robert take place is
the "hom(m)osexual" bond, it is not surprising to find that in both
of the fields in which the men are in apparent opposition, the
stakes involved are essentially the same. Their (displaced) desire is
jointly directed at the female element or the other—whether in the
guise of the "mother country" or, quite literally, the woman both
want to possess so as to contain her "castrating" power—by
which their male identity must be guaranteed.

Once the centrality of the heterosexual paradigm is recognized,
the confusion of the male "antagonists" is fully accounted for. The
respective positions Harrison and Robert represent in relation to
phallic power suggest that the one in effect needs the other in order
to make up for the lack each suffers in either one of the realms
in which masculinity traditionally obtains. In their oppositional
differentiation from the female, they are each other's supplements.
Robert's affair with Stella would seem amply to testify to his
(hetero)sexual adequacy: his lack of phallic power is located in the
realm of the sociosymbolic. Harrison, on the other hand, admits
being "naturally off [his] ground" as to what he calls "all that." He
is, however, eminently confident with regard to his sociopolitical
prowess: he virtually "brag[s] . . . about [his] power to tip scales"
(39). Despite the difference in the areas in which their anxiety over
their masculinity is situated, the strategies by which either man
attempts to contain it and to compensate for or redress his sense of
lack are strikingly similar: both exploit their command of critical
information and the concomitant possibility of concealment in
order to gain access to the mode of dominant power/knowledge of
which the other appears to be in control. Although Harrison and

Robert are equally caught up in power/knowledge relations, and hence are not free as subjects in relation to them, their gender accords them a degree of symbolic dominance over Stella, who merely functions as a plot space or obstacle in the narrative of masculine desire. Kept in the dark by both men, Stella only gradually finds out the nature of the "secret knowledge" around which the interlocking male plots revolve. (So does the reader, for that matter).

Even so, Stella is conscious of her own function in between them. Underlining the inextricable links among desire, knowledge, and power, she explains to Robert the basis of Harrison's "obsessive" desire for her: "'He says he knows what he wants; I suppose he wants what he doesn't know'" (283). Her awareness of her status as an object of exchange is further established when she accounts for Harrison's ultimate rejection of her:

"The fascination for [Harrison] in this thing with me could have been so much less me than himself his own all-powerfulness [*sic*]—a one-sided love's unnatural: there must be vice in it somewhere. If so, he would see my 'yes,' at *that* point, only in one way: my having called his bluff. Not that he might jib at breaking a bargain—me his: a new lease of safety for you—but, what value could I have left for him once he'd watched me see he couldn't do what he'd said? Very little, odiously little, none." (284)

These words confirm that the system in which Woman has value only as the object of male exchange finds its origins in the cultural taboo on homosexuality. As a product of a phallogocentric unconscious, the "dark continent" of female sexuality is the condition upon which male (phallic) self-presence depends. It is only by remaining his "castrated" Other that Woman can guarantee the Self-presence of the Same. Translated into sociopolitical terms, it is thus by denying women subjective agency, by ensuring the unequal distribution of its "currency" through/in the heterosexual contract, that the symbolic power/knowledge system can sustain itself. Once having exposed Harrison's power as essentially dependent on her ignorance, Stella would have lost her function in authenticating his masculine/phallic superiority, and therewith whatever value she may have had.

Stella's recognition of her place within the patriarchal configuration comes almost at the end of the novel's main plot. As the culmination of a process of increasing self-awareness, the heroine's expanding insight into the operations of dominant power/knowledge in the story of her life has been anticipated by explorations of the function of heterosexual difference in the larger text of history. It is her son's patrilinear heritage that plays a critical role herein. In order to see the connections, we have to move back to an earlier point in the narrative, to Stella's visit to Ireland.

The Paternal Home and History. The Irish estate Mount Morris functions in the novel—unlike Holme Dene but like Danielstown in *LS*—as the seat of patriarchal power. The Irish Big House thus extends the line of critique set out in the Holme Dene episode by further exposing the cultural image of femininity-cum-domesticity as both the product and the condition of a phallogocentric symbolic order.

Stella decides to visit Mount Morris after her second meeting with Harrison. Although Robert feels extremely threatened by the prospect of her leaving their private orbit, she ignores his objections and perseveres in the undertaking. Her intentions appear to be threefold. First, she wants to escape from Harrison. Second, she wishes to verify the counterspy's existence and the validity of his claims by finding out whether his boasts of an acquaintance with Cousin Francis have any grounds. Third, and no less important, Stella is anxious to redress the wrong she feels she has inflicted upon Roderick by not having immediately informed him about his uncle's death; thus she will attempt to ensure that he can take possession of his property as soon as the army releases him. She also wants to see whether Mount Morris is really the "white elephant" she fears, or whether Roderick's future position might help put an end to her son's "high" but dubiously "abstract" ideas.

This would simultaneously resolve the question of her own guilt, for, as we have seen, Stella fears that these spring from a flaw in Roderick's character for which she partly blames herself because she has deprived him of a conventional home. Underlying these motives lies her not-quite-conscious desire to return to the past in order to gain some focus on her own historical present. The process of self-exploration is sparked off when, during her second encounter with Harrison, the heroine is surprised to find herself suddenly thinking about Victor. Her reflections enable her to understand the discursive production of both private and public histories. The narrator merges with her thoughts to observe:

One could only suppose that the apparently forgotten beginning of any story was unforgettable: perpetually one was subject to the sense of there having had to be a beginning *somewhere*. Like the lost first sheet of a letter or missing first pages of a book, the beginning kept on suggesting what must have been its nature. One never was out of reach of the power of what had been written first. Call it what you liked, call it a miscarried love, it imparted, or was always ready and liable to impart, the nature of an alternative, attempted recovery or enforced second start to whatever followed. The beginning, in which was conceived the end, could not but continue to shape the middle part of the story, so that none of the realizations along that course were what had been expected, quite whole, quite final. That first path, taken to be a false start—who was to know, after all, where it might not have led? (133)

Although Stella "in fact . . . dread[s]" coming face to face with the beginning of her story, she feels forced to seek illumination of its fraught middle by visiting the place where she started her career as a gendered subject (160). At Mount Morris, where twenty-one years earlier she had spent her honeymoon, she experiences a crucial moment of revelation.

The episode in Ireland is cast in terms of a transition or, more precisely, a turning point in the heroine's quest. As she enters into the quiet of a country unaffected by war, it appears to Stella that "this was another time, rather than another country that she had come to" (163). Away from what has by now become a familiar scene of destruction, she is filled with a sense of "barbaric joy" about the "prodigality" of ordinary life (167). But the quiet is deceptive: in the "arrested energy" of the room in which Cousin Francis had had "his being," Stella is met with the man's desire both to contain the past and to control the future. Amid the relics and mementos recording the patrilinear history of Mount Morris, she finds a number of "cards, white, still fresh, peremptory to the eye" on which Francis had "blockprinted" his "injunctions, admonitions, and warnings" in case of any foreseeable emergency, up to and including his own death (163–64). Regretting that she has "not any such clear directions to her own life," Stella temporarily indulges in a longing to "stay here forever, playing this ghostly part." The sight of her physical attributes, "her gloves, shaped by her hands, her bag, containing every damning proof of her identity" (164), irretrievably recalls her to her material existence.

Paradoxically, the room's "indifference" produces a "startling" sense of "familiarity" in Stella. This becomes less of a paradox when we consider that Cousin Francis's room newly confronts Stella with the operations of patriarchal power, with the "directions" of the system of heterosexual difference that, as Teresa de Lauretis has pointed out, is in effect the "term of sexual indifference."[4] At the very moment when time appears to stand still, the house "as a whole . . . rose to the surface in [Stella], as though something weighting it to the bottom had let go" (164–65). The imagery here suggests that, by repressing the story of "her false start" as a gendered subject, she has prevented herself from consciously perceiving the connections between this beginning and her present situation. The encounter with the familiar setting of her early history provides Stella with the sense of direction she had felt to be lacking: "Expectancy rather than memory from now on guided her—she could not tell at which moment of her return journey the sensory train had started itself alight. Now she seemed to perceive on all sides round her, and with a phantasmogoric clearness, everything that for the eye the darkness hid" (166).

Stella's apprehension of the "hidden" subtext of her story not only issues in relief: when Harrison's existence is incontrovertibly proven by the old caretaker Donovan, she knows that she can now no longer remain oblivious to the import of her persecutor's accusations. Thus the perfect stillness of Mount Morris prompts her to reflect on what a direct confrontation with Robert might entail, for such a confrontation seems to have become inevitable. She feels that she would rather hear him confirm Harrison's allegations than see their love betrayed by another lie—"the first lie spoken not being, in most cases, the first lie acted." The possibility that Robert may have been "incalculably calculating, secretly adverse, knowing, withheld . . . all this time, from the start," strikes her as more horrifying than a frank confession would be. But by allowing her "sensory train" to "start alight" and thereby gaining rather than losing her self as she had feared, she has broken the spell of the myth of heterosexual romance that had induced her to set the repressive mechanism in motion in the first place. That her strategy of denial is no longer available to her dawns upon Stella the moment she tries to tell herself that her lover's honesty would be the "consummation" of their love (173). Having realized that her dreaded "loss of face" was in fact the product of an internalized cultural myth, she recognizes the oppressive effects of the social contract she sees everywhere inscribed in Cousin Francis's room. Her disillusionment signifies both a loss and a liberation:

Indeed, it was most of all with the sense of some sense in herself missing that she looked, from mirror to mirror, into misted extensions of the room. She was proof against it. Constrained to touch things, to make certain that they were not their own reflections, she explored veneers and mouldings, corded edges, taut fluted silk with the nerves of her fingers; she made a lustre tinkle, breathed on the dome over a spray of birds, opened the piano and struck a note, knowing all the time she was doing nothing more than amuse herself, if she *could* amuse herself, and was outside the society of ghosts. (173)

Stella's appreciation of her no longer self-evident position within the heterosexual matrix allows her to grasp the inscription of her self in a material world beyond the enclosure of her relationship with Robert. Her insight into the contextualized nature of her identity in the larger text of history has implications that reach beyond her immediate predicament. Wandering about, sensing the presence of the "ghosts" of so many other women's lives in the paternal home, she comes to a further understanding of the extent to which not only her past but also her present has been determined by dominant technologies of gender.

Inspecting the reflection of the "romantic face that was still hers," Stella sees herself "for the moment immortal as a portrait." "Momentarily . . . the lady of the house," she fleetingly regrets the "look of everything she had lost the secret of being" (173–74). Clearly, the heroine can no longer believe in her appointed role in the text of patriarchal culture. Her initial sense of loss is reversed when Stella recalls that history generally, and that of the paternal home in particular, is written by and in the service of dominant social groups, that is, men. Merging with her consciousness, the narrator subsequently puts forth an outspoken condemnation of traditional womanhood. By simultaneously illuminating how the prevailing regimes of power/knowledge succeed in making women collaborate in perpetuating their compulsory silence, the passage effectively exposes the constraining effects of ideological operations:

After all, was it not chiefly here in this room and under this illusion that Cousin Nettie Morris—and who knew how many more before her?—had been pressed back, hour by hour, by the hours themselves, into cloudland? . . . Virtue with nothing more to spend, honour saying nothing, but both present. Both, also, rising and following the listener when she left the drawing-room; she had been unaccompanied by them along no path she took. Therefore, her kind knew no choices, made no decisions—or, did they not? ... No, knowledge was not to be kept from them; it sifted through them, stole up behind them, reached them by intimations—they suspected what they refused to prove. ... So, there had been the cases of the enactment of ignorance having become too much, insupportable inside those sheltered heads. Also in this room they had reached the climax of their elation at showing nothing. ... Victory of society—but not followed, for the victors, by peace—for remaining waiting in here for them had been those unfinishable hours in which they could only reflect again. ... Their however candid and clear looks in each others' eyes were interchanged warnings; their conversation was a twinkling surface over their deep silence. Virtually they were never to speak at all. (174–75)

Identifying the moral stakes involved in women's (self-)imposed silence, Stella is alerted to the gendered underpinnings of her own "enactment of ignorance." Recognizing herself to be entwined within the same ideological structures that have sent Cousin Nettie to the confinement of Wistaria Lodge—the mental asylum where she has been "left undisturbed ... for years" (68)—she sees a renunciation of her passive and submissive attitude as the only morally justifiable route for her to take now.

The heroine's conscious assumption of her answerability signals the unresolvable contradiction of her position as a female subject in the dominant cultural plot. Claiming her right to speak in relation to Robert and Harrison means a defiance of traditional gender rules. But as a mother to her son, Stella cannot simply dismiss a symbolic order in which his masculine identity can only be ensured by the "deep silence" of the members of her own sex. Furthermore, even if she repudiates the oppressive story of patriarchy, what she believes to be Robert's alienation also prompts her to acknowledge the subject's need for a meaningful sociosymbolic context. Her only hope, therefore, is that the inescapability of the narrative of history need not necessarily imply the immutability of its meanings. Hence her cautious supposition that there "could still be something more," that the fact "that her own life could be a chapter missing from this book need not mean that the story was at an end; at a pause it was, but perhaps a pause for the turning-point?" (175). Warily, Stella admits that Roderick's inheritance may yet turn out to be a positive thing, for through his inheritance, "he had been fitted into a destiny; better, it seemed to her, than freedom in nothing" (175). Her relative compliance with the "directive" of patrilinear tradition, however, does not mean that Stella loses sight of the fact that history works differently for women than for men. It is therefore only in a moment of wishful thinking that she can envisage her future daughter-in-law entering Mount Morris "disembarred" of much of the oppressive patriarchal heritage, capable of changing the meaning of "old things" by "push-[ing them] into a new position" (176).

Stella's hesitant acquiescence to Roderick's "requisitioning" does not diminish her distrust and profound scepticism toward the self-assuming and constraining operations of a Law that legitimizes "Cousin Francis's egotistic creative boldness with regard to the future" (175). Indeed, the sight of a picture showing "a liner going down in a blaze with all lights on," which is "stuck crooked into an alien frame," returns her to her reflections on the muted lives of generations of women confined to the paternal home. The text does not explicitly make the connection between Cousin Nettie's "madness" and the image of destruction and alienation that the picture of the sinking *Titanic* evokes. Such a connection is nonetheless established by the fact that Stella wonders about the "significance of this drawing-room picture of Cousin Nettie's"—and thus, significantly, does not associate it with Francis, whose "being" is otherwise so omnipresent (176).

The pivotal function of the Irish interlude in Stella's quest is underlined by its thoroughly disorienting effect. Waking up the morning after her arrival at Mount Morris, she feels as if her "place in time had been lost." "Forced to grope for . . . the day of the week, the month of the year, the year . . . as though for her identity," she wonders whether these "deep sleeps of hers [were] periodic trances . . . birth-sleeps . . . of some profound change"

(176). In her "unearthly disassociation from everything," the heroine experiences the "peace of the moment" as one "in which one
sees the world for a moment innocent of oneself." She is soon to
discover, however, that "one cannot remain away." Pervading her
with its "rapture of strength," the natural world restores Stella's
sense of connection, filling her with "some expectant sense to be
tuned in to an unfinished symphony of love." While taken up by
the perpetual movement of nature's cycles, she appreciates that
she, by virtue of her own historical existence, "had brought time
with her into the wood" (177). When she seems to be passing
through an endless moment of timelessness, the heroine comes to
an understanding of both nature and herself as essentially time
bound. Her revelatory experience thus occurs when she temporarily apprehends herself as standing outside history. In this way, the
text highlights the female protagonist's dual position within the
plot text of history and the mythical time of masculine desire.

Stella is forced to acknowledge that she is not only a creature of
the times but also a creator of the meanings produced within
them. Her visionary experience underlines the contingency of all
meanings. As if to reaffirm the mutual inscription of the story of
subjectivity and the text of history, the moment when it appears
that "the answer [to her dilemma] had already provided itself and
did not matter" (177) turns out to coincide with Montgomery's
"terrible victory" in Egypt, an event that signifies the "war's turning" (178). This is followed by the narrator's comment (and the
epigraph to the preceding chapter): "There cannot be a moment in
which nothing happens" (178). While foregrounding the irreversible import of Stella's revelation, the echo of her private experience
in one of the war's landmarks underscores, for her as much as for
the reader, the inextricable links between private and public history, between Self and (the) Other/s, between subjective and objective "reality."

The sight of Donovan bringing her the war news also gives
further impetus to Stella's earlier thoughts about the structural

influence of heterosexual difference (or "sexual indifference") in the process of meaning production or signification. It strikes her that the caretaker suffers from the "loneliness of a man among women," being unable to share his knowledge or his feelings. From the fact that his daughter Hannah appears unaffected by the miraculous news, Stella infers that Donovan's words have no meaning to her. Indeed, the "oblation to victory being taken by her to be now ended, [Hannah] stepped down quietly from the parapet and began to wander towards the house," that is, the closed space where she, on account of her gender, properly belongs (179). The girl's enforced "enactment of ignorance," her relegation to a cultural position in which her beauty is enhanced by her very "apartness from what was going on," has reduced her to the status of an undifferentiated nonentity. Quite literally performing her role as untransformable matter, the girl, who has "inherited the colour of trouble but not the story," has neither consciousness of herself nor of the world: "Having not a thought that was not her own, she had not any thought." When Stella sees Hannah "standing there in the sunshine, indifferent as a wand," her fear of being herself reduced to mere "matrix" in the "hom(m)osexual" power/knowledge plot returns with compelling force (179). Gathering the strength actively to assume symbolic authority over her story, she returns to London "fixed upon what she meant to say" (180).

Shifting Positions. Just before her train's arrival in London, Stella "stop[s] to stare at herself, as though for the last time, in the panel mirror over the seat" (180). Underlined by the travel imagery that marks the transitional aspect of her quest, this action suggests that the heroine is taking leave of an earlier self. Attesting to her position as the subject of the narrative, and not as a mere plot space incapable of transformation, Stella's shift in perspective brings about a profound sense of disorientation. She wards off the accompanying fear of loss of self by displacing her changed view of herself onto the world around her: when she is met by Robert at the station, she is struck by his "*egaré* disassociation from other people" (181). The temporary interruption of their *dialogue intérieur* has produced a first rift in their *égoisme-à-deux*. Stella has conclusively lost her habitual place in the heterosexual matrix.

Driving through London in the company of Robert and his sister Ernestine, Stella is shocked by her lover's obvious "fondness for his sister," which appears "ineradicable" because of "some element of perversity" in it. Such a confirmation of the sexually overcharged nature of the relations among the Kelways also reminds us of the vaguely incestuous ring to the narrator's description of the lovers' own relationship. Although Stella is the focalizer here, the narrator points out that Ernie evokes the "sort of attraction jealousy can create" (184), suggesting "some element of perversity" in Stella's own present sense of sexual (dis)orientation. These suppositions are supported by classic psychoanalytic theory. Jealousy, Freud informs us, is "rooted deep in the unconscious, it is a continuation of the earliest stirrings of the child's affective life, and it originates in the Oedipus or brother-and-sister complex of the first sexual period."[5] Adding that "in some people" jealousy in its "normal" variety is "experienced bisexually," he moves to the more problematic phenomenon of "projected jealousy" and concludes his discussion by focusing on "delusional jealousy," in which all three varieties are to some degree present. In this case, Freud submits, the object "is of the same sex as the subject," indeed, this type of jealousy "is what is left of a homosexuality that has run its course." In the latter mode, jealousy serves as a defense against a "strong homosexual impulse."[6] Although Freud's discussion is limited to male homosexuality/jealousy, the concordance of precisely these two intertwined affective reactions in the heroine, and at precisely this point in the narrative, intimates that Stella's "revelatory moment" has issued in a shift in perspective not only in sociopolitical terms but also, though less consciously, in psychosexual ones.

In light of the above, it is not surprising that the heroine's sense of disorientation is enhanced by Ernestine's presence. The impenetrable darkness surrounding the car in which the three are locked together accentuates the deep "dark" level on which her sense of self is thrown into confusion. Stella has difficulty repressing an urge to "make the escape leap ... many prisoners had made." Realizing that she no longer knows where she stands, she exclaims: " 'We have never been wherever *this* is before!' " (185). Since Stella is projecting her internal bewilderment onto the outside world, Ernestine's ensuing departure hardly alleviates her plight. In the process of repositioning herself in the context of the heterosexual contract, the heroine is forced to admit that she "cannot be alone with [Robert] all at once." Therefore, instead of confronting him with Harrison's story as she had intended, Stella first tries to unravel the shifts in her appreciation of herself and, by extension, of their relationship. She points out to Robert that, having once served as a protection, perhaps even as its condition, the self-contained aspect of their affair now seems to her its basic liability:

"We are friends of circumstance—war, this isolation, this atmosphere in which everything goes on and nothing's said. Or we began as that: that was what we were at the start—but now, look how all this ruin's made for our perfectness! You and I are an accident, if you like—outside us neither of us when we are together ever seems to look. How much of the 'you' or the 'me' *is,* even, outside of the 'us'? The smallest, tritest thing I could be told about you by any outside person would sound preposterous to me if *I* did not know it. So I have no measure." (188)

Her subsequent inquiries concerning Harrison's allegations are met with a flat denial on Robert's part. Realizing the constraining effects of the myth of heterosexual romance, Stella acknowledges that she has no "measure" against which to judge the veracity of any of his assertions regarding a discursive field transcending the horizon of their relationship. This allows Robert to set in the counterattack. He accuses Stella of having been secretly "watching" him while he "show[ed]" her everything. Ostensibly abandoning her resolutions, she responds by apologizing for her show of mistrust. But despite this apparent act of resignation, it is clear that Stella perceives that it is indeed her limited access to the male-dominated field of power/knowledge that prevents her from assessing either man's charges. This is reflected in the precise terms in which she casts her predicament: " 'One can live in the shadow of an idea without grasping it. Nothing *is* really unthinkable, really you do know that. But the more one thinks, the less there's any outside reality—at least, that's so with a woman: we have no scale' " (192).

For the moment, the rapport between the lovers seems restored when they once again retreat into their "private illusion," entering a restaurant in which they can experience the "sensation of custom, of sedateness, of being inside small walls" (193). Significantly, it is here that the narrator steps in to make her grave comment—partly quoted at an earlier point—on the interpenetration of private and public history:

No, there is no such thing as being alone together. Daylight moves round the walls; night rings the changes of its intensity; everything is on its way to somewhere else—there is the presence of movement, that third presence, however still, however unheeding in their trance two may try to stay. Unceasingly something is at its work. Even, each beat of the other beloved heart is one beat nearer the destination, unknowable, towards which that heart is beating its way; under what compulsion, what?—to love is to be unescapably conscious of the question. To have turned away from everything to one face is to find oneself face to face with everything. (195)

Testifying to the public nature of the most private emotions, the passage suggests that Stella has arrived at the point of no return in her coming to consciousness. That this process is primarily a practice of *gender* consciousness is inadvertently brought to light by Robert himself.

When Stella endeavors to convey what the Mount Morris drawing room and the picture of the *Titanic* have made her see, she is cut short by her lover's attempt to reinstate precisely the oppressive patriarchal power she is about to denounce. Robert evidently fears that it is his masculine superiority that is slipping away from him. Threatened by any transgression of their unspoken contract, he suddenly recognizes the precarious nature of their unformalized relationship and seeks refuge in the founding structure of the Law, asking Stella to marry him. Her reaction is, in view of her contradictory social position, understandably ambivalent. While observing that "Roderick would like it," since he "really could not go on and on having a disreputable mother" (196), she also immediately grasps the connection between the "unhappy talk in the car" and Robert's unexpected proposal, and hence obliquely articulates her doubts by saying, " 'In a way I wish you hadn't chosen tonight' " (197). These words, intimating that Stella is either more upset or knows more than she is at present willing to concede, arouse Robert's congenital suspicion of "secret" female power. The violence of his reactions conveys the neurotic groundings of his fears. Undermining the validity of his emphatic proclamations of innocence, he aggressively attempts to bind Stella more closely to him. In trying to force the Law upon her, Robert succeeds in achieving the opposite of his intended goal.

Her lover's desire to subject her to his will is motivated by Stella's reassertion of her self other than solely in relation to him. Such a stance endangers his masculine identity. Instead of remaining only the Other to his Self, Stella has unexpectedly introduced a reality exterior to their relationship, a reality, moreover, in which she assumes the position of speaking subject in her own right. Its "perfectness" having thus been impaired, Robert's self-evident position within their private universe is no longer automatically guaranteed by the hitherto exclusively affirmative power of Stella's look. As noted before, the significance of the gendered look or gaze has formed the focus of attention in many feminist theoretical debates. Despite their higher level of abstraction, these discussions have not really changed the basis of Virginia Woolf's acute analysis, presented as early as 1929. Woolf claims that "women have served all these centuries as the looking-glasses possessing the magic and delicious power of reflecting the figure of man at twice its natural size."[7] Hence, within the patriarchal paradigm, the female look exists to authenticate the male subject in his identity: the woman sees the man in order for the man to be capable of seeing himself. The man, on the other hand, sees the woman only insofar as she performs this function. The male look therefore seeks to fix the female in the position from which she can operate as the mirror to his ego. While the woman recognizes the man in his subjective identity, she is not, in her turn, recognized as such by him. As the Other to his Self, the female subject is practically invisible in any other position than that from which she can verify the male subject's presence.[8] Since binary thought implies that one element's presence depends on the suppression or marginalization of its opposite, the central position of the male necessitates the absence of the female. The nominal and institutionalized marginalization of women in society serves to obscure and therewith neutralize their power in creating male psychosexual identity. This explains the enormous threat to the male ego that the female subject represents once she assumes a position other than that traditionally ascribed to her.

This (oversimplified) line of thought illuminates Robert's paranoid response to Stella's increased gender consciousness. Taking up a position outside the bounds of their relationship, she at once appears to embody the "uncanny" power of Woman in all its ambivalence: after all, as the mirror through which his male Self must be confirmed, the female Other by necessity simultaneously incorporates the power by which masculinity can be withheld or undermined. Hence Robert's frantic need to reinstate Stella in the position of absence necessary for the maintenance of his self-presence/identity. The insularity of their life together has hitherto served to safeguard the interior balance of power: Stella's love has provided him with the sense of masculine self that he feels has been denied by the emasculating look of his mother. Only by aggressively asserting his phallic power can Robert counter the fear of castration and contain its underlying homosexual impulse, which he, and phallogocentric culture generally, displaces onto the "dark continent" of female sexuality. He must try to fix Stella back into the required position. This is exactly what he endeavors: "Now, with an effect of deliberation, he fixed his eyes on her face— though somehow not, it appeared, on *her*." Since this passage is focalized through Stella, it is evident that she fully understands that Robert's attempt to (re)position her as his Other implies that her newly recovered subjective Self would thus be obliterated. Having finally successfully overcome Victor's earlier ventures at "effacement," Stella is not prepared to give up her subjective position now. Robert's refusal to acknowledge her as anything but his Other does not lead her to resign her Self to invisibility so much as it leads to a profound sense of alienation: her lover's "eyes appear to her [not] to be his own—they were black-blue, foreign, anarchical" (198).

By asserting her self within the symbolic order, Stella has called into question the traditional subject-object distinction predicated upon heterosexual difference. In breaking the silent agreement upon which, in his opinion, their relationship has thus far rested, she has made Robert aware of the fact that its foundations have never been more than a "question of faith." Now that she has acted in "bad faith" toward the social contract, Robert feels compelled to enforce the Law by which his masculinity is formally guaranteed. Seeing "only one way of knowing" whether she is still available to him, he desperately tries to subject her to the official conditions of patriarchy. By endeavoring to coerce her into marrying him—Stella reproachfully exclaims that he is "simply forcing things"—Robert takes recourse to one of the customary strategies by which the Law of the Father sustains itself. He seeks to reinscribe a policy of containment through (violent) appropriation. Stella does not accept Robert's "browbeating" and responds with "brimming-over reproach" (198), inquiring whether "any of her own reasons to hesitate [over marrying him] have got to go by the board?" (199). While resisting Robert's proprietary claims, Stella is shocked to find herself "talking like this to [him]." Their dispute has obviously aroused conflicting feelings in her. The fact that the heroine is "in two minds" about her lover's proposal in fact reveals that she is caught between her own need for recognition and his refusal to recognize her except within the strict terms of the heterosexual contract. When she admits, " 'I may not have been sure where I was, but now I certainly don't know where I am' " (198), it is clear that she is deeply confused about her own self. Robert seizes at the opportunity offered by her apparent disorientation and seeks to reassert his control by suggesting that Stella's interrogation in the car was merely inspired by fear, " 'fear for me—but also of me, a little bit?' " Slightly recovering her grip on her self, Stella denounces this further show of force only to be met with Robert's abrupt demand for a declaration of love. The heroine's response underlines the ambivalence of her position: "Eloquently she answered nothing whatever, not even looking up" (200). Such an inability or unwillingness to speak may suggest a silent submission, or rather a submission to silence. In view of the significance of specularity in the constitution of masculinity, however, the fact that Stella does not grant Robert the look of affirmation that he at this crucial moment seeks to elicit not only indicates that she is no longer willing to take up her appointed position within the heterosexual matrix; it also leaves her final stance within the narrative of love characteristically undecided. The next time the lovers speak to each other, their dialogue ends with Robert's similarly equivocal death.

Silence and Madness: Cousin Nettie's Escape. Several intervening chapters precede Robert's dramatic off-stage disappearance from the narrative scene. Directly following upon Stella's assertion of herself in other than oppositionally gendered terms, the first of these represents one of the most outspoken condemnations of dominant regimes of power/knowledge in Bowen's work.

The episode is introduced by a letter of Roderick's, informing Stella about his intended visit to Cousin Nettie. The reluctance with which the owners of Wistaria Lodge have let him enter their stronghold is indicative of the extent to which "civilized society" depends for its stability on strategies of exclusion. Established rules of "discretion" serve dominant groups to remove from the public eye that which does not fit in properly with their standards of normality. Exemplified by the mental as compared to the paternal home, such codes of behavior present a difference of degree rather than kind: the asylum, "this powerhouse of nothingness, hive of lives in abeyance," strikes Roderick as "no more peculiar than any other abode" (203).

He finds Cousin Nettie seated "with finality," her back to a window from whose view there is to be gained "no impact, no mystery, no horizon, simply a nothing more." The reason why Nettie should cling to the "unassailing sensation of having nothing but nothing behind her back" (206) is revealed when the narrator merges with Roderick's consciousness to disclose the nature of her "oddness": "All Cousin Nettie's life it must have been impossible for her to look at the surface only, to see nothing more than she should. These were the eyes of an often-rebuked clairvoyante [*sic*], wide once more with the fear of once more divining what should remain hidden" (207). What should remain hidden in the culture's unconscious is, of course, the "dark secret" of female sexuality: only as an enigma can this "fact of nature" serve to maintain the myth of masculinity. Unable to withstand the power of institutionalized structures of containment, Nettie has preferred to absent and thus efface herself with a vengeance from a sociocultural context in which she, on account of her sex, was not allowed to be and see (for) herself.

When Roderick mentions Mount Morris, it emerges that his aunt's position as the lady of the house had been forced upon her from the start: " 'You see I am only in half-mourning . . . mourning a cousin—[Francis] was my cousin, you know. There should have never never been any other story' " (208). Reluctant to play her appointed role in the story of patriarchy, Nettie had appeared "odd" in the eyes of "everybody." Unable to articulate herself in any other than the language of her oppressors, she had eventually reached her conclusion: " 'Then that must be what I am.' " Since "there seemed to be nowhere for [her] than here or there," she had preferred the asylum to Mount Morris (213). Nettie clearly discerns the liabilities of her gender in the process of self-determination. When Roderick hints at Cousin Francis's role in connection with her confinement, she says: " 'All my cousins make decisions; I have been used to that all my life. . . . It was only for me that there was nothing to do but what I did' " (213). Although the internalized identity of the "madwoman" has supplied her with the safety of Wistaria Lodge, Nettie's escape has not been achieved without inflicting a profound sense of guilt. Telling Roderick that she cannot blame Francis and is trying not to blame herself, she implores him not to blame her either. To his assurance that he does "not specially want anybody to do anything," she retorts: "'Oh, but you brood about what they should be doing. Whenever you remember you are unforgiving.'" Since Roderick has become "the master" of Mount Morris, he might try to force her to come back (208).

Nettie's sensible conversation gainsays any suggestion of mental illness. She herself locates her "madness" unequivocally in the system of gendered heterosexuality:

"Day after day for me was like sinking further down a well—it became too much for me, but how could I say so? You see I could not help seeing what was the matter—what [Francis] had wanted me to be was his wife; I tried this, that, and the other, till the result was that I fell into such a terrible melancholy that I only had to think of anything for *it* to go wrong, too . . . so I took to going nowhere but up and down stairs, till I met my own ghost." (216–17)

Nettie saw that her oddness prevented her from being what she was called upon by everybody to be: a "normal," that is to say, a heterosexual woman. Unable to speak her "abnormality," she made herself try to conform to the Laws of Nature. While exposing the precariousness of the binary frame of sex, this account underscores Kaja Silverman's contention that melancholia rather than hysteria "represents the norm for the female subject" in patriarchy.[9] What clinical psychological discourse succeeds in obscuring is the social and political interests underlying and informing the regulatory regimes of compulsory heterosexuality and phallogocentrism. This is confirmed when Cousin Nettie declines to tell Roderick more about Mount Morris, suggesting that he go and see for himself. She adds: " 'Of course there's this to be considered— you're a man. So you may keep going, going, going and not notice' " (216).

The violence inherent in the founding social contract is reflected in the fact that Nettie's withdrawal has led to a practice of virtual self-mutilation. An effective use of imagery discloses its results. Upon entering the room, Roderick notices that his aunt is working at a "piece of canvas" whose "design, very possibly not of her own choosing, had been machine-stamped on." After her outburst about Francis, she "once more, pick[s] up the woolwork, with a conventional sigh," but

only to turn the canvas from front to back, examine her stitches closely, then hold out the whole at arm's length for a look in which showed absolute disconnexion, as though the secret or charm of the continuity had been lost now, and she for one did not care. But no, she dare not afford *that*—she at once set out, with stork's beak scissors, sedulously to snip off straggles of wool from the rough side. But the scissors, out of some impish volition of their own, kept returning to peck, pick, hover destructively over the finished part. So she disengaged herself from them in a hurry, dropping them in her lap. (209)

Nettie has clearly seen that there was no connection between her self and the prescribed, artificially enforced design of the heterosexual matrix. Indeed, from her distant perspective as the odd one out, she had threatened to break the spell of its illusory self-evidence, of "naturalness" itself. Fearing the sanctions that would follow upon her disobedience of the Law, she had tried to snip off those aspects of herself that failed to meet its conditions. But since psychosexuality largely obtains within the realm of the unconscious, her will power had proven incapable of subduing the "straggles" that made it impossible for her to fit in. Anticipating the uncontrollable strength of her own disruptive desires, Nettie had "disengaged" herself from the sociosymbolic order altogether.

By stirring up her memory, Roderick has reactivated precisely those aspects of herself that Cousin Nettie had felt compelled to subdue, to silence. Only by deliberately reinstating this grid of self-effacement can she "keep the conversation within bounds" and perpetuate the safety of nothingness (209). The postcards making up "quite a little gallery" on her walls, all of which feature children "engaged innocently in some act of destruction," yet form a poignant reminder of the violence with which their owner succeeds in preserving the "neutralizing prettiness" of her gilded prison (210). Nettie's situation is a trenchant illustration of the ways in which dominant gender discourses succeed in making women participate in their own subjection to the Law.

Complicity does not mean ignorance, however. It is precisely because of her ability to "divine" the potentially harmful effects of discursive power that Nettie has opted for silence. Having told Roderick the story of his parents' divorce, she proclaims that it is a "pity . . . that there should be any stories" at all. She rejects his suggestion that "something has got to become of everybody": " 'No, I don't see why. Nothing has become of me: here I am and you can't make any more stories out of that' " (214). Insofar as she has allowed herself to be "neutralized" under the sway of patriarchal power and thereby precluded her reinscription into the history of Mount Morris, Nettie's contention is undeniably correct. Her appearance on another discursive level, as a character in the text of *HD,* nonetheless demonstrates that she forms no exception to the rule. The system of signification upon which her existence as a character depends is ultimately the same as that in which subjectivity obtains in so-called real life. Nettie's story testifies to the fact that the symbolic is, in the final instance, inescapable. But as a disruptive element in two of the novel's central cultural intertexts, the myth of heterosexual romance and the narrative of patriarchal history, the character also constitutes a configuration of a subversive sexuality in the text of *HD* and thus effectively challenges the closed intellectual system of dominant culture as such.

Reciprocal Inscriptions. The next scene begins in Stella's flat. Harrison happens to be present when Roderick phones his mother to vent his confusion about the new light Cousin Nettie has cast on his parents' divorce. On the point of taking her out to dinner, Harrison becomes Stella confidant—almost, but not quite, by accident. Although the gist of the ensuing talk has been discussed at an earlier point, there are several aspects of Stella's "confession" that deserve further attention here.

As usual in Bowen, the scene's spatial setting carries particular significance. Announced by a "dimmed sign, OPEN," the restaurant to which Harrison takes Stella presents itself as a counterpart to Holme Dene, with its forbidding notice on the driveway. In contrast to the family abode, the restaurant offers an open space. While the connection between these two chronotopes, representative of the private and the public domains, respectively, is primarily established in oppositional terms, their point of intersection is formed by the "uncanny" sexual subtext informing both. Unlike the earlier scene, in which we have seen an exploration of the closed system of heterosexuality, this sequence obliquely inquires into sexuality in its "OPEN" though culturally "dimmed" articulations. It is precisely in its explicit other worldliness that the space of the OPEN café acquires its significance as a subcultural realm. In their readings of this scene, earlier critics have correctly emphasized the weird atmosphere reigning in it. While Lee calls it a "nightmar[e]," Heath describes it as a "hallucinatory vision," and Lassner defines the episode as a whole as a "descent into hell."[10] I will take up the latter's suggestion only in order to move in quite a different direction.

As Gillian Spraggs has recently argued, hell has been the literary landscape for "those who rejected the gifts of God's Creation" to pursue "unnatural practices" ever since Dante's description of the *Inferno* in *The Divine Comedy*.[11] While the medieval category of "those who are 'violent against God'" comprised both "usurers" and homosexuals, in the course of the centuries hell became the "territory allocated specifically to homosexuals." Despite the fact that traditional Christianity has lost its firm grip on public Western culture, the "landscape of Hell continues to haunt the collective imagination," even in a largely "post-Christian society."[12] It is as the appropriate context for unrepenting sinners against God/nature (or sodomites) that hell has entered the tradition of lesbian literature. While, as Spraggs shows, hell has taken on a diversity of guises and meanings in contemporary literary texts, it was Radclyffe Hall's depiction in *The Well of Loneliness* (1928) of the gay bar in post–World War I Paris that set the pattern for a series of similar literary images turning the nether world of the underground bar into one of the central topoi of lesbian sexuality. But even if we disregard these specific intertextual allusions, Dante's depiction of hell as a desolate open plain "heated continually by huge flakes of flame which descend from above" reverberates throughout the scene at the OPEN café.[13] With its echoes of sodomy and usury, the space appears a fitting setting for Harrison, who is, after all, a "usurer," although the "currency" with which he ingeniously seeks to make a profit is not money but information, or rather, power/knowledge. It is, however, chiefly on account of his "hom(m)osexual" aspect that her diabolical interlocutor forces Stella to reconsider her views on her self and on her place in the world.

Upon entering the OPEN café, Stella is overwhelmed by a unnerving sense of exposure. Marking its physical quality, the heroine's sensation is signaled by the sight of a "zip fastener all the way down one back," which makes "one woman seem . . . to have a tin spine." In its X-ray directness, the OPEN café confronts Stella with her own enhanced powers of vision:

> Wherever she turned her eyes detail took on an uncanny salience—she marked the taut grimace with which a man carrying two full glasses to a table kept a cigarette down to its last inch between his lips. Not a person did not betray, by one or another glaring peculiarity, the fact of being human: her intimidating sensation of being crowded must have been due to this, for there were not so very many people here. The phenomenon was the lighting, more powerful even than could be accounted for by the bald white globes screwed aching to the low white ceiling—there survived in here not a shadow: every one had been ferreted out and killed. (225)

Driven out of her shaded existence, Stella is, for the first time it seems, looking with startling penetration at her Self in relation to (the) Other/s she had heretofore disregarded. Vaguely aware of its sexual undercurrents, she realizes that her process of self-consciousness is becoming a highly disturbing if not alarming experience. Since it is her relationship with Harrison that forms the enabling context of her (self-)discoveries, she is compelled to acknowledge that she can no longer dismiss him as a "nobody": she finds herself "look[ing] at and into [his] eyes with curiosity" (227). The resulting "echo of intimacy" betokens the sexual drive behind her quest for (self-)knowledge. Precisely because Harrison has let her give him "no place in the human scene," the feelings he arouses in Stella do not fit in with the scenario of normative heterosexuality. Such a sudden wave of affect toward the man she finds so difficult to "tape" proves to be "enough ... to set up resistance in her." In her subsequent outburst, Stella indirectly reveals that

Harrison, by not inviting her to play her accustomed gender role, has forced her to face long-repressed aspects of herself:

> "I simply do not care what I say to you. You're right: almost no one has heard this particular story—to be quite precise, no one I care for has. Not, if you want to know, most of all Robert—I should be ashamed, for one thing, to let him know that ever, however long ago, I could have cared so much for face. *There may be other reasons; if so I do not know them.* And not up to now—hence that scene this evening—Roderick. Between you and me, everything has been impossible from the first—so, the more unseemly the better, it seems to me. With you from the very beginning I've had no face: there's nothing to lose. There's an underside to me that I've hated, that you almost make me like: you and I never have had anything but impossible conversations: nothing else is possible." (227–28; italics mine)

As my emphasis suggests, the "underside" to Stella's subjectivity is largely unconscious in content. While underlining its locus in psychosexuality, the cultural "impossibility" of her repressed feelings renders it very appropriate that Stella acknowledges her disconcerting debt to Harrison in a subcultural spatial context chosen by him. Identifying the OPEN café as a "lie-detecting place," she is impelled to face parts of her personality that she had sought to obscure from even her own view. However terrifying, it is these substantial if not constitutive elements in the text of her self that have gone "into [her] making" (226).

Apart from recognizing her own "underside," Stella is ready to admit that there is not "any such thing as an innocent secret" (228). The implications are manifold. For one thing, the recognition forces her to see that, by having "arranged things to suit [her]self," she has denied Roderick a viable view on her character. Having "grown up swallowing what he's thought [she] did," he must have "somehow . . . made the person he thought did that into the person he's loved" (229). By concealing her past, she has allowed her son to construct her in the conventional image of the "disreputable mother" (196), providing him with a "false" heredity that he has sought to counterbalance with an "idealization of pattern." For another, Stella's insight into the disastrous effects of secrecy and concealment critically affect her uneasy considerations about Robert. The significance of the OPEN café as the counterpart to Holme Dene is at this point quite explicitly extended to the script of gendered heterosexuality: identifying Mrs. Kelway's screened domain of "fibs and subterfuges" as the "uncanny" breeding ground of obsessions and suspicions, Stella can no longer remain blind to the incriminating light such a place of origin sheds on that which it has produced, that is, on Robert. Once she has realized the implications of Mrs. Kelway's contemptuous (ab)use of language in its confounding effects on her lover's sense of masculine self, the inference that the latter's neurotic fears can only have led to political corruption becomes inescapable. When Harrison informs her that her lover has given himself away through slight changes of behavior since the upsetting talk in the car, she has no other option than to believe him.

Stella picks this moment to examine her eyebrows in her mirror. While indicating a need for reassurance about her continued existence, the mirror also forms another veiled allusion to the "dimmed" presence of lesbian sexuality haunting this textual space. In the essay cited earlier, Spraggs argues that the psychoanalytic notion of same-sex love as always to some degree marked by narcissism derives from the fact that much of Freud's work forms a "systematisation and refinement of folk belief." She notes that the "idea that a woman who loves another woman is merely loving herself in a mirror" has been part of "received masculine wisdom for centuries."[14] Stella looks at herself in the mirror at the moment when she faces the virtual collapse of the romantic illusion or, more precisely, when her place in the heterosexual matrix seems irretrievably lost. This reinforces my earlier suggestion that the heroine's confrontation with her hidden "underside" has given her a hold on a part of her self that falls outside the closed space of female heterosexuality. Her customary retreat into abstraction is no longer feasible; the irreversibility of Stella's insight is reflected in a "deadness . . . about her tone." At the same time, however, in the OPEN café, which allows for a "seeing of everybody by everybody else with . . . awful nearness and clearness," she also faces up to a new perspective on herself that, though disconcerting, provides her with an unwonted and necessarily "dimmed" sense of identity autonomous from the dominant cultural paradigm (232). This supposition is confirmed in the remainder of the sequence.

Filled with loathing for Harrison for making her feel so helpless, Stella finds herself moved by a passionate desire to hurt and humiliate him. She reasserts herself by aiming at the very basis from which his power derives: his phallocratic superiority. Noticing a young woman who is trying to catch Harrison's attention—"ungirt, artless, ardent, urgent" Louie Lewis, whom we remember from the novel's opening scene—she invites the latter to their table, so that the tête-à-tête between Harrison and herself is abruptly brought to an end (235). Drawing an immediate circle of intimacy around herself and the other woman, Stella renders Harrison's symbolic power momentarily ineffectual by excluding him from the conversation. Emphatically disengaging herself from him, she in effect sidesteps the system of heterosexual difference and, behaving "indifferently as though Harrison were nothing more than a stuffed figure" (237), she declares his symbolic power irrelevant. Aggravated beyond endurance, Harrison breaks all conventions of civilized behavior and lashes out at Stella and Louie alike. Startled into a realization of the factual reach of his power, Stella checks herself and tactfully makes an attempt at appeasement. She points out to Louie that Harrison is "in trouble." Her next words reveal that she has not only sobered up to the potential of her antagonist's aggression but has also taken into account the contingency of all meanings:

"Nothing ever works out the way one hoped, and to know how bitter that is one must be a worker-out. . . . This is the truth. . . . He cannot bear it; let's hope he will forget it—let's hope that; it is the least we can do; we're all three human. At any time it may be your hour or mine—you and I may be learning some terrible human lesson which is to undo everything we had thought we had. It's that, not death, that we ought live prepared for." (240) [15]

Although her appeal to their common humanity appears sincere, Harrison, vexed by the fact that he has allowed the "hom(m)osexual" underpinnings of his schemes to be exposed, is not so easily placated. Hurt in his masculine pride, he too reasserts himself— and with a vengeance.

Stella, strengthened by her perception of the stakes in her antagonist's power/knowledge games, further challenges Harrison by conveying that she is finally prepared to exchange her body for her lover's safety. He, in his turn, declares Stella's femininity of no value: he flatly rejects her and proceeds by sending away both women. Fully aware of the unviability of their bond in the outside world, Harrison can safely suggest that "the two of [them] go along together." It is thus ultimately his superior sociosymbolic power that allows the counterspy to regain control over the situation. This he underscores by contemptuously snapping at Stella, "pale again with stupidity," to "get the bill." The scene concludes with Harrison's rhetorically asking whether she "think[s] a bill pays itself" (240).

Suspended Action/The Act of Suspension. Despite her insight into the ways in which both Harrison and Robert utilize their superior symbolic power, Stella cannot help being subordinated to their plot. In her relation to each man, she ends up feeling that she has "no idea how we left it" (285). Whereas she uses this phrase with reference to the scene at the OPEN café, it equally pertains to the inconclusive end of her affair with Robert. The latter's appreciation of the remark reveals that what he regards as her "ineffectuality" is indeed the condition of his love for her:

The expression on those lips of hers was familiar—its many contexts, vagrant, social, so very much not mattering, had become too many for

[Robert] to count. It had come as the end, or rather the fading-out, of so many stories at the end of so many days; or, as a sort of confession as to why many stories, now that she came to tell them, had no ending. So much had had to be left in the air, so often, that her manner of saying so, every time, always had the same intonation—of fatalism of fleeting but true regret [*sic*]. She had been given the slip once more. "I've no idea how we left it." Ineffectual little expression, blent of boredom and chagrin, it had become conventional; but, at the same time, a sort of convention or shorthand of lovers' talk, stamped with a temperament and endeared by use. She had said this so many times: again it was said tonight— and the monstrous, life-and-death disproportion between tonight's context and all that host of others did not, could not, stand out as it should. She did not sound, so could not seem to be feeling, very much more inadequate than she ever had felt. Which was enough to make Robert laugh. (285)

Robert's amusement will turn out to be not quite justified: what he reads as his lover's—endearing—helplessness, that is, the inability to reach the conventional moment of (dis)closure in the course of a traditional narrative, is not merely a sign of the culturally imposed restraints on Stella's symbolic efficacy. It also represents a strategy of subversion—one that, as we shall see shortly, operates on both the intra- and the extradiegetic levels of the text.

Robert's death, jointly announced with the "Allied landings in North Africa," gains significance by coinciding with this milestone event in the text of history. Its promise of liberation notwithstanding, the latter event rapidly results in "people . . . turning away from the illusion" of an approaching victory (291). Signaling that Stella's ordeal is not over yet, the concurrence further demonstrates that the structure of crisis is an ontological condition of both history and subjectivity, an inherent aspect of these equally indeterminate processes.

Stella's suspended position at the end of the spy plot thus not only marks a transgression against narrative conventions; it additionally reflects the contingent and provisional nature of any temporary fixings in the process of meaning production. This is substantiated by the fact that the novel does not end with the inconclusive endings of either the love story or the spy plot. When we next meet Stella, she is sitting on a train, the suggestion of transition again signifying the continuation of her process of self-consciousness. The emotional shock caused by Robert's death proves to have alerted the heroine anew to the inscription of her story and its possible meanings within the larger sociohistorical text: her "eyes themselves [are] exposed for ever to what they saw, subjected to whatever chose to be seen" (294). Although Stella feels that it "would have been easy to recline, to become suffused by indifference, to be thankful that all was over," her shift in perspective on what is actually a "different" self necessitates a reconsideration of all her (dialogic) relationships. She appeals to her son in the hope of grasping the meanings of her lover's acts and their consequences.

Roderick's unquestioning love, the "pity, speaking to her out of the stillness of his face" (296), gives the heroine the strength to accept that "it was not [over], yet": the "rest was not yet ready to be silence" (298). Feeling that "one has no right to tell anybody anything as to which there's nothing to be said," Stella knows that she must talk to her son nonetheless, for meaning can only be arrived at in language, in dialogue: "'Of course there is something to be said. There must be. There's *something* to be said'" (299). It is Roderick who inadvertently hits upon the only "truth" that the material crisis of the times has left intact, exposing the illusory nature of any claim to transcendent Truth:

I couldn't bear to think of you waiting on and on and on for something, something that in a flash would give what Robert did and what happened enormous meaning like there is in a play of Shakespeare's—but, must you? If there's something that *is* to be said, won't it say itself? Or mayn't you come to imagine it has been said, even without your knowing what exactly it was? ... Robert's dying of what he did will not always be there, won't last like a book or picture: by the time one is able to understand it it will be gone, it just won't be there to be judged. Because, I suppose art is the only thing that can go on mattering once it has stopped hurting? (300)

After this shattering analysis of the founding assumptions of the central regimes of Western thought, Stella's story is temporarily disrupted by the narrator's summarizing the two years following "Robert's end."

We learn that "few outward changes" marked the "subsidence of the under soil" that caused "gradients [to] alter, uprights [to] cant a little out of the straight . . . without the surface having been visibly broken." This indicates that the changes in the text of the heroine's ostensibly "straight" self have taken effect on the largely invisible level of the unconscious. Such shifts surface in the fact that she, leaving the artificial enclosure of her accustomed habitat behind her, "moved across London into another flat." While "Harrison vanished" altogether, the Kelways, not surprisingly, "stayed where they were" (301). The protagonist's response to Harrison's disappearance underscores that, despite the placid surface of her appearance, "internally, tensions shifted":

After the night climax in Weymouth Street, Harrison made no move to contact Stella, and she did not know how to contact him: their extraordinary relationship having ended in mid air, she found she missed it— Harrison became the only living person she would have given anything to see. Ultimately, it was *his* silent absence which left her with absolutely nothing. She never, then, was to know what had happened? (301)

Not satisfied with leaving things in midair this time, Stella is determined to speak or, to put it differently, to author the meanings of her experience. She is once again frustrated by her lack of power/ knowledge, for, ignorant of Harrison's whereabouts, she is unable fully to grasp the significance of either their relationship or Robert's death. When the third-person narrative perspective is in its turn interrupted by a long passage of direct speech in which Stella hesitatingly gives her account of that last elusive night, the text appears to reestablish her in her role of symbolic ineffectuality, literally presenting her as merely a "good witness" (305).

Unlike her protagonist, the narrator does not feel hampered by a lack of symbolic agency. An extraordinary passage of journalistic prose disrupts the narrative line for a second time. The major historical events of the years 1942–1943 are recounted and linked up with the characters featured in the novel's two subplots. Only then do we reencounter Harrison, "back again," appearing on the doorstep of Stella's new flat. Amid the deafening "overhead throbbing and the bark of guns" announcing the final phase of the war, he and Stella find themselves "star[ing] at one another" (315). Stella invites him in, pointing out with a "vagrant, echo-aroused smile" that "nothing," not even the cat she is holding in her arms, is hers. The similarities between her present situation and that of two years ago would seem to suggest that Stella has reverted to her long-standing practice of disengagement. But her desire to speak and her need to know indicate that a change has taken effect.

Since Harrison is, as always, reluctant to communicate any information, it is the heroine who speaks first:

"I wish you had come before. There was a time when I had so much to say to you. There once was so much I wanted to know. After I gave up thinking I should see you again, I still went on talking and talking to you in my own mind—so I cannot really have felt you were dead, I think, because one doesn't go on talking and talking to any one of *them:* more one goes on hearing what they said, piecing and repiecing it together to try and make out something they had not time to say—possibly even had not had time to know. . . . Yes, I missed you. *Your* dropping out left me with completely nothing. What made you?" (317)

Indicative of the critical role played by this "nobody" in the heroine's story, it is thus Harrison rather than Robert in relation to whom Stella has continued to position herself. Urging him to tell her what happened on the fatal night of her lover's death, she finds out that the counterspy had been "switched" out of the game the night before (319). This coincidence confirms the "hom(m)osexual" identification between the two male characters. Deprived of her hope that Harrison might yet solve the riddle at the center of the spy/love plot, Stella must face the inconclusive nature of this or, for that matter, any story. While the "lofty drumming of the raider" seems to promise that "one kind of utter solution was in the offing," she is forced to accept that "no, it was not to be that way," for in the end "nothing fell." She concedes that perhaps there is "no right *or* wrong to it after all" (319). By thus withholding the moment of "*closure* which is also disclosure," the text not only frustrates Stella's hope of a "dissolution of the enigma";[16] it also undermines conventionalized reading expectations. By leaving the endings of the fiction of heterosexual romance as well as the male spy plot literally in midair, *HD* effectively subverts these joint narrative tracts of masculine desire, rendering their resolution basically irrelevant.

The recognition of the arbitrary nature of her story and its moral allows Stella to reconsider her relationships with both Harrison and Robert. Pointing out that there is no going back to the past, since "one never is where one was," she is led to wonder whether Harrison "were . . . then, somehow, love's necessary missing part" (320). Rather than binding her more closely to him, the acknowledgment of his constitutive role in the narrative of love releases Stella from the spell that Harrison's presumed power to resolve its plot had continued to cast on her. Exploding the myth of his all-powerfulness by exposing its fundamentally interdependent character, she conclusively rejects her position as object in the system of male exchange: "You and I are no longer two of three. From between us some pin has been drawn out: we're apart. We're not where we were—look, not even any more in the same room. The pattern's been swept away, so where's the meaning? Think!" (320). Exposing the fragility of the heterosexual contract, Stella liberates herself from its constraints. Empowered with a new sense of symbolic agency, she can finally afford to call Harrison's bluff. She asks him point-blank "what [he] *did* . . . want, then, when it came to the point." His failure to respond corroborates Stella's earlier suspicions about the stakes of the male characters' power/ knowledge game. She further challenges Harrison's heterosexual (in)adequacy by maintaining that he "did not know what to do" at the time. His embarrassed reaction to such a check on his masculinity enables her finally to solicit the incontrovertible proof of his "hidden" sexual aims. When she suggests that he "stay tonight," she is met with utter silence on his part, even though he has made a number of insinuating remarks to this effect himself. Stella's speculations about her object status within the male "hom(m)osexual" plot are presently verified. No longer functioning as the Other in the system of Same-sex exchange, she has lost whatever value she may have had. Harrison, the obsessive schemer, furthermore clarifies that he never expected her "to do anything for nothing" (321). Therewith the central aspect of Stella's "riddle" is resolved: by calling into question Harrison's heterosexual potential, Stella has hit upon the very basis of anxiety underlying the myth of masculinity and, a fortiori, upon the crucial function of the "dark continent" of female sexuality in sustaining phallogocentric culture.

The heroine's subsequent announcement of her intended marriage to a "cousin of a cousin" provokes an "expression of a violent, fundamental relief" from Harrison. While releasing him from any obligations in a field in which he, we recall, is "naturally off his ground," this also provides him with the opportunity to reassume his place in the "hom(m)osexual" economy. He immediately starts voicing his concern about her safety "on behalf of an unknown somebody else," claiming that it is "far from fair to the chap" that Stella continues to expose herself to the danger of the air raids (321–22). Although this attempt to draw her back into his scheme succeeds in exciting the "old irritation" in her, Stella is no longer liable to its confining designs. When Harrison starts admonishing her to take her "prospects" into account, she retorts that "prospects have alternatives." Affirming her unwillingness to accept the closure of the heterosexual contract in marital or any other terms, Stella concludes their dispute by declaring that she has "always . . . left things open" (322). Underlining the ambivalence of her own (sexual) orientation, these words bring Stella's story to an appropriately indeterminate end. In the remainder of the text the last stages of the war are recorded and the two subplots are wrapped up. Since Stella's suspended position in the novel's main plot is offset by the conclusion of one of the subplots, I will briefly examine its development before showing the interconnections between them.

Discourse in Crisis

Slipping Authority. As we have seen, the note of uncertainty on which Bowen's early novel *LS* ends primarily concerns the heroine's plight: the lack of resolution is situated on the intradiegetic level of the text only. The ultimate termination of Danielstown by the narrator indicates that at this point in her career, Bowen still believed in the power of language to impose "meaningful shape" onto an otherwise incoherent reality. Such faith in the practice of signification had suffered a severe blow by the time she wrote *HD*, the novel marking the midstage of her career. The author's preoccupation with the ambivalence of discursive operations was validated in a most disturbing manner by a war of "dry cerebration" whose origins she located in "conversations" carried out "inside windowless walls." Language, and in particular the regulatory regimes of phallogocentrism and compulsory heterosexuality, surface both explicitly and obliquely in the war novel's main plot: in Mrs. Kelway's contemptuous denunciation of words as "dead currency" and their connection with her function as castrating force in the myth of masculinity, in her son Robert's paranoia and corruption as a result of the closed system of binary thought, in Harrison's cunning exploitation of platitudes in the service of a collapsing moral order, and in Stella's worries about her own place and that of her sex in the "august book" of history, as well as her realization of the constraints imposed on her by her culturally prescribed role in the narrative of love. Although subdued in its actual manifestations, sexuality operates as a structuring force in the narrative exploration of these issues. It is in one of the subplots, however, that the inherent ambivalence of discursive effects and their moral implications are explicitly addressed in terms of the technologies of gendered sexuality.

The central character in this minor story is Louie Lewis, a lower-middle-class woman whose husband Tom is with the army in India.[17] The first impression we receive of her is Harrison's perception of her mouth: "Halted and voluble, this could but be a mouth that blurted rather than spoke, a mouth incontinent and at the same time artless" (11). Louie's inarticulacy is at once foregrounded in its connection with her "artless" and "incontinent" body. Lacking in verbal power, she asserts herself by exploiting a "sort of clumsy not quite graceless pre-adolescent strength," being "ready, nay, eager to attach herself to anyone who could seem to be following any one course with certainty" (11, 15). To her flat in Chilcombe Street she brings, after a day's work at the factory, the soldiers she has formed the habit of picking up.

Louie has, "with regard to time, an infant lack of stereoscopic vision": to her "everything seemed to be going on at once." The suggestion that the character has failed to internalize the meanings of sexual difference *as a result* of her inarticulacy thoroughly undermines the state-of-nature hypothesis that presupposes a precultural or prediscursive binary frame of sex. Her lack of a "normal" gender identity does not mean, however, that Louie is free of the apparatus by means of which the sexes are produced; nor is she so naïve as to fail to notice "all men to be one way funny like Tom—no sooner were their lips unstuck from your own than they began again to utter morality" (17). Her very inability to understand this "funny" quality in men alerts us to the gendered aspects of (sexual) morality and symbolic power. Denying her the right to an active sexual desire of her own, the men whose needs Louie is willing to fulfill seek to contain the physical—and potentially castrating—power she embodies by first enjoying and then denouncing it on moral grounds. The disparity in terms of symbolic agency renders Louie helpless. Ignorant and inarticulate, she is by definition the loser in the battle between the sexes, for even if she does not provoke male "sexual anger" by being "disobliging," it seems that "everything still ended in her being told off" (19).

Louie is lost in the "unsettling" maze of London and the complex cultural mores of city life. While living through her body, she has not mastered the language in which (self-) representations obtain and hence has not acquired any consciousness of herself in gendered terms. She is "swept along in one shoal of indifferent shadows against another." Having failed in the "business" of losing her "innocence," Louie has no place in the fallen world of human history: whenever she is unable to express herself comprehensibly, a "look of animal trouble" passes over her face. Her inability to make herself known, the reason why "to be seen [is] for her not to be," springs from the fact that she is not recognizable as a human, that is, gender-differentiated, being: she "bulk[s] ahead through the dark with the sexless flat-footed nonchalance of a ten-year-old" (145–46). In her virtual presymbolic state, she often visits a "mirrored" café, where she can enjoy the "satisfaction of seeing, in bright steaminess, herself, Louie, walk in, look round, and sit down" (147). She thus appears to be detained in what Lacan defines as the "mirror phase," the period in which the infant has acquired a primitive notion of itself as a being separate from the mother through its identification with its own mirror image; it is nonetheless only upon its entry into language, into the symbolic order, that full subjectivity can be achieved.[18] Louie's sense of "being of meaning only to an absent person," that is to say, of overall "unmeaning," is temporarily relieved by the arrival at Chilcombe Street of ARP warden Connie, a figure who defies the duality of sexual categories.

The "uniformed newcomer," who combines a "brick-red postbox mouth" with a "scissor-like stride in . . . dark blue official slacks," is an interesting attempt on Bowen's part to create a character endowed with conflicting gender attributes. Occasionally bordering on the ridiculous, the portrait is adorned with several of the stereotypical trappings of the "mannish lesbian."[19] Connie's "unfixed" sexual identity renders her an eligible counterpart to the sexless Louie. For before Connie becomes drawn to the latter's "vacuum," the "preadolescent" has been most aware of her lack among "real" women:

The actual trouble at the factory was, that you had to have something to say, tell, swop, and Louie was unable to think of anything. She felt she did not make sense, and still worse felt that the others knew it. *Women seemed to feel that she had not graduated*; where *had* she been all her life, they wanted to know—and, oh, where had she? It is advantageous being among all sorts if you are some sort, any sort; you gravitate to your type. It is daunting if you discover you are still no sort—the last hope gone. (149; first italics mine)

Whereas Louie's sexlessness results in indiscriminateness, Connie takes up a position in between sexual "sorts," partaking of both. With her "doughty shoes" and her "dark spare behind," she has no difficulty "stand[ing] upright" and making her presence known by "swearing as though the house were hers: in that line she was royal" (150). Her "masculine" self-assertion is directly related to the gender bender's favorite pastime, a voracious reading of newspapers. Her appropriation of the (printed) word has further enabled her to assume her unLawful position within the symbolic order.

Eager to please her new friend, Louie seizes upon "Connie's addiction" as something to "imitate." "Having begun by impressing Connie," however, she finds that "newspapers went on to infatuate [her] out-and-out" (151). Anticipating the dangers of the uninitiated's unquestioning faith in the language of the Law, the narrator wryly observes: "In the beginning was the word; and to that it came back in the long run. This went for anything written down." The effects of Louie's new habit give us a fair insight into the constraining operations of dominant ideology. Having "begun in the middle," the gullible creature has no frame of reference to assess any of the official war accounts. Imbibing the news as gospel truth, she allows her experiences to be falsified and successively altered: "Once you looked in the papers you saw where it said, nothing was so bad as it might look. What a mistake, to have gone by the look of things!" The "innocent" prove to be a primary target for ideological interpellation:

For the paper's sake, Louie brought herself to put up with any amount of news—the headlines got that over for you in half a second, deciding for you every event's importance by the size of the print. . . . But it was from the articles in the papers that the real build-up, the alimentation came— Louie, after a week or two on the diet, discovered that she *had* got a point of view, and not only *a* point of view but the right one. Not only did she bask in warmth and inclusion but every morning and evening she was praised. Even the Russians were apparently not as dissatisfied with her as she had feared; there was Stalingrad going on holding out, but here was she in the forefront of the industrial war drive. As for the Americans now in London, they were stupefied by admiration for her character. Dark and rare were the days when she failed to find on the inside page of her paper an address to or else an account of herself. (152)

Unable to qualify the nutrition provided by the papers, Louie is horrified to find that such ego sustenance does not pertain to all aspects of her life, especially not in the field in which she is most "lacking":

Was she not a worker, a soldier's lonely wife, a war orphan, a pedestrian, a Londoner, a home- and animal-lover, a thinking democrat, a movie-goer, a woman of Britain, a letter writer, a fuel-saver, and a housewife? She was only not a mother, a knitter, a gardener, a foot-sufferer, or a sweetheart—at least not rightly. Louie now felt bad only about any part of herself which in any way did not fit into the papers' picture; she could not have survived their disapproval. They did not, for instance, leave flighty wives or good-time girls a leg to stand on; and how rightly—she had romped through a dozen pieces on that subject with if anything rather special zest, and was midway through just one more when the blast struck cold. Could it be that the papers were out with *Louie?*—she came over gooseflesh, confronted by God and Tom. (152)

The slightly derisory tone of the passage does nothing to detract from the acute analysis it presents of the ways in which the regulatory regimes of phallogocentrism and compulsory heterosexuality jointly operate in the service of dominant power/knowledge. While subscribing to the psychological necessity of sexual positioning, the final lines irrefutably situate the bounds of officially endorsed female identities within the confines of the two principal constructs underlying Western civilization: the mutually reinforcing discourses of patriarchy and Christianity.

Once "reinstated" by yet another favorable self-representation, Louie's feeling for newspapers "enters a deeper phase." Coming to "love newspapers physically," she adopts the role of the nurturing wife/mother towards the Word of the Father. While she is moved by a "solicitude for their gallant increasing thinness" and "long[s] to feed [and] fondle" them, Connie, on the other hand, having the "*droit du seigneur* over any newspaper entering the house," treats them with "sensual roughness." Set up in these divergent positions in relation to the symbolic/phallus, Louie, displaying the features of symbiotic dependence conventionally connoted as "feminine," feeds on and is at the same time devoured by the Law's "everlasting arms." Connie, "suspicious[ly] reading between the lines," maintains a certain aloofness and thus occupies the imaginary position of autonomy that, as a rule, is the "masculine" prerogative (153). This allows the latter some critical distance and thus a measure of symbolic agency, preventing her from being as totally immersed in established truths and meanings as her young friend. The mocking tone of voice in which the narrator relates Connie's "informed" views on the war and the world nonetheless make

clear that she, too, is subjected to ideology's interpellating operations and is indeed effectively deluded into subscribing to the jingo-
ist notions transmitted by the powers that be.

Although Connie's "masculine" aspects are throughout foregrounded, she is not presented as a caricature of the male. Her
superior attitude toward Louie and her self-important professional
stance are set off against equally conspicuous "feminine" attributes: the "bobby-pins" trimming her "fringe," the "lace blouse"
she combines with her "uniform slacks," the "pearl ear-ring" going
with her "tunic" (156–57). Rather than representing the stereotypical *femme manquée,* the figure thus defies the binary terms of
sexual difference. As such, she enables Louie to feel less oppressed
by her palpable lack of self-awareness. If one or both of these
characters come in for an arguably objectionable form of narrative
scorn, the active principles of Connie's personality contrast favorably with Louie's condemning helplessness. Even the girl's tears are
not intended to invite our pity: since "tears need volition to form
and fall," they amount to no more than a "glaze on this idiot's
cheekbones" (156). By appropriating a role within the sociosymbolic order, Connie, in contrast, has empowered herself to subvert
some of the established system's rules. She does so both at the ARP
post (where she shows a "feminine" warmth and kindness) and in
her relation to Louie. While occasionally treating her protégée like
the archetypal husband, the gender bender does not pass any of the
moral judgments that the younger woman justifiably fears from
"God and Tom." The former's overall attitude intimates a sense of
protectiveness rather than reprobation.

The unorthodox same-sex relationship is clearly preferable to
Louie's heterosexual one-night stands. We furthermore note that
the relationship is mediated by, if not founded on, the word. But,
while the text thereby situates female homoeroticism within the
symbolic order, rather than enclosing it within a presymbolic or
preoedipal stage, it also suggests its confinement to a particular
(lower) social class. The displacement of lesbian sexuality to a

lower level in the cultural hierarchy is reinforced by its being shifted to a lower narrative level of the text: while haunting the edges of the novel's major plot, the lesbian "specter" surfaces directly only in one of the subplots.

Crossing Lines. We have seen that Stella's and Louie's stories intersect at the OPEN café. The bar's intertextual value as a sexually overdetermined subcultural space renders its function as the characters' meeting point particularly significant. When the younger woman returns home that night, she is filled with a wish to "speak of Stella" but feels hampered by her inability to use words properly. Louie has never before felt the need to make herself "known" in any other than the biblical sense. After all, as she points out to Connie: "'There's always this with a man—it need not have to come up what you cannot say'" (246). But if male interest in female silence/ignorance has thus far allowed Louie to believe that "there never used to be any necessity *to* say," tonight she "felt what she had not felt before—was it even she herself who was feeling?" (246, 248). Her encounter with Stella, whose "shaped lips" had been "shaping what they ought not" (247), has given this "nothing" a disconcerting glimpse of unknown possibilities. By provoking in Louie a strong need to "make [her]self understood" (246), Stella has left the guileless creature in a state of emotional confusion. The girl's bewilderment shows all the ambivalence of an overwhelming erotic desire, wavering between a longing to be one with as well as to know this other:

Louie felt herself entered by what was foreign. She exclaimed in thought: "Oh no, I wouldn't be *her!*" at the moment when she most nearly was. . . . She felt what she had not felt before—*was* it, even she herself who was feeling? . . . Here now was Louie sought out exactly as she had sought to be: it is in nature to want what you want so much too much that you must recoil when it comes. . . . Louie dwelled on Stella with mistrust and addiction, dread and desire. (247–48)

When Louie reads about Robert's fall from the roof the next day, her desire initially strengthens. In her naïvety, she inadvertently hits upon the truth underlying the cover story by confusing its two featuring male characters: the "ill-fated officer's behaviour ... seemed to her in its rabid suspiciousness, its unloving ruthlessness and its queerness [!], to have been that of Harrison exactly" (305). The suggestive terms in which the tabloid papers depict Stella's entanglement in the enigmatic triangle, however, do not fail to affect the mindless girl. Since her moral conceptions are shaped by the popular press, these relays of bourgeois convention lead Louie to a despair of what she has learned to accept as "female virtue."

Stella's face had "attract[ed] aspiration" in Louie, had made her feel "to be in a presence," but the circumstance that she is publicly denounced makes it seem that "it was Stella who had fallen into the street." Her susceptibility to the seductive power of words and her unreflective faith in their ostensible transparency thus allows for another falsification of the girl's experience. The narrator steps in to condemn the moral framework conducive to such denunciations and clarifies Louie's reaction:

It was the blanks in Louie's vocabulary which operated inwardly on her soul; most strongly she felt the undertow of what she could not name. Humble and ambiguous, she was as unable to name virtue as she had been, until that sudden view of Harrison's companion, to envisage it. Two words she *had,* "refinement," "respectability," were for her somewhere on the periphery. In search of what should make for completeness and cast out fear she indistinctly saw virtue as the inverse of sex: at the same time, somehow, it had distress, of one kind or another, as its sublime prerogative—Had not Louie herself felt distress in Stella, owing to Harrison? ... She could not but be out of her sphere here, nonplussed, a wanderer from a better star. It had been much to find in the world one creature too good for the world.

She had not been too good. Here, and not in one paper only, was where it said about her, the bottles, the lover, the luxury West-End flat. She had had other men friends; there nearly had been a fight. It all came down to a matter of expansiveness; there was no refinement. ... There was nobody to admire; there was no alternative. No unextinguished watch-light remained, after all, burning in any window, however far away. (306–7)

The passage underscores that the ethical value of Woman in patriarchy is—paradoxically—located in her sex(lessness). It furthermore confirms that it is by virtue of the system of compulsory heterosexuality that established gender relations can be maintained: by rendering erotic relations among women at once unnameable and "morally" impossible, this regulatory regime operates so as to preclude any potential disruption of the social contract.

Left "in a vacuum" by her disillusionment, Louie returns to her "vagrant habits" (307) and ends up pregnant. She once again appeals to Connie for (self-)authentication: "'I don't know how I should feel: I could equally laugh or cry. Whatever *is* this?—I've got to see from you'" (324). Since his wife's "passiveness biggen[s] with her body" (326), Connie accepts the task of informing Tom about Louie's condition. Her exonerating letter is made redundant by the news of Tom's death. When the "whole of the story narrow[s] down to Louie," we have reached the text's concluding pages. In September 1944, the young mother arrives at Seale-on-Sea with her newly born son. The final scene—two years after the novel's opening—presents Louie holding up her baby to see "three swans . . . flying a straight flight . . . disappearing in the direction of the west" (330).

Rather than a distinctly positive symbol, representing the "unconscious natural will to survive and produce life"[20] or affirming that "only the very simple . . . can find happiness . . . in the cycle of nature,"[21] the novel's concluding image forms a questionable counterpart to Stella's position of indeterminacy.[22] Although the heroine's stance conveys a sense of despair at Western civilization, expressing a deep suspicion of the regenerative potential of an oppressive, phallogocentric order, Louie's recourse to nature as a "thoughtless extension of her now complete life" (329) can hardly be considered to suggest a viable alternative. As an image of "naturalness" or "simplicity" the character is indeed highly suspect, considering Bowen's forthright rejection of such notions. Furthermore, as the epitome of symbolic inadequacy, Louie has consistently been placed in a decidedly negative light. The fact that her son is "christened Thomas Victor" reaffirms her unself-conscious subjection to the constraints imposed by prevailing technologies of gender. Her story shows that the assumption of a "naturally" sexed body as a precultural or prediscursive given is no more and no less than an ideologically produced effect. Serving as the legitimating ground of a system of hierarchical power relations, it is this very state-of-nature hypothesis that renders the female subject into the ideal vessel for reproduction—not only quite literally but also with regard to the discourses through which the power of the paternal heir is sustained. Confined to her "state of nature," Louie unwittingly perpetuates the self-same structures by which she is reduced to a virtual nonentity. The figure therefore becomes a highly unlikely representation of potential redemption.

If the novel's endnote is sufficiently bleak, Stella's stance is qualified by a degree of potentially redemptive self-awareness. As I have argued above, the inconclusive resolution of the novel's main plot forms a defiance of narrative conventions predicated on the mythical plot of masculine desire. But the double displacement of an alternative mode of desirous exchange, that is, the relegation of lesbian sex/textuality to a lower level in the narrative hierarchy as well to a lower level in the class system subtending the diegesis as a whole, suggests that the conservative postwar climate in which the novel was produced put severe restrictions on what Bowen had been able to write about quite unreservedly in the 1920s and 1930s: female same-sex relationships. Stella's insistence on the open-endedness (rather than a subversion) of the story of heterosexual romance hence also appears to indicate that the social formation in which the novel was written placed stricter bounds on the construction and negotiation of particular meanings than before. Still, while the heroine's quest attests to the author's enhanced wariness of any of the established regimes of power/knowledge, Stella's suspended position nonetheless conveys ambivalence rather than despair at the enabling potential of narrative discourse. In the following chapters we will see how Bowen's ideas about the operations of language evolved in its most constitutive and simultaneously most elusive aspects, that is, in its produced/producing effects on psychosexuality.

6

Subtexts of Psychosexuality

What a slippery fish is identity; and what *is* it besides a slippery fish?

—*Eva Trout*

The Inscription of Creation in Eva Trout (1969)

Structuring Stylistics. Eva Trout or Changing Scenes (hereafter, *ET*), as the full title of Bowen's tenth and final novel reads, was published forty-odd years after her first (*The Hotel,* 1927) and twenty years after the appearance of her seventh (*HD*). Since 1949, two volumes of nonfictional writings, a historical work, two more novels, a travel book, a children's book, and her last collection of short stories had been published.[1] The only work to appear in print after *ET* was *Pictures and Conversations* (1975), the unfinished set of autobiographical essays published posthumously two years after Bowen's death in 1973. At once suggesting a departure from earlier narrative scenes and marking a change in the author's sociohistorical setting, the novel's subtitle also heralds an alteration in the textual surface itself, a shift in terms of style and/or narrative method. Whereas the last two emphases are certainly borne out by the text, the suggestion of a change in narrative scene is somewhat misleading. The controlling theme of *ET* signifies a different angle on Bowen's lasting subject matter rather than a deviation from it. Since the author considered the object of the novel to be the "non-poetic statement of a poetic truth," the essence of which is "that no statement of it is final," it is not surprising to find her returning to her abiding preoccupations in what was to become her last story.[2] *ET* is, quite appropriately, also an exploration of "origins." Placed in relation to *LS* (1929) and *HD* (1949), which mark the beginning and the middle of Bowen's writing career, respectively, the novel inevitably acquires additional significance by virtue of being this writer's final statement of her "poetic truth." It represents Bowen's last novelistic effort to explore the constitution of (female) sexuality/subjectivity.

Although *ET* offers no change in terms of thematics, it does represent a shift in perspective when compared to *HD*, a difference in outlook that is similar to that between the author's war novel and her "recall book," *LS*. As we have seen, the early novel's emphasis on the constraining effects of the ideological patterns of outside "reality" upon the developing subjectivity of the young heroine provides the "internal combustion" upon which, according to Bowen, the "movement [of] plot depends."[3] The war novel, on the other hand, presents the dynamics of crisis situated in external rather than internal forces, in the material collapse of the sociosymbolic structures in relation to which the middle-aged protagonist is forced to (re)define herself. In *ET*, both external and internal "reality" are rendered as continually "Changing Scenes." The flux, the disruptive or destabilizing elements of the interdependent processes of history and subjectivity are newly articulated both in the novel's textuality and in its eponymous heroine. *ET* confronts us with a protagonist who is not so much in transition as "larger-than-life." Her unfocused existence is reflected in the variety of spatial and temporal settings against which her story evolves. The sense of fragmentation resulting from the novel's haphazard plot development is amplified by its discursive surface. Especially in the early chapters, the narrative voice is uncharacteristically equivocal, while the overall stylistic mode is impressionistic rather than controlled and precise. Ostensibly unable to contain, either the story or its protagonist, the text highlights the crucial role of language in the proliferation *and* the dispersal of meaning. Since the distinction between outside and inside dislocation—already tenuous in the earlier novels—is now entirely abolished, the disconcerting effects of such (discursive) decenteredness are fully dramatized on both the extra- and the intradiegetic levels of the text.

Before going into the significance of the novel's stylistic attributes, I want to mention a further aspect in which *ET* perpetuates a line of exploration running through and connecting all of the author's previous work. Two major Bowen themes, the operation of the past in the present and its relation to the question of identity, are once again central preoccupations. In *ET*, these two thematic lines intertwine in such a way that, instead of focusing on the interpenetration of the sociohistoric past and the individual's present, the text zooms in on the protagonist's personal history as the constitutive force in the process of meaning production. Cast in psychoanalytic terms, the narrative of *ET* is a case history that specifically concerns the heroine's (non)acquisition of a (hetero)sexual gender identity. Covering Eva's life span up to and including her death at age thirty-two, the novel resembles *LS* and *HD* in that it presents an "adolescent" heroine who—as an "open psychic structure"—personifies the condition of crisis inherent in subjectivity as such.[4] This is, paradoxically, at the same time the aspect in which Bowen's last novel differs crucially from the earlier ones. Eva Trout is neither struggling to attain nor compelled to realize the precarious nature of an established sense of self. Her "case" shows the effects of a suspended process of symbolic inscription. More accurately, her story depicts what happens when a (female) subject does not effectively enter the phallogocentric order and so fails to take up her proper position within the Law.

Its significance as a case history notwithstanding, the suggestive value of the protagonist's name, the title of the novel's first part ("Genesis"), and the central place of the oedipal plot or "family romance" in Eva's story[5] raise the novel from its particular to a more general level. Rather than constituting a narrative of psychological development in the tradition of classic realism, *ET* engages the metanarratives of Christian (patriarchal) culture and of psychoanalysis as two of the founding conceptual schemes of twentieth-century Western society. While firmly set in the here and now, the novel transcends its boundaries as a traditional social comedy or bildungsroman by advancing a fundamental critique of Western metaphysics in a story of development that is cast in virtually epic terms.

These observations may to some extent explain why a critic like Hermione Lee denounces *ET* as an "unfocussed and bizarre conclusion to [Bowen's] *opus*." While identifying the author's late techniques as signs of an increasing concern with the "concept of the breakdown of language," Lee refrains from further exploring the issue, putting down the narrative and stylistic idiosyncrasies of Bowen's last two novels as "failures of assurance" resulting in deplorably "clumsy procedures."[6] Such criticisms are echoed in Patricia Craig's assertion that in *ET*, the "author has let her mannered manner run away with her." Failing to place the novel in its larger philosophical perspective, Craig concludes that "as an attempt to render a modern nerve-ridden society, it goes even more awry" than its predecessor, *The Little Girls* (1964).[7] Whether or not Bowen had the intention, in writing *ET*, of rendering a "modern nerve-ridden society" is not my point here. What is important, however, is that it would appear to be these critics' (conventionalized) reading expectations rather than any flaws residing in the text that motivate their disapproval. In other words, their unwillingness or inability to approach *ET* from any but a particular (realist) perspective precludes both critics from investigating the operations of the textual discourse insofar as these fall outside the boundaries of any narrowly defined genre:[8] instead of looking at what the text actually does effect, they reject *ET* for failing to be what they had come to expect—both in the context of an established literary tradition and on account of Bowen's previous work.[9] Foreseeing the likelihood of such inconsequentially disparaging comments, Victoria Glendinning pertinently observes that Bowen's last is a "formidable novel," though "difficult only for readers who longed for the old Elizabeth of *The Death of the Heart.*"[10]

In many respects *ET* is vitally Bowenesque. The often-rebuked verbal mannerisms embedded in a typical blend of comedy and social realism and the narrative irony conjoined with lyrically evocative elements serve to compose a characteristic "Bowen-landscape."[11] In one notable respect, however, the novel forms a stylistic departure from earlier works. At this late point in her career, the author had, to borrow the words of her friend and adviser Spencer Curtis Brown, set herself "the technical puzzle of writing a book 'externally.'" Whereas Bowen continued to express an "uncharacteristic uncertainty" about the results of her stylistic experiments with regard to *The Little Girls* (1964), she appears to have found her last attempt at technical innovation a "complete fulfilment."[12] It may well be that it is precisely the unnerving effect of this technique, Bowen's decision to "forgo the controlled, elaborate commentary and the sharp, minute inward presentation of character,"[13] that accounts for the sense of unease the novel creates, as reflected in such negative evaluations as Lee's and Craig's. Bowen's choice for external narration is not an artistic flaw or a sign of despair so much as a conscious subversion of the ideology of narrative itself.

As Lennard J. Davis has argued, the novel generally depends on the myth of reality of its characters. The fundamental difference between characters and human beings is that the former exist for a particular purpose within a created discursive structure whereas the latter do "not require a text to exist."[14] The way in which human beings can be known or remain a mystery differs fundamentally from the ways in which characters can be (un)known. Human personality is complex, mysterious, and in the final instance unknowable, and what is more, it is without purpose. The novel, in its capacity to offer the possibility of shape, can provide a bridge to overcome the reader's sense of alienation by creating "illusions of complete personalities" with which we can identify.[15] Fiction, Davis argues, serves to rationalize the incomprehensibility of human subjectivity. The character of Eva Trout, "inexplicably large, and largely unexplained,"[16] defies the reader's desire for identification and, since psychological identification is a necessary part in the process of subject formation, critically affects us in our own sense of self. Insofar as identity formation is an ideological process in which novelistic discourse is structurally inscribed, a character as baffling as Eva Trout not only exposes the impossibility of knowing either oneself or any other human being; it also undermines the ideological economy of classic realism as such.

In addition to denying the reader the reassuring illusion of complete and knowable personality in terms of characterization, the ambivalent narrative voice in *ET,* which, as Lee remarks, "seems as much intent on obscuring characters and events as on establishing them," creates a further disturbing effect.[17] In traditional realist fiction, the narrator is the character with whom readers identify most strongly.[18] The narrative voice is conventionally accorded a high level of authority and a position of relative independence in relation to the material organized in/

by the text. The reader's desire is primarily directed at this position of superiority, at what Bowen called the writer's "overlordship."[19] The narrator's discursive power/knowledge is willingly submitted to by the reading subject, for it presents us with the illusion of control that is by definition lacking in our "real" lives. The reader of *ET,* however, is denied the possibility of sharing an authorial narrator's knowledge and the concurrent position of power that s/he desires. Moreover, as Curtis Brown points out, in *ET* Bowen no longer shows "characters reacting to a situation" but a "character creating the situations herself."[20] Since the narrative voice does not assume the customary measure of control over her awesome protagonist, the joint effects of the narrative's doubly subversive strategies can only produce a profound sense of alienation and unease in the reader. What is more, the level at which these dislocations essentially obtain is that of psychosexuality. These reflections render any vehemently negative reactions to *ET* unsurprising.

Bowen's deviations from her accustomed stylistic practices are neither expressions of "dissatisfaction with out-dated formulae" nor illustrations of her "late *malaise.*"[21] They are, rather, intrinsically entwined with the questions she set out to explore in her last novel. In this context, it is important to bear in mind the significance of a writer's sociohistorical situation, which to a considerable extent determines both the process and the product of her/his creative activities. *ET* was written in Hythe on the Kent coast, in the little house Bowen had bought after the enforced sale of Bowen's Court, the Irish family home that she— as the first female heir in a long line of male predecessors—had inherited after her father's death. The author's ingrained sense of exile can only have been deepened by this ultimate dislocation, which doubtless goes some way to account for the fragmented structure of what proved to be her final narrative text. With a protagonist who expresses herself "like a displaced person," whose homelessness compels her to endless wanderings around the world, *ET* unmistakably reflects the author's own sense of displacement. But Kent, and the English coast generally, had also been the scene of Bowen's early youth, making up the landscape she had shared with her mother during the last five years of Florence Bowen's life. If the author's conclusive deracination from her native Ireland therefore represents the culminating stage in a lifelong experience of rootlessness, it also constituted a break with her paternal past that enabled Bowen to go back to an earlier part of herself, to a past permeated with the (repressed) memory of her mother.[22] Twenty years before she finally moved to Hythe, Bowen had written to Charles Ritchie (to whom, incidentally, she dedicated *ET*): "I suppose I like Hythe out of a back-to-the-wombishness, having been there as a child in the most amusing years of one's childhood—8 to 13. But I can't see what's wrong with the womb if one's happy there, or comparatively happy there."[23] The house she eventually bought was called "Wayside," but she renamed it "Carbery" after the long-lost property of her mother's family. Toward the end of her life, Bowen apparently felt an urge to return to her maternal past, which gives *ET* an underlying sense of "back-to-the wombishness." As an exploration of origins, the novel's cultural-ideological context acquires marked significance.

Insofar as *ET* allows us to discern aspects of the author's search for her life's starting point/meaning, it is also an investigation of the production of meaning itself. Bowen wrote the novel in her late sixties, when the idea of authorship no longer held the magical promise of her childhood, that is, the prospect of acquiring the autonomy and control she in those years associated with adult subjectivity. What lingering faith in the constructive potential of language remained while she was writing *HD* in the late 1940s was severely undermined by the very subject matter of this novel, World War II and its dislocations. What is more, when she was working on *ET,* the epistemological crisis marking the middle of the twentieth century was already well under way. This was a period in which the concept of the "transcendental cogito" at the heart of positivist philosophy and liberal humanism had come increasingly under attack. (Post)structuralist thought had incontrovertibly shown the radically decentered nature of subjectivity, while the critique of ideology had fully exposed the pivotal role of discourse in the construction of the multiple meanings of self and world. Surely a self-conscious writer like Bowen, whose appreciation of the constitutive function of language had always been acute, must have been deeply affected by the implications of the theorizations engendered by/in such cultural conditions. Instead of "incorporat[ing] the idea of a future without any verbal 'style' at all," as Lee would have it,[24] Bowen's last two novels and their thematically inscribed stylistic features testify to her profound awareness of the epistemological climate by which both she and her art were produced. The structural decenteredness of *ET* therefore places the text squarely in a postmodern sociocultural context while simultaneously attesting to the author's undiminished ability to respond to the changing conditions of her times. Marking the shifting configuration of what she regarded as her "unique susceptibility to experience," the novel underscores what her friend Eudora Welty declared after the author's death: "[Bowen] was a prime responder to this world."[25]

At this point I should qualify some of my foregoing comments concerning the novel's structure and style. By taking earlier critical appreciations as my starting point, I may have inadvertently reinforced rather than redressed what I consider to be a serious critical oversight. Although it can justifiably be maintained that *ET* is a far more loosely narrated novel than either *LS* or *HD,* there is, in this respect, a notable difference between the two sections into which the text falls apart.[26] Ostensibly merely stylistic in nature, the discursive distinctions between parts 1 and 2 in fact reflect a thematically significant division that is reinforced by the narrative's twofold structure.

Part 1, with the heavily allusive title "Genesis," consists of twelve fairly short chapters. Presenting a variety of scenes depicted in an impressionistic manner, these sketches communicate a somewhat nebulous, even surreal atmosphere. Bowen's stock techniques—broken syntactic patterns, half-sentences, unusual sentence structures, and so on—are prominently in evidence. The chronological order of narrative events is frequently disrupted by flashbacks and reminiscences. The erratic third-person narrative perspective at several points gives way to diary entrances and letters. Character development occurs, in addition to patchy dialogue, mainly through other characters' observations and their responses to one another, and by way of external description. The rare occasions when we do share the protagonist's thoughts are marked off in the textual surface by appearing fully italicized. The matter-of-fact title of part 2, "Eight Years Later," at once indicates a movement away from the vaguely mythical and epic plane evoked by that of part 1, a narrowing down to the ordinary world of everyday "reality" and linear history that forms the characteristic chronotope of traditional novelistic discourse. Although roughly equal in length to the first, the second half of the text coheres into four longish chapters in which the story unfolds more or less in chronological order. Here, too, the narrative perspective is often substituted by the characters' correspondence. Instead of disrupting the story line, however, these epistles serve to string plot and action more tightly together. Odd syntactic patterns and obscure dialogues do occur, but far less frequently and less obtrusively than in part 1. The resulting shift in mood is adequately reflected in the respective opening passages:

"This is where we were to have spent the honeymoon," Eva Trout said, suddenly, pointing across the water. She had pulled up the car on a grass track running along the edge of a small lake. She switched off the engine—evidently, they were to gaze at the castle for some time. (11)

Eight years later, Eva and her little boy, Jeremy, boarded a Pan-American Boeing 707 at O'Hare Airport, Chicago. Destination: London. (147)

The difference between these sequences in terms of contextual information is striking. The novel opens with a scene in which, in addition to the protagonist, several unidentified characters are suggested to be present. The questions of where the scene occurs and why these figures are present are apparently as unclear to the characters as they are to the reader. The second passage, in contrast, does not plunge us into the middle of a scene but provides us with exhaustive factual information in the manner of a newspaper report. The conciseness of the message and the somewhat peremptory tone in which it is conveyed render the sequence almost "unliterary" in quality.

The stylistic discrepancy between the novel's two parts first of all underlines the contrast between the "productive" as distinct from the "reflective" function of language. We further note that in the first passage it is protagonist Eva who speaks the opening words, while in the second it is the narrator who assumes the position of speaking subject. This signals the crux upon which the distinction between the two sections hinges. The reason why the second half of *ET* appears more "narrative" in character than the first basically lies in the shifting position of the narrator. As the difference underlying all surface distinctions, it is the authorial narrative voice in its relative absence from the first and emphatic presence in the second part of the novel that produces the textual divergence marking the novel's overall structure. What is more, the position of power/knowledge that the narrator assumes in part 2 entails a marked deviation from the novel's reputed "external" method of narration. The narrator henceforth not only describes but also merges with the consciousnesses of her characters so as to allow both herself and the reader to explore their "inner landscapes."[27] As a *structural* feature, this alteration in the narrator's role brings to the fore the novel's major preoccupations: the question of discursive power/knowledge, the (in)adequacy of phallogocentric language to articulate (female) sexuality/subjectivity, and the constraints imposed in/by the symbolic order on the "ex-centric" subject's dialogic production of (her)self.[28] My purpose in this and the following chapter is to show and discuss the links between these issues and the novel's underlying sense of "back-to-the-wombishness" or, to put it in more general terms, its treatment of the place of the mother/daughter relationship in the process of (female) subjectivity per se, as well as in relation to nonnormative sexualities.[29]

Originating Masterplots. As one of the founding myths of Western culture, the biblical story of origins, "Genesis," is primarily a story of loss. The first book of the Old Testament recounts the loss of Man's innocence, his expulsion from paradise as a result of Eve's transgression of the Father's Law. While Eve is actively culpable for the fall from God's grace, Adam is guilty mainly by implication. Eve, however, is not only the instigator of loss, depriving both herself and Adam of their Edenic bliss; she is also, paradoxically, the agent who sets human history going by entering into "carnal knowledge." As prime sinner *and* as the motivating force of (pro)-creation, her double function in the text of patriarchy is thus structurally inscribed: Woman is at once madonna and whore, the bearer of (Man's) millions and the cause of his destruction. The masterplot of Judeo-Christianity is fundamentally Man's story, the history of his sufferings springing from this primal loss at the hands of Woman.

The history of the world is a story of symbolic differentiation, and the distinction underlying all symbolizations is (hetero)sexual difference.[30] The persistence with which the text(s) of patriarchy reinscribe sexual difference in binary terms, establishing Man in his role as the superior/active principle in opposition to the passive inferiority defining Woman,[31] serves both to retain the latter in her function as Other to the Same and to obscure the essentially dual position of the female principle per se. The paradox incorporated by the ur-mother of differentiation, that is, Eve's (pro)creative and her destructive powers, form interdependent elements in the foundation of phallocracy and, by extension, embody the contradiction by which the constitution of the male subject is ensured. As the "condition of existence" for both culture and masculinity, femininity and the female body represent an active force whose power must be contained through their designation as the site of negativity.[32] The threat posed to male positivity by the Mother's (pro)creative potential is screened by the phallogocentric privileging of Eve's guilty aspect, Woman's displacement to the site of the abject.[33] It is precisely as a locus of contradiction, the "dark continent" of human (i.e., male) subjectivity/sexuality, that the category of Woman is perpetuated in/by a second major myth underpinning contemporary Western culture, (Freudian) psychoanalysis.

The bridge covering the conceptual gap between the oedipal plot of psychoanalysis and the biblical plot of creation is the abject female (body). Insofar as "the feminine" has a place within these master discourses as a productive condition of existence, its role is exclusively passive, whether as holy virgin, mother nature, or any other of the receptive topoi of everyday Christian lore, or as the object of masculine desire whose lack (of the phallus) is compensated for by a desire (re)directed at its attainable substitute, the (male) child. In addition to repressing the female aspect as an *active* principle in the process of (symbolic) creation, both discourses obscure the fact that Man as well as Woman was cast from the Garden of Eden, that is, that both sexes suffer the alienation that the Christian myth of origins seeks to naturalize.[34] Freud's Oedipus story is also a story of loss, of the infant's loss of the mother as its first love object, which is partially redressed by the promise of future phallic power—for the oedipal boy, that is. The

Law imposed by the wrathful God of the Old Testament becomes the paternal prohibition of incestuous desire, the disruptive presence of the third factor whose threat of castration breaks up the mother/child dyad to instate the family triangle. In Lacan's rereading of Freud, the Law of the Father is literally identified as the child's initiation into the symbolic order, which constitutes him/ her *as* a subject by opening up his/her unconscious as repressed desire. In Lacan's scheme, Woman, in fact, does not exist, except as the absolute other in phallogocentric representation. It is the suppression of the Mother and of an active female sexuality that allows phallogocentric master narratives to establish the Father in his central position of authority—whether in the form of God's wrath in the story of Man's fall or, alternatively, as the originating factor of meaning and subjectivity that brings about the infant's primary split from the mother.

Since in Western culture the members of both sexes are subjected to the Law of the Father—indeed, since heterosexual difference is a retroactive effect of its very operations—the biblical myth of creation necessarily serves as a subtext to any of its reinscriptions, in theoretical as much as in literary texts. Bowen emphatically situates the story of Eva Trout's "Genesis" within this specific cultural context. But precisely because the patriarchal story of origins hinges on the structural inscription of sexual difference, a female author's explicit intervention in the master text(s) signals a revision rather than a reinscription. As Madelon Sprengnether suggests:

Women writers' versions of the Fall are different from men's in that for women it is a mother/daughter story, and the Fall is portrayed in terms of the loss of the mother. This shift is not perhaps immediately apparent because women read through the Genesis story as well as men, but these fictions have a different twist.[35]

Discussing a number of contemporary fictions of female development, Sprengnether shows that, as "narratives of origin," they provide us with a different perspective on the fall. Central to these alternative stories of loss is not the family triangle but the mother/daughter relationship. In psychoanalytic terms, it is thus the (loss of the) mother that inaugurates the process of female subjectivity—rather than the intrusive Father. Eve is hence reinstalled in her active role in the story of creation. As "rival fictions" to the masterplots, these narratives "challenge some of our most cherished stories of cultural and personal development, calling into question some of the ways in which woman has been represented in psychoanalytic theory as well as literature."[36]

In the light of such considerations, *ET* acquires a significance that has gone largely unnoticed. While unmistakably announcing itself as a story of origins in both of the senses distinguished by Sprengnether, the novel has not been read as such, and one of the reasons for this oversight may be that writers and critics alike "read through" the masterplots of patriarchal culture. And as she goes on to point out, the critical effort required to "discover an unexpected text in the guise of a familiar story, one that is capable, in turn, of altering our cultural awareness . . . involves a kind of inner displacement . . . a psychic disengagement from the biblical master plot that provides an aura of familiarity and from the oedipal master plot that sustains it" (299). Before making such an effort, I will conduct a short detour along the Freudian oedipal trajectory and indicate the very different roles played by the mother in the psychosexual development of subjects of either sex.

Freud's Little Man.   In his lecture "Femininity" (1932), Freud recapitulates his earlier work in the field of female sexuality and psychosexual differentiation.[37] Addressing himself specifically to the "riddle of femininity," he maintains that the task of psychoanalysis is not to "describe what a woman is" but to inquire "how she comes into being, how a woman develops out of a child with a bisexual disposition" (149).[38] Earlier, Freud had established the Oedipus complex as the first clearly recognizable stage in a child's psychic development.[39] During this "phallic phase," when he has learned how to derive pleasure from his genitals, the little boy's libidinal energy remains invested in his primary love object, the mother. Placed in a position of rivalry with the father, he experiences the *positive* form of the complex, consisting in a "desire for the death of the rival—the parent of the same sex—and a sexual desire for the parent of the opposite sex."[40] The recognition of the former's superior phallic power and the accompanying threat of castration (which gains reality value only upon the discovery of his mother's "lack") compel the little boy to turn away from the oedipal situation. He subsequently identifies with the father's position of authority, and, with the prospect of his own future phallic power, suspends his desire for the mother/female object until its fulfillment during mature (hetero)sexuality. Although the boy's Oedipus conflict involves a struggle that is not fully resolved until its reemergence and the formation of a secondary object during puberty, the "normal" trajectory of male sexual development is relatively straightforward in that both his erotogenic zone—the penis—and his original object are retained throughout its various stages.

The central place of the threat of castration in the resolution of the boy's Oedipus complex at once signals the more complicated course of the little girl's psychosexual development.[41] Initially, her trajectory runs more or less parallel to the boy's: she, too, takes the mother as her original love object and enters the phallic phase upon discovering the erotogenic pleasure she can derive from the sexual organ that functions as a "penis-equivalent," her clitoris. During the phallic phase, Freud says, "the little girl is a little man."[42] In order to pass through the *positive* or, as he gradually came to define it, the "normal Oedipus complex," the little girl has to accomplish two complex tasks.[43] First, she has to abandon her primary love object and redirect her desire to the member of the opposite sex within the family triangle, the father. Secondly, the vagina (as the "truly feminine" sexual organ) should at some point substitute the clitoris as the woman's "leading erotogenic zone." Freud's question of female sexuality becomes a question of "femininity." Remarkably—considering his insistence on sexuality as a *constructed* phenomenon—Freud, in this context, returns to the anatomical basis of sexual difference: "How does [the little girl] pass from her masculine phase to the feminine one to which she is biologically destined?"[44] In his attempts to answer this question Freud developed several notions that gave rise to heated discussions among his then fellow analysts. Since the revival of feminist interest in his work in the mid-1970s,[45] these notions have continued to preoccupy psychoanalytic and critical feminist theorists alike.

In "The Dissolution of the Oedipus Complex" (1924), Freud still assumed that, since the threat of castration does not operate in the case of the little girl, her Oedipus complex is not so much dissolved as "gradually given up." Once the little girl has assumed the feminine position in the family triangle, the "accomplished fact of her castration" urges her to transform her lack of the penis into a "desire . . . to receive a baby from her father," a wish that is eventually abandoned because it is never fulfilled. The two wishes—for a penis and for a child—remain "strongly cathected in the unconscious," thus preparing the girl for her future role (321). Clinical evidence forced Freud to reconsider his ideas. As we have seen, whereas it is the threat of castration that compels the little boy to exit the *positive* oedipal situation, it is this same "fact" that forces the little girl to enter it. When she discovers not only her own but also the mother's lack of a penis, the girl's love for her turns into hatred. As well as being held responsible for the girl's own castrated condition—the mortification about her highly inferior "penis-equivalent," Freud informs us, actually causes the girl to lose interest in her own "phallic" pleasure—the mother also turns out not to be what she was expected to be: the complete, "*phallic* mother."[46] The girl's discovery of her mother's "lack" allows her to drop her as a love object and to (re)direct her desire toward the father. Precisely the tenacity, however, with which some of his female patients clung to their attachment to the father led Freud on to the notion of what has become known as the "masculinity complex," that is, an enduring wish in the girl to obtain a penis/be a man. What he discovered in those cases where a woman's affinity with the father was particularly ardent was that it usually had been preceded by a "phase of exclusive attachment to the mother which had been equally intense and passionate." Freud had to acknowledge that the period of the girl's attachment to her first love object might in fact not be concluded by the oedipal conflict but might extend into and well beyond this phase: "We had to reckon with the possibility that a number of women remain arrested in their original attachment to their mother and never achieve a true change-over towards men." In order to preserve the central place of his main discovery (the Oedipus complex) in the development of either sex, Freud situated the little girl's "masculine" phase in a space anterior to the "normal positive Oedipus complex," a space he designated the "negative complex" or,[47] alternatively, the *pre-Oedipus*.[48] It is this phase, as the site of the girl's exclusive attachment to the mother and as an explicitly *active* stage in her libidinal development, that has become the focus of recent feminist theorization. This, in turn, provides us with a rewarding approach to *ET*.

(Pre)oedipal Love and the Symbolic Mother

Eva's Story: Take One. The opening chapter of *ET* presents us with the heroine, aged twenty-four, in a scene of her own design. She has brought a "carload of passengers" to gaze at a castle, a "Bavarian fantasy" whose "sightless" facade shows with "photographic distinctness" against the January Worcestershire sky (11). The "giantess," as Eva is referred to, has taken the Danceys, inhabitants of the neighboring vicarage, on an outing to her former school (12). The scene at once establishes Eva as a true heir to the Trouts' "genius for unreality" (44) and discloses her will to be "the patient, abiding encircling will of a monster" (92). This enigmatic figure, whose behavior is "monolithic ... not, somehow, the attitude of a thinking person" (12), is staying as a paying guest with her former teacher Iseult Smith—now Mrs. Arble—and her husband, Eric. The extended visit at Larkins is also part of the heroine's own design (16). "Motherless from the cradle" (39), Eva has, after her father's recent death, been placed in the care of the latter's (male) lover. Since the "big heiress" is not to come into Willy Trout's fortune till she has reached the age of twenty-five, her "wicked guardian" Constantine Ormeau had been very pleased when his charge expressed a "wish to take up residence" at Larkins. Since Constantine considers a "Trout ... of any kind ... a liability" (38), the Arbles evidently "solved a problem" (16). However, Constantine's forebodings about what he regards as Eva's "dreadful gift," her "endless capacity for making trouble, attracting trouble, strewing trouble around her ... beget[ting] trouble," soon appear to materialize nonetheless (44).

For reasons that will become clear shortly, Eva feels betrayed by Iseult and informs her guardian that she wants to leave the Arbles—whose shaky marriage has visibly been put under pressure by the ex-pupil's presence. Fearing resistance from Iseult, Eva secretly arranges for young Henry Dancey, the "topmost intelligent one" of the vicar's four children, to sell her beloved Jaguar while she herself sets out for Broadstairs on the south coast. After taking up residence in a huge, baroque villa called "Cathay," Eva, who has left fairly obvious clues as to her whereabouts, is successively called on by Eric, Constantine, and Iseult, each of whom she suspects of seeking to restore his or her former power over her. At the end of the ex-teacher's visit in late summer, by which time Eva has come into the possession of her fortune, the "she-Cossack" announces that she will be "having a little child" by next Christmas (121).

Eva's flight from her guardians seems temporarily at an end when, in the penultimate chapter of part 1, entitled "Interim," we are faced with a letter dated October 1959 from an unknown American professor who has apparently fallen in love with the "monstrous heiress" on a plane to New York (63). (The letter, which remains "unclaimed," is followed by the parenthetical narrative comment that it was eventually returned to the sender, who is never again mentioned.) In the course of the preceding chapters, we have become familiar with Eva's rather bizarre history. Some light has also been shed on her relations with the two characters figuring centrally in it—Iseult and Constantine, both of whom seem to be as much baffled by the erratic actions of their protégée as they are terrified by her elusive personality.

Eva Trout is preeminently an "ex-centric." She was born as the only child of the popular but astute businessman Willy Trout and his pretty wife, Cissie. The former, as his shrewd lover "unerringly sensed," had it "in him to deviate," while the latter was perhaps "delightful" but certainly "*not* normal" (17, 41). Two months after Eva's birth, Cissie fled from her husband's "obsession" with Constantine and was "almost at once killed in a plane crash" (18). Willy Trout dies equally abruptly: twenty-three years later, his "inexhaustible capacity to suffer" ends in suicide. Eva has spent the greater part of her childhood "under the shadow" of her father's "hated love" for Constantine. At various moments the text suggests that she blames her "wicked guardian" for both of her parents' deaths. The "ambience" of her childhood is thus one in which love, violence, and death are inextricably linked to "abnormality" and sex/uality (92)—Eva's case history is not merely a question of "heredity," as Constantine suggests (40).

The supposition that the psychoanalytic masterplot is one of the principal subtexts underlying *ET* is borne out by the narrator's position of one-upmanship in relation to Iseult so far as the analysis of Eva's case history is concerned. A fact "little

known" about Eva, we are told, is that she had already attended
a school before she was sent to Lumleigh, where she met her
"brilliant teacher": "Even Iseult (then Smith) had, during the
great research, uncovered practically nothing on that subject—
she had perhaps not probed deeply enough?" (48). The place
where Eva was "for the first time . . . exposed to her own kind"
had been an experimental educational enterprise funded by Willy
in order to get a friend of Constantine's—"inspirational Kenneth
of the unclouded brow and Parthenon torso"—out of the way.
A "mixed school" at the lakeside castle with Kenneth as
headmaster had presented itself as the solution to what for Willy,
"in the throes of a jealousy aggravated by a chronic mistrust of
Constantine," was rapidly becoming a "nightmare" (48). Amid
the "wealthy little delinquents" of the school's assorted
population, Eva had plainly been an outsider. This had partly
been due to the fact that she was known to be the "donor's
daughter" (48). What primarily made Eva appear an alien to the
young "veterans," however, had been her ostensible sexlessness:
"At fourteen [she] was showing no signs of puberty" (49). This
would appear to indicate that Eva had not come under the sway
of that particular technology of sex, the discourse of adolescence.
We recall that it is during this phase in the "normal" trajectory
of psychosexual development that the earlier "oedipal
stabilization of subjective identity" is disrupted by the
reemergence of repressed imaginary material.[49] Eva, however,
having been raised within an "inverted" family triangle, had not
been initiated into heterosexual difference at all, and hence had
not acquired any sense of a recognizable sex/self to begin with.
When one of her fellow pupils asked her: " 'Trout, are you a
hermaphrodite?' " she had merely responded: " 'I don't know' "
(51). Only now, in her confrontation with "juveniles—a species
known to her so far only in parks in the distance or hotels
fleetingly," Eva began to discover (sexual) difference (49).

The text gives us another unmistakable clue about its conceptual subtexts: one of the pranks of Eva's companions had been to "[set] up an Oedipal trap" for a teacher "by arranging an effigy of his mother in his bed" (51). In the Freudian framework thus evoked, Eva had up till this time remained unaware of her own "castrated" condition. Since the preoedipal absence of the mother and the exclusive company of two male adults—whose sexual relations virtually cancel out the female element—precluded her from taking up her "proper" position within the family triangle, she had not been compelled to enter the oedipal complex—negative or positive. Because subjectivity can only come into being, first, by the primary split from the mother during the mirror stage, and second, by the *repression* of the desire for the "forbidden" female love object during the oedipal stage, she, accordingly, had not acquired any sense of self. Once she was placed in a context where "mixedness . . . was the whole idea," the first stage of Eva's subjective process was set in motion:

As for her comrades, she took them with equanimity. She was senior to any of them (in actual age) by a month or two; one of them was taller than she, the rest rather miniature: even the smallest seemed wondrously *physically complete* to Eva, who had been left *unfinished*. So these were humans, and this was what it was like being amongst them? Nothing hurt. From being with them, she for the first time began to have some idea what it was to be herself; but *that* did not hurt. (51; italics mine except for the last)

In the normative terms of the oedipal trajectory, this stage of Eva's psychosexual development would seem to equal what Freud defines as "primary narcissism," an intermediary phase between autoerotism and object love.[50] The phase roughly coincides with the Lacanian mirror stage, the period during which the child acquires its first (imaginary) sense of identity by recognizing its own mirror image as distinct from its mother's. Only when this primary split is followed by a secondary one, that is, the constitution of the unconscious upon the child's entry into the symbolic, does s/he come into existence as a "full" subject.[51]

Fredric Jameson has stressed the inseparability of the Lacanian Imaginary and Symbolic orders while still maintaining that it is possible to conceptualize the former as "a kind of preverbal register whose logic is essentially visual."[52] The Imaginary is a "uniquely determinate configuration of space" that is "not yet organized around the individuation of [a] personal body . . . yet which nonetheless swarms with bodies and forms intuited in a different way." The visibility of such objects is "not the result of an act of any particular observer," since they "carry their specularity upon themselves like a color . . . or the texture of their surface."[53] These are what Melanie Klein has called "part-objects," primary objects (breast, feces) whose psychic investment is transferred to an endless number of more indifferent objects. It is the uniquely human capacity for imaginative transformation that allows for the "affective valorization" of such inanimate objects. In Lacan's words:

> It is normally by the possibilities of a game of imaginary transposition that the progressive valorization of objects is achieved, on what is customarily known as the affective level, by a proliferation, a fan-like disposition of all the imagination equations which allow the human being, alone in the animal realm, to have an almost inifinite number of objects at his . . . disposition, objects isolated in their form.[54]

Jameson emphasizes that it is the "primacy of the human *imago*" in the mirror stage that enables such identificatory investment. The whole process depends on the "possibility of symbolic associations . . . of an inanimate thing with the libidinal priority of the human body." There is a substantial difference, however, in the relationship between self and other during the mirror stage as compared to the later (Symbolic) Self/Other distinction. In the Imaginary there is a "kind of situational experience of otherness as pure relationship," one in which bodies "primarily entertain relationships of inside/outside with one another," a spatial configuration in which the "child can occupy either term indifferently, or indeed . . . both at once."[55]

Each of the elements inherent in the Imaginary process of the mirror stage is present in Eva's initial experiences at the castle, the first object with which she "fell in love . . . at first sight" (52). The "genesis" of her dawning sense of self is cast in terms of an awakening:

This was the hour. Through the curtainless window day stole in, fingering its way slowly, as though blindly, from thing to thing. Redness, though still like a watered ink, began to return to the top blanket, under which lay outlined her body. This redemption from darkness was for Eva, who had witnessed it nowhere else, a miracle inseparable from the castle. Her bed had its back to the window, but a looking-glass faced it—in that, she could see existence begin again. Seeing is believing: again, after the night of loss and estrangement, after the malicious lying of her misleading dreams in which she was no one, nowhere, she knew herself to be *here*. Here again was the castle, and she in it. (53)

Another "part-object" had presented itself in the guise of Eva's eleven-year-old roommate, Elsinore. This "fairy-like little near-albino," whose "washed-out beauty gave her an air of age," would indirectly cause the castle school—"Home for inflicted children"—to come to an end (52, 53). Suffering from "sensuous desolation," Elsinore had walked into the lake one day, and although she had been pulled out in time, her ensuing illness added another scandal to the already numerous mishaps marring the establishment's reputation. In the absence of a proper sickroom, the girl, who had gone from "convulsions . . . into coma," had continued to lie in her "sad bed distant only from Eva's by the width of the window" (55). Eva, who was told that "[*she*] must not touch her," had begun her silent watch over Elsinore (55). Rendered in conspicuously ritualistic terms, the episode acquires the significance of an initiation ceremony. The "octagonal chamber," where the curtains stand out in a "cabalistic pattern" and whose ceiling forms an "umbrella-shaped canopy of shadows" virtually absorbs its "two consenting prisoners." "Locked-up" in a place that "began in a cardboard way to belong to history," Eva, at fourteen, had been gradually enfolded in a form of love that evokes the primordial mother/child dyad in which otherness consists in "pure relationship":

What made Eva visualize this as a marriage chamber? As its climate intensified, all grew tender. To repose a hand on the blanket covering Elsinore was to know in the palm of the hand a primitive tremor—imagining the beating of that other heart, she had a passionately solicitous sense of this other presence. Nothing forbad love. This deathly yet living stillness, together, of two beings, this unapartness, came to be the requital of all longing. An endless feeling of destiny filled the room. (56)

The "stillness" of this scene of love suggests its Imaginary or pre-Symbolic nature. The ambivalence of the archetypal symbiosis—representing the source of life *and* carrying the threat of engulfment—that qualifies Eva's experience indicates that such "unapartness" had to come to an end if the process of her subjectivity was to continue. It was, quite appropriately, Elsinore's "corrupt mother" who had accomplished this first split necessary to inaugurate the subjective process: with her "coming-into-the-room" to take her daughter away, "all here ended" (57). The rupture of the dyad, this ultimate experience of "otherness," had formed the culmination of Eva's mirror stage. In Lacan, the subject's imaginary identification with its reflection in the mirror constitutes a loss of the "Real"—the undifferentiated "sameness" with all introjected objects—that effects a fundamental loss of self never to be restored.[56] The loss of the (real) object inflicts a "narcissistic wound," calling into being the defensive mechanism of disavowal, or *Verleugnung*.[57] This aptly characterizes Eva's reaction to the separation from Elsinore: "From that instant, down came oblivion—asbestos curtain" (57).

By situating the subject within the libidinal economy—instituting the desire for the lost object—the primary split sets the subject on its way to the second decisive moment for the constitution of full subjectivity, the entry into language. This part of the (Lacanian) subject's trajectory roughly coincides with the Freudian "phallic stage," when the girl child desires the mother and wants to get rid of the father, a stage alternately designated as the *pre-Oedipus* or the negative Oedipus complex. The implications of Freud's deployment of these distinct terms are, contrary to what my indiscriminate use of them may have suggested, in fact far reaching. In her influential study of the female voice in psychoanalysis and film, *The Acoustic Mirror* (1988), Kaja Silverman in fact takes the alternation of these terms as a starting point for what amounts to an entire recasting of the oedipal masterplot. She points out that Freud, in *The Ego and the Id* (1923), still suggests that the "subject is generally obliged to negotiate his or her way between two versions of the Oedipus complex, one of which is culturally promoted and works to align the subject smoothly with heterosexuality and the dominant values of the symbolic order," the other of which is "culturally disavowed and organizes subjectivity in fundamentally perverse and homosexual ways" (120). Freud defines the two versions here as the positive and the negative Oedipus complex, respectively. In "Femininity" (1933), the terms "*pre-Oedipus*" or "preoedipal phase" have completely supplanted the notion of the negative Oedipus complex. Everything that customarily precedes the girl's attachment to the father, that is, her passionate desire for the mother, has thus been situated within the *pre*oedipal or Imaginary order. Effectively excluded from the Symbolic, the preoedipal mother has become a site of celebration for (especially French) feminists as the locus of an essential "feminine" characterized by plurality, contiguity, and simultaneity.[58] Silverman's argument, in contrast, hinges upon her attempt to restore the girl's first attachment to the mother to its place *within* the symbolic by resituating the negative complex within the oedipal situation per se.

Such a relocation of the girl's affective investment in the mother requires a reconsideration of Freud's notion of "castration." Juliet Mitchell has shown that Freud's notion of the *castration complex* marks the turning point in his understanding of sexual difference.[59] It is the threat of castration that concludes the (boy's) Oedipus complex and that "institutes the superego as its representative and as representative thereby of the law." The concept of castration "operates as the law whereby men and women assume their humanity and . . . gives the human meaning of the distinction between the sexes." Castration hence "embodies the law which founds the human order itself." [60] The "natural categories of sex" are therefore culturally produced "reaction formations," effected within as much as to sustain the binary frame of sexual difference. Both femininity and masculinity are marked by castration anxiety for, as Mitchell correctly emphasizes, Freud insists that the girl's recognition of the "fact" of her castration only acquires significance by the prohibition of the Law: only when the father steps in to forbid the girl's access to the mother's body, assuming a position of sole possession for himself, does the fact that the girl lacks a penis become a source of loss and mourning. In other words, only within the terms of phallogocentrism does the girl experience her own body as lacking. The *symbolic* meaning of the notion thus determines the subject's "normal" heterosexual object choice: "For Freud, identification with the appropriate parent is a *result* of the castration complex which had already given the mark of sexual distinction." [61]

Including the mother within the oedipal scenario proper substantially qualifies the concept of castration. In Freud, the castration crisis forces the little boy to exit the positive Oedipus complex whereas it compels the little girl to enter it. This may well be, Silverman concedes, but the mother's resituation within the "general equation" implies that castration becomes the "impetus" whereby the girl enters "only into the *positive* Oedipus complex, and not the Oedipus complex *tout court.*" It follows that, since castration undeniably has an "inaugural part to play" in the male subject's entry into the positive as well as in the female subject's entry into the negative complex, "in both cases . . . desire for the mother is initiated only through *symbolic castration.*" [62] Castration thus leads not merely to desire but to "desire specifically for the mother." The subject's entry into language entails both the loss of the original object and the traumatic separation from the mother: "Accession to language marks not only the eclipse of the real, and the child's division from the mother, but the inscription of the Oedipus complex for both boy and girl."[63] The location of the secondary loss in the separation from the oedipal mother renders male and female subjects equally castrated. The female subject is henceforth split between two "irreconcilable" desires, since her desire for the mother, or another female object, is one that virtually falls outside the symbolic.

Silverman frankly acknowledges that her theoretical paradigm "closes off the pre-Oedipal domain both as an arena for resistance to the symbolic and as an erotic refuge." But, she argues, to relegate the mother/daughter bond to the preoedipal phase is to "suggest that female sexuality precedes language and symbolic structuration." The invaluable positive effect of her analysis of the negative Oedipus complex is precisely that it "contextualizes [the daughter's passion for the mother] and the sexuality it implies firmly within the symbolic." This makes it possible to "speak for the first time about a genuinely oppositional desire—to speak about a desire which challenges dominance from within representation and meaning, rather than from the place of a mutely resistant biology or sexual 'essence'" (123–24). The negativity of the negative Oedipus complex arises from its opposition to the phallus, or the Law; it is not the "trace of some more primordial union of mother and child." The "homosexual-maternal" or negative facet of female subjectivity/sexuality can, after all, only pose a threat to the phallic order by challenging *dominant* meanings from within, that is, only when the "unconscious mother" of feminism is recognized for what she is: an oedipal rather than a preoedipal figure.

A central aspect in Freud's notion of femininity is the concept of repression. Silverman insists on maintaining or even maximizing this dimension of femininity on account of its "enormous . . . transformative potential" (149). For what has been repressed has

in the main been associated with the unconscious only: the negative Oedipus complex, which comprises not only the desire for but
also the identification with the mother. Freud's concept of the
"phallic phase" in the little girl's sexual development reinforces
his assumption of the opposition/reversal scheme in the libidinal
economy: "Desire for one parent presupposes identification with
the other." Lesbian sexuality thus always implies masculine identification. Silverman shows that several of Freud's own texts argue
"against the necessary divergence of identification and desire."
From these inconsistencies she infers that it is possible to "conceptualize . . . a period after the girl's separation from the mother . . .
but before the onset of the positive Oedipus complex, during which
her identity is formed through the incorporation of the mother's
imago" (152), that is, as an (as yet) nonlacking, phallic mother.

At this point a notion introduced earlier in Silverman's argument acquires particular significance. Coining a phrase, she uses
the term "acoustic mirror" to denote the infant's early perception
of the mother's voice. We recall that during the Imaginary phase of
the child's development it knows no boundaries between self and
other and experiences incorporated objects as if they were parts of
her/himself. In traditional families in the West, the mother's voice
is usually the first to demarcate the child's auditory universe. The
perception of the mother's voice leads to introjection—it is heard
from inside. This is accounted for by the double organization of
the auditory/sound system: a sound enunciated is also heard. The
child could thus be said to "hear itself initially through that voice—
to first recognize itself in the vocal mirror supplied by the mother"
(80). Not only is the mother's face the visual mirror in which the
child learns to recognize itself but also her "voice is the acoustic
mirror in which it first hears itself." It is this "conjunction of
identification and eroticism" that forms the repressed element of
femininity (150).

The essential role of the mother in defining the child's sexuality/
subjectivity entails that the little girl's identificatory investment

during the negative Oedipus complex is primarily an incorporation of activity. The equation of femininity and passivity is a "consequence only of the positive Oedipus complex and the cultural discourses and institutions that support it" (153). Only upon her entry into the positive Oedipus complex is the girl's loved object devalued or shown to be "lacking." When cultural pressures enforce her to continue to identify with lack while at the same time to displace her desire onto the father, the result inevitably is melancholia. This, rather than hysteria, Silverman contends, appears to be the "norm for the female subject—that condition of melancholia which blights her relationship with both herself and her culture" (155).

Silverman's theoretical paradigm bears on Eva Trout's story in several ways. The text unequivocally underscores the fundamental role played by the symbolic mother or the female/maternal voice in the infant's psychosexual development. A first, quite startling, suggestion of this is the fact that Eva, having been only two months old when Cissie departed, "maintains she remembers hearing her mother shriek" (40). This suggestion is taken up when Iseult Smith appears on the oedipal stage to become, in her function of "acoustic mirror," the focus of Eva's desire.

Eva's Story: Take Two. Since nobody tells her, Eva had never learned whether Elsinore had lived or died, and "not told, she became unable to ask" (57). After the castle school had been closed down, she had been taken by her father and Constantine on their "global business trips." At the end of two years of traveling—from Mexico to the Far East, from Hong Kong to San Francisco, New York, and Hamburg—Eva had informed Willy that she "should like to learn" and wants to go to an "English boarding school: one for girls" (57). Thus, at almost sixteen, Eva had entered Lumleigh. She had at once exhibited all the signs of the drive for knowledge linked by Freud to an early stage in infantile sexuality, the so-called anal phase, which is determined by sadomasochism and the infant's sexual curiosity. "An ambiguous force," says Toril Moi, recapitulating Freud's scattered statements on "epistemophilia," the "drive for mastery signals the child's need to dominate itself and its world."[64] Both the intensity of the drive and its ambiguity are readily apparent from Eva's behavior and the reactions it had evoked: "Eva's attention did not wander once a lesson began: steadily, earnestly, emphatically, and so searchingly as to appear reproachful, it remained focused on whichever of the teachers held the floor. Some of them found it mesmeric. Miss Smith did not" (58). At this equivocal stage in her psychosexual development, Eva had met the woman who would be of paramount importance to its subsequent progress. Since the whole of the heroine's early history is revealed in flashbacks, before we actually witness this first encounter between Eva and Miss Smith, we have already become familiar with the latter's recollected version of the critical episode.

In an early chapter, entitled "Mr and Mrs Arble," Iseult is introduced as a "highly intelligent person, young still, of pleasing appearance and good character, as to whom there existed but one mystery: why had she thrown herself away? (She apparently had)" (16–17). Throughout the chapter, the narrative voice behaves unpredictably: ostensibly delivered as "facts," what we learn about Iseult's relations with her ex-pupil gradually emerges as the former teacher's own retrospective account of affairs. Having made an "abiding impression" on Eva, who had "never lost touch with her," Iseult "seemed destined to have Eva—destined, she sometimes wondered, never to lose her? Everything had indicated Iseult." Through such shifting focalization—the narrator almost imperceptibly moving in and out of the character's consciousness—the text succeeds in revealing Iseult's pivotal function in Eva's "Genesis" while simultaneously disclosing the older woman's propensity for repression and rationalization:

Iseult Smith had gone out of her way to establish confidence, for her own reasons—she proposed to tackle Eva's manner of speaking. What caused the girl to express herself like a displaced person? The explanation—that from infancy onward Eva had had as attendants displaced persons, those at a price being the most obtainable, to whose society she'd been largely consigned—for some reason never appeared: too simple, perhaps? Much went into the effort to induce flexibility. But Miss Smith had come too late on the scene; she had had to give up. Eva by then was sixteen: her outlandish, cement-like conversational style had set. Moreover—the discouraging fact emerged—it was more than sufficient for Eva's needs. She had nothing *to* say that could not be said, adequately, the way she said it. What did result from the sessions was, on the girl's side, awe for the dazzling teacher; also, Eva was left in a daze of gratitude. Till Iseult came, no human being had ever turned upon Eva their full attention—an attention which could seem to be love. Eva knew nothing of love but that it existed—that, she should know, having looked on at it. (17)

Although Iseult's "own reasons" are never exactly defined, the text suggests that her need to "give up" on Eva had sprung not from her pupil's dull-wittedness so much as from the force of the girl's passionate attachment to her, or rather, from the teacher's own reciprocal feelings. Behind the placid surface of "Miss Smith, as she then was" had lain the powerful sexual drive that she had sought to sublimate through intellectual activity:

Supremacy set apart this wonderful teacher. She could have taught anything. Her dark suit might have been the habit of an Order. Erect against a window of tossing branches she stood moveless, but for the occasional gesture of hand to forehead—then, the bringing of the finger-tips to the brain seemed to complete an electric circuit. Throughout a lesson, her voice held a reined-in excitement—imparting knowledge, she conveyed its elatingness. The intellectual beauty of her sentences was informed by a glow; words she spoke sounded new-minted, unheard before. With her patient, sometimes ironic insistence upon fact, as fact, went what could be called her opposite capacity—that of releasing ideas, or speculation, into unbounded flight. (58)

Caught within a cultural scheme in which the desire for knowledge is effectively split off from its bodily inscription by being set up in extrapolation from heterosexual difference, Iseult's talent for rational thought (or her "masculine" aspect) had eventually been curtailed by her equally strong "opposite capacity." While capable of restraining her "feminine" bodily desire when confronted with Eva's emerging "life-long devotion" (17), in the end it had been the "cerebral young woman's first physical passion" that had induced her to abandon a "star career for an obscure marriage" (18). In patriarchy the masculine mind and the feminine body are mutually exclusive.

My reading of the teacher/pupil relationship in terms of love and sexual desire is based on the central place of language in their interaction. From the perspective of Silverman's recast oedipal scenario, Eva had been about to enter the negative Oedipus complex. Since it is only in the positive complex that the girl is forced to appreciate Woman as lacking, Iseult had embodied for Eva the still-complete, "phallic" love object. The teacher's manifest intellectual powers had established her in the position of the active symbolic mother whose voice functions as the "acoustic mirror" in which the child recognizes herself. The text thus prefigures and underscores Silverman's subversion of the Lacanian masterplot—in which it is not the mother but the Father who plays the decisive role in the child's initiation into the symbolic order. Even if Miss Smith herself might appear to consider such a central position for the female voice a (feminist) utopia—she had remarked upon seeing her own and Eva's shadows cast ahead of them: "'Yes, we're like coming events!'" (59)—we have seen that the notion of the symbolic mother principally implies a reconceptualization of the existing state of affairs in Western culture. It had thus fallen to Miss Smith to take Eva, "unable to speak—talk, be understood, converse" (63), into the realm of language. She had accordingly set out to teach her pupil to think: "'Try joining things together: this, then that, then the other. That's thinking; at least, that's beginning to think'" (62).

Iseult is explicitly presented as the agent precipitating Eva's coming to (self-)consciousness. The girl had first responded to this gift of herself with incredulity, then by falling in love with her teacher:

Slowly credulity overtook her. Then, through one after another midsummer night, daylight never quite gone from the firmament, cubicle curtains round her like white pillars, she was kept amazed and awake by joy. She saw (she thought) the aurora borealis. Love like a great moth circled her bed, then settled. (63)

From the "first manifestation," taking "place at five ten in the evening," Iseult had been vaguely aware of the nature of the seemingly "occult pact" into which she and Eva had entered: "Of Eva she was to ponder, later: 'She did not know what I was doing; but did I?'"(61). Eva had notably suffered under her subjection to the law of desire and when Miss Smith had noticed her pupil's "look of subjection, bewilderment, fatalism," she had responsibly declared that they "mustn't exhaust one another." Still, in reply to Eva's half-hearted apology, the teacher had admitted that she was not "really" sorry either, though conscious of the implications: "Miss Smith leaned back, considered what she had said, but did not emend it" (64).

Despite her passion for Miss Smith, Eva had been and remained wary of the symbolic order into which she was being initiated. When Iseult had urged her to "think," she had questioned the purpose of such efforts:

Eva fitted her knuckles together. She frowned at them. "Then, what?"
"Then you go on."
"Till when?"
"Till you've arrived at something. Or found something out, or shed some light on something. Or come to some conclusion, rightly or wrongly. And then what?—then you begin again."
"Why, however?" Eva asked, not unreasonably.
Miss Smith whirled her fingers over her forehead: a parody of despairingness. She laughed aloud, an abandon which was endearing. "Honestly, how can I tell you? It's what is done, Eva. Try—" (62)

In addition to disclosing the precise nature of Iseult's project, the sequence adequately illustrates the (Derridean) concept of discourse as an endless process of differentiation and deferral. As such, it exposes the precarious foundations of Western metaphysics, which, in Silverman's words, "locates the subject of speech in the same ontological space as the speaking subject" in order to create the "illusion of self-presence."[65] Lacan, in contrast, emphasizes that "speech produces absence, not presence." Since, Silverman advances, the symbolic order can never be anything than "Other," the "discoursing voice is the agent of symbolic castration." The ambiguity of the voice thus originates in its enabling function: while creating the illusion of the subject's self-presence, it in effect signals the irretrievable loss of the first object. In other words, the subject can come into being only insofar as the object is lost. The voice is hence the "site of division between meaning and materiality," situated in the "partition between the biological body and the body of language, or . . . the social body."[66]

Miss Smith, in her paradoxical position of *female* subject of power/knowledge, had seemed as yet untouched by the experience of "carnal knowledge." In her zealous intellectuality, her "unfeminine" celibacy, she had been all spirit/mind, untainted by the materiality of the (female) body: in her room at Lumleigh, "little betrayed the fact that anybody inhabited" it. Indeed, "something disembodied" the teacher, so that "neither then nor later did Eva look upon her as beautiful or in any other way clad in physical being" (64, 61). Later, Iseult had come to look upon herself as someone "soiled" by "having lived a thousand lives . . . through books . . . internally" (93). While at that point acknowledging that any idea of oneself is "inconceivable" (91), she had been, at the time when her "*noli-me-tangere*" had actually been unneeded, still under the illusion of self-presence produced by/in language:

In fact, at that time, that particular spring at Lumleigh, the young teacher was in a state of grace, of illumined innocence, that went with the realization of her powers. They *transcended* her; they filled her with awe and wonder, and the awe and wonder gave her a kind of purity. . . . About Iseult Smith, up to the time she encountered Eva and, though discontinuously, for some time after, there was something of Nature before the Fall. (61; italics mine)

The sequence implies that it had been (her desire for) Eva who/that had urged Iseult to get on with the "business" of life, that is, losing one's "innocence." By evoking the novel's second major subtext, the biblical story of creation, the passage furthermore suggests that it had also been Eva, not yet "soiled" by language, who had brought to bear upon Iseult the delusive nature of her sense of self-presence.

Since a female author's revision of the Fall from grace revolves around the mother/daughter relationship, and specifically around the loss of the mother, Miss Smith's endeavors to bring her pupil "nearer the surface" of the "deep waters" in which Eva had apparently wished to "go on being submerged" had recalled to her the primordial scene of dyadic "oneness," the Imaginary bliss that is violently ruptured upon the subject's entry into language. Iseult had been forced to realize her symbolic castration, which entails a first awareness of the illusory nature of her sense of self-presence or identity. This is obliquely yet unmistakably communicated by a narrative comment. When the teacher asks her pupil what she is actually "afraid of," the narrator steps in to remark: "Eva might have said: 'That at the end of it you'll find out that I have nothing to declare' " (64). In other words, Eva had threatened to expose that not only her own subjectivity but subjectivity generally is no more than a necessary fiction with no intrinsic meaning or essence.

As soon as Eva had inadvertently reminded Iseult of the primary split, and therewith of the fictitious groundings of the self, the teacher had begun to withdraw from her, behaving "noncommittally—tolerantly, if anything" (66). The negative affect associated with the scene of primary loss, the enforced recognition of her alienation-in-language, and the reemergence of her repressed sexual desires for a female object had henceforth been connected with Eva in Miss Smith's un/consciousness. This explains the persistence of her fearful fascination with her former pupil. Her illicit same-sex longings are palpably at odds with the intellectual system from which Miss Smith derives her "symbolic authority." As such, the character's dilemma exemplifies precisely the irreconcilablity of desires informing "normal" female sexuality as delineated by Silverman. At the time, however, Iseult's excitement at discovering her intellectual powers had still been strong enough to subdue and neutralize any unwanted physical impulses. Taking recourse to her customary strategy of disavowal, she had retreated to the "unearthly" pleasure of speculative thought, leaving Eva on the verge of full subjectivity so as to enable the continued *Verleugnung* of her own symbolic castration. In the final instance, the Law of the Father—splitting off the (male) mind from the (female) body, as well as discounting a female same-sex object choice—had caused Iseult to break the unLawful "occult pact" with her pupil. She had done so, however, in a manner not provided for by the classic oedipal scenario. Instead of assuming her "castrated" (feminine) position, the teacher had persevered in her intellectual (masculine) role. Although, in psychoanalytic terms, Eva had suffered the loss of her symbolic mother, she had not come under the sway of the castration complex, for Iseult had not undergone the devaluation that serves to usher the girl into the positive Oedipus complex. Indeed, to the end Eva had declared: " 'All that I know of me I have learned from you' " (66). The heroine's secondary loss thus not only involved the traumatic separation from her love object; it also entailed her entry into full subjectivity by way of the *negative* oedipal complex, which, as Silverman maintains, opens up a "desire specifically for the mother." [67]

Femininity Subverted. After school Eva once again had joined her father and his lover on their travels, resuming her place within the inverted family triangle. In the ensuing years she "constantly sent picture postcards to Miss Smith from wherever she found herself" and "caught glimpses of [her] when back in London" (18). After the teacher had given up her career to marry, her former pupil had often visited Larkins. In short: Iseult had remained an "influence" (17). This suggests that Eva, not having been compelled to (re)direct her desire within a heterosexual libidinal economy, had persisted within that new conceptual space, a period after the separation from the mother but before the inception of the positive Oedipus complex. We recall that during this phase the girl both identifies with and desires the object of the same sex. The repositioning of the negative complex within the general oedipal situation makes it possible to conceive of a lesbian object choice as the identification with an *active* female sexuality—instead of Freud's "masculinity complex"—as well as a nonregressive (for fully symbolic) form of desire. Since Freud's notion of femininity rests upon repression of the (unconscious) desire for the mother and its redirection toward the father, Eva obviously cannot be classified in the conventional binary terms of sex. Her perseverance in a position that falls outside the (phallogocentric) symbolic determines her enduring "ex-centricity."

When Eva had returned to her former teacher some time prior to the point where the novel opens, she had been motivated by a desire that defies the Law. Iseult, in contrast, seems to have adopted the role of impotence and passive inferiority appropriate to her sex. Having renounced her masculine brain or active intellectual powers, her "movements as a housewife" resemble "those of a marionette" (23). The internalized equation of lack and femininity has resulted in extreme self-disparagement: Iseult feels not only that she has "murdered [her] life" but that she has "murdered for nothing" (91). This suggests that her desires have not been fulfilled within the heterosexual contract to whose constraints she has "willingly" subjected herself. The confrontation between the former teacher and her ex-pupil is hence disconcerting to both. Eva, perceiving her love object's embrace of her cultural devaluation, is mortified. Overwhelmed by an "enormous sadness," she first wishes that Iseult would "vanish." In the end, as we have seen, she decides to flee from the scene of disenchantment herself. Iseult, on the other hand, is painfully reminded by Eva of the " 'I' " she had been and "was to have been" (91). But once she "know[s] herself fallen in hate with" by "this organism [that] had so much loved her," she is also stirred by "that original vivisectional interest which had drawn her to her uncouth pupil" in the first place (33).

Eva's rejection of Iseult's morbid self-effacement does not spur her into following the course set out by the oedipal masterplot proper. Instead of identifying with a position of powerlessness in her turn, she mocks the Law by continuing to assume an active or "phallic" position, one that is conventionally predicated upon the possession of a penis. Her discovery of Iseult's "castrated" condition does not prompt her to enter into the positive Oedipus complex, but issues instead in an almost total detachment from the symbolic order per se: outlandish Eva is and remains an outlaw. Having left Larkins, she arrives at Broadstairs "appear[ing] less feline than paramilitary" and takes control of Cathay in a manner recalling "Russian troops said to have passed through England in the late summer of 1914" (76). Once settled in, she is filled with an "abysmal content," for "*this* she possessed" (82, 80).

The heroine's defiance of the conventional role casting in the sexual play of gendered sexuality brings her power struggle with Constantine to a head. The latter persists in trying to subdue his charge to the "form" by telling her that she is "not normal," or "something worse" (101). Eva, however, instead of subjecting herself to the "hom(m)osexual" rules he seeks to impose, succeeds in making Constantine "shift . . . his position." When her wicked guardian comes to pay his "late call" at her house, he tries to practice his "vanishing" act upon Eva, a "performance [that] had always been for the benefit of Willy—who could act back in no way." Constantine presents her his countenance with "one of its master-pieces of non-expression," but the victim's daughter, "conjuring from a pocket a voluminous handkerchief, printed with dragons," succeeds in breaking the spell, "vociferating: 'Stop *that*. *I* won't have it.' " By effectively resisting the manipulative symbolic powers of her father's former lover, Eva shows that she is not in the same position as Willy had been (104). Whichever of his extensive range of discursive tricks Constantine deploys—blackmail, threat, cajolery—she turns out to be out of his reach, "not where she had been" (105). Having renounced further identification with the position of the now-devalued oedipal mother, Eva has obviously not taken up that of the father either—as Freud's opposition/reversal scheme would require. Altogether "elsewhere" (105), she continues in that new conceptual space allowing for a "genuinely oppositional desire . . . which challenges dominance from within representation and meaning."[68]

Since desire and subjectivity are interdependent, we may safely assume that her self-contained position provides Eva with an equally radically deviant sense of self. This assumption is sustained when she catches sight of herself in the mirror: "There, indeed, was Eva! One felt reinforced. The Evas exchanged a nod, then stayed rapt in mutual contemplation" (105). Instead of instilling her with a sense of inferiority or lack, her mirror image confirms Eva's increased power of self-determination. Rather than indicating its Imaginary or preoedipal quality, the sense of (same-sex) self Eva derives from her mirror image is shown to be fully grounded in the symbolic. This is confirmed when Iseult, visiting Cathay several months later, finds the place filled with "outstanding examples of everything auro-visual on the market this year, 1959" (118). She, too, notices that her ex-pupil has been "transformed" (108):

Iseult received again that puzzling impression of gained weight—exactly physical, or exactly not? The always ample and giant movements, slowed down (or could that simply be the heat?) gave signs of having prestige for the girl who made them: she rated herself, all she did and was, decidedly higher than she had done. She was in possession; in possession of *what*?

Astronomic wealth, and its so far products in here, rationally should have supplied the answer: they not only failed to, they somehow did not begin to. (119)

It is obviously not the/her Father's word/worldly goods that have provided the heroine with an enhanced sense of self; rather, it appears to be the "irrational" (female) body that has put her "in possession" of a (nonnormative) identity. After Eva has lavishly reimbursed her former teacher for any damage she may have caused, the "Amazon at bay" leaves for New York (74).

The undelivered letter referred to earlier supports my supposition that Eva has assumed a radically ex-centric sexual identity. Its author, Professor Holman (a hilarious portrait of fatuous and verbose self-importance) appears to have been fascinated by Eva because neither she herself nor the "primitive object" of her journey, her "coming reunion with [her] child," seemed to him "credible" (123, 124). Judging by his phallocentric standards, "Mrs Trout" clearly does not fit in with the patriarchal myth of motherhood:

You diverged, you are not to know how widely, from the mother-image hitherto entertained by me. Your lengthy and unencumbered physique with its harboured energy more seemed to me, and not at the first glance only, that of the dedicated discus thrower. The then total reversal of my ideas could not be without some emotive effect. (123)

While failing to meet expectations with regard to one major aspect of femininity, Eva also defies the heterosexual matrix in another. Although such a figure "assaults [Holman's] sense of all possibility," the professor yet believes a husband to Eva "must be posited" (127). He confesses, however, to being "unable to conceive who, or what in manner of being, or in some senses wherefore, can be Mr Trout." As a "being" that strikes Holman as "autonomous . . . absolutely," Eva is not to be defined in relation to a male counterpart. She exceeds the binary frame of sex.

The final chapter of part 1 reveals that Eva has found a way to

sidestep the Law of the Father in what is perhaps its very foundation. Instead of accepting the role to which she is "biologically
destined" to perform as the receptacle or bearer of man's progeny,
she has made arrangements to buy herself a child on Chicago's
black market. But before she sets out to collect her infant son, Eva
has an eerie encounter with the past. Sitting down in a coffee shop,
she finds herself opposite Elsinore, her "waif beauty . . . as it had
been, not child's or woman's" (131). While all seems to be "blotted
out" and "silence roar[s] in her ears," Eva remembers:

*The dark: the unseen distance, the known nearness. Love: the here and
the now and the nothing-but. The step on the stairs. Don't take her away,*
DON'T *take her away. She is all I am. We are all there is. . . . Right—
then* TAKE *her away, take your dead bird. You wretch, you mother I
never had. Elsinore, what happened? Nobody told me, nobody dared.
Gone, gone. Nothing can alter that now, it's too late. Go away again.*
WHAT ARE YOU DOING HERE? *Better not—* (133)

Elsinore, having spent her life "princip'ly mortifying [her]
mother," begs Eva to take her with her. In her "despairing clutch
upon Eva, round Eva," the "terrible, obstinate self-determination
of the dying" makes itself felt (142). In profound turmoil, Eva
realizes that Elsinore has come back "too late" and "at the wrong
time."

   This curious episode underscores that subjectivity is a process
based in loss, both in the form of the original object or the Real
and in terms of the first female love object. While Eva is beyond
the first phase of identity formation, the primary loss continues to
exert its ambivalent power in representing both blissful fusion and
annihilation. The sequence additionally reaffirms the central place
taken up by the mother in the process of (female) psychosexuality.
Having suffered the secondary split, albeit without internalizing
the "proper" sense of castration, Eva's desire has remained a desire
specifically for a female object. A female subject's abiding desire
for an object of the same sex is irreconcilable with the symbolic
Law. The passage concluding Eva's "Genesis" reminds us of our

heroine's ineluctable inscription in the patriarchal order and hence of the fact that she is bound to the (Judeo-Christian) law she is on the point of further trespassing against. Back at her hotel, Eva picks up the Gideon Bible and "put[s] her thumb in it: *'This is the law,'* she read, *'of the burnt offering, of the meat offering, and of the sin offering, and of the trespass offering, and of the consecrations, and of the sacrifice of the peace offerings—'* " (143). The ominous sense of foreboding expressed in these lines is, as we shall see in the next chapter, borne out when Eva returns to England in the company of her eight-year-old son, Jeremy.

7

Sexual/Textual Transgressions

> When I write, I am re-creating what was created for me.
> —"Out of a Book"

Scriptural Encodings

Ex-centric Outlaws. It is no coincidence that Eva and Jeremy spend their first eight years together in the United States.[1] As a country less exclusively rooted in the Judeo-Christian tradition, or at least with a much shorter (patriarchal) history than any European country, America is not only the mythical land of opportunity; its proverbial melting-pot culture also makes the New World the topos of accommodation to all sorts of displaced persons. There is, however, a further aspect that renders these surroundings highly plausible for Eva and her adopted son: the boy turns out to be a deaf-mute. If his mother's disengagement from the established order finds expression in her suspicion of language and a fascination with "auro-visual equipment," Jeremy's literal inability to speak would seem to position him as the sociosymbolic outcast par excellence. The United States, where the spoken and written word are increasingly being replaced by the visual discourse of movie and television screen, provides mother and son with a cultural context eminently suited to their needs.

The American fixation on images appears to have allowed Eva and Jeremy to remain in an Imaginary realm beyond inside/ outside distinctions. A few weeks after her return to England, the heroine reflects:

Yes: during the at-large American years, insulated by her fugue and his ignorance that there could be anything other, they had *lorded* it in a visual universe. They came to distinguish little between what went on inside and what went on outside the diurnal movies, or what was or was not contained in the television flickering them to sleep. From large or small screens, illusion overspilled on to all beheld. Society revolved at a distance from them like a ferris wheel dangling buckets of people. They were their own. Wasted, civilization extended round them as might acres of cannibalized cars. Only they moved. They were within a story to which they imparted the only sense. The one wonder, to them, of the exterior world was that anything should be exterior to themselves—and *could* anything be so and yet exist? (189; first italics mine)

Eva, who has taken the Law into her own hands, has assumed the position of master/God over a world ostensibly unaffected and unconstrained by the phallogocentric symbolic. Such a scene of "joyful complicity," innocent of words, evokes the preoedipal stage or, alternatively, the pagan world before the fall. Eva's reminiscences, of "sunrises with Jeremy capering naked on [her] bed like Cupid cavorting over the couch of Venus" and of the "sublimated monotony" that had "cocooned them, making them near as twins in a womb," form resounding echoes of the novel's major cultural subtexts (189, 188). The couple's shared "cinematographic existence, with no sound-track" thus reflects the presymbolic dyad in which mother and child are as yet undivided. But neither a pre-Christian Eden nor innocence are ever unproblematical or, indeed, tenable notions in Bowen. While Jeremy had been "scanning" the images, "seeking for portents," Eva had been forced to discern "premonitions of manhood in his changeable eyes" (189). If she had thus far succeeded in "lording it" in an imaginary enclosure in which "their continuous manner of being ... had had a sufficiency which was perfect," the unmistakable onset of the mirror stage in her son's psychosexual development has made her realize the illusory nature of her exclusive power to author her son's and her own lives: in the final instance, the symbolic order proves inescapable (188). Acknowledging that Jeremy, "scion of Willy Trout," must be given his Lawful place on the discursive map, Eva has been prompted to return to England.

The "uncontrollable eloquence" of Jeremy's look, the openness he and Eva have in common, their "alikeness," which has about it "something more underlying, being of the kind which is brought about by close, almost ceaseless companionship and constant, pensive, mutual contemplation" (147), evoke Eva's union with her son in terms of the Lacanian Imaginary in which all "otherness" is experienced as pure relationship. The boy's deafness has not forced Eva, who never wished to speak since she failed to the "object" or the "good," to start doing so on his behalf. Although she has provided Jeremy with a succession of visual mirrors in which to recognize himself, she has not acted as the "acoustic mirror" for him to *hear* himself in. Eva has assumed the role of symbolic mother with respect to all forms of signification except for language/discourse. The secondary split, the definitive rupture of the mother/child dyad upon the entry of the third factor has not taken place.

Thus far, the exclusive extraverbal communication with his mother has precluded any sense of lack on the part of Eva's son. Neither the loss defined by Lacan as the subject's "alienation-in-language" nor the physical affliction that factually prevents him from entering the realm of discourse has caused him to feel in any way wanting. Rather, the boy, "handicapped, one was at pains to remember, imposed on others a sense that *they* were, that it was *they* who were lacking in some faculty" (158). Jeremy has not himself experienced the symbolic castration that he makes others aware of when he and his mother arrive in her native country. But whereas Eva has recoiled from the symbolic order on account of its perceived "castrating" operations, in the sense that it failed to accommodate her ex-centric desire/subjectivity, her son has not acquired any sense of a separate self to begin with. While Eva's inability to speak is, if not exactly a matter of choice, at least to some degree determined by her own agency, Jeremy's physically imposed silence has caused the process of his subjectivity to halt at its initial (mirror) stage.

Upon their arrival in England, Eva sets out to recover the threads of the past in which she wishes to entwine her son. She learns that Iseult and Eric Arble had separated almost immediately after her departure for America, basically on account of Eric's rumored connection with the "reputed foetus" that was to become Jeremy (242). Iseult has been living in France and has not been heard from since, while Eric runs his own business in Luton with the help of a "Norwegian companion" who has borne him two children (170). Finding Larkins deserted, the prodigal daughter visits the neighboring vicarage, where she again encounters Henry Dancey, the vicar's eldest son. This old and almost only friend from the past, now donning the "form of a young man," is the first to make clear to Eva that her return to the Old World will have incisive consequences for herself as well as for her relationship with Jeremy. When he discovers that she had "been sold a pup," he cruelly points out: "'You can't get your money back; you're wrong with the law'" (152–53). Eventually, it will fall to Henry to play a mediating role in Eva's dealings with the Law, for he himself, though twenty-four and at Cambridge, is not yet quite fixed within the established order, nor has he fully embraced its founding tenets. This is reflected both in his fraught relations with his father—the vicar who, in his professional capacity, is a preeminent upholder of the Law—and in the young man's visible uncertainty about his own masculine subject-position. Henry is still practicing his part as a male intellectual-to-be. The manner in which he is presented adequately conveys the performative nature of this, and by implication any other, aspect of identity:

[Henry] took up a preparatory new position—leaning, this time, lightly against the chimney-piece, hands in pockets, one foot trailing over the other, on which he stood. The pose put him back some way into equilibrium. Each of his ways of standing, youthfully mannered, had at the same time about it its own authority: each gave emphasis. Now, the nonchalance he enacted quite soon returned to him. (153)

This insecurity in his prescribed role within the play of gendered heterosexuality permits the Reverend Dancey's "ivory other self, his fine-carved son" (157) to apologize for his harsh condemnation of Eva's "crime." He does, however, bring to bear upon the outlaw the reality that her wish to inscribe herself and her son in the historical present must involve an engagement with the past as well as the future.

Henry is not the only one who informs the heroine that she cannot continue in her ex-centric position if she is to create a space for herself and Jeremy in the Old World. His intellectual sensibility and the precariousness of his sense of gendered self, however, enable the brilliant young man to articulate in very precise terms what kind of danger Eva (re)presents. While the fact that she has placed herself beyond the Law makes her ethically speaking a "Typhoid Mary," the most "awful thing," he proclaims, consists in her "artless" behavior: in her refusal to relate to the world according to form, she "leave[s] few lives unscathed. Or at least, unchanged." Eva, in her unwillingness to practice the "art" of playing out her part in the dominant cultural scenario, "roll[s] around like some blind indeflectable planet," therewith "plung[-ing] people's ideas into deep confusion" (179). These remarks highlight that the heterosexual matrix is most seriously threatened by those subjects who are unfixed in their relations to it, who assume deviant sexual positions. Henry therefore insists on "projecting a role" for Eva, suggesting that, being conspicuous anyhow, she might as well be so on purpose and set up a "spectacular London house" to fill with "those known as 'people'" (177–78).

Constantine, too, asserts that Eva cannot pursue what he disparagingly calls her "harlequinade." With his "physical smooth collectedness, imperviousness, his look of being once and for all assembled" (167), the former guardian appears not at all uneasily poised between the contradictory pulls of the Law. While one would expect him to be an "outsider" on account of his homosexual object choice, he has in fact negotiated the most securely "assembled" place inside the dominant order. The essentially "hom(m)osexual" organization of society is thus underscored rather than gainsaid by his position. Exerting his power/knowledge as a successful businessman, Constantine at the same time entertains—merely ostensibly unLawful—relations with his new friend, a "young East End priest." Explaining to Eva that his "angle on many things has been a good deal altered" as a result of this new friendship, Constantine casually adds that Father Clavering-Haight [!] is "Anglican naturally" (174). This seemingly inconsequential observation accentuates the mutually reinforcing operations of the regulatory regimes of phallogocentrism and compulsory *female* heterosexuality. While his gender position allows the former guardian to persist in his deviant "habit of living" and yet maintain an "undintable surface" (167), Eva's ex-centricity, he contends, is altogether intolerable. Still impressed by her "unusual, many would say, phenomenal, force of character," Constantine suggests that his former charge marry so as to accommodate her "er, dynamic energy, seeking an outlet" (176). Clearly, it is an active female or lesbian sexuality that poses the most serious threat to the "hom(m)osexual" economy. The reason why Eva's access to "normality" would seem to be restricted to the conventional role of the female sex derives from the fact that she has, to all intents and purposes, assumed one of its positions while refusing the other. Since motherhood is practically interdependent with femininity within the Freudian paradigm, Eva's adoption of Jeremy has *nolens volens* inserted her into the oedipal masterplot. Constantine communicates the impossibility of the situation in unequivocal terms:

You keep [Jeremy] in Cellophane. You make a plaything of him; at best, a playmate. He may well go on hugging his disability, it's a form of immunity. He does well with it—you make life too charming for him: an Eden. High time he was cast forth from it; as things are, that could only be done across your dead body. None the less, he has a Black Monday Morning coming to him, I shouldn't wonder. (175)

While underlining the fact that the symbolic order is both an irretrievably fallen world and revealing the sociopolitical interests underpinning its founding structure, Constantine's macabre concluding words will turn out to have distinct prophetic value.

Delayed Subjection. Through the shift in the narrator's position in the second part of *ET,* we gradually become familiar with the heroine's appreciation of herself and of the world to which she has returned, a world in which gendered subjectivity and intersubjective relations are constructed in/through language. Having hitherto ensconced herself with her son in an extralinguistic "illusion," Eva faces a renewed confrontation with dialogic interaction—her conversations with primarily male acquaintances—that inevitably leads to a realization of her symbolic castration. Finding herself in the "grip of a nervous vacuum" one morning, she reflects:

What was this lack she had felt?—it was foreign to her. How came it that she could feel it? The fact was, since her return to England her mistrust of or objection to verbal intercourse—which she had understood to be fundamental—began to be undermined. More than began; the process had been continuous. Henry, Mr Dancey, Constantine, Henry again, and now finally Father Clavering-Haight: each had continued the other's work. Incalculable desires had been implanted. An induced appetite grew upon what it fed on. She was ready to talk. (188)

Newly induced to take up her appointed gender role, this time indeed by assorted representatives of the third term within the

Law, Eva is lured into the Self/Other economy of "hom(m)osexual" desire.

The colloquy with Constantine's new friend Father Tony, which immediately precedes these reflections, nonetheless supports a reading of Eva's desire as the reemerging desire for the primary love object, the symbolic mother, that is, Iseult. Urged by the "sardonic" priest, Eva admits that she resents her former teacher because she feels betrayed by her. The terms in which she relates the story of her loss echo Silverman's appreciation of the subject's symbolic castration, that is, the loss of the Real and the separation from the mother, events whose "traumas are so complexly imbricated as to be virtually synonymous," so that both the loss and the separation acquire the "force of major surgery."[2] Ascertaining that there was no "sapphic relationship" between them (Iseult "always was in a hurry"), Father Tony inquires what then the nature of Eva's "supposed injuries" may have been. The heroine responds:

"She desisted from teaching me. She abandoned my mind. She betrayed my hopes, having led them on. She pretended love, to make me show myself to her—then, thinking she saw all, she turned away. She—"
"—Wait a minute: what were your hopes?"
"To learn . . . to be, to become—I had never been." She added: "I was *beginning* to be. . . . Then she sent me back . . . again—to be nothing. . . . I remain gone. Where am I? I do not know—I was cast out from where I believed I was." (184–85)

Although she had accepted the rejection from her private Eden by acknowledging that she "became too much" for Iseult, Eva, as we have seen, had remained profoundly attached to her symbolic mother. Only later, when she recognized that she had become a witness to the older woman's internalized sense of castration, that the teacher "hated the work she had feared to finish" and that it had been she herself "who *was* that work," did Eva's passionate attachment turn into resentment. She has remained in the negative oedipal situation ever since, and it is only now, when she wishes to become a full subject within the *patriarchal* symbolic order, that cultural pressures compel her to enter the *positive* complex and thus to redirect her desire to a member of the opposite sex.

We recall that Freud himself found that the girl's attachment to her first love object can extend until well after the age at which the oedipal complex normally should have run its course. The cultural or ideological determination (as distinct from its presumed "naturalness") of a woman's heterosexual object choice that this discovery signifies became a central issue in the great psychoanalytic debate among Freud's contemporaries and was of special concern to his female colleagues. If not effectively concluded within the Oedipus complex proper, this shift in the female subject's object choice came to be situated by classic psychoanalysis within the adolescent crisis—in the narrow (clinical) sense of the term. As Hélène Deutsch put it: "Thus the task of adolescence is not only to master the Oedipus complex, but also to continue the work begun during pre-puberty and early puberty, that is, to give adult forms to the old, much deeper, and much more primitive ties with the mother, and to end all wavering in favor of a definite heterosexual orientation."[3] When the text of *ET* links the definitive loss of the first object to the institution of heterosexuality and thus of the phallogocentric order itself, the two underlying masterplots of origin once again converge.

In her engaging study, *The Mother/Daughter Plot*, Marianne Hirsch addresses the issue of sexual object choices in the context of the mother/daughter relationship.[4] In a chapter entitled "The Darkest Plots: Narration and Compulsory Heterosexuality," she borrows Adrienne Rich's well-known phrase to explain the frequent appearance of a mediating male character in female stories of the fall.[5] In modernist female fiction, Hirsch argues, "male presence provides a mediating space which clarifies the liminal position of women's discourse and of female relationships in the realm of the father" (114).[6] The mediating male, as well as his nineteenth-century predecessor, the "nurturing" fraternal/paternal figure in female novels where any maternal attachment is either absent or repressed, yields a useful perspective on Eva's burgeoning desire for Henry Dancey.

Our heroine's readiness to speak, with its concurrent sense of lack, reevokes her original oedipal desire. Since a same-sex object choice and the ex-centric subject-position it implies are ideologically disavowed, the only possibility for her to attain fully differentiated subject-status within the Law is to position herself in relation to a male object. This would, paradoxically, also provide her with an access to the female object, for if she, with the help of male mediation, can "finish" what her symbolic mother has left "unfinished," Eva will no longer function as the reminder of the latter's own lack and hence will no longer form a source of mortification and hatred. What is more, Hirsch's notion of a "fraternal" alliance would seem particularly pertinent to Eva's relations with Henry, whom she has, after all, known since childhood (he being twelve and she twice as old), when they acted as allies in opposition to Eva's powerful guardians. Since Henry is not (yet) immutably fixed in his masculine position within the Law, he is eminently suited to take up the "nurturing" role traditionally connoted feminine.

The restrictions imposed by a subject-position within the binary terms of sexual difference are at once borne down on Eva when she visits Henry at Cambridge. While he and Jeremy are absorbed in a game of "cat's cradle," she sits "locked in an anguish nobody could explain." The "beautiful agonizing mirage of the university," which is "inescapable from," represents the symbolic order she has hitherto shunned:

This was a forever she had no part in. The eternity was the more real to her for consisting of fiery particles of transience—bridges the punt slid under, raindrops spattering the Cam with vanishing circles, shivered reflections, echoes evaporating, shadows metamorphosizing, distances shifting, glorification coming and going on buildings at a whim of the sun, grass flashing through arches, gasps of primitive breath coming from stone, dusk ebbing from waxen woodwork when doors opened. Holy pillars flowed upward and fountained out, round them there being a ceaseless confluence of fanatical colours burningly staining glass. Nothing was at an end, so nothing stood still. And of this living eternity, of its kind and one of its children, had been Henry, walking beside her. (180–81)[7]

While discerning its transient character, Eva is confronted with the inaccessibility of Henry's seemingly unshakeable "world of learning." The gendered distribution of power/knowledge makes itself painfully felt: Eva is "set upon by the swamping isolating misery of the savage," beginning to suffer from the "blighting melancholia" (Silverman) that is the "norm" for a female subject (180–81).

The enforced loss of her autonomous position outside the Law has instant repercussions on Eva's relations with Jeremy. Although she tells herself that her step into the realm of discourse has been taken "for his advancement," she acknowledges that she has "not computed the cost for him of entry into another dimension." While it is quite inconceivable what the deaf-mute boy has been "thrust into the middle of," the "worst was its not being so for her. He was alone in it. Void for him, this area was at the same time dense with experiences which by claiming her made her alien" (189). Their love has never been more "mutually imploring," but Eva currently feels that Jeremy "manacle[s] her." By breaking her silence, she has broken her "pact" with her son: they are no longer "alone together" (190).

Eva realizes that it is not, as Father Tony suggested, Jeremy who is entirely in her power but rather the other way around. Grudgingly assuming her feminine position, she is beset by its accompanying sense of guilt. Her remorse about the irreversible ending of the "inaudible years" (188) is reinforced when it proves increasingly difficult to fulfill the compensatory promise of finding her son a home in the "promised land, the abiding city" of her native country (163): "That England was to provide one had been implicit" (190). Cathay is "not the answer." Marking the shift in Eva's position, the house had proved a "case of an absence" turning out to be "fatal." Once a space she "possessed," it has now become one where "unmeaningness reigned" (163). She and Jeremy are no longer the only ones to impart meaning to their story.

At the very moment when Eva feels that an externally derived "tragedy" is "trying to sit down opposite at [her table]," Iseult reappears on stage. She phones Eva at Paley's, the hotel in which the heiress's suite maintains its "provisional look of permanence" (163). The former teacher's impressive verbal "performance" gives Eva occasion to reflect on her own and Miss Smith's personalities. At first, she wonders whether this had been Miss Smith, or someone "impersonating" her: "X had certainly documented herself faultlessly: not a trick missed. But yet in another way she had fallen short, betraying an insufficient grasp of the character, its ins-and-outs ... something ... had not rung true" (192–93). Then another possibility occurs to her: "The impersonator of Miss Smith had been Miss Smith, a deceased person purporting to be a living one." Eva realizes that she apparently knows a different, former Miss Smith and that she knows her better than the woman who is trying to revivify this persona. Bringing home the performative and unstable groundings of identity, the dialogic encounter issues in a further reconsideration of the notion of subjectivity. The narrator merges with the heroine's consciousness to reflect:

Anyhow, what a slippery fish is identity; and what *is* it, besides a slippery fish? If Miss Smith had not rung up Eva, nobody else had: "X" could be counted out. What *is* a person? Is it true, there is not more than one of each? If so, is it this singular forcefulness, or forcefulness arising from being singular, which occasionally causes a person to bite on history? All the more, in that case, what *is* a person? (193–94)

In order to find an answer to these ontological questions, Eva decides to visit the National Portrait Gallery. Her uneasy premonitions are confirmed:

They *were* all "pictures." Images. "Nothing but a pack of cards"?—not quite, but nearly enough that to defeat Eva. . . . Every soul Eva knew became no longer anything but a Portrait. There was no "real life"; no life was more real than this. This she had long suspected. She now was certain. (195–96)

When Eva returns to the "real world," she does so with a thorough understanding of the constructed nature of cultural identities and of the inescability of the masterplots from which human actors must take their meanings: "One plot unravelled, another knitting. . . . Yet here the personae were, as before. As ever" (196). While denying her the illusion of self-presence, the experience provokes a renewed determination to exert her agency with regard to the creation of a self, to author the story of her life. She is soon to learn, however, that the very discursivity of the meanings of self and world implies that both are always already inscribed in a symbolic network that is external to as well as beyond the reach of any individual. Henceforth, Eva is irreversibly taken up by the phallocratic masterplots.

Inscription into the Masterplots. Arriving at the studio where Jeremy has lately been spending the afternoons sculpturing, Eva finds that he has been abducted by a woman who had presented herself as her friend. He is returned to Paley's a few hours later, but Eva's panic and desolation during the hours of her son's absence, with her eyes "fixed on nothing but nothingness" (202), induce her to leave London. Settling in Paris, she is for the first time "not sure where to go next" (203).

At the point where Eva is "beset by the quandaries of the rootless rich, for whom each choice becomes a vagary," we have reached the final chapter of part 2, and thus of the novel as a whole. The chapter's title brings the narrative line full circle. "This is Where We Were to Have Spent the Honeymoon" is literally the opening sentence with which the unaccountable heroine had introduced herself—characteristically, since the putative marriage was the product of her "passion for the fictitious for its own sake" (242). This emphatic circularity heralds a tightening of the plot while at the same time reinscribing into the narrative the myth of heterosexual romance. The episodes making up the final section of the text are qualified by a rising mood of urgency and looming crisis.

Once they have taken up residence at the Ritz, Jeremy, whose numerous "paroxysms" have been becoming a source of worry to her, surprises Eva by being "implacably good" and "conciliating." She herself recovers some of her self-assurance: "One knew nobody: Paris was one's own." But while her son watches "this further movie" with interest, Eva is forced to perceive that the breach between them has become irreparable: "An unbridgeable ignorance of each other, or each other's motives, had been cleft between them, and out of the gulf rose a breath of ice" (205). There are several indications suggesting that it is not only Eva's hesitant steps into the realm of the symbolic that have caused the former channels of their wordless communication to become blocked. The mysterious interlude away from his mother is clearly absorbing the boy's attention in retrospect: he turns to Eva "irradiated by some secret" (205). The stranger with whom Jeremy— otherwise not "confiding"—had gone away "willingly," will later turn out to have been Iseult. While suggesting that the latter has succeeded in initiating Jeremy into the "secret" (sexual) subtext of Western culture, the central position that Miss Smith continues to occupy in Eva's story is further brought to the fore in a number of letters exchanged between her and Constantine.

We learn that the former teacher, during the eight years of her own and Eva's absence from England, had been keeping up a one-sided correspondence with the figure nearest in access to her ex-pupil. Addressing herself to Constantine the way she used to address her typewriter—curious to see "what it was about to tell her" (91)—she has thus established him in the position of the "mediating male" while at the same time proceeding with her

autoanalysis, relaying to him her case-history-in-progress. A further string of letters reveals that Eva's whereabouts have, through
Henry, inadvertently been passed on to Miss Smith; this precipi-
tates yet another move, for the figure of her lost love object continues to haunt the heroine's narrative itinerary.

At Fontainebleau, Eva contacts a couple—"doctor and doctor
wife"—who specialize in cases such as Jeremy's. Until their coming to the Old World, each of the various specialists she had
consulted had run up against the boy's inner resistance. Eva's
willingness to speak, however, has plunged the boy into a hitherto
unknown isolation. He retaliates against the rupture of their dyadic union by responding remarkably well to the Bonnards' treatment. When we learn that the success of the doctors' method
depends on "certain factors, in the main psychic," the teleological
masterplot of Freudian psychoanalysis no longer operates merely
as one of the novel's (hidden) subtexts. After a month with the
Bonnards—residing in a house "bound round by a patriarchal
wisteria"—Jeremy begins to formulate words and starts to "accord to the lips of speakers, other than Eva, a level, exacting,
scientific attention denied formerly." He has been "won over" by
his therapists. The narrator merges with Eva's consciousness to
explore the causes of this radical change:

> What *had* decided him? One could recollect that, since the flight to Paris,
> in fact since the eve of the flight to Paris, he had, for all his angel
> amenability, been withdrawn as never before. To be as others, simply to
> be *as* others, had never tempted him—what, as the terms of his lordly,
> made-magical life were, could (as Constantine had asked) be the induce-
> ment? But now, by what means had the idea of *exceeding* been made
> known to him, or made itself known to him? . . . He was interacting
> ideally with the Bonnards. (215)

Iseult will later proudly disclose that she was the first to tempt the
boy out of his "cage," luring him out of his "dream" into "razor-
edged actuality, layers deep" (245). Taking up the work she had
left "unfinished" with Eva, she has thus reassumed her former

role, initiating her ex-pupil's son in lack, therewith instituting his desire/subjectivity.

Jeremy's symbolic inscription forces him to acknowledge (hetero)sexual Otherness (supplanting the "otherness" characterizing the mirror stage). He is subsequently inserted into the oedipal family triangle proper by his "psychological engineers," the Bonnards. The "accustomed communications" with Eva break down: his "responses were not less willing, but less ready." No longer "one" with her son, Eva is presently compelled to touch Jeremy in order to get his attention. In the process of becoming the female Other to his male Same/Self, she realizes that the gulf between them is even more marked since the language that is "to be his first" is foreign to her. Eva is able to "master" the "vocabulary" of the French novels [!] she starts reading on Jeremy's account, "but not their content." While the myth of romance remains alien to her, the mother/child dyad has conclusively come to an end: "His and her universe was over" (216).

Dr. Bonnard, a self-defined "environmentalist," rejects the "horrible doctrine of Predestination" and is therefore primarily interested in what Eva has supplied Jeremy with, the "character of what [she] ha[s] given him" (222). Extending his professional interest to Eva herself, he endeavors to "make her try to define [her situation] for him" (221). This issues in an unequivocal exposure of Eva's excentric position within the heterosexual matrix. Dr. Bonnard first asks Eva what had made her "prefer mimicry to what could have been the actual continuance of flesh-and-blood" (222). His use of the word "mimicry" calls to mind the debate on the "masquerade" of femininity within recent feminist theory, especially in relation to the male gaze, or specularity in general.[8]

As a concept theorizing "femininity," "masquerade"—a term also echoed in Constantine's designation of Eva's existence as a "harlequinade"—was first used by one of Freud's contemporaries, the female psychoanalyst Joan Rivière, as early as 1929. In "Womanliness as a Masquerade," Rivière relates the case history of a patient considered to be representative of a "particular type of intellectual woman."[9] Rivière's professionally highly successful patient suffered from an extreme need for reassurance from her male colleagues, as if she feared retribution for usurping the masculine position culturally acknowledged to be rightfully theirs. She furthermore devoted herself to her feminine activities with unnecessary and degrading zeal, "'disguising herself' as merely a castrated woman." Her patient's aim, Rivière infers, "was chiefly to make sure of masquerading as guiltless and innocent":

Womanliness therefore could be assumed and worn as a mask, both to hide the possession of masculinity and to avert the reprisals expected if she was found to possess it. . . . The reader may now ask how I define womanliness or where I draw the line between genuine womanhood and the "masquerade." My suggestion is not, however, that there is any such difference; whether radical or superficial, they are the same thing. (38)

Feminist film theorist Mary Ann Doane takes up Rivière's concept of femininity as a means to "compensate for the theft of masculinity" on the part of the woman who assumes the "position of the subject rather than its object," positing that "masquerading" offers a radical strategy against "patriarchal positioning." If womanliness is a masquerade, Doane argues, the possibility either to wear this "mask" or to remove it is necessarily implied. Rather than representing the unrepresentable, the "masquerade of femininity" would thus "double representation," produce an "excess of femininity," and thereby threaten the male system of specularity in which woman can only be the object of the male gaze.[10]

While highly tempting in its promise of political empowerment, Doane's argument rests on a perhaps overly optimistic assumption of agency in the "deep-seated, psychically entrenched play" by means of which sexual identities are constituted.[11] Even if we take sufficiently into account that the performative acts in/through which genders are produced do not entail that they are merely roles to be adopted or rejected at will, the supposition that femininity can be performed to excess presupposes the prior existence of a female subject who can choose (not) to perform her ascribed gender role. Such a notion of the masquerade of womanliness, in other words, by assuming a radical noncoincidence of sex and gender, is founded on the state-of-nature hypothesis by means of which dominant discourses naturalize as fixed and immutable what are in effect no less unstable, constituted effects: the "natural" categories of sex, of man and woman. The stakes involved in maintaining the duality of gender are, not surprisingly, revealed by the two male characters who at this point (re)assume their roles as "guardians" over Eva's story. Considering their vested interests in, respectively, the social and the economic structures of the "hom(m)osexual" economy, it is not by accident that Dr. Bonnard and Constantine refer to Eva's outrageous sexual "play" in similar terms of simulation and/or imitation. While quite differently situated within the dominant field of power/knowledge in terms of desire, these characters are joined in their gender investments in a social order subtended by the binary frame of sex.

Established gender relations cut across the straight/gay binary, for, as Judith Butler points out, the male homosexual in Western culture serves as the exception to confirm the rule, occupying a discursive space within the heterosexual matrix as prohibited object in relation to which the law of nature can assert itself. Whereas "homosexualities of all kinds ... are being erased, reduced, and (then) reconstituted as sites of radical homophobic fantasy," it is precisely as "prohibited objects" that male homosexualities are in effect perpetually (re)constituted by official discourses as well as "reverse-discourses" within the "grid of cultural intelligibility." Lesbians, in contrast, are "not even named nor prohibited within the economy of the law." The mandatory falsification of lesbianism in phallogocentric culture shows that it is not compulsory heterosexuality per se, but compulsory *female* heterosexuality that is the condition upon which the "natural" order of things or, to be more precise, the social contract depends. Only by being relegated to a "domain of unthinkability and unnameability" can the lesbian be culturally present: as an "abiding falsehood," as a "copy, an imitation, a derivative example, a shadow of the real."[12] It is in its virtual discursive absence (effectively reinscribed by derivative terms like "female homosexual") that the category lesbian must function as the abject of the cultural unconsciousness.

By conspicuously performing the "unthinkable," Eva embodies a threat of exposure to both gay and straight upholders of the law. Since the most explicit sexually specific definition of the heroine given in the text is that of "hermaphrodite," the "monstrous" creature is eminently suited to subvert what Butler calls the "onto-logically consolidated phantasms of man and woman." Her sexual "mimicry" is hence exactly the kind of "drag" that Butler (drawing on the work of Esther Newton) claims "enact[s] the very structure of impersonation by which *any gender* is assumed."[13] In order to ensure their self-presence as male, that is, as genuine, authentic, real subjects, Eva's guardians must set off her "abnormal" per-formance as a harlequinade against the "real thing": "natural" heterosexuality, which, as we have seen, is in fact the term of "hom(m)osexuality."[14]

Eva's mimicry is clearly not a strategic performance of "feminin-ity to excess" with which she self-consciously attempts to subvert the phallocratic order. Still, the "drastic" means by which she has donned the aspect of motherhood without going to "all that trou-ble" of heterosexual intercourse indicates that her "womanliness" is no more and no less than a masquerade. Iseult's perplexity at Cathay, leading her to wonder "in possession of *what*" her ex-pupil appeared to be, is retrospectively placed in a significant light: at that moment, Eva had already set the scheme in motion by which to procure Jeremy. That her feminine drag inadvertently serves both to disguise and to maintain the phallic powers ideologi-cally denied her emerges when Dr. Bonnard asks Eva whether she had "wished . . . to be Jeremy's father as well as his mother." "Not greatly startled," she replies that this has "possibly" been the case (222).

The suggestion that the heroine's ex-centricity consists first and foremost in her rejection of a gendered sexuality is substantiated by Iseult. In what is "not a 'confession'" to Father Clavering-Haight, the former teacher gives an account of herself in relation to Eva and, by extension, to Jeremy. Claiming to have worked a miracle with the boy during her stolen hours with him, Iseult explains that her interest in the "for so long hypothetical child" had "always had a particular undertow": "'It was inextricable from my feeling for Eva. I care for her. . . . Implanted in her there is something which surmounts any harm we have done each other. It is something in which I was instrumental.'" Acknowledging her critical role in furthering Eva's psychosexual development and disclosing the "negative" affect underlying her "positive" interest in Jeremy, Iseult, having been forced to disavow her desire for her pupil under cultural pressure, had, in a slightly twisted version of the oedipal plot, come to "conceive of [Eva's child] in his own right, to in some way desire for his own sake [*sic*]" (242). Her forbidden desire for Eva had thus resulted in the desire for a substitute object at one remove: her love object's own (substitute) desire for a child. The renunciation of her masculine position as a subject of power/knowledge has had a doubly castrating effect on Miss Smith. Not only has she abandoned her intellectual drives, but the repression of her lesbian desire has also led to an "emotional hysterotomy" (225). The fact that Iseult's "inside's gone" is directly linked to her desire for Eva, whom, she regretfully sighs, "loved [her], once" (212).

In addition to exposing the basis of her enduring "obsession" with her former pupil, Iseult's nonconfession justifies a reading of Eva's harlequinade as a performance of a nonnormative sexuality with radically subversive potential. Situating her ex-centricity explicitly within the binary frame of sex, the former teacher explains why the heroine's child could only have been a boy:

"For one thing, a second Eva would have been not only unthinkable but impossible. For another, she belonged in some other category. 'Girl' never fitted Eva. Her so-called sex bored and mortified her; she dragged it about after her like a ball and chain. Why should she wish to reproduce it when she chose a child? Also, remember, thanks to her father and Constantine she had grown up apart from women, other than hirelings. She did not need women. Their vulnerability antagonized her—as *I* found. She had had enough of her father's vulnerability. She had watched him being destroyed—.... That Willy image, it became her object to repair, or reconstitute—" (243)

This sequence almost literally foreshadows Butler's radical reconceptualization of sexuality as a compulsively repeated "string of performative acts," of a sexually determined self as the (re)produced effect of a discourse that "nevertheless claims to 'represent' that self as prior truth."[15] Eva has rejected femininity per se— whether in the guise of her father's victimization at the hands of his lover or in the form of Iseult's self-mutilation under pressure of phallocratic ideology. Falling outside the grid of cultural intelligibility, she is indeed "unthinkable." Positioning oneself beyond the Law, however, exacts its price. This is currently making itself felt.

Hitherto, Eva has maintained a complete disregard for the interpellating Other/s making up the dialogic network of the symbolic. After her disappointment in Iseult, the self-sufficient nature of her "pure relationship" with Jeremy had temporarily subdued any reemerging wish for an Other in relation to whom/which to constitute her Self. The breakdown of that "perfect union" is bringing about a drastic change in this respect. It is the environmentalist Dr. Bonnard who informs Eva why it is important to consider "what is thought of [her], or was":

One is so much made by it. Whether one resists it or not, it has so much power. It is so hard not to comply with it, not to fall in with it—not to be overcome by it in the very battle one has against it. The way one is envisaged by other people—what easier way is there of envisaging oneself? There is a fatalism in one's acceptance of it. Solitude is not the solution, one feels followed. Choice—choice of those who are to surround one, choice of those most likely to see one rightly—is the only escape. But for some of us it is an escape difficult to make. (223)

Eva's expanding desires preclude a further dismissal of (the) Other/s upon which her subjective differentiation depends. Her instructor, true to the creeds of his profession, puts great emphasis on the critical role of specularity in the subjective process. The "gendered nature" of the gaze gives the doctor's words all the more significance: the enclosure from which Eva is urged to "escape" has, after all, been an exclusively "visual," even "cinematographic" one. Not only will she henceforth be cast into a symbolic field in which the authority of the look is a male prerogative—so that the range of her "choice" is considerably reduced—but her son Jeremy is entering the Realm of the Father too—and in anticipation of a different position. The boy, we shall see, assumes his "phallic" power with a vengeance.

Closing Circles. The imposing presence of the castle of Fontaine-bleau during her exchange with Dr. Bonnard underscores the links between Eva's growing desire for Henry and her earlier experiences at the castle-school. In the throes of the reemerging oedipal crisis, which now seems to be approaching its positive stage, her sense of apprehension is as yet vague. When she tells Dr. Bonnard that she is "frightened, as though [she] were about to die" (224), the implications of accepting her proper role within the heterosexual matrix are invoked in unmistakable terms. Moved by her need for recognition, Eva is allowing herself to become defined in the binary terms of gender, which threatens to put an end to her ex-centric self. A return visit to the scene of her first love in the company of Henry enhances rather than alleviates the heroine's anxiety.

The episode is presented as if performed on stage. Set against the castle, which "seemed to be leaning a little back, like a propped-up canvas," the two figures floating on the lake in their "bright shirts . . . admired each other, dreamily, as they did the scenery" (229). The unreal atmosphere is not as idyllic as it seems, for the "stained, sham castle" resounds with "revengeful unheard echoes . . . as though by frivolling with the past the building incurred the past at its nastiest" (230). The actors themselves are aware of the illusory quality of their gambol in front of this "pleasure-ship," which, as Henry observes, is too "dreamed-up ... to do" (231), thereby underlining the mythical character of the heterosexual plot—a plot, moreover, that is to be superimposed on the passionate echoes of a prior, more "primitive" sexual scenario. When, despite their repeated attempts, the couple fails to get into the castle, Henry implores his companion to tell him "what's supposed to be going to happen," adding somewhat uneasily: "'You are the authority—if there is one?'" By letting the past go unheeded, however, Eva is losing her autonomous self, and therefore is no longer the sole author of her story. The biblical reverberations punctuating the text underscore with stark precision the nature of the larger plot that is rapidly unfolding:

The torrents of the future went roaring by her. No beam lit their irrisible waters. The Deluge: dead arms flailing like swimmers. Where were they on their way to being swept to, she, Henry, Jeremy? Who had opened the sluice-gates, let through this roaring? The boy, doing so by the same act by which he heaved the lid from his tomb of silence? Jeremy, whose destiny she had diverted? One does not do such a thing with impunity, the priest had said. The doctor had warned her. . . . She absently turned to Henry, at this moment, caverns of apprehension. (233)

The passage underlines Jeremy's critical function in establishing both himself and Eva in the oedipal triangle. The joint appearance of the priest and the doctor as the angels of retribution furthermore testifies to the reinforcing operation of the novel's underlying masterplots, against whose founding laws Eva has trespassed in a most intolerable manner. When the heroine subsequently gets entangled in a briar bush, provoking from Henry the exclamation that she will be "like Abraham's ram" (234), we are reminded of the portentous passage from the Gideon Bible that, her own "Genesis" concluded, inaugurated the story of her unLawful motherhood.

Despite her growing sense of alarm, Eva's "indomitable will" and her bent for the fictitious urge her to "precipitate" the next installment of her own subversive plot. Back in England on the advice of the Bonnards, who felt it best for Jeremy to be "quite away from [her]" for a while, she informs Henry that she intends not merely to love but also to marry him. By his reactions Henry unwittingly highlights his role as a fraternal figure in Eva's alternative oedipal scenario. He protests that the plan would make him "almost another Jeremy," for to Henry—"such a split-up character"—Eva remains "outsize, larger-than-life" (236). His fear of his father's condemnation of a further "brush with Mammon" (232), that is, Eva, leads him to reject the plan as crazy. Although Henry tries to disguise his sexual insecurity by declaring that he "*could* make love to [Eva]," although they have never "so much as touched" (237), he reveals, on their way back, that the traditional balance of power in fact does not apply: too nervous to drive Eva's new Jaguar, he is forced to hand back the wheel to her. Reasserting herself as the director of her harlequinade, Eva proceeds by asking Henry to act the part of her "bridegroom . . . for one occasion," by "*appear*[ing] to depart with [her] on a wedding journey" from Victoria Station, "seen off by friends." To his shocked objection as to the "poor fun" she is "master-minding" him into, she responds: " 'For once, one day only, part of one day only, you would at least be mine *in the eyes of the world*' " (238; italics mine). Despite his blunt refusal to feature in her "*comédie noire,*" the young man begins to be irked by "that fatal old fascination of cooking a plot with Eva" (239), therewith authenticating her in the role of author/director. After a protracted period of soul-searching (his internal struggle with the/his Father is beautifully done), Henry complies with the request of the "Iron Maiden" of his youth (232).

While engrossed in the preparations for the play she is staging for herself and Henry, Eva is distracted by another plot, this one "imposed on her" by the Bonnards. As the "inspired authorities" with regard to Jeremy, these "dedicated zealots" have ordained her to reassemble the former suite at Paley's so as to make it look plausible for her son's unexpected visit to London (253). The irreversible effects of the boy's initiation into the Law of the Father are clear the moment he makes his entry with a "touch of the executive, however junior." The narrator explains:

They were seeing each other after their first, their one separation since Jeremy had (virtually) been born to Eva. And what was disconcerting was, not that there was any question of disillusionment, on either side, but rather that the minute was reigned over by a startling, because unavoidable, calmness—a calmness to which there was no alternative. One could have called it a disinfected one. . . . Anything primitive, was gone. . . . The dear game was over, the game was up. (254)

Foregrounded by the emphatic presence of linear time ticking away toward the narrative climax, the scene of the post-Imaginary reunion between mother and son signals the teleological violence inherent in the oedipal tract: Eva and Jeremy are henceforth engaged in the primordial battle between the sexes. Becoming an "onlooker" at her son's acquisition of his masculine identity—a project "supervised by himself"—Eva's suspicions about his "therapy" increase:

What sort of dupe had the noble Bonnards imagined this boy to be? As stars in Eva's firmament, they declined slightly—a fundamental misgiving shook her. Alternatively, were their machinations five fathoms deep? This *recherche* for the basic they had made such a point of . . . what of it? Unloading Jeremy on her, for that adduced reason . . . his directors, his psychological engineers *could* have had an undeclarable motive: what? To bring about this undoing. To rid not only the child of Eva but the child and Eva of one another. (255)

The passage exposes the "hom(m)osexual" interest in the mother/child separation. While ensuring the female subject's availability as the authenticating Other to the Same/Self, the enforced split also guarantees the female subject's dispossession of symbolic power.

As the "directors" of the oedipal plot proper, which essentially concerns the demolition of a libidinal economy in which the female subject occupies an actively phallic position, the Bonnards' mode of treatment attests to the phallogocentric inscription of the narrative of classic psychoanalysis. By defining woman as lack (on which man's presence depends), the Freudian masterplot serves to obscure the symbolic castration intrinsic to male and female subjectivity alike. Jeremy's "preoccupation" therefore strikes Eva as something "alien or even hostile to" to the "limpid seriousness of childhood." His separation from his mother is, after all, the loss of the Real as much as the loss of his presymbolic self. Although the boy is cast in his prospective role as the subject of power/knowledge, his "centredness" has "something forbidding—sundering? repellent?" about it: he is henceforth cut off from the excess to rational (masculine) consciousness. To this exposure of the male subject's origin in lack, the narrator wryly adds: "History, one was forced to remember, is forged by the overriders of handicaps, some evident, some not known till the end" (256). While emphasizing the oedipal undertow of the narrative of patriarchal history, the remark acquires a specifically menacing ring in the light of scattered references to a revolver that subsequently begin to surface in the text. Having found its way into the hotel's storeroom via Iseult, the gun had ended up amid the "stunning amount" of belongings Eva was to reassemble into a scene of "domesticity" at Paley's. Immediately attracted to the "one extraneous parcel" in the room, Jeremy has stealthily taken possession of this unmistakable phallic attribute (253).

The novel's final scene contains all the elements of a grand finale. Under the dome of Victoria Station, this "temple of departure," one after the other character reappears to witness the triumphant concluding act of the heroine's harlequinade. In addition to Henry, Constantine, Iseult, and Eric Arble, we witness an unidentified "drift of people" radiating the "waveringness of a phantom company." These anonymous extras accentuate the spurious nature of the scene about to be enacted: the conventional "happy ending" to the story of heterosexual romance. Since these nameless characters function as a chorus, their presence also hints at the mythical origins of the tragic cultural script onto which the protagonist/director persists in superimposing her own blasphemously revised versions. Still, it is precisely *as* myths that the patriarchal founding texts are so compelling. This is unambiguously brought to the fore when Henry, discerning the "tribal likeness" among the members of the crowd and their "look, or air, which in its own way was like a wedding garment," astutely reflects that an "unreal act collects round it real-er emotion than a real act, sometimes" (261). Then, with the aspect of a genuine tragic heroine, Eva makes her appearance. Her grandeur provokes an awed silence:

Not far off, in one of those chance islands of space, she stood tall as a candle, some accident of light rendering her luminous from top to toe—in a pale suit, elongated by the elegance of its narrowness, and turned-back little hat of the same no-colour; no flowers, but on the lapel of the jacket a spraying-out subcontinent of diamonds: a great brooch. A soft further glow had been tinted on to her face; her eyes were increased by the now mothy dusk of their lashes. She was looking unhurriedly, all but abstractly in the direction of Henry. (261–62)

The imagery in this passage splendidly underscores the sexual over-determination of the heroine's magnificence. While her body and posture are defined in unequivocally phallic terms, the striking use of the word "subcontinent" to describe Eva's brooch recalls Freud's designation of female sexuality as the "dark continent" of psychoanalysis. We are also reminded of the archeological image he used to describe his discovery of the negative Oedipus complex or the pre-Oedipus: acknowledging its hidden and subversive power, Freud declared that the passionate bond between mother and girl child was "like the discovery, in another field, of the Minoan-Mycenaean civilization behind the civilization of Greece."[16] The suggested link is confirmed when Eva reveals that the "spraying-out . . . diamonds"—which invite excited comments from everyone present—had been her mother's (262). While her phallic surface appearance reflects Eva's ex-centric position within the Law of the Father, its concealed or underlying foundation is thus shown to be the bond with the first love object, the mother.

Eva reaffirms her role as stage manager by confessing to Constantine that she has herself invited the "Happy Band" of "mist-like phantoms . . . still seeking, unflaggingly" along the platform (264). The surreal atmosphere is given a distinctly contemporary dimension when a rumor starts spreading of "film . . . being shot." This is the perfect moment for Jeremy to appear "on the stage, or the platform." The "audience-minded" crowd stands back to allow him the "space and free play [of] the child star." When the boy lifts the gun out of his dispatch case "in a manner evidently rehearsed," it is clear that he is engaged in playing out a different scenario than the one set up by his mother (266). But Eva's control as director of her harlequinade is undermined in other respects as well. Henry informs her that he is "not going to get off" the train as planned. Seeing the day thus being turned into a genuine "coronation day," Eva sheds the first tears of her life. When the couple steps back onto the platform they are as yet ignorant of Jeremy's arrival. Constantine gives them his blessing and wishes them a "pleasant future." This, he adds, "will resemble the past in being the result, largely, of a concatenation of circumstances." Such conceptualizations are all but alien to Eva, so she asks her former guardian what "concatenation" means. These are "her last words." "At the sight of Eva," Jeremy speeds "like a boy on the screen towards the irradiated figure, waving his weapon in salute." Holding out her arms to receive him, Eva turns round at a "cry of terror" from Henry:

> That instant, the revolver went off. She fell, while the shot rang round Victoria Station.
> Jeremy could not stop running on. A woman bystander to whom nothing was anything had the quickest reflex—she snatched him back before he could fall over the dead body. (266)

The fact that it is a "woman bystander" who prevents the full disclosure of the final irony of Eva's/the text's end indicates the complicitous position of female subjects in patriarchal ideology. Yet, by almost literally fulfilling Constantine's prophesy, Jeremy also reaffirms the central function of the (loss of) the mother in the process of both male and female subjectivity. Induced by the primary split, his act is one of retaliation against the infliction of a narcissistic wound, the traumatizing rupture of the Imaginary dyad that installs the subject *as* subject by opening up her/his un/consciousness. Having been inscribed in an alternative as well as into the master narrative, however, Jeremy's oedipal trajectory has become exceedingly complicated. The boy's act of aggression against Eva therefore signifies on several intertwining levels at the points where these two conflicting plot lines intersect.

Jeremy's sense of betrayal is enhanced by the fact that, instead of showing herself to be lacking, his mother had suddenly assumed the position of speaking subject in relation to which his own affliction came to represent a "doubled" symbolic castration. Furthermore, by assuming the roles of mother as well as father in the family triangle, Eva had situated herself in both—or neither—of the conventional (oppositional) gender positions with regard to the phallus/sexual desire. Hence, her son's initiation into the "normal" oedipal complex under the guidance of the Bonnards had rendered the love object he was forced to renounce simultaneously into the rival parent. By killing Eva, he has rid himself not only of the castrating mother but also of the masculine figure endowed with superior phallic power, equally representing the threat of castration. Finally, and no less importantly, the boy's entry into the symbolic order has not only led him to assume his proper position within the oedipal situation but has also set him up in his function as future defender of the Law. Embracing his role as the agent of prohibition and retribution, he punishes Eva for having committed *the* archetypal cardinal sin. The position of phallic/creative power she has been usurping is, after all, in both the Christian and the oedipal myths of origin, the prerogative of the

Father/male. Both the heroine's sexual ex-centricity and her harlequinade of womanliness are shown to be intolerable in a symbolic order in which male presence can only be defined in relation to female absence.

The Mother's Tongue and Female Authorship

Cracking Surfaces. The history of Bowen's last heroine would seem adequately to support Victoria Glendinning's contention that at the end of her career, the author "dispensed with the civilized surface of behaviour": in *ET*, "there is no longer a cracked crust over the surface of life." The biographer's inference that Bowen finally "allowed the danger, despair, and passion which had always lain under the surface to be expressed"[17] acquires further interest when we regard her last novel as a story of origins in the several senses suggested in the opening section of the preceding chapter. Its underlying "back-to-the wombishness" qualifies *ET* as an exploration of origins in which the "danger, despair, and passion" expressed on the surface level are directly linked to the daughter's passionate desire for and separation from the mother. As traumatic experiences in themselves, these psychic events take on particular edge in the light of Bowen's personal tragedy, the premature death of her mother. On the intra- as much as the extradiegetic levels of the text, *ET* represents a fictional recreation, and thus a reworking, of what we can safely assume to be a repressed part of the author's un/consciousness. While the protagonist's history testifies to the central place of what I have termed Bowen's maternal past on the narrative or intradiegetic level, the pivotal role of the narrator illuminates its significance on the extrafictional or extradiegetic level.

As mentioned before, the absent mother or the figure of the "terrible" older woman are recurring features in Bowen's work. The essential ambivalence of these figures has never been more explicitly brought to the fore than in *ET*, whether she appears in the guise of ever-absent Cissie, of Elsinore's "corrupt mother," of Iseult Smith, or, indeed, of the eponymous heroine herself. The novel's formidable protagonist, however, is present not only in her role of mother but also as a daughter (of sorts). As such, she would seem to be the perfect embodiment of "sexual ambiguity, disguise, and polynymia," that is, of the crisis-subjectivity that Julia Kristeva assigns to the character of the adolescent. As we have seen, the open psychic structure represented by this mythic figure functions as a locus of its creator's repressed desire. To repeat Kristeva: "There is a certain identification of the narrator with his seductress or seducer, even more so, since these adolescents escape all categories—even those of coded perversions—and impose themselves on novelists as metaphors for what . . . calls to him, the mirage of pre-language or unnamed body." [18] The multiplicity of the metaphor in question, "outsize" and "monstrous" Eva, whose "perversion" is explicitly "coded" as "hermaphroditism," resides precisely in her dual role as mother/daughter, a heterogeneity that Marianne Hirsch attributes to the female character per se. Even so:

The multiplicity of "women" is nowhere more obvious than for the figure of the mother, who is always both mother and daughter. Her representation is controlled by her object status, but her discourse, when it is voiced, moves her from object to subject. But, as long as she speaks as mother, she must always remain the object in her child's process of subject-formation; she is never fully a subject. [19]

From the fact that mothers are mainly "absent, silent, or devalued" in female fictions in the classic realist tradition, Hirsch infers that the conventions particular to this genre "shut out various forms of indeterminacy, instability, and social fragmentation, including . . . maternal perspectives and experiences." She goes on to suggest that the "thoroughness with which female realist writers eliminate mothers from their fictions" may partly result from "hostility, resentment and disappointment on the part of these writers themselves, as well as with their total self-identification as daughters." [20]

The character of Eva Trout combines, or perhaps *doubles* the elements of ambiguity and polyvalence inhering in either of these mythic figures—the adolescent as much as the maternal. In both functions, the heroine therefore constitutes a highly ambivalent object of authorial identificatory and desirous investment. Since *ET* transcends conventional generic boundaries while still remaining firmly inscribed in the realist tradition, one would expect the figure of the mother to be both present and absent in/from the text, to find her occupying the position of both subject and object of narration. Although the latter expectation is readily confirmed, the text remains ultimately divided as to the former. Surfacing in a structural decenteredness, the resulting sense of contradiction is foregrounded by the shift in narrative method that distinguishes the novel's two parts.

In using the author's biography as a dialogizing background against which to explore the fictional text's "unconsciousness," it is not my intention (posthumously) to analyze Elizabeth Bowen nor to resurrect the traditional Author-God conclusively put to death by poststructuralist theory.[21] What I am concerned with is the (theoretical) construct of the speaking/writing subject, and more precisely, the concept of the female author. By incorporating a number of textual modes—such as letters, diary fragments, (non)confessions—that are essentially discursive inscriptions of the characters' selves, while still being situated explicitly in the text of history, *ET* presents itself emphatically *as* text in its postmodern context. As a self-consciously intertextual construction in which a multiplicity of heterogeneous discourses intersects on various levels, the novel directs us to the author as an intra- as much as an extratextual configuration. To clarify my point, I must digress briefly into auteur theory.

Despite the preoccupation with female language, the category of the author has remained relatively untheorized within feminist literary studies.[22] In line with dominant trends within general critical theory, the author is largely seen as a textual effect whose "origin" is ideology. Although the psychic spillage between the speaking subject and the subject of speech is usually regarded as an inevitability, the authorial bearer of the discourse is generally firmly rooted "outside" the text.

In feminist cinema, and in film theory generally, the problematization of the author has been a central concern from the 1960s onwards. Silverman, for example, addresses the question of female authorship from the double perspective of cinematic and psychoanalytic theory.[23] Fully conceding the critical primacy of the author "inside" the text, Silverman opposes the view that the biographical author should be dismissed from the theoretical arena entirely. Instead, she proposes a "new model for conceptualizing the relation" between these two authorial instances. Designating the second instance the "author 'outside' the text," she argues that this figure can "come into existence as a . . . self-affirming subject only through the inscription of the author 'inside' the text," and is thus fundamentally different from the one "laid to rest by Barthes in 1969" (193). Such inscription, we recall, obtains through identification and the desire for mastery, occurring on both the intra- and the extradiegetic levels of the text. In other words, the author "outside" is always present, both in the form of "any representation or network of representations" through which s/he is "constituted as speaking subject" and in the "body" of the text, that is, as the "'nodal' points" existing in recurrent elements in narrative strategies, movement, verbal style, and so on.[24]

The reconstruction of the author "inside" the text requires analysis of all levels of narration and focalization as well as of their interrelationships. We have noted that the narrator in novelistic discourse is the character with which readers most readily identify. But the narrator as a persona created by the text is at the same time the figure in relation to which the textual author stands on a level of "diegetic equivalence."[25] If the sexually ambivalent adolescent as well as the absent or "terrible" mother form two of the "nodal" points in Bowen's texts, the relationship in *ET* between its narrator and its protagonist—in which these two figures coalesce—would seem to offer an excellent way of approaching the two indissolubly intertwined author effects conceptualized by Silverman.

The Itinerary of Recovery. As a narrative of creation, the Oedipus myth is the story of the *son*'s relations to father and mother, to male and female origin. *ET* presents an alternative myth, the story of the daughter and her relation to the mother. As Hirsch points out, the extreme complexity of the psychic interaction between mothers and daughters necessitates that the literary critic adopt a psychoanalytic perspective when approaching such stories. I therefore once again turn to psychoanalysis. In *Beyond the Pleasure Principle* (1920), Freud tries to account for his patients' need to recover or reexperience traumatic events rather than merely remember them. The compulsion to repeat, he says, is connected with the drives or instincts and should be conceived as an *"urge inherent in organic life to restore an earlier state of things* the living entity has been obliged to abandon under the pressure of external disturbing forces." Freud infers that the drives are the "expression of the *conservative* nature of living substances" and that they are "historically determined."[26] The movement of the drive is thus directed at a point before, and since the ultimate moment before the subject's beginning is death, the movement of the drive is directed at the as yet unknown but imposed end.

Peter Brooks, taking "Freud's Masterplot" as a starting point for a discussion of the movement of narrative, asserts that metonymic repetitions, deviations and detours making up the middle of a story—or the body of the text—in the end serve to produce the unity of meaning/significance in the shape of metaphor.[27] Drawing on Lacan, who "equated metonymy and desire," Brooks concludes that it is the desire for totalized meaning that moves the narrative of contiguous syntagmatic relations through the element of *time* toward metaphor, which is "in this sense totalizing."[28]

What is more, narrative beginnings become significant only in light of the ending. In other words, it is the desire for illumination of beginnings and of the haphazard course of events constituting the (metonymical) middle of a story that lies behind the desire for the totalizing metaphor of meaning/ending. In this perspective, the movement of narrative is by definition informed by a specifically masculine desire.[29]

Its self-conscious inscription in dominant myths of creation sufficiently validates a reading of *ET* as an exploration of origins, with the understanding that the author's gender gives a twist to the traditional course of this narrative mode. As a female revision of the story of loss/the Fall, Bowen's last novel constitutes a search for meaning as well as for a past anterior to her inscription into history as a writing subject. Approaching the end of her life, the author clearly felt the need to retrace "beginnings" in order to shed light on the "middle" part of the story of her self. Since she closely associated her profession with her "grown-up" status, the textual reinscription of the adolescent as a metaphor of sexual ambivalence signifies an attempt to recover a subjective state prior to her assumption of symbolic authority as a (heterosexually) gendered subject. That is to say, the process of writing the novel led to the restoration of a self preceding the moment when Bowen assumed the sociocultural role of the author in which she located the center of her adult sense of identity. Moreover, as a topos of incompleteness, the literary figure of the adolescent represents an open psychic structure *only* retrospectively or, in the words of Kristeva, only "through the eyes of a stable law."[30] Fully established in her position of (adult) symbolic authority, Bowen resurrected as an object of identificatory investment an imaginary figure who is placed outside the symbolic due to her ex-centric, that is, lesbian, desire. In the character of "unfinished," inarticulate Eva Trout, she constructed a metaphor of a sexually amorphous subjectivity—"a slippery fish"—residing neither within nor without the patriarchal symbolic—a figure whose libidinal energy is not organized in correspondence with the normal/normative positive Oedipus complex. The textual configuration of this mythic figure, we recall, is directly connected to the reemergence of the Oedipus crisis and the desire for the first love object, the mother. By opting for a method of "external narration" throughout the scenes of origin ("Genesis"), Bowen not only created a discursive space for the repressed desire for a same-sex love object but also allowed the subject of this desire to speak (for) herself. In other words, the text allows for the self-articulation of the "unthinkable" lesbian subject. The shift in narrative method following upon the originary scenes is closely entwined with the contradictions inhering in Eva's double role.

The respective subtitles of the novel's two parts are in themselves misleading. The suggestive value of the first would lead one to expect the familiar Bowen narrator, the aloof yet benevolent organizing voice fully in control of her discourse and her material, the Author-God creating and directing the fictional world from her position of "overlordship." The arbitrary title of the novel's second part, "Eight Years Later," suggests, in contrast, an inscription of the narrative into the larger text of history, a fragmented plot whose contingent development lies outside any speaking subject's control. But as we have seen, these initial expectations are immediately thwarted by the ways in which the two sections open, the one setting up the protagonist as the subject of speech, the second installing the narrator in her position as the dispassionate reporter of narrative events. The contradiction inhering in such a reversal of discursive agency is sustained by the overall stylistic differences distinguishing the text's two sections.

The implied authority of the God of the Old Testament is thoroughly undermined by the fragmented, or perhaps more accurately, shiftless, operation of the narrative in part 1. The haphazard sequence of scenes, superimposed by a textual surface that is ambiguous if not obscure, and a blurred, unfocused narrative perspective, turn "Genesis" into a fully dispersed discourse. Still, at the end of this narrative trajectory without definable origin, a discourse giving voice to what is essentially a "no-voice," we find the heroine almost in triumph, or at least in "possession." When in part 2 both structure and style tighten, the narrator is unmistakably present in her role of authority, while the plot evolves in a straightforward teleological line to culminate in a painstakingly orchestrated narrative climax. While the author/narrator regains her position as the organizing voice, offsetting the equivocal tone of the preceding discourse of incohesion, the protagonist is not only supplanted in her role as director—moved from the position of subject to that of object of narration—but is finally obliterated from the text altogether. The point of transition between the two sections is literally formed by the chapter entitled "Interim," where Eva is flying to what will turn out to be another universe. The stage of transition from her adolescent (or daughter's) position to that of the mother is mediated by the direct observations of a male character, Professor Holman. Henceforth, the heroine's agency decreases: she loses control over her story and is forced to give up her ex-centric gender role in exchange for a place within the heterosexual matrix.

We recall that the figure of the adolescent enables the novelist to recover repressed or unconscious psychic material while simultaneously allowing for a reorganization of her psychic space through the act of symbolic inscription itself. Writing adolescence thus provides a link between desire and discourse. Since the writer's affective investment in the sexually ambivalent figure is located in the adolescent search for a (secondary) love object, this unfocused psychosexual stage coincides with an allusive eroticism in which "nothing but *signs*" are articulated.[31] In "Genesis," the relationship between the author/narrator and her inarticulate protagonist is one of desire as well as identification. Operating in a clearly homoerotic libidinal economy, the narrator's investment is directly related to the passionate energy cathected to the (incestuous) first object, the mother. While the incest taboo and the cultural disavowal of a female same-sex object choice—mutually inscribed in the founding myths of patriarchy—force the female subject to abandon the original object and to repress her primary desire, the recovery or reexperience of traumatic events ultimately serves to enable her to gain mastery over them. In this perspective, the textual reinscription of her primary desire, while allowing Bowen to recover a repressed/disavowed past, would simultaneously seem to serve as a screen against the threat of "shapelessness" and "amorphousness" she associated with the preadult or nonwriting aspects of herself.

In part 1, such measures of symbolic containment would seem to have offered adequate protection against the threat of psychic dissolution presented by the "polynymia" of the adolescent's "forbidden" desire. This evidently does not hold true for the novel's second part. When Eva shifts her position from adolescent/daughter to phallic mother, that is to say, when she becomes the creator of difference herself, the author emphatically (re)assumes her position as the organizing discourse and transforms her creation from a subject into the object of narration. In the final instance, it is the fundamental ambivalence of the maternal figure that accounts for the resolute assertion of the narrator's "overlordship" in the novel's second part. Embodying blissful fusion as well as the threat of annihilation or, to put it differently, functioning both as the object of desire and as the agent of rupture and betrayal, the figure of the mother apparently requires a more vigorous exertion of symbolic power than the mere textual reinscription that suffices to gain mastery over that other mythic figure, the crisis-subjectivity of the adolescent.

The Power to Speak the Ex-centric. The ultimate erasure of the heroine from the text of Bowen's last novel obtains significance in yet another sense, connected with but distinct from that outlined above. It has become clear that the oedipal scenario, and more particularly the complexities of the female trajectory within it, resounds on both the conscious and the unconscious levels of this text. We must bear in mind, however, that at least on the former, it is an Oedipus reversed: instead of following the course of the male hero of the original myth by killing the father, the son (Jeremy) kills the mother (Eva). Whereas the extradiegetic elimination of the maternal character symbolizes the mastery of the conflictual affect cathected to this figure, the essential duality of the female protagonist is not only retrospectively sustained but is structurally inscribed in the text's twofold division.

In part 1, the figure of Eva functions in a same-sex economy as an object of desirous investment for the author/narrator and as a subject of desire in her own right. She is allowed to speak (for) herself. Her very inarticulacy reflects her ex-centric position in relation to the heterosexual—or rather, "hom(m)osexual"—organization of the phallogocentric symbolic. In the course of part 2, her need to exist in a recognizable manner with regard to (the) Other/s forces Eva to enter into the Law of the Father and to assume a conventional gender position. She nonetheless tries to maintain her phallic powers as the director of her harlequinade. The ensuing development of the plot, as much as the narrator's "overlordship," reveals that such a subjectivity as Eva's cannot exist in a conventionally teleological narrative plot. In other words, the narrative itself moves as a counterforce to the creation of a female subject who seeks to exert the active powers that dominant discursive regimes relegate to members of the male sex. While the movement of discourse itself is shown to be quite ineluctable, the constraints it imposes on female sexuality are simultaneously critically exposed by/in Eva's dissolution at the end of the narrative. In the final instance, she is destroyed by her son (as a representative of the Law) as much as by the narrator who assumes her power as Author-God.

Rather than manifesting a despair at a "breakdown of language" as such, as Lee has suggested, it would appear that Bowen's last novel expresses a more specific sense of disillusionment, that is, a loss of faith in the possibility of articulating at once the two aspects of her identity that she had tended to separate throughout her life: the "wholly personal, or womanish" and the "writing part" of herself.[32] I have suggested that, in her search for origins in *ET,* Bowen explored her prewriterly past, a period suffused with the memory of her mother, and discovered the implications of her adoption of the father's discourse. In a culture whose founding conceptual schemes revolve around the absence of the mother as the site of symbolic origin, the narrative of passionate attachment between mother and daughter must ultimately remain hidden. The ex-centric desire informing this "dark continent" would seem to be necessarily inexpressible for the female subject who wants to speak with authority.

Bowen's final "statement of [her] poetic truth" would appear to testify to the impossibility of fully grasping the meaning of the two modalities of (her) self in conventional symbolic terms. In this context, it is interesting to note an aspect that I have thus far mentioned only in passing. In addition to relating the protagonist's "case history," the novel also renders another, by giving room to the voice of the protagonist's symbolic mother/love object, Iseult Smith. While underlining the presence of psychoanalysis as one of the text's discursive undercurrents, the frenzied attempts on the part of this verbally and intellectually highly gifted woman symbolically to inscribe herself amount to what I have earlier called self- or autoanalysis. Still, neither in the form of her nocturnal addresses to her typewriter, her extended correspondence with Constantine—duly accepted as fascinating "psychological material" (227)—nor her nonconfession to Father Tony does the teacher succeed in fully apprehending the text of herself. She is eventually forced to admit with a note of despair: "'How inconceivable oneself is!'" But Miss Smith's role in *ET* as the emotional and intellectual victim of her conflictual gender position is most poignantly brought to the fore by the disclosure that the book she had intended to write while away in France "was born dead" (228). Her search for herself in the texts of her symbolic Fathers—she intermittently cites or alludes to Proust, Dickens, and D. H. Lawrence, and at one point claims to suffer from a "Hedda Gabler complex" (192)—fails, since these master discourses not only do not reflect but in effect exclude the "womanish" part of her experience. Iseult's thwarted self-explorations principally concern her passionate obsession with Eva. The central place of lesbian desire and thus of the mother('s body) in the construction of female subjectivity/sexuality per se, as well as the *Verleugnung* of such a bond in/by dominant regulatory regimes of power/knowledge, are thus forcefully exposed.

Still, as Hirsch points out, it is precisely in the "interplay between absence/silence and determining significance" that the maternal is located.[33] The elimination of the figure of the mother from the text therefore remains ambiguous. It might be argued that the novel's ending constitutes a subscription to the phallogocentric master narratives in which the repression of the mother is the condition for the daughter's creative symbolic space. In contrast, Eva's annihilation might equally be seen as a genuine subversion of the oedipal family romance. It is, after all, at the very moment when she seems willing to take up her appropriate position within the heterosexual matrix that the heroine is exterminated from the narrative, while at the same time the "subcontinent" of the mother/daughter bond is discursively inscribed. In this sense, the novel's conclusion represents a refusal on the part of the narrator to play out the oedipal plot of (hetero)sexual difference, while still retaining her own position as symbolic agent in an order sustained by this and other such myths. In other words, the text maintains the double vision embodied in the dual role of the protagonist herself. In this sense, it is thus not so much Eva, or the figure of the mother, but the sexually overdetermined structure of the narrative *form* that is eventually exploded. The coexistence and joint operations of the novel's two parts—the shifting settings and scenes determining the movement of the first, offset by the linear development characterizing the second—therewith acquire the significance of a truly ex-centric narrative space. This space is not a utopian extrasymbolic or feminine space (as opposed to a masculine sequential temporality), but a dynamic in which both modalities operate at the same time: that which Teresa de Lauretis has termed the "space-off," the "movement from the space represented by/in a representation, by/in a discourse, by/in a sex-gender system, to the space not represented yet implied (unseen) in them."[34] It is perhaps only such a space, in which the contradiction of a subversive female sexuality is perpetually held in suspense, that can accommodate the last of Bowen's formidable heroines.

8

From Marginality to Ex-centricity

She and I belong to the same sex, even, because
there are only two: there should certainly be more.
—*The House in Paris*

(Post)modernist Identifications

Poststructuralist theories of difference and the cultural break occasioned by postmodernism have rendered any foundationalist claims to universal validity politically suspect and theoretically untenable: no category by which individual human beings (however provisionally) define themselves can any longer be maintained to ground the subject. Whether specified in terms of gender, race, class, sexual orientation, or any of the categories subsumed under the by-now notorious phrase "and so on," no single element of differentiation can be assumed to form the only, or even the primary, founding aspect of any identity defined in exclusionary terms. Feminist discourse has functioned centrally in this epistemological shift in perspective on human subjectivity.[1]

The insistence on a differentiated otherness notwithstanding, the feminist project in the 1990s continues to take as its starting point the historical existence of "women" or, similarly, to base itself on the theoretical notion of the female subject. Indeed, a feminist politics cannot simply do away with all concepts of (female) identity. To the extent that gender functions as one—but clearly not the only one—of the most pervasive structuring forces that concretely affects each of us in our individual lives, this category of identification must continue to be posited in order to allow for a critical analysis of its highly complex and diverse operations. Still, a postmodern feminist critique needs to address gender in its specific and intertwining relations to other ideological structures and to analyze their joint effects on theoretical, sociopolitical levels as much as on that of subjective experience. This should serve to preclude the (inadvertent) takeover by mainstream feminism of various disruptive othernesses, including, most notably, differences in sexual orientation as well as ethnic and racial differences in terms other than black.

The postmodern celebration of difference has led not so much to the "dispersal of the subject" as to a recognition of its multiple inscription in a range of contingent and intersecting discursive structures. Far from resulting in a "view from nowhere,"[2] postmodernism has necessitated a conscious and explicit contextualization of any discursive position or critical perspective.[3] Contemporary literary theory starts from the premise that signifying practices play a constitutive role in the formation of what is in effect an idealization: that "slippery fish" called identity. Current feminist theory has become, in the words of Teresa de Lauretis, no more and no less than a "politics of self-representation."[4] But the insistence on the heterogeneity of the processes of signification that both structure and deconstruct such representations has also compelled feminism to be a "politics of location" in the widest sense of the term. Rather than a "resistance to the recognition that one is always *somewhere*," as Susan Bordo argues in a defensive account of its presumed apolitical pluralism, the postmodern "project of embracing heterogeneity" signifies a self-conscious acknowledgment of the contextual boundaries that overdetermine any enunciatory act.[5]

Any act of speech, any form of reading/writing is de facto

situated within a contingent and shifting set of material social relations and is thus, by definition, *interested*. By exposing the constraining effects of dominant discursive regimes, feminist theory and practice have foregrounded the significance of the enunciating subject's situatedness within a symbolic network of unequal power relations—in particular the founding structures of patriarchy: phallogocentrism and compulsory heterosexuality. Since, as Bordo correctly points out, the "inescapable fact of human embodiment" renders it physically impossible to do critical justice to the myriad of structuring forces simultaneously operative in a given society, in an individual subject, or even in a single literary text, it is in the interest of a feminist critique to continue to take the category of gender as one of its central objects of investigation. The focus on gender, however, need not entail a denial or obscuring of other, equally important factors of differentiation. In current lesbian theory, therefore, the "contextual imperative" means a relative privileging of the category of sexuality in order to analyze the ways in which this "axis of exclusion" functions through,[6] against, and/or in conjunction with other forces of sociodiscursive stratification.[7] As a politics of location and self-representation both *within* and *without* a phallogocentric discursive realm, postmodern critical theory and practice should thus attend to the private, the specific, and the particular as much as to the fundamentally public and institutionalized discourses by which "identities" are socioculturally produced and subjectively inscribed.

In the preceding chapters I have employed various strategies and methodologies generated by feminist theory and practice over the past decades. Since any chosen perspective will be invested with a critic's specific sociopolitical and subjective interests, I have selectively focused on theoretical perspectives that appeared to offer the best practical tools with which to explore an equally selective number of Elizabeth Bowen's novels. Although indisputably contingent, these choices have not been arbitrary. Inspired by the dynamics of the transferential process in which writer/text/reader are mutually engaged, they both result from discursive interplay and derive from the nature of the task I had set myself in writing this book: critically to reassess the accomplishment of a largely neglected female author, to bring to bear on her texts the notion of fiction as the "'non-expository' theory of practice,"[8] and to practice lesbian feminism as a "politics of identity," as a "political-personal strategy of survival and resistance that is also, at the same time, a critical practice *and* a mode of knowledge."[9] The end focus of my theoretical itinerary may appear to suggest that I regard psychoanalysis ultimately as forming the most viable approach to the "complex notion that the female subject is a site of differences [that] remain concretely embedded in social and power relations."[10] Although the intrinsic temporality of any kind of narrative—even one situated within a self-consciously antiteleological context—inadvertently implies a movement toward progress, such a dialectic is certainly not intended. Rather, by focusing on different ways to address the vexing questions central to a radical feminist project in what have already been called "postfeminist" times, it has been my purpose to underline the necessarily interdependent relations between various ways of theorizing *and* practicing a critique that is a political as much as an epistemological enterprise. Even so, the apparent narrowing of focus in the last chapter, my reading of *ET* as a case history of sorts, does indicate some of the assumptions underlying my reading/writing practice. These are connected with what seems to emerge as *the* critical concept in current theoretical debates as well as in the literary texts it has been my attempt to de/reconstruct, that is, the notion of identity.

My privileging of psychoanalysis in the preceding two chapters is related both to the literary text around which my argument is organized and to the aforementioned theoretical questions. As a narrative—as opposed to a science or clinical methodology—of psychic formation in which representation and identification play determining roles, psychoanalysis bears directly on the problems currently facing feminist theory. Moreover, the central place of sexuality in the Freudian account of subjectivity has inevitably led to an abiding interest among feminist theorists in psychoanalytic theory—and no less importantly, in the critiques to which Freud's work has given rise.[11] By approaching his writings as sociohistorically specific *texts,* and by disclosing their inconsistencies and blind spots, their phallogocentric gaps and biases as well as their analytic potential, such critiques have rendered psychoanalysis into one of the most productive intertexts among many modes of contemporary theory. This is partly because psychoanalysis deals with the (re)constructions of meaning. In clinical practice, the process of psychoanalysis consists in the listening to and the telling of stories: analyst and analysand are mutually engaged in the (re)production of meaning through fictionalization. As such, psychoanalysis provides one of the most feasible conceptual schemes with which to explore identity formation as a discursively produced/producing effect, or, put slightly differently, as a sexually overdetermined signifying process.

Freud's case histories reveal that he realized that, since any story is both told and received from/within a particular perspective, neither point of view can ever be disinterested or objective. With the reemergence of critical interest in his work in the early 1970s, feminist film theorists were among the first to acknowledge the relevance of the psychoanalytic account of the formation of sexual identities as a semiotic phenomenon. Calling attention to the interrelations between the "processes of psychoanalysis and cinema," the debate on the gendered nature of the gaze directed the theoretical focus to what E. Ann Kaplan has called the "materialization of the signifier." The ensuing insight into the close links between social experience and art allowed critics to "read daily life as structured according to signifying practices."[12] In this way, the much disputed ahistoricity of psychoanalytic theory, and therewith its use(lessness) for feminism as a *sociopolitical* practice, has been newly held up for discussion. But even if a substantial part of psychoanalytic discourse had not been related as case histories,

Freud's metatheoretical narratives, and the major concepts he evolved in them, explicitly draw on *fictions,* that is, on the founding myths of classical antiquity. In other words, psychoanalysis unequivocally attests to the discursive nature of the social, political, and personal investments that inform the narratives by means of which we construct ourselves and the world—and vice versa. That Freud was largely incapable of looking beyond the boundaries of his own narrow sociocultural context has effectively been pointed out by many of his critics, but this need not detract from the radical insight he offers into the material ontology of the human psyche.

As a technology in the Foucauldian sense, psychoanalysis virtually "invented" what in the early twentieth century came to be accepted as the individual's inner psyche. Elizabeth Bowen's position within the literary and intellectual circles of London and Oxford in the 1920s and 1930s, not quite within but close enough to what is now known as Bloomsbury, allows us safely to assume that she was familiar with Freud's basic assumptions.[13] Her early novel *LS* was in fact written at a time when psychoanalysis was increasingly gaining ground as a lay discourse, proffering a sophisticated yet accessible account of the psyche as an inner space whose unconscious drive energy was assumed to have an autonomy and authority of its own. When Bowen's work is placed within this sociohistorical context, it is not really surprising to find that the author initially posed one of the central questions addressed by/in all her novels, that is, the constitution of (female) subjectivity, in terms of a binary opposition between inner and outer reality. Her preoccupation with the interior of the inner soul, with what William James in 1890 first defined in the metaphor of the "stream" or river of thought, of consciousness,[14] irrefutably situates Bowen within the cultural climate of modernism. At the same time, however, we recall that Lois Farquar's struggle for identity is not depicted as an exclusively intrapsychic process but is cast as a conflict between inner and outer space. In this sense, the novel would seem to extend the preoccupations of the positivist and deterministic naturalist writers of the nineteenth century, whose focus was predominantly on the "conflicts of individual aspiration and social obligation," on the "clash of traditions and self-fulfillment."[15] What thus amounts to an apparent contradiction in the author's position also pertains to the operation of language itself. While Bowen to a certain degree shared the overwhelming fear of the inadequacy of language and the loss of faith in "objective reality" that characterize the works of a large number of modernist writers, she never adopted the accompanying dream of an "order in art independent of or else transcending the humanistic, the material, the *real*."[16] Her concern with language therefore never results in the aesthetic introversion crucial to much modernist art. These ambivalences, however, do not legitimize relegating Bowen to the margins of the major cultural movement of the early twentieth century or denouncing her fictions as reactionary returns to the confinement of an idealized Edwardian past. Rather, they indicate Bowen's complex inside/outside position with regard to the prevailing artistic and intellectual tendencies of her times. Her early concentration on her characters' inner psychic space and her simultaneous insistence on their situatedness in the historical here and now install her firmly within the larger cultural context—although in an ex-centric position.

It has become clear that Bowen's concern with the problematical relations between inner and outer "reality" was strengthened rather than weakened by the shifting sociohistorical coordinates in which she successively found herself. The rising level of self-consciousness qualifying both her fictional and her critical writings testifies to a deepening awareness of the located nature of her self and her art. World War II evidently formed a watershed experience in this respect: her deep-seated conviction of the inseparability of the private from the public and her acute insight into the critical operations of gender in both were confirmed and acquired particular poignancy when the author explored these questions in the guise of the moral dilemma controlling *HD*.[17] The author's last novel, in which the boundaries between inner and outer space are blurred to the extent that their interactive forces become practically interchangeable, at once displays a growing emphasis on externality with regard to narrative technique and embodies a most private or inner-directed story as a case history and/or story of origins in which sexuality takes center stage. Forming a pivotal and representative aspect of the contradictory or, perhaps more accurately, of the idiosyncratically ambivalent quality of Bowen's novelistic discourse, this structural feature of *ET* attests to what I consider the novel's essentially postmodern character, exemplifying an ex-centricity already prefigured in the paradoxical duality of *LS*.

To validate my claim to a postmodern quality in Bowen's later work, I must briefly return to the sociocultural climate in which she started her writing career. In her nonfiction, Bowen repeatedly underlined the profound influence of Marcel Proust on her ideas about literature. She adhered to the French novelist's notion of art as a "central illumination," as the only means by which disconnected and contingent reality can be patterned.[18] She did not, however, harbor a belief in the work of art's ability to "transcend its locality"; nor did she subscribe to a notion of the writer's style as a "symbolist totality."[19] Indeed, Bowen's deliberate inscription in the tradition of social realism represents a refusal to accept the modernist tenet of a fundamental disjunction between social reality and literary language, of an absolute aestheticism repudiating any notion of mimesis or description that, in its turn, resulted in the autotelic and hermetic antinarratives typical of high modernism. The author's deviant stance connects her work with another, less centrally acknowledged aspect of the by-no-means-homogeneous modernist movement.

As Richard Sheppard points out, the antiart forms of dadaism and surrealism evolving contemporaneously with modernism do not convey a fundamental despair at the communicative ability of language but actually reinstate language as one among many means of communication.[20] Positing verbal signification as a medium with a power of its own, indeed as a constitutive force over which human beings have limited control, these movements went counter to the modernist tendency to celebrate the author's ability to create a newly ordered universe out of social chaos. As the ultimate forms of modernism, these countercultural movements, whose aims were social and existential rather than purely aesthetic, should, Sheppard maintains, be regarded as the precursors of postmodernism. Such insistence on the necessity of accepting the new situation and developing alternative sociocultural countercurrents from within finds expression in Bowen's particular blending of diverse generic and discursive styles, that is, in her sustained attempt at transforming established narrative forms and techniques in order to articulate radically altered views on the subject and/in society. In the words of one of her characters: "One has to live how one can."[21] The countercultural abandonment of the claim of mastery over meaning and the universe implies a politicization of literary discourse. This renders Bowen's assertions of the inextricable links between private and public reality, and of the critical function of narrative discourse in constructing both, into radical gestures—in political as much as in artistic terms.

In accordance with the Proustian notion of writing/reading as indefinite processes of self-definition, Bowen's texts reflect a concept of identity that, in the final instance, is irreducible to either inner or outer space, or to any one term in an endless range of similar binary oppositions. The resulting ambivalences, surfacing on both the representational and the discursive levels of her narratives, produce a sense of instability and crisis palpable from her earliest novels onward. It is, however, especially in her later work that conventional interpretive strategies are thoroughly undermined. By both invoking and defying traditional reading expectations, these novels generate disturbing effects that, as we have seen, may unsettle even the "professional" reading subject. However, rather than retracing a line of argument that can be found throughout the foregoing chapters, I want to conclude by dwelling on the significance of the literary enactment of such irreducibility in the context of (feminist) discourses on sexuality.

Sexual In/Difference

In her introduction (1976) to the Penguin edition of *The House in Paris* (1935), the British novelist A. S. Byatt declares that this is a novel about "sex, time, and the discovery of identity."[22] Such a claim would appear to hold true for all of Bowen's novels. Although her treatment of sex is always subdued, occurring as it were off-stage, its consequences and implications feature center stage in the stories of most if not all of her characters' lives. Moreover, as I have tried to show, sexuality plays a critical role not only in terms of plot and narrative movement but also insofar as the texts constitute the author's discursive explorations of (her own) subjectivity.

Byatt connects her first to her second emphasis with the assertion that "sex has a history" (9). This critical point is not only borne out by Bowen's preoccupation with the here and now but also by her shifting perspective on sexual identities. It is the third of Byatt's emphases that functions as the point of intersection at which all of the author's major concerns converge. The central place of the question of sexuality in Bowen's work accounts for my final theoretical focus on psychoanalysis. By conceptualizing subjectivity, psychosexuality, and discourse in close interrelation with one another, psychoanalytic theory allows for an exploration of the libidinal processes informing the fictional text on its various levels of operation. It therewith opens the possibility of reading Bowen's novels with regard to what Barthes would call their "readerly" as well as their "writerly" aspects. In the remainder of these pages, I will concentrate on what has hitherto come only obliquely under discussion: the significance of the author's stylistic idiosyncrasies in relation to the ex-centric content of her novels.

As indicated above, I have, from an avowedly interested perspective, sought critically to read Bowen's texts not only with regard to (heterosexual) gender but also in terms of (lesbian) sexuality. In this sense, I have tried to move beyond a feminist critique such as that of Lassner, whose main argument revolves around a notion of sexual difference cast in strictly binary terms, as woman's difference from man. While valid in itself, and clearly an improvement on critics who leave the question of gender virtually out of account, such a heterocentric conception of identity is in the final instance too reductive to generate a sufficiently comprehensive view on Bowen's texts. For even if we disregard the fact that this exclusionary notion of sexual difference has become increasingly problematic in theoretical terms as well, Teresa de Lauretis correctly reminds us that the early feminist "emphasis on sexual difference as gender . . . has rightly come under attack for obscuring the effects of other differences in women's psychosocial oppression."[23] It would seem that it is both Bowen's Anglo-Irish origins and, paradoxically, her gender that have operated in precisely such an obscuring manner. Failing to meet the requirements of dominant (male) literary movements, she has, to all intents and purposes, been landed in the position of literary exile: off mainstream modernism, off Bloomsbury, off the Anglo-Irish tradition even. Fully to disentangle the web of causes for her marginalization would require analyses of more than just gender or nationality differences. Hence, by highlighting the aspect of sexuality, I do not wish to claim pride of place for this element of otherness as a structuring force in the author's texts. Having said this, I would still maintain that it is the ex-centric nature of her fictions' underlying desire, apparent from the first novel onward, that, in intricate interaction with the other noted aspects of difference, has made it particularly difficult for critics to assess the radicalness of Bowen's accomplishment.

While no other critic of Bowen has, as far as I know, related the stylistic aspects of her work to a radically subversive desire, I am, of course, not the first to draw attention to the importance of same-sex relationships in the lives of her heroines, or of lesbian sexuality generally in her novels—both Lee and Glendinning fleetingly attend to these issues.[24] The American/Canadian novelist Jane Rule, however, has devoted an essay specifically to the construction of lesbian experience in Bowen's novels.[25]

Rule describes a pattern of "lesbian experience bracketing the heterosexual experience of marriage and children" in which "marriage is both the unlikely and inevitable center at either end of which is the more likely and less destined involvement of women with their own kind" (115). She maintains that the presence of lesbian characters and relationships is particularly prominent in the author's early work. While subsequent novels "concentrate on the emotional life of women," it is only in her last novels, Rule posits, that Bowen returned to a "concern for relationships between women" (115), suggesting that this shift in emphasis is directly related to the death of the author's husband in 1952. Bowen's concentration on heterosexual relationships in the 1940s, however, would seem to be not a shift in emphasis so much as an exceptional move; nor does it strike me as having directly to do with her marital status. After all, when in her first novel, *The Hotel* (1927), she created the relationship that was to set the pattern for many of her ensuing fictions—the passionate involvement of a young girl with an older woman—the young writer had in fact just been married.[26] Moreover, as another instance of her practice of "transposed autobiography," the displacement of lesbian sexuality to one of the subplots in her war-time novel *HD* reflects an urgency to examine male-female interaction in a specific sociohistorical context, resulting in views that appear rather bleak if not downright destructive. As Glendinning informs us, *HD* was written during the period when Bowen's affair with the Canadian diplomat Charles Ritchie was reputedly at its height.[27] If biographical information is to shed any light on altering sexual orientations in her fiction, it would thus seem that Bowen's extramarital affairs provide more conclusive evidence for shifting concerns in this field.[28] But whatever the worth of the possible connections between the author's life and her art in the realm of sexual relations, it is obvious that the issue of lesbian sexuality surfaces in most of her texts.

In the essay referred to above, de Lauretis contends that the feminist "act of assuming and speaking from the position of a subject" has opened up a "critical space" allowing for lesbian identity to be spoken and "conceptually articulated."[29] Yet, the exclusive focus on gender as both cause and end of women's social oppression has resulted in a "sexual indifference" within feminism itself, in the institution of a conceptual framework in which "female desire for the self-same, an other female self, cannot be recognized." De Lauretis hence asserts that the "condition of possibility" of lesbian representation consists in the "critical effort to dislodge the erotic from the discourse of gender." Drawing on the works of a range of lesbian artists and writers to support her claims, she shows that it is at their textual/discursive level that such a dislodgement can and does variously occur. This leads her to the conclusion that a thorough rethinking of "what, in most cultural discourses and sociosexual practices, is still . . . a gendered sexuality," requires the critical analysis of discursive attempts to "escape gender, to deny it, transcend it, or perform it in excess, and to inscribe the erotic in cryptic, allegorical, realistic, camp, or other modes of representation, pursuing the diverse strategies of writing and of reading the intransitive and yet obdurate relation of reference to meaning, of flesh to language."[30] It is in my attempt to disentangle the "indissoluble knot" of sexuality and reproduction in Bowen's texts that the significance of psychoanalytic theory incontestably manifests itself. For rather than exploring the question of female subjectivity primarily in terms of "gendered sexuality," Bowen's novels constitute a discursive quest for nonnormative sexual identities on both the sociohistorical and the profoundly intrapsychic levels of experience.

As the quotation heading this chapter suggests, Bowen was fully aware of the untenability of the binary frame of sex, of a "natural" sexual difference resulting in stable categories of heterosexual gender. Her need to move beyond such narrow boundaries of (self-)determination is reflected in the fact that her protagonists are never fixed in their identities—that, to use her own words, "Bowen-characters are in transit *consciously*."[31]

The sexual overdetermination of these characters' *différance* surfaces explicitly in the central place taken up by the paradigmatic figure of sexual ambivalence, the female adolescent. I have argued that this figure operates not only as a subject of desire in relation to other female characters and the author "inside" the text but also as the object of desire on the extradiegetic level, as an object of erotic investment for the author "outside" the text. Classic psychoanalytic theory has shown that desire and identification are inextricably linked in subjective formation. Within the traditional family triangle, these distinct moments in the economy of desire obtain in diametrically opposed directions. By insisting on the noncoincidence of the gender positions among which the processes of desire and identification take effect, the reversal/opposition scheme of the oedipal conflict serves to reinforce and maintain established "hom(m)osexual," that is to say compulsorily heterosexual, gender relations. A feminist critique of Freudian theory such as Silverman's, reinstating the negative Oedipus complex within the realm of the symbolic, has made it possible to reconceptualize female sexuality in terms of a radically subversive desire, as the process and the product of both erotic investment in and identification with the parent of the same sex.[32]

Subjectivity is, as Lacan has shown, an imaginary construction. Silverman's metaphor of the "acoustic mirror" expands the psychoanalytic conceptualization of the psychosexual process from the visual/specular to the auditory/acoustic realm of perception. This conclusively qualifies the relevance of the female subject's physical lack of a penis and thereby also the concept of femininity—or rather of masculinity—upon which both the Freudian and the Lacanian theories of "hom(m)osexuality" depend. But instead of constituting literally perceived images of the child's as yet unformed self, these various "mirrors" in which it first learns to recognize itself represent fantasy images of the child as other, as objects that the mother projects onto the screens of a differentiated other, the symbolic realm of outer reality. From the earliest stages onward, the subject thus identifies with what are in effect so many culturally inscribed fantasies of the parent for whom s/he needs to exist in order to come into being at all. This renders sexual identity into a fantasmatic formation that has little to do with anatomy.[33]

Although the gendered nature of the mother's fantasies plays a critical role in the psychosexual development of the child, it is possible to conceive, at this very early stage of subjective formation, of (female) sexuality as "dislodged" from (female) gender identity. Moreover, within the Freudian paradigm, the mother's desire for the child serves as a substitute for the phallus that is denied her as an adult female subject. This implies that the girl's primary sexual identifications are with phallic images, not with the lack of femininity. In longing to be what the mother desires, to fulfill the promise of being the mother's object, the child's own desire is opened up. It is in this sense that the operation of desire is indissolubly linked to identification. Since the girl's desire during the negative stage of the oedipal complex is directed at the phallic, sexually *active* mother, both her identificatory energy and her erotic desire are directed at a phallic, or rather a nonlacking, position. The splitting off of the one from the other during the positive oedipal phase in order to meet the requirements of the heterosexual matrix occurs only when the girl's first love object undergoes the devaluation of normative femininity. What is, within this perspective, a surprising empirical fact, that is, the cultural prevalence of female *hetero*sexuality, attests to the pervasive operations of dominant regimes of power/knowledge. It also goes to show that the concept of a gendered sexuality per se serves to maintain the "hom(m)osexual" order in which the taboo on lesbianism would appear to take precedence even over that of incest.[34]

The point of my short theoretical detour is not a sociopolitical but a literary-critical one. A conception of female identity as a fantasmatic process in which the figure of the mother occupies a central place serves to connect the stylistic aspects of Bowen's work to both its literary-historical context and its underlying desire. To elucidate these connections, I must turn to an essay by Shari Benstock, in which she rereads the history of modernism from the perspective of contemporary lesbian theory.[35] Benstock begins by clarifying that her object, the "exploration of *Sapphic modernism*," would not have been possible ten years ago on account of the fact that the "denial of all forms of lesbian experience, including artistic and aesthetic experiences, and the suppression of lesbianism by and within history have defined it as an excluded Other within cultural tradition."[36] While acknowledging the difficulties of definition surrounding the term (male) modernism itself, she concentrates her argument on the variety of "(female) modernisms," making a (provisional) distinction between those authors who "followed traditional models of form and style, but whose subject matter was Sapphism" and those who "filtered the lesbian content of their writing through the screen of presumably heterosexual subject matter or behind experimental literary styles" (184–85). I would argue that, as the products of an "expatriate" par excellence, Bowen's texts do not exactly fall within either of these categories but belong to both at the same time, exemplifying that which lies behind the two sides of what Benstock designates the "psychosexual fault line" of subjectivity.

Drawing on Lacanian psychoanalysis, Benstock uses the term "fault line" to suggest the "structural relation" between the conscious and the unconscious that is textually "marked in a pattern of cracks and fissures, evidence of the cultural imprint that the unconscious constantly unsettles and undermines." Since a subject's cultural position is by definition a sexual position, the inscription of sexuality in the literary text "reveals the psychosexual positioning by either tracing [the fault line's] contours or attempting (however unconsciously) to trace its patterns" (188). Precisely in the context of highly (self-)conscious modes of writing such as post/modernism, the tensions of a simultaneous tracing and encoding of these contours can be clearly discerned. The mark of psychosexual double inscription and the violence with which the lesbian as psychosexual other is socioculturally repressed, Benstock posits, emerges in the writing of female modernist texts in their "use of tropes and images, which are themselves disguises of the unconscious," and in their "linguistic excess" (189). Such a focus on the "structural terms of figuration itself" not only places the works of more or less officially "canonized" female writers into a radically different light but also succeeds in further moving feminist theory "beyond its concerns with representation-of-woman-as-figure." The grammatical unconventionalities and syntactic deviations in the texts of "sapphic modernists" attest to what is pertinent to symbolic practice in general, that is, the fact that "representation is always premised on the loss of that which cannot be represented." By employing strategies of disruption such as elliptical forms, experimental punctuation, and, particularly prominent in Bowen, double or triple negatives, these texts figure "woman-in-culture" as the site of absence or negativity, and therewith "mark the impossibility of figurability and the failure of representation" itself. Such techniques of "grammatical-rhetorical 'deviation,'" Benstock contends, are not merely articulations of the "experimental or avant-garde, but the Sapphic" (191–92).

Silverman's recasting of the Freudian paradigm enables us to take Benstock's argument one—crucial—step further. The relocation of the negative Oedipus complex within the symbolic, as a stage of psychosexual development preceding the heterosexual acculturation of the positive Oedipus, establishes the girl's desire for her first love object as an inaugurating moment in the process of her subjectivity. The interrelated operations of desire and identification render female sexuality into a fantasmatic formation that, instead of representing a preoedipal or unconscious stage of development, is firmly situated within the realm of the signifier/phallus. Rather than expressing the position of "woman-in-culture" in terms of heterosexual gender, the inscription of such a desire by way of techniques of "deviation" signals the negative presence of lesbian sexuality/identity *within* the text of phallogocentric culture. The gaps, fissures, and disruptions qualifying the texts of "sapphic modernists" are not articulations of a femininity that, within the terms of a binary sexual difference, can only be defined as lack or absence. They are, rather, the markers of a radical female or lesbian sexuality resolutely situated on this side of the "psychosexual fault line," a sexuality whose phallic nature contains such subversive potential that it must be doubly disavowed.

By defining the "sapphic erotic power" informing the texts of female modernists as the force of a sexual *un*conscious, Benstock inadvertently reinforces the "sexual indifference" inherent in a concept of sexual identity conceived of in strictly binary, that is to say heterosexually gendered, terms. Instead of articulating an "unfigurable" sexual unconscious, the lesbian desire operating in these texts would appear to constitute the socioculturally repressed erotic content of the writing. The stylistic idiosyncrasies are (self-) conscious deviations, representative of a negativity that is both ideologically disavowed and symbolically present. The textuality itself *speaks* as a psychosexual other of Western culture, that ex-centric figure hovering in the "space-off" of patriarchy, both present and absent by virtue of embodying an identity in which normative sexuality and gender do not coincide.

Such considerations place the stylistic idiosyncrasies of Bowen's fiction—as much as the frequency with which critics have found fault with these "mannered" ex-centricities—in an entirely different light. The suggestion of a "sapphic erotic power" as the underlying force of her fiction is supported by the fact that alterations in the perspective on gender relations and sexual identities on the representational level of her texts are reflected in similar modulations on their discursive level. While all of the novels display to a considerable degree the strategies of deviation and disruption that Benstock discusses, it is possible to trace an increase in the prominence of her characteristic disruptive techniques over the course of the author's career. Placed in their chronological order, Bowen's novels reflect not only a growing tendency to "dispense with the civilized surface of behaviour" in terms of plot and characterization but also a gradual expansion of textual dislocations in which the "danger, despair, and passion which had always lain under the surface" are increasingly discursively articulated.[37] An exceptional position is, in this respect, again taken up by *HD*. In considering *HD*'s exceptional position, it is important to bear in mind that Bowen found her war-time novel extremely difficult to write. Having completed the struggle, she felt that she had tried to put language to what she feared might be an "impossible use" and acknowledged a "certain strain" that a number of critics had also recognized in its writing. These equivocations acquire particular significance when one considers that *HD* was the most "narrative" of Bowen's novels, that is, the one in which she attempted most strictly to conform to the rules of conventional narrative practice. The author's retrospective unease about the novel's linguistic/stylistic aspects appears to suggest that *HD* is exceptional to her oeuvre not only in that it deals with the construction of female experience in primarily heterosexual terms but also with regard to the normative desire articulated in its contorted and evasive discursive surface.

Ex-centric Interpellations

The operation of an ex-centric mode of desire in Bowen's texts affects the processes of identity/identification on several interrelated levels. First, there is the question of address. In directing attention to the place of enunciation—by inscribing it into a variety of genres, by setting up a narrator in the position of control while a subversive desire is simultaneously allowed to speak through this mask, through shifts in narrative development, the use of obscuring imagery, broken syntactic structures, double and triple negatives, and similar forms of technical "deviation"—the ex-centric text urges the reader to resituate herself in relation to the enunciation as such. While equally articulating itself on a representational level in ambivalent rather than merely oppositional terms, the text projects a reading position that is thus both accessible and unsettling. In other words, the movement of the text invites the reader to identify with the ex-centric position of double inscription that it projects, to assume both "normal" and "abnormal" sex/textual positions simultaneously. Since sexual identity is a fantasmatic formation produced in/by discourse, the imaginary effort that such a positioning requires forces the reader to invest her attention in the reassuringly conventional as well as in the disconcertingly disruptive aspects of the text.

"Attention," as Eva Trout discovered, and as Marilyn Frye confirms, "is a kind of passion."[38] Frye elaborates: "When one's attention is on something, one is present in a particular way with respect to that thing. This presence is, among other things, an element of erotic presence. The orientation of one's attention is also what fixes and directs the application of one's physical and emotional work."[39] This adequately accounts for the unease that Bowen's work has provoked among critics. By problematizing the unmarked reading position in the process of textual identification, the ex-centric text alerts us not only to *its* unsaid but also to the repressed psychosexual other in ourselves and in the cultural text generally. Moreover, the rhetorical-syntactic strategies of ellipsis and interruption point to that which is symbolically inscribed as the sign of absence, that is, a mode of female sexuality that defies the regulations of the heterosexual matrix. By encoding the movement of female same-sex desire in its discourse, the ex-centric text reveals the critical function of the socioculturally repressed aspects in the process of female subjectivity/sexuality per se.

Reading it as a "structure of the unconscious," Benstock maintains that the "sapphic" is "not a language, but it structures language; it is mysterious and shadowy, not directly accessible, not immediately available to view." The metaphor she uses to designate this other "realm" is the image Freud introduced to describe his discovery of the libidinal bond between mother and daughter during the earliest stages of psychosexual formation: the "Minoan-Mycenaean civilization behind Greece," a notion that we have found to be of such crucial relevance to the most ex-centric of Bowen's fictions (*ET*) and to her creation of the novel's "larger-than-life" eponymous heroine. Moreover, a recasting of Freud's paradigm such as proposed by Silverman allows for an even more subversive reading of the "shadowy" power structuring the "sapphic" text than Benstock proposes. Rather than figuring as a pre-symbolic or unconscious realm, this discursive space then represents the negative Oedipus complex, the socioculturally repressed stage in the development of female sexuality, whose significance lies precisely in its location in the oedipal situation generally. Functioning as, in Benstock's terms, an "echo chamber of simulacra and phantasms," this textual realm provides a space to re-present not so much what has been lost with the inscription of (female) subjectivity in the symbolic order as such, but what has been repressed upon the girl's insertion into the positive Oedipus of compulsory heterosexuality.[40]

Instead of situating the "sapphic" in an archaic presymbolic, the ex-centric text thus obliquely reinscribes the repressed psychosexual other of heterocentric culture in the fissures and knots of referential discourse. In this way, such texts constitute configurations of a lesbian sexuality extrapolated from a mother/daughter relationship that is both oedipal and profoundly other than the dominant structure, that is, the lethal tract binding father and son.

As the site of a negative oedipal textuality, the ex-centric text allows us to conceptualize a genuinely "feminine symbolic" as a doubly inscribed discourse that, while radically transgressing the bounds of phallogocentric epistemology, is yet firmly rooted in the realm of the signifier.

Signaling the erotic aspects of same-sex relations in the process of female subjectivity, the inscription of the desire pertinent to such a negative realm in Bowen's texts makes it possible to give her a central place in an ex-centric tradition rather than a marginal place in a dominant one. If the self-defined exile-author belongs anywhere, it would seem to be among the "sapphic modernists" who "position themselves *structurally* in the interstices, gaps, and overlaps inherent in literary orders."[41] Insofar as Bowen's work reflects a preoccupation with a "breakdown of language" (Lee), it is the crisis inherent in a subjectivity that can only speak itself from a position of double inscription, both within and without structural forms and sexual norms. On a representational as much as on a discursive level, Bowen's novels testify to a thoroughly ambivalent "unique susceptibility" to self and world. The concept of identity that eventually emerges from her fiction is in the final instance recognizable as the gradually unraveling "indissoluble knot" of "gendered sexuality." The contradictory qualities of her work, in terms of plot, characterization, narrative development, and the idiosyncrasy of the discourse itself, attest to the fundamental disjunction underlying the "dark continent" of female sexuality. Bowen's genuine ex-centricity consists in her textual enactment of precisely this irreducibility.

Notes

1. Introduction

1. Patricia Craig's more recent *Elizabeth Bowen* (1986) is a short and altogether superficial book.
2. Glendinning 11, 15.
3. Elizabeth Bowen, *Seven Winters* (1942; 1984), 8.
4. Ibid., 9.
5. Elizabeth Bowen, *Bowen's Court* (1942; 1984), 451.
6. Elizabeth Bowen, "Pictures and Conversations," 23.
7. Ibid., 27.
8. Elizabeth Bowen, "The Mulberry Tree," 188, 186.
9. Ibid., 188, 189.
10. Glendinning 35.
11. Ibid., 44.
12. Elizabeth Bowen, Preface to *Early Stories* (1951), ctd. in Glendinning 54.
13. Elizabeth Bowen, *English Novelists* (1945), 25.
14. Jocelyn Brooke, *Elizabeth Bowen* (1951).
15. Mary McCarthy, *On the Contrary*, 275–76. Ctd. in Rosalind Miles, *The Female Form: Women Writers and the Conquest of the Novel* (1987), 18.
16. Miles 18–19.
17. Douglas Hewitt, *English Fiction of the Early Modern Period, 1890–1940* (1988), 196–97.
18. Hermione Lee, *Elizabeth Bowen: An Estimation* (1981).
19. William Heath, *Elizabeth Bowen: An Introduction to Her Novels* (1961).
20. Harriet Blodgett, *Patterns of Reality: Elizabeth Bowen's Novels* (1975).

21. Phyllis Lassner, *Elizabeth Bowen* (1990).
22. Elizabeth Bowen, "The Achievement of Virginia Woolf," 81.

2. *Technologies of Female Adolescence*

1. In her essay "Out of a Book," Bowen uses the phrase "so-called real life" (264), whereas the narrator in her last novel, *Eva Trout,* at one point asserts that "there is no 'real life' " (195).
2. Elizabeth Bowen, preface to *Encounters,* 85.
3. Ibid., 85, 84.
4. Ibid., 86.
5. I am using the term "(the) Other/s" to comprise (in)animate "signifi-cant others" as well as the ideological structures and semiotic systems that preexist the individual subject, and in relation to which whom/which s/he is compelled to define her/himself.
6. Ibid., 87.
7. Elizabeth Bowen, preface to *Stories by Elizabeth Bowen,* 77.
8. Ibid. Bowen invariably refers to "the writer" with the male personal pronoun; I will come back to this.
9. Preface to *Stories by Elizabeth Bowen,* 77.
10. Ibid., 78. Italics mine.
11. This phrase is a derivation from what Michel Foucault in his essay "What Is an Author?" defines as the "author-function." This term elucidates the fact that certain discourses in our culture are endowed with a measure of authority and significance that is denied to other discourses. Since the author's name operates as a "certain mode of being in discourse," the "author-function" is "characteristic of the mode of existence, circulation, and functioning of certain discourses in society" (148, 149).
12. In my discussion of Bakhtin's ethics of experience in everyday life, I am largely drawing on a series of texts entitled *The Architectonics of Answerability* (1918–1924). For detailed bibliographical information on and documentation of the Russian linguist/philosopher's published and unpublished works, see Katerina Clark and Michael Holquist, *Mikhail Bakhtin* (1984), esp. 146–70, 352–58.
13. The term "timespace" (or "chronotope") in the subheading for this section is used by Mikhail Bakhtin to designate a "formally constitu-tive category of literature," and serves to highlight the "inseparability

of space and time." See "Forms of Time and of the Chronotope in the Novel: Notes toward a Historical Poetics," 84.

14. It is surprising that Bakhtin, whose work in fact constitutes a celebration of difference, does not include sexual differences in his "architectonics" of subjectivity. The s/he distinction therefore is mine.

15. Clark and Holquist 64.

16. Bakhtin thus prefigures Emile Benveniste's concept of "discourse," that is, language as a system of differential relations and therefore other by definition, in which the subject assumes a position in order to identify her/himself. See the latter's influential study *Problems in General Linguistics* (1971). For an illuminating discussion of Benveniste, see Kaja Silverman, *The Subject of Semiotics* (1983), 43–53.

17. In "The Bounded Text," in *Desire in Language* 36–63, Julia Kristeva takes the (Bakhtinian) utterance to be the smallest "ideologeme" of the text. Defined as the "intertextual function read as 'materialized' at the different structural levels of each text," it is the ideologeme that gives the text "its historical and social coordinates" (37). The notion implies that all texts are by definition intertexts, whose meanings derive from the available discursive structures in which they were produced and from the discursive structures accessible to the reader in/by whom its meaning(s) are (re)produced.

18. Louis Althusser, "Ideology and Ideological State Apparatuses," 36.

19. Ibid., 56.

20. Michel Foucault, *The Order of Things: An Archeology of the Human Sciences* (1966; 1973).

21. See Michel Foucault, *The Archeology of Knowledge and the Discourse on Language* (1969; 1972).

22. In "Explanation and Culture: Marginalia," 103–17, Gayatri Chakravorty Spivak uses the term "masculism" to designate "old-fashioned humanism, which considers the study of woman to be a special interest and defines woman in terms of man" (107, 283 n. 9).

23. Teresa de Lauretis, "The Technology of Gender," 1–30. De Lauretis adopts the term in "technology" analogy to Foucault's notion of the "technology of sex," a notion he developed to theorize the nineteenth-century "invention" of sexuality. She advances a concept of gender as the "product of various social technologies, such as cinema, and of institutionalized discourses, epistemologies, and critical practices, as well as practices of daily life" (2). I am using the term in this sense.

24. In her more recent article "The Essence of the Triangle or, Taking the

Risk of Essentialism Seriously," de Lauretis reviews her earlier position on the notion of sexual difference, and argues instead for maintaining it on the grounds of its "constitutive role ... in feminist thought" (3).

25. The term was originally used by Gayle Rubin in "The Traffic in Women: Notes toward a Political Economy of Sex," 157–210.

26. See Althusser 44–51.

27. Michel Foucault, *The History of Sexuality*. Vol. I, *An Introduction* (1976; 1990), 127.

28. For instance, as described by Michèle Barrett and Anne Phillips in their introduction to *Destabilizing Theory: Contemporary Feminist Theory* (1992), 4.

29. Butler effectively contests the "immutable character of sex" in a chapter of her book *Gender Trouble: Feminism and the Subversion of Identity* (1990) entitled "Subjects of Sex/Gender/Desire." She posits that this "construct called 'sex' " was "always already gender, with the consequence that the distinction between sex and gender turns out to be no distinction at all" (7).

30. Butler, *Gender Trouble*, xi.

31. Monique Wittig, "On the Social Contract," 40.

32. Ibid., 40–41.

33. Jane Gallop, *Around 1981: Academic Feminist Literary Theory* (1992), 188, 199. Introduced by Gayatri Spivak ("French Feminism in an International Frame," 149), the practice of "symptomatic reading," Gallop explains, can be set off against "new critical close reading," which "embraces the text in order to more fully and deeply understand its excellences." Coming out of "psychoanalytic method by way of deconstruction ... 'symptomatic reading' squeezes the text tight to force it to reveal its perversities." Demystifying and hence diminishing the power of authoritative texts, a "symptomatic" reading practice can at once be "respectful, because closely attentive, and aggressive, because it wrests secrets the author might prefer to keep" (7).

34. Cora Kaplan, "Pandora's Box: Subjectivity, Class, and Sexuality in Socialist Feminist Criticism," 148. Ctd. in Gallop, *Around 1981*, 196.

35. The "suggestive" term "implant" was originally used by Foucault in his *History of Sexuality*. Ctd. in de Lauretis, "The Technology of Gender," 12.

36. De Lauretis, "The Technology of Gender," 18–19.

37. All page references to Bowen's novels discussed in this and the following chapters will appear in parentheses in the main text.
38. For a revealing account of the interrelations between these two texts and the historical context of the Anglo-Irish Ascendency, as well as for an alternative reading of the novel, see Lee's chapter "Only Children: *Bowen's Court* (1942) and *The Last September* (1929)" in *Estimation,* 13-56. For further readings of *LS,* see Heath, *Introduction,* 32–46; and Austin 37–41.
39. Lee, *Estimation,* 48–49.
40. Ibid., 45.
41. Heath, *Introduction,* 36.
42. In "The Big House," 195–200, Bowen analyzes the phenomenon of the Anglo-Irish Big House. I shall make further reference to this essay below.
43. In *Female Adolescence: Psychoanalytic Reflections on Literature* (1986), Katherine Dalsimer notes that the location of the actual moment at which adolescence became recognized as a "distinct phase of life" has led to considerable disagreement among historians. She gives several examples of scholars who dismiss the idea that the term originates in the late nineteenth century on account of evidence derived from documents dating from the sixteenth, seventeenth, and eighteenth centuries (4).
44. Teresa de Lauretis, "Feminist Studies/Critical Studies: Issues, Terms, Contexts," 8.
45. For an overview of publications on the issue see Dalsimer 1–12. Her footnotes provide useful bibliographical references.
46. These are "Fragment of an Analyis of a Case of Hysteria" (1905), also and better known as the "Dora-case," and "The Psychogenesis of a Case of Homosexuality in a Woman" (1920).
47. Gallop, *Around 1981,* 186.
48. Dalsimer 2. For further appreciations of the female adolescent in literary texts, see Barbara A. White, *Growing Up Female: Adolescent Girlhood in American Fiction* (1985); and Pamela Pattynama, *Passages: Vrouwelijke Adolescentie als Verhaal en Vertoog* (1992).
49. Erik H. Erikson, *Identity: Youth and Crisis* (1968), 128.
50. Although Erikson's work is noteworthy as one of the first psychological studies to take the socioideological aspects of identity seriously into account, his decidedly masculist (and racist) bias is particularly disturbing. Confined to the penultimate chapter of his book—preced-

ing his final section on "Race and the Wider Identity" (295–320)—
the adult horizon for female adolescents is described as "Womanhood
and the Inner Space." Appearing as the privileged site of reproduction, girls are to become women "by dint of the fact that their somatic
design harbors an 'inner space' destined to bear the offspring of
chosen men" (266). The reductiveness of Erikson's argument is especially conspicuous when, maintaining that it is the "ideological potential of a society which speaks most clearly to the adolescent who is so
eager to be affirmed by peers, to be confirmed by teachers, and to be
inspired by worth-while 'ways of life,'" he locates the destination of
the adolescent's need for "trust in oneself and others" exclusively in
"men and ideas to have *faith* in," conveniently glossing over the fact
that all such categories ("peers," "teachers," " 'ways of life,' "
"men," and "ideas") will invite very different kinds of investment
from male and female adolescents, respectively (130, 128–29). What
is most objectionable, however, is the heterosexism informing Erikson's analysis of adolescence, which evolves into glaring homophobia
when he (faithfully following Freud) defines homosexuality as a "state
not uncommon in a milder and transient form in all adolescence,"
and then proceeds by unabashedly denouncing it as a pathology from
which some his patients "suffer more lastingly and malignantly"
when they fall "victim to the pressure emanating from . . . homosexual cliques" (186). In a gesture known as declaring guilt by association, Erikson at a certain point in fact counts among "negative group
identities" all spontaneous "cliques," including "neighbourhood
gangs, dope rings, homosexual circles, and criminal gangs" (196).

51. Erikson 105. I discuss the crucial role of the "symbolic mother"—as
opposed to the presymbolic or preoedipal maternal figure—in relation to the construction of female subjectivity/sexuality in chapters 6
and 7. See also Cora Kaplan, "Language and Gender," 69–93; and
Kaja Silverman, *The Acoustic Mirror: The Female Voice in Psychoanalysis and Cinema* (1988), 72–100.

52. Lassner rightly identifies Danielstown as the "novel's focus." She
continues by reading the house as a "symbol of maternal omniscience
and omnipotence." Laura's story clearly undermines such a reading.
What is more, the passage Lassner quotes in this connection also
confuses the function of the Big House in the novel's sociopolitical
context. By conflating the "lovely unloving country" upon whose
"unwilling bosom . . . [Danielstown] is set" (66) with the house itself,
she not only misses the crux of the Irish/Anglo-Irish political conflict,

but equally fails to discern that it is the (patriarchal) Ascendency, by *imposing* itself on the Irish country and hence assuming the position of omnipotence symbolized by the Big House, that operates as an oppressive and eventually (self-)annihilating force (28–29). The significance of these issues for Lois's story will gradually become clear.

53. Heath, *Introduction*, 71–102.

54. Elizabeth Bowen, "Out of a Book," 264–69.

55. Contemporary psychoanalytic theory perpetuates the traditional rationality/irrationality opposition predicated upon the male/female opposition by defining the two psychic dispositions upon which subjectivity rests in similarly oppositional terms. Julia Kristeva, for instance, designates the realm of the Law of the Father (Lacan) the "symbolic" as against the unarticulated presymbolic impulses or *choric* psychic material of the "semiotic" order associated with the maternal body.

56. The phrase "historical present" derives from Marx; Judith Butler inserts it into the "genealogical project" of her book *Gender Trouble* to indicate that any critical analysis is by neccessity situated inside the field of political and discursive structures constituting the "contemporary field of power" (5).

57. Interview, Elizabeth Bowen and Jocelyne Brooke, "Broadcast transcribed from a telediphone recording 3rd Ocober 1950," MS (Harry Ransom Humanities Research Center, University of Texas at Austin).

58. Elizabeth Bowen, "The Big House," 27.

59. Preface to *LS*, 99.

60. Judith Butler, "Imitation and Gender Insubordination," 13–14.

61. Ibid., 15.

62. Ibid.

63. Her contradictory emotions and ambivalent perception of love eventually cause Lois to renounce Gerald. Lee reads this as the "failure of love in Lois," which she considers to represent the "most spectacular image of impotence and isolation" in *LS* (*Estimation*, 48). I would suggest that it is not "love" as such but the constraining effects of its sociocultural meanings that Lois ultimately cannot but reject.

64. Teresa de Lauretis, "Perverse Desire: The Lure of the Mannish Lesbian," 15.

65. Butler, "Imitation," 18.

66. Wittig, "Social Contract," 41.

67. Butler, "Imitation," 21.

68. Ibid.

69. The explicitness with which Gerald's reactionary views are condemned here as well as elsewhere in the text renders Lee's evaluation of his character decidedly puzzling. Describing Gerald as the "perfect ideal of the English boy," she posits that he is the novel's "one purely romantic figure" (*Estimation,* 47). Quite apart from its obvious unwarrantability, such a reading obscures the sociopolitical issues explored through the character, and thus implicitly downplays the ideological critique presented by the novel as a whole.

70. The passage provides further evidence against Lassner's interpretation of Danielstown as a symbol of the voracious mother. It is clearly as the seat of patriarchal power that the Big House, imposing itself on her "unwilling bosom," keeps Ireland politically in thrall.

3. *Authoring Sexual Identities*

1. "Pictures and Conversations," 34.

2. In the context of her discussion of time and place in Bowen's work, Lee aptly draws attention to *The Shelbourne Hotel* (1951) and *Bowen's Court,* in which the author makes a "great point . . . of the relationship between architecture and behaviour." Lee correctly points out that the "symbolic value" of the Big House in Ireland is linked to Bowen's joint obsession with the "idea of style" and the "idea of power." The tragedy of the Anglo-Irish, she suggests, evolves from their "lack of insight into the ambiguity and isolation of their position." This is reflected in the ultimate fate of Danielstown: Lee interprets the violent destruction of the house at the end of the novel as the expression of the "relative ineffectuality of the Anglo-Irish gentry in the 20th century" (*Estimation,* 27–39). Although I agree with her evaluation of the Big House in sociohistorical terms, I reject Lee's concluding inference that the inadequacy of "Danielstown" to deal with the situation of war parallels Lois's emotional inadequacy to deal with the "occasion" of love. If not yet sufficiently explained by my alternative reading of the protagonist's predicament so far, my reasons for disagreeing with this statement will shortly be further clarified.

3. Teresa de Lauretis, "Semiotics and Experience," 159.

4. In view of the scene's function as the moment of "awakening" or "revelation" in the traditional adolescent quest, it is amazing to find Lee absolutely silent on the passage. Heath, in contrast, does define

the scene's dramatic meaning as a coming-into-consciousness of the protagonist. He stresses the "ambivalence" of Lois's "revelatory moment," which he correctly identifies as "involving both sexuality and death." But since he reads Lois's sudden discovery of Hugo's illicit desire for Marda as the decisive moment, as a discovery that draws her into a "conspiracy of adulthood and adultery," he arrives at the conclusion that Lois now "know[s] something of the thinness of the wall separating life and death, Marda and Hugo" (*Introduction*, 40). Heath's exclusive focus on the dichotomy between the life and death principles, cast in familiarly phallocentric terms, allows him both to ignore the "ambivalence" of sexuality as such—the death drive being intrinsic to it—and to obscure the very palpable sexual desire between the two female characters operating throughout the scene.

5. Much feminist work in the fields of psychoanalysis and film has been devoted to the significance of the gendered look or gaze. Cf. Teresa de Lauretis's *Technologies of Gender* (1987); Mary Ann Doane, Patricia Mollencamp, and Linda Williams, eds., *Re-vision: Essays in Feminist Film Criticism* (1984); Judith Mayne, *The Woman at the Keyhole: Feminism and Women's Cinema* (1990); and Silverman's *The Acoustic Mirror*.

6. Butler, "Imitation," 20.

7. Sigmund Freud, "Some Psychical Consequences of the Anatomical Distinction between the Sexes" (1925), 337.

8. The image of the "home" as the foundation of constricting patriarchal power is here explicitly linked up with the Law(e) of compulsory heterosexuality. This supports my reading of the symbolic value of the Big House/Danielstown as opposed to Lassner's perception of the "home" as the voracious, smothering mother.

9. Dominant discourses such as religion, education, the media, medicine, and law even today define "adult" lesbian sexuality largely in terms of deviation or perversity. That such definitions serve to ensure the stability of the dominant cultural order is clear from the fact that a film like Paul Verhoeven's *Basic Instinct* (1992), appealing as it does to deep-seated cultural anxieties surrounding lesbian sexuality, has become an instant box-office success on both sides of the Atlantic. A perhaps even more disturbing example of lesbophobia is provided by a recent act issued by the Dutch government denying official parental rights to the nonbiological parent in a lesbian couple.

10. I go into these issues in more detail in chapters 6 and 7.

11. In her reading of this sequence, Lassner attributes significance to Lois's encounter with Daventry mainly because it sets up a contrast between him and the heroine's young "lover," Gerald. Her heterocentric perspective leads her to the conclusion that the "sexual impetus"—which she quite unaccountably ascribes to the latter—is lost in the encounter with the senior subaltern's "impotence" (49).

12. "The Big House," 197.

13. Elizabeth Bowen, *To the North* (1932), 99.

14. Ibid.

15. Bowen's last novel, *Eva Trout* (1969) forms an exception to this pattern. I discuss the possible reasons for this deviation in chapters 6 and 7.

16. "Pictures and Conversations," 36.

17. Ibid., 41–42.

18. Gayatri Chakravorty Spivak, "Feminism and Critical Theory," 85.

19. Catherine Belsey, *Critical Practice* (1980; 1988), 65.

20. The term "extradiegetic" originally derives from Gérard Genette, *Narrative Discourse* (1972; 1986). In *Recent Theories of Narrative* (1986), Wallace Martin explains the terms "diegetic" and "extradiegetic" under two different headings. He describes "diegesis" as an "element of narration," comparable to "summary" or "telling" and applicable when a "narrator describes what happened in his/her own words (or recounts what characters think and feel, without quotation)." In this scheme the "extradiegetic" level falls under the category of "authorial narration," indicating whether a narrator is her/himself "inside" or "outside" the story s/he narrates (124, 135). In *Narrative Fiction: Contemporary Poetics* (1983; 1986), Shlomith Rimmon-Kenan defines "diegesis" as the narrative "events themselves," while the "extra-diegetic" refers to the "highest level" within the hierarchy of narratives within narratives characteristic of novelistic discourse, that is, the "one immediately superior to the first narrative and concerned with its narration" (91). I will be using the term in the latter sense. In her book *The Narrative Act: Point of View in Prose Fiction* (1981), Susan Sniader Lanser offers the (less precise) term "extrafictional voice" to designate the authorial instance, who/which, though "absent" from the narrative text, is always present as the "most direct counterpart for the historical author" (123).

21. Preface to *LS*, 100. The threat of destruction in itself was nonetheless of lasting impact. This is clear from the way Bowen describes her

reaction to her father's letter preparing her for such an eventuality. Staying in Italy, she read his letter "beside Lake Cuomo, and, looking at the blue water taught myself to imagine Bowen's Court in flames. Perhaps that moment disinfected the future: realities of war I have seen since have been frightful; none of them have taken me by surprise" (*Bowen's Court*, 440). Eventually, we recall, her family home was demolished. This "clean end"—unquestionably one of the author's most traumatic experiences—did not take place, however, until very much later. For an account of the loss of her family home and what its destruction meant to her, see the afterword (1963) to *Bowen's Court*, 448–59.

22. The temporal distance separating the narrative events of *LS* from the time of the novel's writing has led to divergent appreciations by Bowen's critics, none of which is particularly satisfactory since they all leave the relations between gender and writing out of account. In line with her general focus on the decline of the Ascendency, Lee, for instance, reads the temporal distance as a stipulation of the fact that the narrative is a description of an era "firmly placed in the past," in which the atmosphere of "melancholy autumnal transience" serves to make "social life . . . feel like a period piece" (*Estimation,* 44). In *Elizabeth Bowen* (1971), A. E. Austin disregards the politico-historical aspect altogether and explains the novel's temporal setting by maintaining that the "story seeks to pinpoint the time when Lois begins to have a life of her own." This entails that a "sense of completion is necessary," since "only in retrospect can we possibly presume to identify turning points or locate significance where, at the time, none was recognizable" (37). Austin's view comes nearer to my own in that it locates the significance of the distance in time squarely within Lois's story, in addition to establishing the link between the novel's autobiographical aspects and the author's need to exert her control over narrative events. The second half of his comment, however, surely holds true for any text and thus fails to address the issue at hand in its specificity. Heath, on the other hand, draws attention to the effect of "timelessness" occasioned by the novel's historical setting. Reading it as an expression of the isolation of the Anglo-Irish, he simultaneously stresses the "reader's position," which, he claims "must be complex enough so that he [*sic*] can see an immediate action within a historical context" (*Introduction,* 35). Heath further approaches the question from a thematic angle, offering several valuable insights whose relevance will appear in the course of my subse-

quent discussion. Lassner disregards the issue of the novel's temporal complexities.

23. "Pictures and Conversations," 53, 52.
24. Ibid., 47, 9.
25. Ibid., 48.
26. Glendinning 23.
27. "Pictures and Conversations," 47, 53, 51.
28. Ibid., 19, 9, 53.
29. Preface to *LS*, 96.
30. Elizabeth Bowen, "Why Do I Write?" 222.
31. Ibid.
32. Ibid., 222–23.
33. The letter forms part of a published correspondence between Bowen, V. S. Pritchett, and Graham Greene, in which they explore their respective motives for becoming professional writers.
34. Ibid., 224.
35. Ibid., 224–25.
36. Heath unfortunately fails to take into account the gendered implications of such notions as "authority" and "control" (*Introduction*, 42).
37. Ibid., 41.
38. Julia Kristeva, "The Adolescent Novel," 8–23. Consistently pursuing a practice that has already evoked much comment from feminist critics, Kristeva concentrates exclusively on male-authored texts. Although regrettable, this does little to detract from the valuable points she brings to bear upon the issues at hand.
39. The sole occurrence of the female adolescent at this point in Kristeva's argument does not invalidate my previous comments on her masculist bias: she specifically and exclusively refers to Nabokov's *Lolita* . . .
40. The terms in which Kristeva casts her "metaphor" underline the close links between sexuality and death while also foregrounding the central place of the female (body) in both. The scene of "revelation" in *LS* testifies to the validity of these points in the context of (writing) adolescence. Still, although I support Kristeva's (implied) emphasis on the critical function of the female body in the intertwined processes of subjectivity/sexuality, I do not follow her in confining its significance to the realms of the presymbolic or (Lacanian) Imaginary. See also chapters 6 and 7.
41. For convincing analyses of the contradictions in Kristeva's work on the maternal figure in relation to female homosexuality, see Sil-

verman, "The Fantasy of the Maternal Voice," in *The Acoustic Mirror*, 101–26; Jane Gallop, "The Phallic Mother: Fraudian Analysis," in *Feminism and Psychoanalysis: The Daughter's Seduction* (1982), 113–31; and Butler, "The Body Politics," in *Gender Trouble*, 79–92.

42. Lee repeatedly mentions as a recurrent theme in Bowen's novels the strong attraction between the character of the "older woman" and the author's young heroines. She never attempts to examine this conspicuous motif, however. Nor, for that matter, does she comment on the fact that all of the novels feature at least one major or minor explicitly lesbian character.

4. *Histories of Narrative Desire*

1. These were *Seven Winters* (1942), *Bowen's Court* (1942), and *English Novelists* (1945), respectively.
2. Elizabeth Bowen, preface to *DL*, 52.
3. *New Statesman*, 23 May 1942. Ctd. in Robert Hewison, *Under Siege: Literary Life in London, 1939–1945* (1977), 88. Italics mine.
4. Preface to *DL*, 47.
5. Elizabeth Bowen, "Sources of Influence," 208; preface to *Stories by Elizabeth Bowen*, 77.
6. Preface to *DL*, 47.
7. "Autobiographical Note, sent to Curtis Brown 11/10/46," MS (Harry Ransom Humanities Research Center, University of Texas at Austin).
8. Elizabeth Bowen, "Pink May," *Collected Stories*, 713.
9. "Pictures and Conversations," 36–37; preface to *DL*, 47.
10. Elizabeth Bowen, afterword to *Bowen's Court*, 453.
11. "Why Do I Write?" 223.
12. Preface to *DL*, 47, 48.
13. "Out of a Book," 264–69.
14. Preface to *DL*, 48.
15. We recall that Bowen had been uprooted from her native soil at the age of seven as a consequence of her father's mental collapse. The following five years she spent living an itinerant existence on the coast of England in the company of her mother, a period that ended with the shattering event of the latter's death. She subsequently lived with a number of different relatives and at boarding schools in England, only to return to Ireland in the ambiguous position of the Anglo-Irish landowner. Cf. Glendinning 18–73.

16. Glendinning 131.
17. Preface to *DL*, 49.
18. Ibid., 50.
19. Ibid.
20. "Why Do I Write?" 228, 224.
21. Preface to *DL*, 49, 50; 51.
22. Ibid.
23. From a letter written in March 1945 to Charles Ritchie. Ctd. in Glendinning 149.
24. Elizabeth Bowen, "The Bend Back" (1951), 54–60.
25. Ibid., 54, 56.
26. Hayden White, *Tropics of Discourse: Essays in Cultural Criticism* (1978), 50.
27. Ibid., 106, 112.
28. "The Bend Back," 57, 58.
29. Foucault, *The Archeology of Knowledge*, 215–37.
30. In *Under Siege*, Hewison submits that one of the difficulties facing the writer caught up in the turbulence of World War II was an "inhibiting awareness that this was a 'period' with a beginning and an expected end, cut off from past and future alike," while the present was "too close and too unpleasant" to serve as writing material (87). He notes a remarkable increase in the publication of autobiographies and childhood reminiscences during the war years. Although he considers this phenomenon to have sprung partly from the intractability of a too-immediate present, he also sees this "outpouring of memory" as a search for the causes of the current crisis, usually resulting in a "part-nostalgical, part-critical" return to the period preceding World War I. Coupling Bowen's name with the author's contemporary, Rosamund Lehmann, Hewison attributes to the latter's war-time stories an "atmosphere of retreat and decay in the genteel-middle-classes, out of place since Edwardian times" (91). Significantly, in grouping Bowen with Lehmann, and at a later point also with Ivy Compton-Burnett, Hewison suggests that all three female authors retreated into the safety of "domestic dramas," whereas their male counterparts (e.g., Joyce Cary and Evelyn Waugh) practiced nostalgia on a suitably larger scale: they produced works that represent an "examination of the liberal-Protestant" and of the "conservative-Catholic . . . English tradition," respectively (91–92). The point may appear to be a minor one, but it is precisely this kind of gendered hierarchization within traditional literary history—so familiar that we barely notice

it—that continues to obscure the significance of the work of female authors. As any reader will be able to testify, such a disparaging assessment of Bowen's work is widely off the mark, especially in view of the questions her war-time fictions explore. Bowen's outspoken notions concerning historiography and sociocultural power relations render Hewison's superficial judgments markedly absurd.

31. In *Tradition and Dream* (1964), Walter Allen, for instance, describes *HD* as "the most completely detailed evocation of [the atmosphere of the place and time] that we have in fiction" (195). Although some contemporary critics expressed their reservations about particular aspects of the novel, the archives of the Harry Ransom Research Center in Texas contain letters from Bowen's friends that show that they all more or less shared Allen's enthusiasm. Glendinning quotes from a letter by Rosamund Lehman, whose eulogistic praise she regards as actually "too emotional, most of it, to be exposed to cold print" (153). For further comments on the critical reception of the novel, see Lee, *Estimation*, 205, 235–37.

32. Although Lee acknowledges the novel's importance as "in many ways the culmination of her work," she considers *HD* to be "not altogether characteristic . . . nor [Bowen's] best novel" (*Estimation*, 164). Heath is rather circumspect and does not pass any final judgment on the novel's "quality," but the appreciative tone in which he casts his analysis—subtle and noteworthy comments with which I nonetheless often disagree—eventually speaks for itself (*Introduction*, 106–24). Since her project is biography rather than criticism, Glendinning's comments, though in the main quite pertinent, are necessarily general in character and somewhat superficial. Lassner merely acknowledges past critics' difficulties with *HD* but does not examine their nature and/or possible causes (120–40).

33. From the letter to Charles Ritchie referred to in note 23 above (ctd. in Glendinning 150).

34. Placing it in the sociopolitical historical context in which it was produced, Lee pays a great deal of attention to the spy story and its significance (*Estimation*, 175–77).

35. Lee, *Estimation*, 165.

36. "Elizabeth Bowen & Jocelyne Brooke [broadcast], October 1950." MS (Harry Ransom Humanities Research Center, University of Texas at Austin). The ungrammaticalities are original and stem from the fact that the interview was transcribed from a "telediphone" recording.

37. This is borne out by the fact that, despite their reservations, most critics in the end appear to agree that Bowen's stylistic "mannerisms" are ultimately highly effective and eminently suited to *HD*'s controlling themes. Cf. Lee's comments to this effect, *Estimation,* 165; and also Glendinning 153. The former further mentions a "funny 1952 New Yorker parody of Elizabeth Bowen" by Peter de Vries to illustrate the extent to which the reputed mannerisms gave rise to irritation and ridicule (*Estimation,* 187n.).

38. Glendinning 152.

39. For reference, see note 36 above.

40. Teresa de Lauretis, "Desire in Narrative," 103–57.

41. For the ways in which this nineteenth-century, predominantly male genre has, in the twentieth century, in its turn been transformed into specifically female itineraries of self-discovery or quests for identity, see Elizabeth Abel, Marianne Hirsch, and Elizabeth Langland, eds., *The Voyage In: Fictions of Female Development* (1983).

42. Jonathan Culler, *Structuralist Poetics: Structuralism, Linguistics, and the Study of Literature* (1975), 210.

43. Belsey 70.

44. Ibid.

45. See Luce Irigaray, "Commodities among Themselves," 192.

46. The term "complification" derives from Maaike Meijer, *De Lust tot Lezen: Nederlandse Dichteressen en het Literaire Systeem* (1988).

47. Lee locates the origins of the "impoverishment of the relationship" between mother and son in the "impoverishment of the times," without exploring the nature and causes of such a *zeitgeist* (*Estimation,* 185). It would appear, as I am trying to argue here, that it is the operation of dominant ideology itself, posing its restrictions on the forms that relationships are allowed to take, that lies at the heart of the ruinous "impoverishment" on the intersubjective level as well as on that of social interaction.

48. For the significance of this term in the context of postmodernism, and especially its horrifying implications, see Jean Baudrillard, "The Procession of Simulacra" (1984), 253–81.

49. De Lauretis, "Desire in Narrative," 119.

50. Sigmund Freud, "The Uncanny," 335–76.

51. Patricia White, "Female Spectator, Lesbian Specter: *The Haunting,*" 149.

52. Here as elsewhere, Bowen's choice of names for houses is particularly

felicitous, as will shortly become clear. Suffice it to say at this point that "holm" denotes an island in a river or lake, whereas "dene" refers both to a wooded and narrow valley and to a sandy stretch of land near the sea.

53. White, "Female Spectator, Lesbian Specter," 149.

54. Sigmund Freud, "Some Neurotic Mechanisms in Jealousy, Paranoia, and Homosexuality," 201.

55. Ibid., 206, 205.

56. In *The Language of Psycho-Analysis* (1988), Jean LaPlanche and Jean-Bertrand Pontalis define "reaction-formation" as the "psychological attitude or habitus diametrically opposed to a repressed wish, and constituted as a reaction against it. . . . Reaction-formations may be highly localised, manifesting themselves in specific behaviour, or they may be generalised to the point of forming character-traits more or less integrated into the overall personality" (376–77).

57. Lassner bases her (alternative) reading of the Holme Dene episode as a critique of patriarchy entirely on the figure of the archaic mother (141–63).

58. Afterword to *Bowen's Court*, 455.

59. See Lassner on the Powerful Mother in Bowen. She traces the origins of the figure straightforwardly to Bowen's biography in a way that I do not always consider quite warranted. Her conclusions about the function of this character end up being somewhat contradictory, although a number of her observations are illuminating. As mentioned before, Lee frequently notes but never satisfactorily explores the recurrent figure of the "frightful" elderly woman in Bowen's work.

60. Sigmund Freud, "The Sexual Aberrations," 85–86.

5. The Discourse of Suspension

1. Lee leaves the connection between Harrison and Robert largely undiscussed. She mentions the fact that the men share their Christian names; she implicitly groups the two male characters together in relation to the secret activities from which they jointly exclude Stella, positing that the novel presents "a woman's view of the male world of 'Intelligence' "; and she is particularly disturbed by what she considers to be "one of the plot's weaknesses," namely, that Stella "should warm to Harrison in any degree" (*Estimation*, 175). This is left without any further comment. Lassner, on the other hand, offers

a number of interesting observations on the spy plot from a gender perspective. She focuses on the "elusiveness" of Stella's character as the reason why "each man bring[s] his plot to [her] for interpretation." Representing "woman" as the suspected "harbour" of "secret meaning," such gender-defined elusiveness is conceived of as Stella's "protection from the spy-plot which, if she became involved, would cast her in its presumed moral dichotomies" (125). This putative feminist reading would seem to reinforce rather than criticize traditional gender assumptions: setting up Stella's ignorance, her limited access to power/knowledge—the "muted" female position that patriarchal ideology assimilates by means of compensation (woman as the source of "secret meaning," the keeper or even the embodiment of "enigma")—as a positive quality, even an asset, Lassner reasserts and validates women's exclusion from power/knowledge.

2. Sigmund Freud, "A Case of Paranoia Running Counter to the Psychoanalytic Theory of the Disease," 149.

3. Michel Foucault, *Discipline and Punish: The Birth of the Prison* (1979), 27–28.

4. Teresa de Lauretis, "Sexual Indifference and Lesbian Representation," 156.

5. Freud, "Some Neurotic Mechanisms," 197.

6. Ibid., 199.

7. Virginia Woolf, *A Room of One's Own* (1929; 1977), 35.

8. I thank Teresa Brennan for discussing these issues with me.

9. Silverman, *The Acoustic Mirror*, 155.

10. See Lee, *Estimation*, 173; Heath, *Introduction*, 123; Lassner 113.

11. Gillian Spraggs, "Hell and the Mirror: A Reading of *Desert of the Heart*," 118.

12. Ibid., 121.

13. Ibid., 118.

14. Ibid., 123.

15. This passage confirms my reading of Lois Farquar's/the narrator's moment of "apprehension" in *LS*. See the section "The Lure of Disintegration" in chapter 3.

16. Belsey 70.

17. Lee finds fault with this minor story on account of the problem of scope it poses to the novel as a whole. She furthermore objects to the characters of Louie and her friend Connie, denouncing them as "simplified caricatures of lower-middle-class types" whose function as "innocent witness[es]" fails, because Bowen "is trying to do too

much" with their "half-conscious, half-comical language" (*Estimation,* 184). My reading of Louie's character renders such a criticism not particularly relevant.

18. For fairly accessible discussions of the Lacanian notion of the subject's developmental stages, see Belsey 60–61; and Toril Moi, *Sexual/Textual Politics* (1985), 100, 162. For more extensive feminist explorations of Lacanian theory, see Jane Gallop, *Reading Lacan* (1985); and Elizabeth Grosz, *Jacques Lacan: A Feminist Introduction* (1990). Helpful also are the relevant sections in Jacqueline Rose, *Sexuality in the Field of Vision* (1986); and Silverman, *The Acoustic Mirror.*

19. The concept of a so-called third sex, the "invert" or the "mannish lesbian," was developed by early twentieth-century sexologists such as Krafft-Ebing and Havelock Ellis. The most obvious literary example of the "invert" is, of course, Radclyffe Hall's creation of Stephen Gordon in *The Well of Loneliness* (1928). For an assessment of the influence and effects of the sexologists' work on literary texts, see Lilian Faderman, *Surpassing the Love of Men* (1981; 1985), 239–53. For a thorough discussion of the character as type, see Esther Newton's seminal essay "The Mythic Mannish Lesbian: Radclyffe Hall and the New Woman," 557–76. For a further (psychoanalytically oriented) exploration of the type, see de Lauretis, "Perverse Desire," 15–26. It is interesting to note that the figure of the ARP warden performs the same duties in the war effort as Bowen herself—it would seem that "tough, cross, kind" Connie, who admits to a "bossy" nature, having been "prey, since childhood, to a repressed wish to issue orders, blow whistles, direct traffic," represents, at however "many removes," her creator's wish to assert herself with symbolic authority (149). Since this sexually ambivalent creature is situated in a class position decidedly beneath Bowen's own, she is put at a reassuringly safe distance so as to prevent any further (biographical) speculation in this respect.

20. Lee, *Estimation,* 184.

21. Heath, *Introduction,* 119.

22. Lee's view is not in fact as unqualified as my comment here seems to suggest. Her criticism of the Louie subplot is, however, not directed at its presumed function within the framework of the novel as a whole but at the ways in which it fails to ring true in its depiction of the lower classes. She eventually prefers to discern an "alternative to despair in the idea of inheritance and in the solid, likeable, literal-

minded character of Roderick" (*Estimation,* 185). Such a reading strikes me as overly optimistic in light of the severe critique of patriarchal ideology the novel presents on its various levels.

6. Subtexts of Psychosexuality

1. These were, in the order listed here, *Collected Impressions* (1950); *Afterthought* (1962); *The Shelbourne Hotel* (1951); *A World of Love* (1955); *The Little Girls* (1964); *A Time in Rome* (1960); *The Good Tiger* (1965); *A Day in the Dark and Other Stories* (1965).
2. Elizabeth Bowen, "Notes on Writing a Novel," 170–71.
3. Ibid., 176.
4. See Kristeva, "Adolescent Novel," 8; and the section "Interpretation, Transference, and Authorial Control" in chapter 4.
5. "Family romance" is a central concept in psychoanalytic theory. Before he published his essay of the same title in 1909 ("Family Romances," 217–26), Freud had already used the term "family romances" on several occasions. As Laplanche and Pontalis explain, the notion refers to "phantasies of a particular type, by means of which the subject invents a new family for himself and in so doing works out a sort of romance." These fantasies are "related to the Oedipal situation"; they, in fact, "originate from the pressure exerted by the Oedipus complex" (*The Language of Psychoanalysis,* 160).
6. Lee, *Estimation,* 205–6.
7. Craig 135.
8. Lee duly remarks on the biblical references in *ET.* She defines as the novel's underlying theme the "interplay between good and evil," a central preoccupation of Bowen's that, in this last novel, is "no longer suppressed beneath a realistic level." Quite unaccountably, in light of these and her earlier considerations on the failure of Bowen's realist mode, she concludes that *ET* "unabashedly presents itself as a fairy tale" (*Estimation,* 209). The reasons why I do not share these puzzling views will soon become clear.
9. Bowen has frequently been classified as either a social realist or as a writer of "sensibility"—a qualification to which she herself strongly objected. I reject both these labels as reductive characterizations of her work. Even if most of her novels, especially the earlier ones, are clearly inscribed in the tradition of classic realism, the distinct "gothic" elements in her work (also conspicuous in her short stories),

and the wider philosophical/ethical frameworks in which the narratives are cast render such classifications unwarranted.

10. Glendinning 227. Heath's *Introduction* to Bowen's novels was completed in 1961. His comments therefore do not extend beyond a discussion of what was at that moment Bowen's last published novel, *A World of Love* (1955). Lassner's analysis of Bowen's stylized discourse or, as she puts it, her "attenuated" narratives, is much more to the point than either Lee's or Craig's: "Bowen's language represents a struggle for autonomy in self-expression, and where her characters express their inability to find a language of self-expression, Bowen's imagery, her own deployment of language, expresses their dilemmas" (162). Although in the final instance conducive to a basically sociological feminist critical interpretation—which I consider reductive in light of textual theory—this appreciation of the critical role of language in Bowen's (gender- and ideology-conscious) texts allows for a clearer understanding of her novels' larger politico-ethical frameworks.

11. Craig quotes a passage from the novel in which Bowen has one character comment on another's style of writing: " 'This mannered manner . . . was not quite the thing, no.' " Reading it as an instance where the author is "surely poking fun at herself, bearing in mind the standard criticism of her sometimes elaborate effects," she disregards the wider implications of such a strategy of self-parody (135). The passage clearly ought to be linked up with what Lee calls the "concept of a breakdown of language" figuring in Bowen's later texts. As such, it places the author squarely within the context of postmodernism, in which self-parody and self-reflexivity form constitutive parts of essentially ethical and aesthetic objectives. Names generally associated with the debate on postmodernism in the United States are Fredric Jameson, Ihab Hassan, Edward Said, Hal Foster, and Andreas Huyssen, among others, whose appreciation of the postmodern largely draws on the work of French theorists such as Jean Baudrillard and Jean-François Lyotard. Male critics addressing the issue of feminism in relation to the postmodern are as yet few and far between. Exceptional examples are Craig Owens, "The Discourse of Others: Feminists and Postmodernism," 57–82; and Robert Stam, "Mikhail Bakhtin and Left Cultural Critique," 16–45. For examples of feminist intervention in the debate on postmodernism, see Linda Hutcheon, *A Poetics of Postmodernism: History, Theory, Fiction* (1988); E. Ann

Kaplan, ed., *Postmodernism and Its Discontents: Theories, Practices* (1988); and my "Contradictions Held in Suspense: Postmodernism and Feminist Critique" (1990). Further instances can be found in *Feminism/Postmodernism* (1990), edited by Linda J. Nicholson; particularly interesting in the context of lesbian theory is Judith Butler's "Gender Trouble, Feminist Theory, and Psychoanalytic Discourse," 324–40. See also Meaghan Morris, *The Pirate's Fiancée: Feminism, Reading, Postmodernism* (1988); and Jane Flax, *Thinking Fragments: Psychoanalysis, Feminism, and Postmodernism in the Contemporary West* (1990). An appreciation of postmodernism in the context of lesbian writing is Sally Munt's "*Somewhere over the Rainbow* . . .," 33–50.

12. Spencer Curtis Brown, foreword to *Pictures and Conversations,* xxxviii–xxxix. Glendinning, too, points out that Bowen remained uncertain about the success of her new approach in *The Little Girls,* while being "satisfied" with the novel in which she succeeded in bringing her new techniques to a higher level of perfection. To indicate the measure of Bowen's success, she mentions that *ET* won the James Tait Black Prize (218–20).

13. Lee, *Estimation,* 204.

14. Lennard J. Davis, *Resisting Novels: Ideology and Fiction* (1986), 112.

15. Ibid., 137.

16. Glendinning 123.

17. Lee, *Estimation,* 207.

18. See Davis 141; Sniader Lanser 142–43.

19. "Pictures and Conversations," 59.

20. Curtis Brown xxxix. Glendinning echoes him almost literally, claiming that "instead of responding and reacting to situations, as most of Elizabeth's heroines do, Eva creates the situations herself" (226).

21. Lee, *Estimation,* 206.

22. As discussed in a different context, after her mother's death, Bowen "could not remember her, think of her, speak of her or suffer to hear her spoken of" ("Pictures and Conversations," 48).

23. Ctd. in Glendinning 222. The biographer in fact reads Bowen's return to Hythe very much as a return to origins, as is reflected in the title of the chapter covering this last period of her subject's life, "Coming Home," 222–40.

24. Lee, *Estimation,* 206.

25. Ctd. in Craig 137.

26. For a different approach to the novel's twofold structure, see my essay "De Grens Tussen Spreken en Zwijgen," 43–57.

27. "Pictures and Conversations" 36.

28. The term derives from Hutcheon 57–73.

29. None of the critics mentioned so far take note of the break in what they present as a sustained narrative method. Thus they fail to take into account the gender-inflected operations of language, which are problematized on the intra- as well as the extradiegetic levels of the text. Lassner briefly discusses the interrelations between gender and symbolic articulacy in *ET*, but does not mention the central place of the mother/daughter relationship within them (162–63).

30. See Ferdinand de Saussure, *Course in General Linguistics* (1966); Claude Lévi-Strauss, *Structural Anthropology* (1967), *The Elementary Structures of Kinship* (1969).

31. Many feminist theorists have pointed out and explored the distinction between Woman or "the feminine" as abstract categories in male conceptual schemes and the material-historical beings called "women," whose existence is consistently marginalized or ignored within such theorizations. De Lauretis, for instance, declares: "By 'woman' I mean a fictional construct, a distillate from diverse but congruent discourses dominant in Western cultures . . . which works both as their vanishing point and their specific condition of existence. . . . By *women* on the other hand, I will mean the real historical beings who cannot as yet be defined outside of these discursive formations, but whose material existence is nonetheless certain" (introduction to *Alice Doesn't*, 5). See also Alice Jardine, "The Woman-in-Effect," *Gynesis: Configurations of Woman and Modernity* (1985), 31–49. Judith Butler's problematization of the "categories of sex" does not so much undermine as actually underscore such distinctions. I will come back to this.

32. For an analysis of woman as the site of negativity, see Julia Kristeva, "Negativity: Rejection," 109–47.

33. See Julia Kristeva, *Powers of Horror: An Essay on Abjection* (1980; 1982), 65.

34. Freud naturally acknowledged this, but his oedipal plot is in the first and the last instance the boy's story; in spite of his (later) attempts to analyze female sexuality, woman ultimately remained an "enigma" in psychoanalytic theory.

35. Madelon Sprengnether, "(M)other Eve: Some Revisions of the Fall in Fiction by Contemporary Women Writers" (1989), 299.
36. Ibid., 299–300.
37. Sigmund Freud, "Femininity," 145–69. This lecture was based on two earlier papers: "Some Psychical Consequences of the Anatomical Distinction between the Sexes" (1925), 323–44, and "Female Sexuality" (1931), 367–92.
38. Laplanche and Pontalis define bisexuality as a "notion introduced into psycho-analysis by Freud, under the influence of Wilhelm Fliess, according to which every human being is endowed constitutionally with both masculine and feminine sexual dispositions; these can be identified in the conflicts which the subject experiences in assuming his own sex." They add that Freud "never thoroughly defined his position with respect to the problem of bisexuality" and that "his thinking about the problem includes a number of reservations and doubts" (*The Language of Psychoanalysis*, 52–53).
39. See Sigmund Freud, "The Dissolution of the Oedipus Complex," 313–22.
40. Laplanche and Pontalis, *The Language of Psychoanalysis*, 283.
41. For the shifting place of the notion of castration in Freud, see Juliet Mitchell's chapter "On Freud and the Distinction between the Sexes," in *Women: The Longest Revolution* (1984), 221–33.
42. Freud, "Femininity," 151.
43. Freud, "Female Sexuality," 371.
44. Freud, "Femininity," 151–52.
45. I here of course refer to Freud's reestablishment within the feminist theoretical arena with the publication of Juliet Mitchell's *Psychoanalysis and Feminism* (1974).
46. Freud, "Femininity," 160.
47. Laplanche and Pontalis define the negative Oedipus complex as follows: "Love for the parent of the same sex and jealous hatred for the parent of the opposite sex" (*The Language of Psychoanalysis*, 283).
48. Freud, "Female Sexuality," 371–72, 377.
49. Kristeva, "Adolescent Novel," 8.
50. Laplanche and Pontalis show that psychoanalytic theory is somewhat ambivalent about the concept of narcissism. Especially in "Mourning and Melancholia," however, Freud presents the phenomenon in a manner consistent with Lacan's *mirror stage,* that is, as the child's "amorous captivation" with its own image. Because the ego takes

form by identifying with an object, the subject/object relationship is not one of intersubjectivity but is rather the "internalisation of a relationship" (*The Language of Psychoanalysis*, 256).

51. See, inter alia, Juliet Mitchell and Jacqueline Rose, *Feminine Sexuality: Jacques Lacan and the école freudienne* (1982); and subsequent elaborations in Rose, "Feminine Sexuality," in *Sexuality in the Field of Vision* (1986), 49–82; and Mitchell, "Freud and Lacan," in *Women*, 248–77. As mentioned before, helpful and simple introductions to Lacan's thought are the relevant sections in Moi's *Sexual/Textual Politics*; and Belsey.

52. Fredric Jameson, "Imaginary and Symbolic in Lacan: Marxism, Psychoanalytic Criticism, and the Problem of the Subject" (1977; 1982), 338–95.

53. Ibid., 353, 354–55.

54. Jacques Lacan, *Le Séminaire*, 1, 98, ctd. in Jameson, "Imaginary," 355.

55. Jameson, "Imaginary," 355, 356.

56. See Jacques Lacan, "The Mirror Stage," in *Ecrits*, 1–7.

57. "Disavowal," or *Verleugnung*, is used by Freud in the specific sense of a "mode of defence which consists in the subject's refusing to recognise the reality of a traumatic perception" (Laplanche and Pontalis, *The Language of Psychoanalysis*, 118).

58. Cf. Luce Irigaray, *This Sex Which Is Not One* (1977; 1985); Julia Kristeva, *Polylogue* (1977), *Desire in Language* (1980); and Hélène Cixous and Christine Clément, *The Newly Born Woman* (1986).

59. Juliet Mitchell, "Psychoanalysis: Child Development and Femininity," in *Women*, 249–78.

60. Ibid., 264–65, 263.

61. Ibid., 273.

62. *The Acoustic Mirror*, 122. The meaning of "castration" in Silverman's framework (predicated on Lacan) is thus threefold: it first of all pertains to the subject/object separation; secondly, it denotes the subject's entry into the symbolic order that, preexisting and anticipating the subject, enforces meanings and desires upon it; and thirdly, the term refers to the split between the subject of enunciation and the enunciating subject.

63. Ibid.

64. Toril Moi, "Patriarchal Thought and the Drive for Knowledge" (1989), 199. Moi discusses Freud's notions of "epistemophilia" and

sublimation in the context of the feminist debate on the rationality/
emotionality or mind/body distinction, a duality by which all
forms of intellectual pursuit end up being defined as masculine. Such
a point of view, Moi maintains, is not only harmful in that it unjust-
ifiably renders women's pursuit of knowledge "suspect," but it also
occludes Freud's insistence on the inscription of the bodily drives
(or "instincts" in the *Standard Edition*) in creative/speculative/
intellectual processes (189–205). Another illuminating feminist reading of the Freudian text on creativity and/or sublimation is Rose's
chapter "Sexuality in the Field of Vision" in her book of the same
title, 225–34.

65. Silverman, *The Acoustic Mirror*, 44.
66. Ibid.
67. Ibid., 122.
68. Ibid., 124.

7. Sexual/Transgressions

1. As both Lee and Glendinning remark, *ET* is the only novel of Bowen's
   to be partly set in America. The latter informs us that Bowen enjoyed
   her frequent stays in the United States immensely and that she "loved
   the 'convenience' of American homes and all-American gadgetry: tea-
   machines, matching towels, American cocktail apparatus, crushproof
   everything, were features of . . . Carbery—the polar extreme from the
   doubtful plumbing, ancient kitchen and temperamental generator that
   had underpinned Bowen's Court" (230).
2. Silverman, *The Acoustic Mirror*, 122.
3. Hélène Deutsch, *The Psychology of Women* (1944), 116.
4. Marianne Hirsch, *The Mother/Daughter Plot: Narrative, Psychoanalysis, Feminism* (1989).
5. Adrienne Rich, "Compulsory Heterosexuality and Lesbian Existence"
   (1980; 1984), 212–41.
6. The problem here as elsewhere in this otherwise illuminating work
   is that Hirsch discusses "compulsory heterosexuality" in exclusively
   metaphorical terms, that is, on the level of discourse only, without
   extrapolating from the mother/daughter bond the material lesbian
   desire that informs Rich's iconoclastic—and controversial—essay.
7. The passage echoes Virginia Woolf's (fictionalized) experience of female exclusion from the male realm of knowledge and learning—
   called Oxbridge—in the first section of *A Room of One's Own*,
   5–25.

8. Luce Irigaray's analysis of the concept of "mimicry" or "mimesis" primarily concerns the *loss* of femininity on account of the very unrepresentability of female sexuality within symbolic language: "The masculine can partly look at itself, speculate about itself, represent itself and describe itself for what it is, whilst the feminine can try to speak itself through a new language, but cannot describe itself from outside or in formal terms, except by identifying itself with the masculine, thus by losing itself" ("Women's Exile," 65). This is an entirely different line of analysis from the one I am pursuing here. For a concise discussion of Irigaray's notion of "mimicry," see Moi, *Sexual/ Textual Politics,* 140–42. See also Gayatri Chakravorty Spivak, "Displacement and the Discourse of Woman," 169–95, for an interesting view on womanliness-as-masquerade. Tania Modleski discusses the discursive production of "femininity" in the context of mass culture in her chapter "Femininity as Mas(s)querade," in *Feminism without Women: Culture and Criticism in a "Postfeminist" Age* (1991), 23–34.

9. Joan Rivière, "Womanliness as a Masquerade," 35–49.

10. Mary Ann Doane, "Film and the Masquerade" (1982), 81–82.

11. Butler, "Imitation," 18.

12. Ibid., 20.

13. Ibid., 21. Butler rather loosely paraphases Esther Newton's line of argument in *Mother's Camp: Female Impersonators in America* (Chicago: University of Chicago Press, 1972).

14. In "Boys Will Be Girls: The Politics of Gay Drag," 32–70, Carole-Anne Tyler subjects the contempory valorization of putatively "transgressive" forms of gender impersonation such as "camp" and "drag" to a highly pertinent critique. She correctly points to the dangers implied by a "gay essentialism" that issues from the invocation of a "gay sensibility" to "keep straight the difference between gay and heterosexual gender impersonation" (54).

15. Butler, "Imitation," 18.

16. Freud, "Female Sexuality," 372.

17. Glendinning 218, 225.

18. Kristeva, "Adolescent Novel," 21.

19. Hirsch, *Mother/Daughter Plot,* 12

20. Ibid., 14, 50.

21. I am here of course primarily referring to Roland Barthes's seminal essay "The Death of the Author," in which he replaces of the notion of the Author-God by that of the highly eroticized textual body; and

to Foucault's conceptualization of the authorial figure as a textual function, somewhere in between description and designation, in "What Is an Author?" 141–60.

22. Notable exceptions are, inter alia, Nancy Miller's "Changing the Subject," 102–20; Cheryl Walker, "Feminist Literary Criticism and the Author," 551–71; and Judith Mayne's section on "Female Authorship" in *The Woman at the Keyhole,* 89–154. Specifically lesbian perspectives on the issue are provided by Mayne's recent essay "A Parallax View of Lesbian Authorship," 173–84; and Reina Lewis, "The Death of the Author and the Resurrection of the Dyke," 17–31.

23. Silverman gives a critical overview of the auteur debate in cinematic theory in her chapter "The Female Authorial Voice," in *The Acoustic Mirror,* 187–212 and notes on 249–51.

24. Ibid., 202.

25. Sniader Lanser 151.

26. Sigmund Freud, *Beyond the Pleasure Principle,* 244.

27. Peter Brooks, "Freud's Masterplot: Questions of Narrative," 280–300.

28. Ibid., 282.

29. For an astute critique of the male bias in Brooks's and other dominant theories of narratology, see Hirsch, *Mother/Daughter-Plot* 52–54.

30. Kristeva, "Adolescent Novel," 14, 9.

31. Ibid., 21.

32. "Why Do I Write?" 222.

33. Hirsch, *Mother/Daughter Plot,* 57.

34. De Lauretis, "The Technology of Gender," 26.

8. *From Marginality to Ex-centricity*

1. Although women speaking from other than so-called mainstream (white, middle-class, heterosexual) cultural positions have rightly warned feminists against falling victim to our own ideological blind spots in order to prevent our theory from becoming yet another teleological discourse, the invaluable political and theoretical benefits of such interventions should not, as Susan Bordo aptly reminds us, cause us to lose sight of the fact that "feminist theory—even the work of white, upper-class women—is not located at the *center* of cultural power" ("Feminism, Postmodernism, and Gender-Scepticism," 141).

2. I borrow this phrase from Susan Bordo who, in her turn, adopts it

from Thomas Nagel. Bordo inserts the phrase into a discussion of current "gender scepticism" within feminist theory. She argues that feminism cannot afford to abandon the notion of gender on the grounds of an "increasingly paralyzing anxiety over falling . . . into ethnocentrism or 'essentialism,'" suggesting that such presumed theoretical rigor may in fact be another masculist ruse to perpetuate its policies of exclusion and neutralization. See Bordo 133–56.

3. For the implications of the quite literal "situatedness" of the (feminist) body in place and time, see Biddy Martin and Chandra Tapalde Mohanty, "What's Home Got to Do with It?" 191–212.

4. De Lauretis, "Feminism, Semiotics, Cinema," 7.

5. Bordo 145, 144.

6. I adopt the phrase "axis of exclusion" from Evelyn Fox-Keller, who used it in connection with race during a lecture given at the University of Amsterdam in January 1993.

7. See Sally Munt's introduction (xi–xxi) to *New Lesbian Criticism: Literary and Cultural Readings* (1992), on the necessity to retain the category of a (contextualized) lesbian identity.

8. Spivak, "Feminism and Critical Theory," 85.

9. De Lauretis, "Feminist Studies/Critical Studies: Issues, Terms, and Contexts," 9.

10. Ibid., 14.

11. Examples of feminist engagement with psychoanalysis abound. In addition to titles cited earlier, see, for example, Shoshana Felman, ed., *Literature and Psychoanalysis* (1980); Teresa Brennan, ed., *Between Feminism and Psychoanalysis* (1989); Richard Feldstein and Judith Roof, eds., *Feminism and Psychoanalysis* (1989); Patricia Elliot, *From Mastery to Analysis: Theories of Gender in Psychoanalytic Criticism* (1991). For recent lesbian feminist interventions in the debate on psychoanalysis, see, inter alia, Diane Hamer, "Significant Others: Lesbians and Psychoanalytic Theory," 134–51; De Lauretis, "Perverse Desire"; Judith Roof, *A Lure of Knowledge: Lesbian Sexuality and Theory* (1991); contributions to *The Phallus Issue* of *Differences: A Journal of Feminist Critical Studies* 4 (1992); and my "Fallische Perversie" (1993).

12. E. Ann Kaplan, "Is the Gaze Male?" 321, 322, 324.

13. The Woolfs' Hogarth Press was the first to publish Freud's works in English translation. Glendinning, while maintaining that her "generation was far less cliquey" than the intellectual and literary society in

which Virginia Woolf took up a prominent position, claims that Bowen was "heir, in literary and aesthetic terms, to Bloomsbury" (75, 77).

14. William James, *Principles of Psychology* (1890), ctd. in Malcolm Bradbury and James McFarlane, "Movements, Magazines, and Manifestos: The Succession from Naturalism," 197.

15. Ibid., 196.

16. Malcolm Bradbury and James McFarlane, "The Name and Nature of Modernism," 25.

17. Significantly, it is in this novel, marking the midpoint of Bowen's career, that the interrelated operations of history, narrativity, and identity are explicitly articulated in terms of an oppositional heterosexual difference. More about this in a moment.

18. See Lee on the influence of Proust on Bowen's fiction, criticism, and her ideas about writing, esp. chapters 1 and 7 (*Estimation*, 13–56; 189–212). See also Bowen's long essay on Proust's novelist character, "The Art of Bergotte," 79–109.

19. John Fletcher and Malcolm Bradbury, "The Introverted Novel," 404.

20. Richard Sheppard, "The Crisis in Language," 323–36.

21. *To the North*, 136.

22. A. S. Byatt, Introduction to *The House in Paris*, 7–16.

23. De Lauretis, "Sexual Indifference," 155.

24. Critic and biographer appear equally anxious to point out that Bowen was not a lesbian herself. Although it is by no means my intention either to contest or to establish the author's "real-life" sexual identity, the lesbophobia inspiring such negations of what clearly cannot be altogether ignored in the author's biography inevitably results in a similar downplaying of "unwanted" aspects of her texts, and thus in serious critical oversights.

25. Jane Rule, "Elizabeth Bowen," 115–25. The fact that Rule, herself an out lesbian novelist and short story writer, is, as far as I know, the only critic to approach Bowen's novels as lesbian texts would seem to confirm my suspicions regarding the heterocentric and lesbophobic assumptions of both "mainstream" feminist and other literary critical practice.

26. For analyses of the "unequal couple" as one of the topoi of lesbian textuality, see Elaine Marks, "Lesbian Intertextuality," 325–78; and Pamela Pattynama, "De Herinnering aan het Oude Verhaal," 88–92.

27. See Glendinning's chapters "Noon" and "After Noon" on the development and significance of this long-standing affair (128–66).

28. Glendinning makes light of Bowen's affairs with women, but her own book supports many indications of their occurrence throughout the author's life. Prevailing regulatory regimes of sexual convention surely account for both Bowen's own and her biographer's reticence on the subject. Still, the author's personal correspondence and an essay by May Sarton, one of a number of adoring young women with whom Bowen momentarily shared instant intimacy, testify to at least a bisexual disposition. See May Sarton, "Elizabeth Bowen," 191–214. The sketch forms part of a collection of essays with, as Glendinning observes, a "startlingly Bowenesque" title (104): *A World of Light: Portraits and Celebrations* (1976).

29. De Lauretis, "Sexual Indifference," 155.

30. Ibid., 157, 159.

31. "Pictures and Conversations," 41.

32. At this point I must briefly elaborate on what I consider a flaw in Silverman's argument, that is, her failure to problematize the notion of identification itself. Silverman rightly takes issue with the Freudian notion of lesbian sexuality as involving the so-called masculinity complex, as the (perverse) result of the castrated girl's identification with the father. Her own unquestioning assumption of a "conjunction of identification and eroticism," however, equally fails to do justice to the complexity of the identificatory process in the construction of a sexed subjectivity (*Acoustic Mirror*, 151). The central place of the operation of desire in the process of identity formation hinges on the subject-object distinction. As a consequence, Silverman's conflation of the girl's identification with the subjective position *of* the mother would in effect preclude a desire *for* her as an object of erotic investment. In order to maintain the indisputable value of Silverman's theory of a female same-sex object choice and at the same time to overcome the limitations imposed by a strictly binary subject-object distinction, it is necessary to reconsider the ways in which identificatory processes obtain. A possibility for such a rethinking will shortly emerge in the main text.

33. See Jean Laplanche and Jean-Bertrand Pontalis, "Fantasy and the Origins of Sexuality: Retrospect 1986," 5–28.

34. For a convincing argument along these lines, see Butler's chapter on "Prohibition, Psychoanalysis, and the Production of the Heterosexual Matrix," in *Gender Trouble*, 35–78.

35. Shari Benstock, "Expatriate Sapphic Modernism: Entering Literary History," 183–203.

36. Although in fact she casts her theoretical net more widely than I can outline here, I will address only those aspects of Benstock's essay directly relevant to my argument. Referring to various feminist theorists who have read the works of female modernists such as Virginia Woolf, Djuna Barnes, and Gertrude Stein as "fueled by Sapphic erotic power," Benstock in fact posits that a theory of Sapphic modernism "could profoundly change not only our notions about modernist art, but also redefine the erotic in relation to the creative sources for all art" (183).

37. Glendinning 218.

38. Iseult's attention, we remember, "could seem to be love" to Eva (*ET*, 17).

39. Marilyn Frye, "To Be and Be Seen: The Politics of Reality," 172.

40. Benstock, "Expatriate," 193, 195.

41. Ibid., 197.

Bibliography

Chronological List of Selected Works by Elizabeth Bowen

Encounters. London: Sidgwick and Jackson, 1923.
Ann Lee's and Other Stories. London: Sidgwick and Jackson, 1926.
The Hotel. 1927. Harmondsworth: Penguin, 1984.
The Last September. 1929. Harmondsworth: Penguin, 1987.
Joining Charles. London: Constable, 1929.
Friends and Relations. 1931. Harmondsworth: Penguin, 1982.
To the North. 1932. Harmondsworth: Penguin, 1984.
The Cat Jumps. London: Gollancz, 1934.
The House in Paris. 1935. Harmondsworth: Penguin, 1983.
The Death of the Heart. 1938. Harmondsworth: Penguin, 1984.
Look at All Those Roses. London: Gollancz, 1941.
Bowen's Court and Seven Winters. 1942. Intr. Hermione Lee. London:
    Virago, 1984.
English Novelists. London: Collins, 1945.
The Demon Lover. London: Jonathan Cape, 1945.
The Heat of the Day. 1949. Harmondsworth: Penguin, 1983.
Collected Impressions. London: Longmans, 1950.
The Shelbourne Hotel. New York: Alfred A. Knopf, 1951.
A World of Love. 1955. Harmondsworth: Penguin, 1983.
A Time in Rome. London: Longmans, 1960.
Afterthought. London: Longmans, 1962.
The Little Girls. 1964. Harmondsworth: Penguin, 1982.
The Good Tiger. 1965. London: Jonathan Cape, 1970.
A Day in the Dark and Other Stories. London: Jonathan Cape, 1965.
Eva Trout or Changing Scenes. 1969. Harmondsworth: Penguin, 1982.
Pictures and Conversations. Ed. and intr. Spencer Curtis Brown. London:
    Allen Lane, 1975.

Collected Stories. 1980. Intr. Angus Wilson. New York: Random House, 1982.

The Mulberry Tree. 1986. Ed. and intr. Hermione Lee. New York: Harcourt Brace Jovanovich, 1987.

Select Alphabetical List of Prefaces and Essays by Elizabeth Bowen

"The Achievement of Virginia Woolf." 1949. In *Collected Impressions.* 78–82.

"The Art of Bergotte." 1975. In *Pictures and Conversations.* 77–111.

"The Bend Back." 1951. In *Mulberry Tree.* 54–60.

"The Big House." 1940. In *Mulberry Tree.* 25–29.

Bowen's Court. Afterword. 1963. In *Bowen's Court and Seven Winters.* 448–59.

The Demon Lover. Preface to American edition. 1946. In *Collected Impressions.* 47–52.

Encounters. Preface. 1949. In *Afterthought.* 82–88.

The Last September. Preface to 2d American edition. 1952. In *Afterthought.* 95–100.

"The Mulberry Tree." 1935. In *Collected Impressions.* 185–94.

"Notes on Writing a Novel." 1945. In *Pictures and Conversations.* 167–93.

"Out of a Book." 1946. In *Collected Impressions.* 265–69.

"Pictures and Conversations." In *Pictures and Conversations.* 1–64.

"Sources of Influence." In *Afterthought.* 205–10.

Stories by Elizabeth Bowen. Preface. 1959. In *Afterthought.* 75–81.

"Why Do I Write?" 1948. In *Mulberry Tree.* 221–30.

Alphabetical List of Other Works Consulted

Abel, Elizabeth, Marianne Hirsch, and Elizabeth Langland, eds. *The Voyage In: Fictions of Female Development.* Hanover and London: University Press of New England, 1983.

Allen, Walter. *Tradition and Dream.* London: Phoenix House, 1964.

Althusser, Louis. "Ideology and Ideological State Apparatuses (Notes towards an Investigation)." 1970. In *Essays on Ideology.* London and New York: Verso, 1984.

Austin, A. E. *Elizabeth Bowen*. New York: Twayne, 1971.

Bakhtin, M. M. "Forms of Time and of the Chronotope in the Novel." In Michael Holquist, ed., *The Dialogic Imagination: Four Essays*. Trans. Caryl Emerson and Michael Holquist. Austin: University of Texas Press, 1981. 84–258.

Barrett, Michèle, and Anne Phillips, eds. *Destabilizing Theory: Contemporary Feminist Theory*. Cambridge: Polity, 1992.

Barthes, Roland. "The Death of the Author." 1968. In *The Rustle of Language*. Trans. Richard Howard. Berkeley and Los Angeles: University of California Press, 1989. 49–55.

Baudrillard, Jean. "The Procession of Simulacra." In Brian Wallis, ed., *Art after Modernism: Rethinking Representation*. Boston: Godine, 1984. 253–81.

Belsey, Catherine. *Critical Practice*. 1980. London and New York: Routledge, 1988.

Benstock, Shari. "Expatriate Sapphic Modernism: Entering Literary History." In Karla Jay and Joanne Glasgow, eds., *Lesbian Texts and Contexts: Radical Revisions*. New York and London: New York University Press, 1991. 183–203.

Benveniste, Emile. *Problems in General Linguistics*. Trans. Mary Elizabeth Meek. Coral Gables: University of Miami Press, 1971.

Blodgett, Harriet. *Patterns of Reality: Elizabeth Bowen's Novels*. The Hague: Mouton, 1975.

Bordo, Susan. "Feminism, Postmodernism, and Gender-Scepticism." In Nicholson, ed., *Feminism/Postmodernism*. 133–56.

Bradbury, Malcolm, and James McFarlane, eds. "Movements, Magazines, and Manifestos: The Succession from Naturalism." In Bradbury and MacFarlane, eds., *Modernism*. 192–205.

———. "The Name and Nature of Modernism." In Bradbury and MacFarlane, eds., *Modernism*. 19–56.

———. *Modernism 1890–1930*. Harmondsworth: Penguin, 1976.

Brennan, Teresa, ed. *Between Feminism and Psychoanalysis*. London and New York: Routledge, 1989.

Brooke, Jocelyne. *Elizabeth Bowen*. Supplement to *British Book News*, no. 28. London: Longmans, 1951.

Brooks, Peter. "Freud's Masterplot: Questions of Narrative." In Felman, ed., *Literature and Psychoanalysis*. 280–300.

Burgin, Victor, James Donald, and Cora Kaplan, eds. *Formations of Fantasy*. 1986. London and New York: Routledge, 1989.

Butler, Judith. *Gender Trouble: Feminism and the Subversion of Identity.* New York and London: Routledge, 1990.

———. "Gender Trouble, Feminist Theory, and Psychoanalytic Discourse." In Nicholson, ed., *Feminism/Psychoanalysis.* 301–24.

———. "Imitation and Gender Subordination." In Fuss, ed., *Inside/Out.* 13–31.

Byatt, A. S. Introduction. *The House in Paris.* 1935. By Elizabeth Bowen. Harmondsworth: Penguin, 1976. 7–16.

Cixous, Hélène, and Catherine Clément, eds. *The Newly Born Woman.* Trans. Betsy Wing. Minneapolis: University of Minnesota Press, 1986.

Clark, Katerina, and Michael Holquist. *Mikhail Bakhtin.* Cambridge, MA, and London: Belknap Press of Harvard University Press, 1984.

Craig, Patricia. *Elizabeth Bowen.* Harmondsworth: Penguin, 1986.

Culler, Jonathan. *Structuralist Poetics: Structuralism, Linguistics, and the Study of Literature.* London: Routledge and Kegan Paul, 1975.

Curtis Brown, Spencer. Foreword. *Pictures and Conversations.* By Elizabeth Bowen. London: Allen Lane, 1974. vii–xlii.

Dalsimer, Katherine. *Female Adolescence: Psychoanalytic Reflections on Literature.* New Haven and London: Yale University Press, 1986.

Davis, Lennard J. *Resisting Novels: Ideology and Fiction.* New York and London: Methuen, 1986.

de Lauretis, Teresa. *Alice Doesn't: Feminism, Semiotics, Cinema.* London: Macmillan, 1984.

———. "Desire in Narrative." In *Alice Doesn't.* 103–57.

———. "The Essence of the Triangle or, Taking the Risk of Essentialism Seriously: Feminist Theory in Italy, the U.S., and Britain." *Differences* 2 (1989): 3–37.

———. "Feminism, Semiotics, Cinema: An Introduction." In *Alice Doesn't.* 1–11.

———. "Feminist Studies/Critical Studies: Issues, Terms, and Contexts." In de Lauretis, ed., *Feminist Studies.* 1–19.

———. "Perverse Desire: The Lure of the Mannish Lesbian." *Australian Feminist Studies* 13 (1991): 15–26.

———. "Semiotics and Experience." In *Alice Doesn't.* 158–86.

———. "Sexual Indifference and Lesbian Representation." *Theatre Journal* 5 (1988): 155–77.

———. *Technologies of Gender: Essays on Theory, Film, and Fiction.* Bloomington and Indianapolis: Indiana University Press, 1987.

———. "The Technology of Gender." In *Technologies.* 1–30.

de Lauretis, ed. *Feminist Studies/Critical Studies*. Bloomington: Indiana University Press, 1986.

de Saussure, Ferdinand. *Course in General Linguistics*. Trans. Wade Baskin. New York: McGraw-Hill, 1966.

Deutsch, Hélène. *The Psychology of Women*. Vol. 1. New York: Grune and Stratton, 1944.

Differences: A Journal of Feminist Cultural Studies. *The Phallus Issue* 4 (1992).

Doane, Mary Ann. "Film and the Masquerade: Theorising the Female Spectator." *Screen* 23 (1982): 74–87.

Doane, Mary Ann, Patricia Mollencamp, and Linda Williams, eds. *Revision: Essays in Feminist Film Criticism*. Frederick MD: University Publications of America and American Film Institute, 1984.

Elliot, Patricia. *From Mastery to Analysis: Theories of Gender in Psychoanalytic Criticism*. Ithaca and London: Cornell University Press, 1991.

Ellis, Havelock. *Studies in the Psychology of Sex: Sexual Inversions*. 1897. Philadelphia: Davis, 1911.

Erikson, Erik H. *Identity: Youth and Crisis*. London: Faber and Faber, 1968.

Faderman, Lilian. *Surpassing the Love of Men: Romantic Friendship and Love between Women from the Renaissance to the Present*. 1981. London: Women's Press, 1985.

Feldstein, Richard, and Judith Roof, eds. *Feminism and Psychoanalysis*. Ithaca and London: Cornell University Press, 1989.

Felman, Shoshana, ed. *Literature and Psychoanalysis: The Question of Reading: Otherwise*. 1977. Baltimore MD: Johns Hopkins University Press, 1982.

Flax, Jane. *Thinking Fragments: Psychoanalysis, Feminism, and Postmodernism in the Contemporary West*. Berkeley, Los Angeles, and Oxford: University of California Press, 1990.

Fletcher, John, and Malcolm Bradbury. "The Introverted Novel." In Bradbury and McFarlane, eds., *Modernism*. 394–415.

Foster, Hal. "Postmodernism: A Preface." In Foster, ed., *The Anti-Aesthetic*. ix–xvi.

Foster, Hal, ed. *The Anti-Aesthetic: Essays on Postmodern Culture*. Port Townsend, WA: Bay Press, 1983.

Foucault, Michel. *The Archeology of Knowledge and the Discourse on Language*. 1969. Trans. A. M. Sheridan Smith. New York: Pantheon, 1972.

———. *Discipline and Punish: The Birth of the Prison*. Trans. Alan Sheridan. New York: Vintage, 1979.

———. *The History of Sexuality*. Vol. 1, *An Introduction*. 1976. New York: Vintage Books/Random House, 1990.

———. *The Order of Things: An Archeology of the Human Sciences*. 1966. New York: Vintage, 1973.

———. "What Is an Author?" In Josué Harari, ed., *Textual Strategies: Perspectives in Post-Structuralist Criticism*. Ithaca: Cornell University Press, 1979. 141–60.

Freud, Sigmund. *Beyond the Pleasure Principle*. 1920. *Essentials* 218–68.

———. "A Case of Paranoia Running Counter to the Psychoanalytic Theory of the Disease." 1915. In *On Psychopathology*. 129–58.

———. "The Dissolution of the Oedipus Complex." 1924. In *On Sexuality*. 313–32.

———. *The Essentials of Psychoanalysis: The Definitive Collection of Freud's Writing*. Trans. James Strachey. Ed. Anna Freud. Harmondsworth: Penguin, 1986.

———. "Female Sexuality." 1931. In *On Sexuality*. 367–92.

———. "Femininity." 1932. In *New Introductory Lectures*. 145–69.

———. "Family Romances." 1909. In *On Sexuality*. 217–26.

———. "Fragment of an Analysis of a Case of Hysteria." 1905. In *Case Histories I: "Dora" and "Little Hans."* Trans. and ed. James Strachey. *Pelican Freud Library*, vol. 8. Ed. Angela Richards. Harmondsworth: Penguin, 1977.

———. "Mourning and Melancholia." 1917. In *Standard Edition of the Complete Psychological Works of Sigmund Freud*, vol. 14. London, 1953–73. 239–55.

———. *New Introductory Lectures on Psychoanalysis*. Trans. and ed. James Strachey. *Pelican Freud Library*, vol. 2. Ed. Angela Richards. Harmondsworth: Penguin, 1973. Rpt. 1988.

———. "The Psychogenesis of a Case of Homosexuality in a Woman." 1920. In *Case Histories II: "Rat Man," Schreber, "Wolf Man," Female Homosexuality*. Trans. and ed. James Strachey. *Pelican Freud Library*, vol. 9. Ed. Angela Richards. Harmondsworth: Penguin, 1979. Rpt. 1987. 367–400.

———. *On Psychopathology: Inhibitions, Symptoms, and Anxiety*. Trans. and ed. James Strachey. *Pelican Freud Library*, vol. 10. Ed. Angela Richards. Harmondsworth: Penguin, 1979. Rpt. 1987.

———. "The Sexual Aberrations." 1905. In *On Sexuality*. 45–87.

———. *On Sexuality: Three Essays on the Theory of Sexuality.* Trans. and ed. James Strachey. *Pelican Freud Library,* vol. 7. Ed. Angela Richards. Harmondsworth: Penguin, 1953. Rpt. 1977.

———. "Some Neurotic Mechanisms in Jealousy, Paranoia, and Homosexuality." 1921. In *On Psychopathology.* 195–208.

———. "Some Psychical Consequences of the Anatomical Distinction between the Sexes." 1925. In *On Sexuality.* 323–44.

———. "The Uncanny." 1919. In Albert Dickson, ed., *Art and Literature.* Harmondsworth: Penguin, 1985. 335–76.

Frye, Marilyn. "To Be and Be Seen: The Politics of Reality." In *The Politics of Reality: Essays in Feminist Theory.* Trumansburg, NY: Crossing Press, 1983. 151–74.

Fuss, Diana, ed. *Inside/Out: Lesbian Theories, Gay Theories.* New York and London: Routledge, 1991.

Gallop, Jane. *Around 1981: Academic Feminist Literary Theory.* London and New York: Routledge, 1992.

———. *Reading Lacan.* Ithaca: Cornell University Press, 1985.

———. *Feminism and Psychoanalysis: The Daughter's Seduction.* Ithaca and London: Cornell University Press and Macmillan, 1982.

Genette, Gérard. *Narrative Discourse.* 1972. Trans. Jane Lewin. Oxford: Blackwell, 1986.

Glendinning, Victoria. *Elizabeth Bowen: Portrait of a Writer.* 1977. Harmondsworth: Penguin, 1985.

Grosz, Elizabeth. *Jacques Lacan: A Feminist Introduction.* London and New York: Routledge, 1990.

Hall, Radclyffe. *The Well of Loneliness.* 1928. London: Virago, 1982.

Hamer, Diane. "Significant Others: Lesbians and Psychoanalytic Theory." *Feminist Review* 34 (1990): 134–51.

Heath, William. *Elizabeth Bowen: An Introduction to Her Novels.* Madison: University of Wisconsin Press, 1961.

Hewison, Robert. *Under Siege: Literary Life in London, 1939–1945.* London: Weidenfeld and Nicolson, 1977.

Hewitt, Douglas. *English Fiction of the Early Modern Period, 1890–1940.* London and New York: Longmans, 1988.

Hirsch, Marianne. *The Mother/Daughter Plot: Narrative, Psychoanalysis, Feminism.* Bloomington and Indianapolis: Indiana University Press, 1989.

Hoogland, Renée C. "Contradictions Held in Suspense: Postmodernism and Feminist Critique." *Dutch Quarterly Review of Anglo-American Letters* 4 (1990): 277–86.

————. "De Grens Tussen Spreken en Zwijgen: Elizabeth Bowen's *Eva Trout.*" In Rosa Knorringa, Anke Burger, and Johanna Bossinade, eds., *Uitgesproken maar niet Uitgepraat: Lezingenbundel Vrouwenstudies Letteren UvA.* Amsterdam: FAG-Vrouwenstudies Letteren UvA, 1987. 43–57.

————. "Fallische Perversie." In Mieke Bal, Wies van Moorsel, Pamela Pattynama, Mieke van Schermbeek, eds. *Allure: Psychoanalyse en Feminisme.* Amsterdam: Amsterdam University Press, 1993. 13–26.

Hutcheon, Linda. *A Poetics of Postmodernism: History, Theory, Fiction.* New York and London: Routledge, 1988.

Irigaray, Luce. "Commodities among Themselves." In *This Sex.* 192–97.

————. *This Sex Which Is Not One.* 1977. Trans. Catherine Porter with Carolyn Burke. Ithaca: Cornell University Press, 1985.

————. "Women's Exile: Interview with Luce Irigaray." Trans. Couze Venn. *Ideology and Consciousness* 1 (1977): 62–76.

Jameson, Frederic. Foreword. *The Postmodern Condition.* By Jean-François Lyotard. Minneapolis: University of Minnesota Press, 1989. vii–xxi.

————. "Imaginary and Symbolic in Lacan: Marxism, Psychoanalytic Criticism, and the Problem of the Subject." In Felman, ed., *Literature and Psychoanalysis.* 338–95.

————. "Postmodernism and Consumer Society." Kaplan, ed. *Postmodernism* 13–29.

Jardine, Alice A. *Gynesis: Configurations of Woman and Modernity.* Ithaca and London: Cornell University Press, 1985.

Kaplan, Cora. "Language and Gender." In *Sea Changes.* 69–93.

————. "Pandora's Box: Subjectivity, Class, and Sexuality in Socialist Feminist Criticism." In *Sea Changes.* 147–76.

————. *Sea Changes: Culture and Feminism.* London: Verso, 1986.

Kaplan, E. Ann. "Is the Gaze Male?" In Snitow, et al., eds., *Desire.* 321–38.

Kaplan, E. Ann, ed. *Postmodernism and Its Discontents: Theories, Practices.* London and New York: Verso, 1988.

Krafft-Ebing, Richard von. *Psychopathia Sexualis.* 1882. New York: Surgeons Books, 1925.

Kristeva, Julia. "The Adolescent Novel." In John Fletcher and Andrew Benjamin, eds., *Abjection, Melancholia, and Love: The Work of Julia Kristeva.* London and New York: Routledge, 1990. 8–23.

————. *Desire in Language: A Semiotic Approach to Literature and Art.*

Trans. Alice Jardine, Thomas Gora, and Léon Roudiez. Ed. Léon Roudiez. Oxford: Blackwell, 1980.

———. "Negativity: Rejection." In *Revolution*. 109–47.

———. *Polylogue*. Paris: Editions du Seuil, 1977.

———. *Powers of Horror: An Essay on Abjection*. 1980. Trans. Léon Roudiez. New York: Columbia University Press, 1982.

———. *Revolution in Poetic Language*. 1974. Trans. Margaret Waller. New York: Columbia University Press, 1984.

Lacan, Jacques. "The Mirror Stage." In *Écrits: A Selection*. Trans. Alan Sheridan. New York: Norton, 1977. 1–7.

Laplanche, Jean, and Jean-Bertrand Pontalis. "Fantasy and the Origins of Sexuality: Retrospect 1986." In Burgin, et al., eds., *Formations of Fantasy*. 5–28.

———. *The Language of Psycho-Analysis*. Intr. Daniel Lagache. Trans. Donald Nicholson-Smith. London: Karnac Books and the Institute of Psycho-Analysis, 1988.

Lassner, Phyllis. *Elizabeth Bowen*. London: Macmillan Education, 1990.

Lee, Hermione. *Elizabeth Bowen: An Estimation*. London and Totowa, NJ: Vision and Barnes and Noble, 1981.

Lee, Hermione, ed. *The Mulberry Tree: Writings of Elizabeth Bowen*. San Diego, New York, and London: Harcourt Brace Jovanovich, 1986.

Lévi-Strauss, Claude. *The Elementary Structures of Kinship*. Boston: Beacon, 1969.

———. *Structural Anthropology*. Trans. C. Jacobson and B. G. Schoepf. Garden City, NY: Doubleday, 1967.

Lewis, Reina. "The Death of the Author and the Resurrection of the Dyke." In Munt, ed., *New Lesbian Criticism*. 17–32.

Lyotard, Jean-François. *The Postmodern Condition: A Report on Knowledge*. Trans. Geoff Bennington and Brian Massumi. Minneapolis: University of Minnesota Press, 1989.

Marks, Elaine. "Lesbian Intertextuality." In George Stambolian and Elaine Marks, eds., *Homosexualities and French Literature: Cultural Contexts/Critical Texts*. Ithaca and London: Cornell University Press, 1979. 353–78.

Martin, Biddy, and Chandra Tapalde Mohanty. "Feminist Politics: What's Home Got to Do with It? In de Lauretis, ed., *Feminist Studies*. 191–212.

Martin, Wallace. *Recent Theories of Narrative*. Ithaca and London: Cornell University Press, 1986.

Mayne, Judith. "A Parallax View of Lesbian Authorship." In Fuss, ed., *Inside/Out*. 173–84.

———. *The Woman at the Keyhole: Feminism and Women's Cinema*. Bloomington and Indianapolis: Indiana University Press, 1990.

Meijer, Maaike. *De Lust tot Lezen: Nederlandse Dichteressen en het Literaire Systeem*. Amsterdam: Sara/van Gennep, 1988.

Miles, Rosalind. 1987. *The Female Form: Women Writers and the Conquest of the Novel*. London: Routledge, 1990.

Miller, Nancy K. "Changing the Subject: Authorship, Writing, and the Reader." In de Lauretis, ed., *Feminist Studies*. 102–20.

Mitchell, Juliet. *Psychoanalysis and Feminism*. New York and London: Pantheon, 1974.

———. *Women: The Longest Revolution: Essays in Feminism, Literature, and Psychoanalysis*. London: Virago, 1984.

Mitchell, Juliet, and Jacqueline Rose, eds. *Feminine Sexuality: Jacques Lacan and the école freudienne*. London: Macmillan, 1982.

Modleski, Tania. *Feminism without Women: Culture and Criticism in a "Postfeminist" Age*. New York and London: Routledge, 1991.

Moi, Toril. "Patriarchal Thought and the Drive for Knowledge." In Brennan, ed., *Feminism and Psychoanalysis*. 189–205.

———. *Sexual/Textual Politics: Feminist Literary Theory*. London and New York: Methuen, 1985.

Morris, Meaghan. *The Pirate's Fiancée: Feminism, Reading, Postmodernism*. London and New York: Verso, 1988.

Munt, Sally. "'*Somewhere over the rainbow* . . .': Postmodernism and the Fiction of Sarah Schulman." In Munt, ed., *New Lesbian Criticism*. 33–50.

Munt, Sally, ed. *New Lesbian Criticism: Literary and Cultural Readings*. Hemel Hempstead: Harvester Wheatsheaf, 1992.

Newton, Esther. "The Mythic Mannish Lesbian: Radclyffe Hall and the New Woman." *Signs: Lesbian Issue* 4 (1984): 557–76.

Nicholson, Linda J., ed. *Feminism/Postmodernism*. New York and London: Routledge, 1990.

Owens, Craig. "The Discourse of Others: Feminists and Postmodernism." In Foster, ed., *The Anti-Aesthetic*. 57–82.

Pattynama, Pamela. "De Herinnering aan het Oude Verhaal." *Lover* 2 (1989): 88–92.

———. *Passages: Vrouwelijke Adolescentie als Verhaal en Vertoog*. Kampen: Kok Agora, 1992.

Rimmon-Kenan, Shlomith. *Narrative Fiction: Contemporary Poetics.* 1983. London: Methuen, 1986.

Rich, Adrienne. "Compulsory Heterosexuality and Lesbian Existence." 1980. Reprinted in Snitow, et al., eds., *Desire.* 212–41.

Rivière, Joan. "Womanliness as a Masquerade." 1929. In Burgin, et al., eds., *Formations of Fantasy.* 35–49.

Roof, Judith. *A Lure of Knowledge: Lesbian Sexuality and Theory.* New York and Oxford: Columbia University Press, 1991.

Rose, Jacqueline. *Sexuality in the Field of Vision.* London: Verso, 1986.

Rubin, Gayle. "The Traffic in Women: Notes toward a Political Economy of Sex." In Reina Rayter, ed., *Toward an Anthropology of Women.* New York: Monthly Review Press, 1975. 157–210.

Rule, Jane. "Elizabeth Bowen." In *Lesbian Images.* Trumansburg, NY: Crossing Press, 1975. 115–24.

Sarton, May. "Elizabeth Bowen." *A World of Light: Portraits and Celebrations.* New York: Norton, 1976. 191–214.

Sellery, J'nan. *Elizabeth Bowen: A Descriptive Bibliography.* Austin: University of Texas Press, 1977.

Sheppard, Richard. "The Crisis in Language." In Bradbury and McFarlane, eds., *Modernism.* 313–23.

Silverman, Kaja. *The Acoustic Mirror: The Female Voice in Psychoanalysis and Cinema.* Bloomington and Indianapolis: Indiana University Press, 1988.

———. *The Subject of Semiotics.* New York and Oxford: Oxford University Press, 1983.

Sniader Lanser, Susan. *The Narrative Act: Point of View in Prose Fiction.* Princeton: Princeton University Press, 1981.

Snitow, Ann, Christine Stansell, and Sharon Thompson, eds. *Desire: The Politics of Sexuality.* 1983. London: Virago, 1984.

Spivak, Gayatri Chakravorty. "Displacement and the Discourse of Woman." In Mark Krupnick, ed., *Displacement: Derrida and After.* Bloomington: Indiana University Press, 1983. 169–95.

———. "Explanation and Culture: Marginalia." In *In Other Worlds.* 103–17.

———. "Feminism and Critical Theory." In *In Other Worlds.* 77–92.

———. "French Feminism in an International Frame." In *In Other Worlds.* 134–53.

———. *In Other Worlds: Essays in Cultural Politics.* New York and London: Routledge, 1988.

Spraggs, Gillian. "Hell and the Mirror: A Reading of *Desert of the Heart*." In Munt, ed., *New Lesbian Criticism*. 115–32.

Sprengnether, Madelon. "(M)other's Eve: Some Revisions of the Fall in Fiction by Contemporary Women Writers." In Feldstein and Roof, eds., *Psychoanalysis and Feminism*. 298–322.

Stam, Robert. "Mikhail Bakhtin and Left Cultural Critique." In Kaplan, ed., *Postmodernism*. 116–45.

Tyler, Carole-Ann. "Boys Will Be Girls: The Politics of Gay Drag." In Fuss, ed., *Inside/Out*. 32–70.

Walker, Cheryl. "Feminist Literary Criticism and the Author." *Critical Inquiry* 16 (1990): 550–71.

White, Barbara A. *Growing Up Female: Adolescent Girlhood in American Fiction*. Westport, CT, and London: Greenwood, 1985.

White, Hayden. *Tropics of Discourse: Essays in Cultural Criticism*. Baltimore and London: Johns Hopkins University Press, 1978.

White, Patricia. "Female Spectator, Lesbian Specter: *The Haunting*." In Fuss, ed., *Inside/Out*. 142–72.

Wittig, Monique. "On the Social Contract." 1980. *The Straight Mind and Other Essays*. Boston: Beacon, 1992. 33–45.

Woolf, Virginia. *A Room of One's Own*. 1929. London: Granada, 1977.

Index